Responsible Graph Neural Networks

More frequent and complex cyber threats require robust, automated, and rapid responses from cyber-security specialists. This book offers a complete study in the area of graph learning in cyber, emphasizing graph neural networks (GNNs) and their cyber-security applications.

Three parts examine the basics, methods and practices, and advanced topics. The first part presents a grounding in graph data structures and graph embedding and gives a taxonomic view of GNNs and cyber-security applications. The second part explains three different categories of graph learning, including deterministic, generative, and reinforcement learning and how they can be used for developing cyber defense models. The discussion of each category covers the applicability of simple and complex graphs, scalability, representative algorithms, and technical details.

Undergraduate students, graduate students, researchers, cyber analysts, and AI engineers looking to understand practical deep learning methods will find this book an invaluable resource.

Mohamed Abdel-Basset is an Associate Professor at the Faculty of Computers and Informatics, Zagazig University, Zagazig, Egypt.

Nour Moustafa currently is a Senior Lecturer and Leader of Intelligent Security Group at the School of Engineering and Information Technology, University of New South Wales (UNSW), Canberra, Australia. He is also a Strategic Advisor (AI-SME) at DXC Technology, Canberra.

Hossam Hawash is a Senior Researcher at the Department of Computer Science, Faculty of Computers and Informatics, Zagazig University, Zagazig, Egypt.

Zahir Tari is the Research Director of the RMIT Centre of Cyber Security Research and Innovation (CCSRI), Royal Melbourne Institute of Technology, School of Computing Technologies, Melbourne, Australia.

Responsible Graph Neural Networks

Mohamed Abdel-Basset
Nour Moustafa
Hossam Hawash
Zahir Tari

CRC Press
Taylor & Francis Group
Boca Raton London New York

CRC Press is an imprint of the
Taylor & Francis Group, an **informa** business

A CHAPMAN & HALL BOOK

First edition published 2023
by CRC Press
6000 Broken Sound Parkway NW, Suite 300, Boca Raton, FL 33487-2742

and by CRC Press

4 Park Square, Milton Park, Abingdon, Oxon, OX14 4RN

CRC Press is an imprint of Taylor & Francis Group, LLC

ISBN: 978-1-032-35989-2 (hbk)
ISBN: 978-1-032-35988-5 (pbk)
ISBN: 978-1-003-32970-1 (ebk)

DOI: 10.1201/9781003329701

Typeset in Palatino
by KnowledgeWorks Global Ltd.

Contents

Preface

The main objective of this book is to provide scholars and readers with in-depth understanding of the "graph intelligence" as a special branch of artificial intelligence. The book provides great emphasis on the role of deep learning in revolutionizing the graph intelligence tasks in a broad range of applications reliant graph-structured data. Given the exploding amount of daily generated data containing complex interaction among different entities, the graph-based solutions gain an increased interest when it comes to developing intelligent applications. With the elasticity and generalization ability of deep learning, this book provides a detailed explanation of different families of graph-based deep learning solutions that have been achieving the state-of-the-art graph representational learning performance. This book is introduced to fill the apparent gaps in practical and conceptual information about the potential of deep learning for modeling complex representations from different types of graphs. On the one hand, there are countless research activities all around the world; new research papers are being published daily; a large portion of conferences such as NIPS or ICLR are concentrating on resolving to graph intelligence tasks. Despite the multiplicity of resources in this subject matter, the academic resources are too specialized and abstract to be understandable without significant hard work. Thus, they cannot deliver the body of knowledge to the nonacademic audience. The practical element of deep learning applications is much worse, as it is not always clear how to get from the abstract technique depicted in a research paper to a functioning application to solve real-world case studies and problems. On the other hand, there are some university courses and blogging platforms that explain graph intelligence with working examples; however, these sources are usually incomplete and focus only on one or two models or a particular family of models. This, in turn, makes it difficult to capture the whole idea of this topic. For the first time, this book combines the advantages of both types of materials to provide a systematic and comprehensive knowledge about the graph intelligence applications.

How to Use This Book

To get you up and running for the hands-on learning experience, we need to set you up with an environment for running Python, Jupyter notebooks, the relevant libraries, and the code needed to run the book itself. The simplest way to get going will be to install Anaconda Framework. The Python 3.x version is required. Before installing the Pytorch framework, please first check whether or not you have proper GPUs on your machine (the GPUs that power the display on a standard laptop do not count for our purposes). If you are installing on a GPU server, you need to install CUDA-enabled Pytorch. Otherwise, you can install the CPU version as follows. That will be more than enough horsepower to get you through the first few chapters, but you will want to access GPUs before running larger models. Online GPU platforms (Google Colab) can also be used to run the examples in this book. Following this, the readers are required to install Pytorch_Geometric and DGL libraries to be able to run the graph intelligence methods discussed across different chapters of this book.

In this book, we will teach most concepts *just in time*. In other words, you will learn concepts at the very moment that they are needed to accomplish some practical end. While we take some time at the outset to teach fundamental preliminaries, like graph theory and graph embedding, we want you to taste the satisfaction of implementing and building your first graph before worrying about more esoteric graph embedding. Thus, to best benefit from topics discussed in the chapters of this book, the readers are recommended to first explore the theoretical discussion and mathematical foundations explained in each chapter, then explore the relative implementation presented for each subtopic within the chapter itself. For more experience, the readers can refer to the supplementary material section to implement and experiment with the graph intelligence concepts and models on a real-world case study from a security application.

1

Introduction to Graph Intelligence

1.1 Introduction

Deep learning refers to a category of machine learning methods, which is based on the concept of artificial neural networks (ANNs). In fact, the vast majority of the essential building blocks of deep learning have been around for decades though deep learning has only recently gained popularity. The concept of ANNs may be traced all the way back to the 1940s. After linearly aggregating the information from the inputs, this model can recognize inputs from two different categories and then make a judgment based on that information. Then, a researcher looked into the idea of making a perceptron that can learn its parameters from training examples given to it. The study of neural networks saw a renaissance in the 1980s. During this time period, one of the significant advances that were made was the successful application of the backpropagation algorithm to the process of training deep neural network (DNN) models. It is important to note that the backpropagation method has multiple roots that date all the way back to the 1960s and were used to train neural networks. Even in this age of deep learning, the backpropagation algorithm continues to be the most widely used method for training deep models. In recent years, the availability of "big data" and powerful computational resources has sparked a resurgence in the field of deep learning research and attracted an unprecedented amount of attention. The development of fast graphical processing units (GPUs) has made it possible for us to train deep models of enormous size, and the accumulation of ever-increasing amounts of data ensures that these models can generalize effectively. Both these benefits contribute to the extraordinary success of deep learning techniques in a variety of research fields, which results in an enormous influence in the real world.

In various areas, DNNs have proven to be more effective than the standard approaches, which are considered to be the state of the art. Early deep learning models showed wide applicability in modeling representational structures such as the image, tabular, time series, and textual data. However, the architectural design of these models was not tailored to graph data. Compared to the abovementioned data formats, graphs have been demonstrating great

DOI: 10.1201/9781003329701-1

capabilities in modeling topological relationships in multi-dimensional spaces. This motivated the deep learning community to extend the traditional deep learning to be tailored to learn from the graph using a new family of DNNs known as "graph neural networks" (GNNs).

This chapter concisely presents essential families of deep learning models, including FFNNs), convolutional neural networks (CNNs), and recurrent networks such as gated recurrent unit (GRU) long short-term memory (LSTM), and autoencoders (AEs). These families act as the fundamentals for graph intelligence models discussed in later chapters of this book. This chapter aims to study deep learning on graphs by explaining the reason for representing real-world data as graphs, thus bridging the gap between deep learning and graphs; it also explains the challenges for deep learning on graphs. By the end of this chapter, we discuss the content covered in each chapter of this book to give the reader more insight into the topics covered.

1.2 Feedforward Neural Network (FFNN)

FFNN is the simplest deep network designed as a simple extension to multi-layered perceptron (MLP) that stacks multiple (more than three) layers of neurons to process input. Each layer is completely linked to the following layer, except the last one. While the connections between neurons in two subsequent layers are one directional, not cyclic, the neurons in the same layer are not connected. The neurons in the FFNN are known as nodes or units.

1.2.1 Architecture

The structure of FFNN consists of input layer, hidden layer, and output layer as depicted in Figure 1.1.

   Input layer: Input data is delivered to the network at this level. For each input to the network, a specific number of neurons must be present in each layer of input neurons. It is impossible to anticipate the final outcome without taking into account all the variables at play. The input layer, on the other hand, is completely devoid of computation and serves only to transport data from the outside world into the network.

   Hidden layer: Input data is processed in this stack of layers, which is located between the input and output layers. The responsibility of this stack of layers is to create complex interactions between inputs and outputs. As a result, values in the input are mapped precisely to the desired output based on their inherent representation.

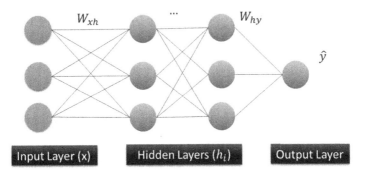

FIGURE 1.1
Systematic diagram of feedforward neural networks (FFNNs).

Output layer: The final output of FFNN is provided by the output layer, which is responsible for receiving the results of hidden layers. To achieve our goals, we must decide how many neurons we need in the output layer.

The parameters of a layer in FFNN are referred to as the weight matrix and bias vector for each layer. Weighted input is augmented by biases, which ensures that a subset of the layered units is always activated regardless of the input concentration. In the case of low-level inputs, biases enable the network to learn and explore new interpretations or patterns by providing network activities.

For each node in FFNN, the input is processed to generate output through the following steps:

Step 1: Nodes receive one or more input elements $X = \{x_1, \cdots, x_N\}$.

Step 2: Weigh each input independently, that is, $x_i \cdot w_i$. The weights are a group of N values that indicate the importance of the respective input values. In other words, weights on connections are parameters that scale (magnify or reduce) the input signal to a particular node.

For instance, when input x_1 is more significant than input x_2, the weight w_1 must be greater than w_2.

Step 3: Apply the combination function to sum the weighted inputs:

$$y = x_1 \cdot w_1 + \cdots + x_N \cdot w_N. \tag{1.1}$$

Step 4: Augment the weighted combination with the bias value to guarantee that even when all the inputs are zeros, the neuron is still activated. Depending on whether the bias is positive or negative, it can increase or decrease the weighted combination in the activation function:

$$y = \sum_{i=1}^{N} x_i \cdot w_i + b. \tag{1.2}$$

Step 5: Pass the weighted combination to the activation function, f, to calculate the output. This activation function decides if the neuron, in FFNN, will fire or not:

$$Z = f(y). \tag{1.3}$$

The following code snippets show the PyTorch implementation of a simple FFNN model:

```
1. #. . . . . . . . . . . . . . class imports . . . . . . . . .
2. import torch
3. import torch.nn as nn
4.
5. # . . . . . . . . . . . . . Model Building . . . . . . . .
   class FeedForewardNeuralNet(nn.Module):
6.     def __init__(self, input_size, hidden_size, num_classes):
7.         super(FeedForewardNeuralNet, self).__init__()
8.         self.fc1 = nn.Linear(input_size, hidden_size)
9.         self.relu = nn.ReLU()
10.        self.fc2 = nn.Linear(hidden_size, num_classes)
11.
12.    def forward(self, x):
13.        out = self.fc1(x)
14.        out = self.relu(out)
15.        out = self.fc2(out)
16.        return out
```

1.2.2 Activation Functions

To regulate whether a neuron or node is activated or not, an activation function is attached to an ANN. According to a comparison with biological neurons, a neuron's activation function occurs at the end, determining if the next neuron will fire. In an ANN, an activation function does the same thing. A structure that can be used as an input by the following cell is created from the output signal of the preceding cell. A neuron's input is important or insignificant to its learning process depending on whether or not the neuron's activation decision has been made. Using the activation function, the ANN can learn complex relationships in a group of input values so that it can produce the desired output (Singh and Manure, 2020). Now, let's discover the principal activation functions (Apicella *et al.*, 2021).

1.2.2.1 Binary Step Function

In a binary step function, a threshold value determines whether a neuron is triggered. The input to the activation function is tested to see if it exceeds a predetermined threshold. Neurons are only activated if their input is sent to the next hidden layer; otherwise, they are turned off:

$$f(x) = \begin{cases} 1 \text{ for } x \geq 0 \\ 0 \text{ for } x < 0 \end{cases}. \tag{1.4}$$

The binary step function has two major drawbacks that limit its useful-ness. First, it can only produce two-value outputs, so it cannot be used to solve multi-class classification problems. Second, it has a zero gradient that makes backpropagation more difficult.

1.2.2.2 Linear Activation Function

An activation function, known as the identity function, is a linear activation function in which the activation is directly proportional to the input:

$$f(x) = ax + c, \tag{1.5}$$

where a and c represent a coefficient and constant, respectively. Linear activa-tion shows two main downsides: (1) backpropagation isn't an option since the function's derivative is static; (2) if a linear activation function is applied, all levels of the FFNN will collapse into one.

1.2.2.3 Nonlinear Activation Functions

With simple linear activation, the model can't create or learn more complex input-output mappings because it lacks the processing power to do so. This problem can be addressed by introducing nonlinearity into the system via non-linear activation. To keep the neuron's output value within a certain range, non-linear activation functions are a primary consideration. For example, if weighted sums of deep learning models with millions of parameters aren't constrained to a certain limit, the value of the estimated weighted sum may increase. As a result, the difficulty of computing typically increases. It is also necessary that nonlinear activations are computationally efficient because they are calculated repeatedly depending on the depth of the deep learning model. The nonlinear activation output should also be symmetrical at zero in order to avoid gradient shifts. Network layers must be able to be differentiated or at least partially dif-ferentiated in order to train deep learning models. To be used as a nonlinear activation function, the function must meet all these requirements.

- Rectified linear unit (ReLU)
  ReLU is a popular activation that shows wide acceptance in deep learning. In addition to be simple to compute, it overcomes the van-ishing gradient dilemma and does not saturate:

$$ReLU(a) = \max(x, 0). \tag{1.6}$$

There is only one drawback of using it that it is not zero-centered. It suffers from the "dying ReLU" issue in which all negative inputs are mapped to a zero output; hence, this formula has no effect. In certain cases, it leads nodes to fully die and not learn anything at all. ReLU also has the issue of explosive activations due to its high upper limit to infinity. As a result, there are instances when nodes are rendered useless.

- Parametric ReLU (PReLU) activation function
  PReLU was introduced as an extension to the ReLU function by adding a linear variable α, the definition of ReLU, such that when the input is less than zero, some information gets through:

$$PReLU(x) = \max(\alpha x, x), \tag{1.7}$$

where α represents the slope of the negative part of ReLU in which the most appropriate value of α is learned through backpropagation.

- RELU6
  Another variant of ReLU that constrains the positive part of the function can be defined as follows:

$$RELU6(a) = \min\left(\max(0, a), 6\right). \tag{1.8}$$

- LeakyReLU activation function
  A variant of PReLU activation that sets the value of α to be 0.1:

$$LeakyReLU(x) = \max\left(0.1x, x\right). \tag{1.9}$$

Both LeakyReLU and PReLU enable backpropagation even for the nonpositive value of the input.

- Exponential linear unit (ELU) activation function
  A variation of ReLU that adjusts the slope of the negative portion of the function to be defined using a log curve with the main aim to evade the dead ReLU problem:

$$ELU(x) = \begin{cases} x & \text{if } x \geq 0 \\ \alpha * \left(\exp(x) - 1\right), & \text{if } x \leq 0 \end{cases}. \tag{1.10}$$

On the contrary, the exponential operation can increase the computational time of the network.

- Sigmoid activation function
  The sigmoid function converts its input value x into another value in the range [0, 1]. As a result, the sigmoid is frequently referred to as a

squashing function as it squashes any input in the range $(-\infty, \infty)$ to a certain value in the range $(0, 1)$:

$$sigmoid(x) = \frac{1}{1 + \exp(-x)}. \tag{1.11}$$

- Hyperbolic tangent (tanh) activation function
  If a neuron looks for an efficient way to squash input x into a value in the range $[-1, 1]$, the tank function is used. Compared to the sigmoid, it just addresses the issue of zero-centeredness:

$$\tanh(x) = \frac{1 - \exp(-2x)}{1 + \exp(-2x)}. \tag{1.12}$$

- SoftMax activation function
  A nonlinear activation function is defined as a mixture of many sigmoid functions. It computes the relative probability of each output class in the range $[0, 1]$:

$$softmax(x) = \frac{\exp(x_i)}{\Sigma_i \exp(x_i)}. \tag{1.13}$$

- Swish activation function
  A self-gated nonlinear activation function, developed by Google's research team, is an extension to sigmoid function and can be defined as follows:

$$swish = x * sigmoid(x). \tag{1.14}$$

In contrast to *ReLU*, Swish activation does not suddenly alter the direction close to $x = 0$ in the same way as *ReLU* does. As a result, the curve gradually shifts from 0 to values below 0 and then backs up again. In the ReLU activation function, small negative values were canceled out. Those negative values, on the other hand, may still be useful for identifying patterns in the data. This is a win-win scenario as large negative values are wiped out due to their scarcity. The non-repetitive nature of the Swish function facilitates the expressiveness of input data and the weight to be learned.

- Gaussian error linear unit (GELU) activation function
  A nonlinear function proposed for transformer networks (TNs), such as BERT, ROBERTa, and ALBERT, is driven by merging estates from dropout, zone out, and *ReLU*:

$$GELU(x) = xP(X < x) = x\phi(x) = 0.5\left(1 + \tanh\left[\sqrt{\frac{2}{\pi}}\left(x + 0.044715x^3\right)\right]\right).$$

(1.15)

- Scaled exponential linear unit (SELU)
  SELU was proposed for self-normalizing DNNs wherein each layer maintains the mean and variance from the preceding layers. Then, it uses these statistics to perform internal normalization by updating the output to have a mean of zero and a standard deviation of one. To shift the mean, *SELU* can map the input to either positive or negative values, which is not viable for *ReLU* function:

$$SELU(x) = \left\{\lambda\left\{\begin{array}{l}\propto\left(\exp(x)-1\right), \\ x\end{array}\right.\right.$$

(1.16)

where $\propto$ = 1.67326 and λ = 1.05070.
To implement nonlinearity in neural networks in a variety of ways, numerous nonlinear activation function variants have been proposed recently. Readers interested in learning more about other activation functions can gain additional information by consulting Apicella *et al.* (2021).

1.3 Convolutional Neural Networks (CNNs)

CNNs are a family of deep learning models that are precisely intended for the image recognition task. The development of the CNNs was stimulated by the study of the visual cortex of the human brain, and they have been applied in image recognition since the 1980s. The convolutional layer and pooling layers are the fundamental building blocks of CNN.

1.3.1 Convolutional Layer

Convolution operations exhibit high similarity with cross-correlation, but the cross-correlation rotates the filter f by 180 degrees before being applied to the input I (Zhang *et al.*, 2021). In this way, the important property of a convolution operation is the capacity to generate a duplicate of the kernel at the location of the desire by convolving a kernel with a discrete unit compulsion. In the cross-correlation, the correlation operation generates a 180-degree rotation of the impulse. As a result, pre-rotating the filter and then doing the identical sliding sum of products procedure should help find the correct,

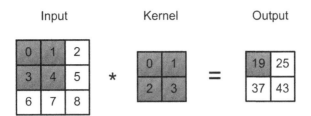

FIGURE 1.2
Illustration of convolution operation on single-channel inputs.

simple result (see Figure 1.2). In mathematical terms, for continuous complex-valued functions, the convolution operation between one-dimensional input I and a convolutional filter F can be defined as follows:

$$(F * I)(i) = \int F(a) \, g(i-a) \, da. \tag{1.17}$$

Likewise, for discrete input sequences, the convolution operation between one-dimensional input I and a filter F can be defined as follows:

$$(F * I)(i) = \sum_a F(a) \, g(i-a). \tag{1.18}$$

In a similar way, when it comes to two-dimensional input, the main concept is the same, but only the dimensionalities of the image and the filter have changed. Thus, the convolution operation between one-dimensional input I and a filter F can be demarcated as follows:

$$(F * I)(i, j) = \sum_a \sum_b F(a,b) \, I(i-a, j-b). \tag{1.19}$$

1.3.2 Pooling Layers

As the network gets deeper, the receptive field of each hidden node in any deep layer gets larger because the network has to progressively decrease the spatial resolution of its learned feature maps by aggregating the features. The nodes must be sensitive to all inputs (global representation). Intermediate convolution can continuously benefit from its ability to efficiently learn valuable hidden representations if it is used to progressively aggregate the hidden features and generate increasingly rough maps. While searching for lower level features like edges, translation invariance is a critical consideration. In this regard, *pooling layers* are discussed in this section to provide two key objectives. First, empower the convolution network to downsample the extracted feature maps across spatial dimensions. Second, enable alleviating the sensitivity of the convolution network to locality.

1.3.2.1 Max Pooling

Layers of pooling work in the same way as convolutional layers do, by scanning all inputs according to a predefined stride and producing a single output for each navigated position. Although the pooling operation lacks a kernel, unlike the kernelized convolution, it has no parameters that must be learned. As an alternative, the input elements covered by the pooling window are used to determine how a pooling operation should be performed. To refer to the pooling layer's output as the maximum input value under the pooling window, Max-pool is used as an acronym. The pooling window, like the convolutional layer, begins by scanning the input tensor row-by-row, starting at the top left corner. The maximum value in the current input subtensor covered by the pooling window is returned by the Max-pool layer at each sliding step. Figure 1.3 presents an example of a Max-pool operation on single-channel input, where each output element is calculated as follows:

$$max(0; 1; 3; 4) = 4,$$

$$max(1; 2; 4; 5) = 5,$$

$$max(3; 4; 6; 7) = 7,$$

$$max(4; 5; 7; 8) = 8. \tag{1.20}$$

1.3.2.2 Average Pooling

Average pooling is a variant of the pooling layer that calculates the average of values in the input subtensor covered by the pooling window as its output. Figure 1.4 displays an example of an average pooling operation using single-channel input, where the output element is calculated as follows:

$$average\ (2; 4; 8; 2) = 4,$$

$$average\ (4; 6; 2; 4) = 4,$$

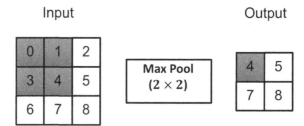

FIGURE 1.3
Illustration of max pooling operation on single-channel inputs.

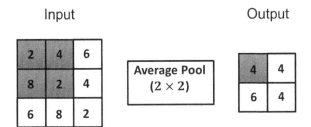

FIGURE 1.4
Illustration of average pooling operation on single-channel inputs.

$$average \ (8;\ 2;\ 6;\ 8) = 6,$$
$$average \ (2;\ 4;\ 8;\ 2) = 4. \tag{1.21}$$

The form of the output can be controlled and adjusted by pooling layers in a manner analogous to that of convolutional layers via the use of padding and stride hyperparameters. By doing so, one can obtain the desired output shape by padding the input and/or modifying the stride size. Instead of adding outputs over the channel dimension as is indicated with the convolutional kernel, the pooling operation is applied to each input channel on its own when multi-channel processing is being done since this is how the multi-channel scenario is handled. As a consequence, it follows that the pooling layer does not have any influence on the number of channels, as the number of channels remains constant for both the input and the output.

The following code snippets show the PyTorch implementation of a simple two-dimensional convolutional model:

```
1.  #. . . . .  . . . . . . . class imports . . . . . . . . . .
2.  import torch
3.  import torch.nn as nn
4.
5.  # . . . . .  . . . . . . . Model Building . . . . . . . . .
6.  class Conv2DNet(nn.Module):
7.      def __init__(self, num_classes=10):
8.          super(Conv2DNet, self).__init__()
9.          self.conv1 = nn.Sequential(
10.             nn.Conv2d(1, 16, kernel_size=5, stride=1, padding=2),
11.             nn.BatchNorm2d(16),
12.             nn.ReLU(),
13.             nn.MaxPool2d(kernel_size=2, stride=2))
14.         self.conv2 = nn.Sequential(
15.             nn.Conv2d(16, 32, kernel_size=5, stride=1, padding=2),
16.             nn.BatchNorm2d(32),
17.             nn.ReLU(),
18.             nn.MaxPool2d(kernel_size=2, stride=2))
19.         #. . . . . . . .Final fully connected layer (FCL). . . . .
20.         self.fc = nn.Linear(7*7*32, num_classes)
21.
```

```
22.     def forward(self, x):
23.         out = self.conv1(x)
24.         out = self.conv2(out)
25.         # . . . . . . . . Output reshaping . . . . . . . . . .
26.         out = out.reshape(out.size(0), -1)
27.         #. . . . . . . . . . . Final Output . . . . . . . . .
28.         out = self.fc(out)
29.         return out
```

The following code snippets show the PyTorch implementation of a simple one-dimensional convolutional model:

```
1. #. . . . . .  . . . . . . . class imports . . . . . . . . . .
2. import torch
3. import torch.nn as nn
4.
5. # . . . . . . .  . . . . . . . Model Building . . . . . . . . .
6. class Conv1DNet(nn.Module):
7.     def __init__(self, num_features=32,num_classes=10):
8.         super(Conv1DNet, self).__init__()
9.         self.conv1 = nn.Sequential(
10.            nn.Conv1d(num_features, 64, kernel_size=3),
11.            nn.ReLU(),
12.            nn.Dropout(0.5),
13.            nn.MaxPool1d(10))
14.        self.flat1 = nn.Flatten()
15.        # Fully connected layer (FCL), Relu Activation . . . . . .
16.        self.linear1 = nn.Sequential(
17.            nn.Linear(768,100),
18.            nn.ReLU())
19.        #.. . . . . . . Final SoftMax layer . . . . . . . . . .
20.        self.linear2 = nn.Sequential(
21.            nn.Linear(100,num_classes),
22.            nn.Softmax())
23.
24.    def forward(self, x):
25.        out1 = self.conv1(x)
26.        #. . . . . . . . . Output is flattened . . . . . . . . .
27.        out2 = self.flat1(out1)
28.        out3 = self.linear1(out2)
29.        #. . . . . . . . . . Final Output . . . . . . . . . .
30.        out4 = self.linear2(out3)
31.        return out4
```

1.4 Recurrent Neural Networks (RNNs)

Recurrent neural network (RNN) is a type of deep network that is structured as a special type of FFNN that uses the previous hidden state as memory, capturing and storing the temporal or sequential information (input) that the network has seen so far. The memorization ability of RNNs makes it an appropriate choice to learn from sequential and/or temporal data.

The weights are shared between layers in each RNN layer, which represents a discrete time step. The recurrent network can generate a useful summary of previous findings through the use of connections among the hidden units, catching interactions between events that occur in the data over time. The general structure of RNN can be illustrated by unfolding the network through time as shown in Figure 1.5. As shown, there are two inputs to the recurrent neuron at each time step t, namely, the new input x_t, and the output it generates at the preceding time step, $\tilde{y}_{t-1}$. Hence, the output of a single recurrent neuron is computed as follows:

$$\tilde{y}_t = \phi\left(x_t \cdot W_x + \tilde{y}_{t-1} \cdot W_y + b\right), \tag{1.22}$$

where ϕ and b represent the activation function and the bias value, respectively.

1.4.1 Vanilla RNN

Vanilla RNN is the simplest form of recurrent network in which a simple memory cell is implemented to control the network's hidden state throughout time steps (see Figure 1.6). Mathematically speaking, the working methodology of RNN cell can be formulated as follows:

$$h_t = \tanh\left(X_t \cdot W_{xh} + h_{t-1} \cdot W_{hh} + b_h\right), \tag{1.23}$$

$$o_t = h_t W_{hy} + b_y, \tag{1.24}$$

$$\tilde{y}_t = softmax\left(o_t\right), \tag{1.25}$$

where W_{xh}, W_{hh} and W_{hy} are weight matrices for the input, recurrent connections, and the output, respectively.

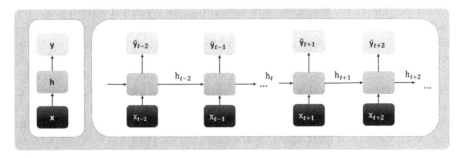

FIGURE 1.5
Unfolded architecture of recurrent neural network.

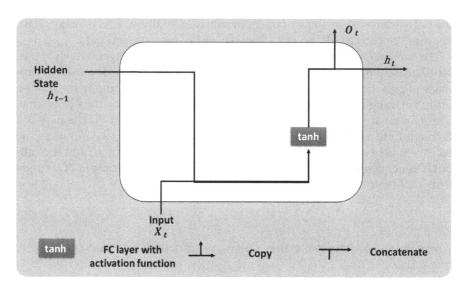

FIGURE 1.6
Architecture of internal vanilla recurrent neural network cell.

1.4.2 Long Short-Term Memory (LSTM)

The LSTM was first introduced in 1997 by Hochreiter and Urgen Schmidhuber (1997). It has been progressively enhanced over the years by a number of research studies (Sak, Senior and Beaufays, 2014; Hofmann and Mader, 2021). LSTM is a variant of a vanilla recurrent network that resolves the issue of vanishing gradient and maintains information in the memory as long as it is necessary. The design of the LSTM cell was doubtfully drawn from computer architecture's logic gates. The LSTM architecture includes a memory cell (or simply a cell) for storing long-term states that have the same shape as the concealed state engineered in some way to capture supplemental information. Some academics and practitioners view memory cells as a unique subtype of the concealed state. To obtain control over the memory cell, the LSTM design requires several gates, each of which serves a distinct function. Specifically, a gate is needed to define which portion of the memory information will be read and output from the memory cell, $C_t \in \mathbb{R}^{n \times h}$. The output gate, $O_t \in \mathbb{R}^{n \times h}$, can be determined by its presence. Another gate is necessary to control the addition of new memory entries. As implied by its name, this is the input gate, $I_t \in \mathbb{R}^{n \times h}$. In addition, a forget gate, $F_t \in \mathbb{R}^{n \times h}$, is necessary to control the mechanism for erasing the cell's contents. This gated design is motivated by the network's requirement for a committed mechanism, which permits selecting when to recall and when to ignore inputs in the concealed state. The architecture of an LSTM cell can be illustrated in Figure 1.7. Given n as batch size, d as the number of inputs, and h as the number of hidden units, the gates in the LSTM cell are calculated as follows:

$$I_t = \sigma\left(X_t \cdot W_{xi} + H_{t-1} \cdot W_{hi} + b_i\right), \tag{1.26}$$

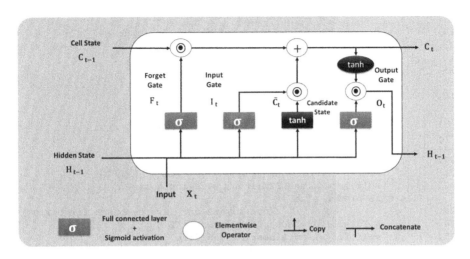

FIGURE 1.7
Architecture of an LSTM cell.

$$F_t = \sigma\left(X_t \cdot W_{xf} + H_{t-1} \cdot W_{hf} + b_f\right), \tag{1.27}$$

$$O_t = \sigma\left(X_t \cdot W_{xo} + H_{t-1} \cdot W_{ho} + b_o\right), \tag{1.28}$$

$$\tilde{C}_t = \tanh\left(X_t \cdot W_{xc} + H_{t-1} \cdot W_{hc} + b_c\right), \tag{1.29}$$

$$H_t = O_t \odot \tanh\left(C_t\right), \tag{1.30}$$

where σ is a sigmoid function, W_{xi} and W_{hi} denote the weight parameters of the input gate for its connections for the input vector and previous hidden state $H_{t-1} \in \mathbb{R}^{n \times h}$, correspondingly. W_{xf} and W_{hf} denote the weight parameters of the forgetting gate for its connections for the input vector and previous hidden state, correspondingly. W_{xo} and W_{ho} denote the weight parameters of the output gate for its connections for the input vector and previous hidden state, correspondingly. $b_i \in \mathbb{R}^{1 \times h}$, $b_f \in \mathbb{R}^{1 \times h}$, and $b_o \in \mathbb{R}^{1 \times h}$ represent bias parameters of input gate, forget gate, and output gate, respectively.

The following code snippets show the PyTorch implementation of a simple LSTM model:

```
1. #. . . . . . . . . . . . . . . class imports . . . . . . . . . . . .
2. import torch
3. import torch.nn as nn
4. from torch.autograd import Variable
5. #. . . . . . . . . . . . . . . Model Building . . . . . . . . .
6. class LSTM_Model(nn.Module):
7.     def __init__(self, num_classes, input_size, hidden_size,
   num_layers, seq_length):
8.         super(LSTM_Model, self).__init__()
```

```
9.
10.         # . . . . . . . . . . . .The size of input . . . . . . .
11.         self.input_size = input_size
12.         #. . . . . . . hidden state . . . . . . . . . .
13.         self.hidden_size = hidden_size
14.         #. . . . . . . . . . . number of layers . . . . . . . .
15.         self.num_layers = num_layers
16.         #. . . . . . . . . . . . number of classes . . . . . . .
17.         self.num_classes = num_classes
18.         #. . . . . . . . . The length of sequence . . . . . . . .
19.         self.seq_length = seq_length
20.
21.         #. . . . . . . . Long short-term Memeory (LSTM) . . . . . .
22.         self.lstm = nn.LSTM(input_size=input_size,
    hidden_size=hidden_size,
23.                            num_layers=num_layers, batch_first=True)
24.         # First fully connected layer (FCL). . . . . . . . . . .
25.         self.fc1 =  nn.Linear(hidden_size, 128)
26.         # Final fully connected layer (FCL). . . . . . . . . . .
27.         self.fc0 = nn.Linear(128, num_classes)
28.         # Rectified linear Unit(ReLU). . . . . . . . . . . . . .
29.         self.relu = nn.ReLU()
30.
31.     def forward(self,x):
32.         h_0 = Variable(torch.zeros(self.num_layers, x.size(0),
    self.hidden_size)) #hidden state
33.         c_0 = Variable(torch.zeros(self.num_layers, x.size(0),
    self.hidden_size)) #internal state
34.         # Propagate input through LSTM . . . . . . . . . . . . .
35.         output, (hn, cn) = self.lstm(x, (h_0, c_0))
36.         # Output reshaping. . . . . . . . . . . . . . . . . . .
37.         hn = hn.view(-1, self.hidden_size)
38.         out = self.relu(hn)
39.         out = self.fc1(out)
40.         # nonlinear activation . . . . . . . . . . . . . . . . .
41.         out = self.relu(out)
42.         #Final Output. . . . . . . . . . . . . . . . . . . . . .
43.         out = self.fc0(out)
44.         return out
```

1.4.3 Gated Recurrent Units (GRUs)

In the previous section, a detailed description of LSTM cells and its uses in various gating mechanisms is provided to deal with the problem of the issue of vanishing gradient faced in the vanilla recurrent network. However, one cloud noticed that the design of LSTM cell has a large number of parameters because of the presence of several gates and states. Thus, while backpropagating the LSTM network, we need to update a lot of parameters in every iteration. This increases our training time. To address this limitation, the GRU was proposed by Cho *et al.* (2014), which functions as a streamlined edition of the LSTM network. However, being different from the LSTM network, the design of GRU cells used just two gates and one hidden state (see Figure 1.8).

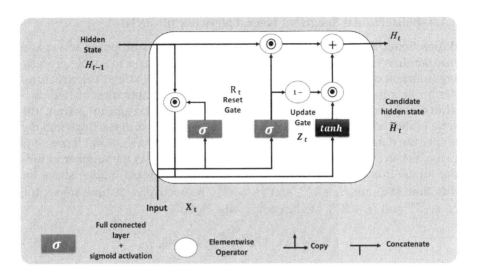

FIGURE 1.8
Architecture of GRU cell.

As with LSTM cells, the first component to know about GRU cells is the control gates that are called the *reset gate, $R_t \in \mathbb{R}^{n \times h}$*, and the *update gate, $Z_t \in \mathbb{R}^{n \times h}$*. In particular, the reset gate is responsible to control the amount of information that the GRU cell might need to remember from the previous hidden state. In a similar way, the update gate is responsible to regulate the degree to which the new hidden state is simply a copy of the old hidden state:

$$R_t = \sigma \left(X_t \cdot W_{xr} + H_{t-1} \cdot W_{hr} + b_r \right), \tag{1.31}$$

$$Z_t = \sigma \left(X_t \cdot W_{xz} + H_{t-1} \cdot W_{hz} + b_z \right), \tag{1.32}$$

$$\tilde{H}_t = \tanh \left(X_t \cdot W_{xh} + \left(R_t \odot H_{t-1} \right) \cdot W_{hh} + b_h \right), \tag{1.33}$$

$$H_t = Z_t \odot H_{t-1} + \left(1 - Z_t \right) \odot \tilde{H}_t, \tag{1.34}$$

where σ is a sigmoid function, W_{xr} and W_{hr} represent the weights of the reset gate for its connections for the input vector and previous hidden state, respectively. W_{xz} and W_{hz} denote the weights of the forgetting gate for its connections for the input vector and previous hidden state, respectively. W_{xh} and W_{hh} denote the parameters of the candidate *hidden state* for its connections for the input vector and previous hidden state, respectively. The symbol $\odot$ denotes the Hamdard product. $b_r \in \mathbb{R}^{1 \times h}$, $b_z \in \mathbb{R}^{1 \times h}$, and $b_z \in \mathbb{R}^{1 \times h}$ denote the bias parameters of reset gate, forget gate, and candidate state, respectively.

The implementation of GRU is almost similar to that of LSTM (see Section 1.8).

1.4.4 Bidirectional Recurrent Neural Network (Bi-RNN)

Bidirectional recurrent neural network (Bi-RNN) was proposed to expand the one-directional RNN with an additional hidden layer to enable processing information in a backward direction. Figure 1.9 illustrates the structural design of a bidirectional recurrent network as a combination of two one-directional recurrent networks—one moves forward, beginning from the start of the data sequence, and the other moves backward, starting from the end of the data sequence with one hidden layer. In mathematical terms, n is given as batch size, d as the number of inputs, and h as the number of hidden units. It is assumed that the forward and backward hidden states for this time step are $\overrightarrow{H_t} \in \mathbb{R}^{n \times d}$ and $\overleftarrow{H_t} \in \mathbb{R}^{n \times h}$, respectively. At time step t, the $\overrightarrow{H_t} \in \mathbb{R}^{n \times d}$ and $\overleftarrow{H_t} \in \mathbb{R}^{n \times h}$ can be computed as follows:

$$\overrightarrow{H_t} = \phi \left(X_t * W_{xh}^f + H_{t-1} * W_{hh}^f + b_h^f \right), \tag{1.35}$$

$$\overleftarrow{H_t} = \phi \left(X_t * W_{xh}^b + H_{t-1} * W_{hh}^b + b_h^b \right), \tag{1.36}$$

where ϕ is the hidden layer activation function. $W_{xh}^f \in \mathbb{R}^{d \times h}$, $W_{hh}^f \in \mathbb{R}^{h \times h}$, $W_{xh}^b \in \mathbb{R}^{d \times h}$, and $W_{hh}^b \in \mathbb{R}^{h \times h}$ denote the weight parameters of the forward and backward layers, respectively. $b_h^f \in \mathbb{R}^{1 \times h}$ and $b_h^b \in \mathbb{R}^{1 \times h}$ denote the bias parameters of the forward and backward layers, respectively. Next, both forward hidden state $\overrightarrow{H_t}$ and backward hidden state $\overleftarrow{H_t}$ are concatenated to calculate the hidden state $H_t \in \mathbb{R}^{n \times 2h}$ to be passed to the output layer. In Bi-RNNs, the information of the hidden state H_t is given as *input* to the following

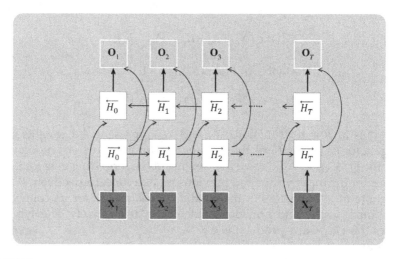

FIGURE 1.9
Architecture of bidirectional recurrent neural networks.

bidirectional layer. At the end of the network, the output is computed as follows:

$$O_t = H_t \cdot W_{hq} + b_q, \tag{1.37}$$

where $W_{hq} \in \mathbb{R}^{2h \times q}$ and $b_q \in \mathbb{R}^{1 \times q}$ denote the weight and bias parameters of the output layer, respectively.

```
1.  #. . . . . . . . . . . . . . . class imports . . . . . . . . . .
2.  import torch
3.  import torch.nn as nn
4.  from torch.autograd import Variable
5.  # . . . . . . . . . . . . . Model Building . . . . . . . . . . .
6.  class BiLSTM_Model(nn.Module):
7.      def __init__(self, num_classes, input_size, hidden_size,
    num_layers, seq_length):
8.          super(LSTM_Model, self).__init__()
9.
10.         # . . . . . . . . . . . . The size of input . . . . . . .
11.         self.input_size = input_size
12.         #.. . . . . . hidden state . . . . . . . . . . . . #..
13.         self.hidden_size = hidden_size
14.         #.. . . . . . . . . . . . number of layers . . . . . . .
15.         self.num_layers = num_layers
16.         #. . . . . . . . . . . . . number of classes . . . . . . .
17.         self.num_classes = num_classes
18.         #. . . . . . . . . . . The length of sequence . . . . . .
19.         self.seq_length = seq_length
20.
21.         #Long short-term Memeory (LSTM). . . . . . . . . . . . .
22.         self.lstm = nn.LSTM(input_size=input_size,
    hidden_size=hidden_size,
23.                         num_layers=num_layers, bidirectional=True,
    batch_first=True)
24.         # First fully connected layer (FCL) for bidirectional LSTM
25.         self.fc1 =  nn.Linear(hidden_size*2, 128)
26.         # Final fully connected layer (FCL). . . . . . . . . . .
27.         self.fc0 = nn.Linear(128, num_classes)
28.         #. . . . . . . . . . . Rectified linear Unit(ReLU). . . . .
29.         self.relu = nn.ReLU()
30.
31.     def forward(self,x):
32.         #.. . . . . . hidden state for bidirectional LSTM . . . .
33.         h_0 = Variable(torch.zeros(self.num_layers*2, x.size(0),
    self.hidden_size))
34.         #. . . . . . internal state for bidirectional LSTM . . .
35.         c_0 = Variable(torch.zeros(self.num_layers*2, x.size(0),
    self.hidden_size))
36.         # Propagate input through BiLSTM.. . . . . . . . . . . .
37.         output, (hn, cn) = self.lstm(x, (h_0, c_0))
38.         #. . . . . . . . . . . . Output reshaping. . . . . . . .
39.         hn = hn.view(-1, self.hidden_size)
40.         out = self.relu(hn)
41.         out = self.fc1(out)
```

```
42.        #. . . . . . . . . . . . nonLinear activation . . . . . .
43.        out = self.relu(out)
44.        #. . . . . . . . . . . . . Final Output. . . . . . . . .
45.        out = self.fc0(out)
46.        return out
```

1.5 Autoencoder

An interesting unsupervised learning algorithm is the autoencoder. Unlike other deep learning (DL) models, the target of the autoencoder is to generate output that is identical to the input [1]. To achieve that, the autoencoder is made up of two major modules known as the encoder and the decoder. The encoder's role is to encode the input by learning the latent representation of the input, and the decoder's role is to reconstruct the input from the encoder's latent representation. Latent representation is also known as "code" or "bottleneck." The encoder module, as shown in Figure 1.10, receives an image as input and then trains to learn the latent representation of that input. The latent representation is then passed to the decoder, which attempts to reconstruct the input image. Given an encoder $g_\varphi(\cdot)$ and decoder $f_\theta(\cdot)$, they are both serious about their auto-encoding operations. The encoder g_φ comprising many neural layers accepts input x and returns the consistent low-dimensional latent representation z. The encoding operation can be mathematically defined as follows:

$$z = g_\varphi(x), \tag{1.38}$$

$$\tilde{z} = \phi(\varphi x + b), \tag{1.39}$$

where φ represents the parameter of the encoder. The latent representation z is passed to a decoder $f_\theta(\cdot)$, containing one or many neural layers, which

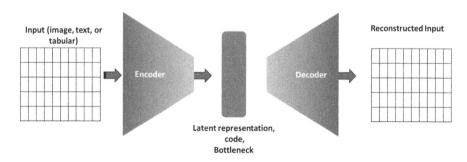

FIGURE 1.10
Architecture of standard autoencoder.

learns to produce output $\tilde{x}$ by reconstructing the original input. This can be mathematically represented as follows:

$$\tilde{x} = f_\theta(z), \tag{1.40}$$

$$\tilde{x} = \phi(\theta z + b), \tag{1.41}$$

where θ characterizes the parameter of the decoder. The autoencoder needs to learn the optimal parameters, θ and ϕ, for both encoder and decoder, respectively, by diminishing some loss function that guesstimates the variance between the actual samples and reconstructed counterparts, which is termed reconstruction loss. For example, MSE is a popular loss for measuring the reconstruction ability of AE:

$$L(\theta, \phi) = \frac{1}{n} \sum_{i=1}^{n} \left(x - f_\theta \left(g_\phi(x) \right) \right)^2, \tag{1.42}$$

where n represents the number of training samples.

```
1. #. . . . .  . . . . . class imports . . . . . . .
2. import torch
3. import torch.nn as nn
4.
5. # . . . . .  . . . . Model Building . . . . . . . .
6. class AutoEncoder(nn.Module):
7.     def __init__(self):
8.         super(AutoEncoder, self).__init__()
9.
10.        #. . . . . . . . . . . . . Build Encoder. . . . . . . .
11.        self.encoder = nn.Sequential(
12.            nn.Linear(32*32, 264),
13.            nn.Tanh(),
14.            nn.Linear(264, 128),
15.            nn.Tanh(),
16.            nn.Linear(128, 64),
17.            nn.Tanh(),
18.            nn.Linear(64, 12),
19.        )
20.        #. . . . . . . . . . . . Latent Representation . . . . . .
21.
22.        #. . . . . . . . . . . . Build Decoder. . . . . . . .
23.        self.decoder = nn.Sequential(
24.            nn.Linear(12, 64),
25.            nn.Tanh(),
26.            nn.Linear(64, 128),
27.            nn.Tanh(),
28.            nn.Linear(128, 264),
29.            nn.Tanh(),
30.            nn.Linear(264, 32*32),
31.        #. . . . . . . . . . compress to a range (0, 1) . . . . . .
32.            nn.Sigmoid(),
```

```
33.              )
34.
35.      def forward(self, x):
36.
37.              #. . . . . . . . . . encoding.. . . . . . . . . . . . .
38.              encoded = self.encoder(x)
39.              #. . . . . . . . . . decoding.. . . . . . . . . . . .
40.              decoded = self.decoder(encoded)
41.              return encoded, decoded
```

1.6 Deep Learning for Graph Intelligence

Since the data that comes from applications that are used in the real world can take on a wide variety of forms, ranging from matrices and tensors to sequences and time series, it is only natural to wonder why we try to represent data using graphs. There are two primary reasons for doing something. To begin, graphs offer a standard method for the representation of data. Data from many different systems and fields can be explicitly denoted as graphs. Some examples of these networks include social media networks, Internet of Things (IoT) networks, citation networks, knowledge graphs, and visual cortex networks. In the meantime, graphs can be constructed out of a wide variety of other kinds of data as well. Second, a vast majority of issues that arise in the real world can be solved by performing a modest number of computational tasks on graphs. The problem of node classification can be summed up as the identification of relevant genes to diseases, the inference of relevant criteria of nodes, the detection of anomalous nodes (such as spammers or terrorists), and the recommendation of relevant medicines to patients. The trouble of link prediction encompasses a wide range of other issues as well, including the forecasting of polypharmacy side effects, the identification of drug-target interactions, and the completion of knowledge graphs.

Nodes on graphs are inextricably linked to one another, which suggests that nodes do not exist in a standalone state. However, traditional machine learning techniques frequently assume that the data is unrelated to one another and is distributed in the same way. As a consequence of this, it would be inappropriate for them to directly tackle computational tasks involving graphs. The development of solutions can primarily go in one of two directions. The classification of nodes will serve as an illustration example for us to talk about these two different directions. Developing a brand-new mechanism that is optimized for use with graphs is one approach. Collective classification is the name given to the classification problem that was developed specifically for graphs (Sen *et al.*, 2008). Collaborative classification, on the other hand, differs from traditional classification, in that it not only takes into account the mapping between a node's features and its label, but it also takes into account the mapping of its neighborhood. The alternative approach involves "flattening" a graph by constructing a set of features to denote its nodes. This allows conventional classification methods to be applied.

Because this path can make use of conventional machine learning techniques, it has quickly risen to the top of the field and is becoming increasingly popular. The ability to successfully construct a set of features for nodes will be essential to the success of this direction (or node representations). The field of computer vision, speech recognition, and natural language processing are just some of the areas that have benefited greatly from the application of deep learning because it is effective in representation learning. As a result, bridging deep learning with graphs opens up opportunities that have never been seen before. On the other hand, deep learning on graphs is fraught with enormous difficulties. To begin, traditional deep learning was developed for regularly organized data such as images and sequences, whereas graphs are infrequent, with nodes in a graph being unordered and able to have distinguishable neighborhoods. Graphs pose a challenge for conventional deep learning because of their irregular nature. Second, the structural information for frequent data is relatively straightforward, whereas the information for graphs is more sophisticated. This is due to the fact that there are many different kinds of complex graphs (illustrated in Figure 1.1), and that nodes and edges can be connected to different forms of rich-side information. As a result, traditional methods of deep learning are insufficient to encapsulate such an abundance of information. Deep learning on graphs is a recently developed area of research that has opened the door to previously unimaginable prospects as well as enormous obstacles.

1.7 What Is Covered in This Book?

Chapter 1: Conceptualization of Graph Intelligence
This chapter provides an introduction to graph intelligence as well as the related concepts in the context of deep learning. Then, the chapter presents background on deep learning by reviewing elementary deep learning models such as FFNs, CNNs, RNNs, as well as AEs. The chapter then discusses the backpropagation methods and related tricks for training deep networks. By the end of this chapter, we briefly discuss the main content covered in each chapter of the book to give the reader concise insight into the systematic flow of topics across chapters.

Chapter 2: Foundation of Graph Representations
Chapter 2 presents a detailed discussion about the graph's representations, the related matrix representations, as well as the imperative events and attributes of graph representation such as centrality, connectivity, and degree. The discussion is then extended to discuss graph signal processing and

graph Fourier transform and how they settle the fundamentals for spectral founded graph intelligence. After that, the chapter examines different types of composite graphs. Lastly, the chapter debated demonstrative computing tasks on graphs, namely, graph- and node-oriented tasks.

Chapter 3: Graph Embedding

Chapter 3 presents a generic framework and new outlook for interpreting graph embedding approaches in an integrated fashion. This framework chiefly involves the counting of four constituents: first, the mapping function to map nodes of the certain graph into the corresponding embeddings in the embedding space; second, an information miner act to mine and fuse information from the graphs; third, a reconstructor to use the node embeddings to reconstruct the obtained information; and, fourth, the objective function that is responsible for measuring the variance between the reconstructed and the mined information. This function is optimized to learn the graph embeddings. Then, the chapter provides a general taxonomy of graph embedding approaches based on the information they seek to reserve counting community, structural role, co-occurrence, and the global status grounded methods while providing the details of archetypal algorithms in each of those categories. Moreover, in this general framework, the chapter debates the demonstrative embedding approaches for composite graphs, comprising bipartite graphs, heterogeneous graphs, and dynamic graphs, signed graphs, multi-dimensional graphs, and hypergraphs.

Chapter 4: Graph Neural Networks

Chapter 4 presents the structural design of graph neural network (GNN) algorithms for node- and graph-oriented tasks. In particular, the chapter discusses two chief constituents of GNN, graph filtering and graph pooling layer, for refining the node features and coarsening the graph to create the graph representation. The chapter presents a taxonomy for both graph filters and graph pooling into categories and reviews archetypal algorithms in each category. By the end, the chapter argues the methodology of learning parameters of GNN for various downstream tasks, such as node classification.

Chapter 5: Graph Convolutional Networks

Chapter 5 debates one of the most well-known families of graph networks, known as graph convolutional networks, which is divided into spectral graph convolutions as well as spatial graph convolution networks. The chapter discusses the main differences between the two categories of graph convolutional networks. Then, the chapter provides a detailed explanation and implementation of the state-of-the-art algorithms in each category.

Chapter 6: Graph Attention Networks

Chapter 6 investigates a new family of attention-based GNNs, which is called graph attention networks. In-line with the theoretical discussion, the chapter provides PyTorch's implementations of the state-of-the-art graph attention algorithms, including graph attention network (GAT), GAT version 2 (GATv2), graph transformers, and graph transformer network (GTN) for heterogeneous graphs. By the end of the chapter, we investigate the potential of graph attention models in a real-world case study of malware detection.

Chapter 7: Recurrent Graph Neural Networks

Chapter 7 explores another popular family of graph networks known as recurrent graph neural networks. The chapter begins by discussing deep learning for sequence modeling and shows the challenges that arise from the ignorance of time dependency. Next, the recurrent graph neural networks are investigated to show how they positively exploit the history of the process to afford a generic solution for generating embeddings at the node level via an information propagation scheme acknowledged as message passing. The chapter provides a detailed explanation and implementation of some state-of-the-art algorithms for recurrent graph neural networks.

Chapter 8: Graph Autoencoders

Chapter 8 discusses a common family of graph networks termed graph autoencoders that concentrate on customizing autoencoders to learn from graphs. The chapter begins by discussing the working mechanisms of a standard autoencoder and how it is extended to graph data. Next, the second part of the chapter discusses the viewpoint of variational graph autoencoders.

Chapter 9: Demystifying Interpretable Graph Intelligence

Chapter 9 provides a taxonomic exploration of the existing approaches to explaining the graph intelligence models. The holistic and taxonomic discussion of interpretability approaches illuminates the similarities and contrasts between current approaches, paving the way for future methodological advancements. The chapter provides some practical implementation of common interpretability methods. By the end of Chapter 9, we extend the discussion to cover the metrics for evaluating the explanation of graph networks.

Chapter 10: Demystifying Privacy Preservation for Graph Intelligence

Chapter 9 is expanded upon in Chapter 10, which does so by giving a more in-depth analysis of important aspects of responsibility for graph intelligence. This is accomplished through a discussion of the privacy issues and threat models for graph neural networks. A fine-grained taxonomy has been designed for each aspect of graph intelligence in order to categorize the corresponding methods and devise generic outlines for the various types of privacy-protection methods. This has been done in order to enrich the readers' knowledge about the topic of privacy preservation in graph intelligence.

1.8 Case Study

The discussion in the previous sections shows a different family of deep networks that have astonishing achievements in the field of cyber-security and threat intelligence, especially in complex environments like IoT systems and smart cities. In this regard, it may be interesting for a large span of readers to practically explore and implement these models in real-world case studies for cyber-security. Motivated by that, the supplementary materials of this chapter are designated to provide an implementation of the abovementioned methods in real-world case studies. The supplementary materials of this chapter also provide the readers with recommendations for further reading about the content of this chapter.

The repository of supplementary materials is given in this link: https://github.com/DEEPOLOGY-AI/Book-Graph-Neural-Network/tree/main/Chapter%201.

References

Apicella, A. *et al.* (2021) 'A Survey on Modern Trainable Activation Functions', *Neural Networks*, 138, pp. 14–32. doi: 10.1016/j.neunet.2021.01.026.

Cho, K. *et al.* (2014) 'Learning Phrase Representations Using RNN Encoder-Decoder for Statistical Machine Translation', in *EMNLP 2014–2014 Conference on Empirical Methods in Natural Language Processing, Proceedings of the Conference.* doi: 10.3115/v1/d14-1179.

Hochreiter, S. and Urgen Schmidhuber, J. J. (1997) 'Long Short Term Memory (LSTM)', *Memory Neural Computation*, 9, 1735–1780.

Hofmann, M. and Mader, P. (2021) 'Synaptic Scaling-An Artificial Neural Network Regularization Inspired by Nature', *IEEE Transactions on Neural Networks and Learning Systems.* doi: 10.1109/TNNLS.2021.3050422.

Sak, H., Senior, A. and Beaufays, F. (2014) 'Long Short-Term Memory Recurrent Neural Network Architectures for Large Scale Acoustic Modeling', in *Proceedings of the Annual Conference of the International Speech Communication Association, INTERSPEECH.* doi: 10.21437/interspeech.2014-80.

Singh, P. and Manure, A. (2020) *Learn TensorFlow 2.0.* doi: 10.1007/978-1-4842-5558-2.

Zhang, A. *et al.* (2021) Dive into Deep Learning. *arXiv preprint arXiv:2106.11342.*

2

Fundamentals of Graph Representations

2.1 Introduction

The graph is a popular data structure that designates pairwise relationships between multiple entities. Graph representation becomes a prevailing representation for a broad range of data modalities from different disciplines, such as social science, biology, chemistry, linguistics, the Internet of Things (IoT), and cyber security. Graphs have been broadly adopted in social science to designate the relationships between persons. In linguistics, graph representations are used to capture the meaning of words and their relationships with other words aiming to capture the syntactical and semantic structures of sentences. In IoT, wireless networks can easily be designated as a directed graph, whereby the required communication links were designated as nodes, while the damaging intrusion links are designated as edges. In cyber security, IoT malware and anomalies can be represented as graphs in accountancy for their intrinsic geometry. In conventional deep learning, the architecture of network topology is not completely exploited because most deep networks are developed to deal with Euclidean (*grid-like*) structure representations (i.e., visual, textual, and tabular data). To evade this shortcoming, graph representational learning is projected to learn from non-Euclidean structured data in the last few years. Hence, research on graphs has fascinated huge attention from numerous industries and research fields.

This chapter finds and defines the fundamental concepts of graph representation as follows:

- The chapter begins by introducing the primary concepts of graphs and deliberates the common grid representations of graphs (i.e., Laplacian matrix and adjacency matrix) and the related attributes.
- Next, the chapter explores the attributed graphs in which each node is accompanied by a set of attributes to offer a clear interpretation of such kinds of graphs by treating each attribute as a function or signal on the graph.

DOI: 10.1201/9781003329701-2

- As the important fundamentals for graph representation learning, the present notions of graph signal processing and graph Fourier analysis are discussed in this chapter.

- Then, the chapter presents shallow dive into the details of different forms of complex graphs that are regularly applied to capture complex relationships between things in real-life applications.

- By the end of this chapter, the reader can explore and understand the representative computing chores on graphs, which are principally functioning as downstream tasks for graph representation learning.

2.2 Graph Representation

The graph is a pervasive data structure and a general way of unfolding and representing interactions between elements of complicated systems. In its simplest form, a graph is a group of nodes (vertices) representing some real-world entities, together with a set of edges representing the relationships between pairs of these entities.

Definition. *A "graph" is a data structure, denoted as $G = \{\mathcal{N}, \mathcal{E}\}$, composed of a set of nodes $\mathcal{N} = \{n_1, \ldots n_N\}$ interconnected with a set of edge $\mathcal{E} = \{e_1, \ldots, e_E\}$, where $N = |\mathcal{N}|$ and $E = |\mathcal{E}|$.*

According to the above definition, the nodes are regarded as the key elements in a graph. For example, in blockchain, bitcoin transactions can be represented as graph nodes, while the flow of bitcoins between transactions can be represented as the edge of the graph. In citation networks, nodes denote papers, while edges denote citations. In IoT networks, nodes denote IoT devices, while edges denote the communication between devices. The number of nodes refers to the size of the graph $N = |\mathcal{N}|$. Besides, if the graph G contains an edge $e \in \mathcal{E}$ connecting node n_i and n_j, then the edge e can be represented as (n_e^i, n_e^j). If the edge in the graph is directed from the node n_i and n_j, then the graph is directed. In contrast, the direction of edges in undirected graphs makes no sense such that $e = (n_e^i, n_e^j) = (n_e^j, n_e^i)$. In this context, one can consider node n_i and n_j as incident to the edge $e = (n_e^i, n_e^j)$. Two nodes can be called to each other only when there is an edge between them.

An appropriate method is equivalently represented to characterize graph representation $G = \{\mathcal{N}, \mathcal{E}\}$ through an adjacency matrix $A \in \mathbb{R}^{|\mathcal{N}| \times |\mathcal{N}|}$. To build the adjacency matrix for graph G, the nodes of the graph are ordered in such a way that the index of each node matches the index of a specific column or row in the adjacency matrix. Then, the existence of an edge between node n_i and node n_j can be represented as $A[i;j] = 1$, if $(n_e^i, n_e^j) \in \mathcal{E}$, else $A[i;j] = 0$. If the graph is undirected, then the adjacency matrix of this graph is symmetric

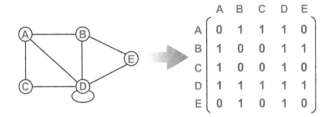

FIGURE 2.1
Illustration of adjacency matrix for undirected graph.

around the diagonal. In the case of a directed graph, the adjacency matrix is not necessarily symmetric. In some kinds of graphs, the edge might be accompanied by some weights, which change the value of entries in the adjacency matrix from binary ones to arbitrary real values.

Definition. *An adjacency matrix $A \in \mathbb{R}^{|\mathcal{N}| \times |\mathcal{N}|}$ is a way of representing a finite graph $G = \{\mathcal{N}, E\}$, as a square matrix of Boolean values, whereby the presence of an edge between node n_i and node n_j can be indicated as $A[i; j] = 1$ or otherwise $A[i; j] = 0$.*

In Figure 2.1, an illustration is given for building 4×4 matrix as the adjacency matrix of undirected graph $G = \{\mathcal{N}, \mathcal{E}\}$, where $\mathcal{N} = \{A, B, C, D, E\}$ and
$\mathcal{E} = \left\{ \left(n_e^a, n_e^b\right), \left(n_e^a, n_e^c\right), \left(n_e^a, n_e^d\right), \left(n_e^d, n_e^d\right), \left(n_e^b, n_e^d\right), \left(n_e^c, n_e^d\right), \left(n_e^b, n_e^e\right), \left(n_e^d, n_e^e\right) \right\}$.

In Figure 2.2, an illustration is given for building 4×4 matrix as the adjacency matrix of directed graph $G = \{\mathcal{N}, \mathcal{E}\}$, where $\mathcal{N} = \{A, B, C, D, E\}$ and
$\mathcal{E} = \left\{ \overrightarrow{\left(n_e^a, n_e^b\right)}, \overrightarrow{\left(n_e^a, n_e^c\right)}, \overrightarrow{\left(n_e^a, n_e^d\right)}, \overrightarrow{\left(n_e^d, n_e^d\right)}, \overrightarrow{\left(n_e^b, n_e^d\right)}, \overrightarrow{\left(n_e^c, n_e^d\right)}, \overrightarrow{\left(n_e^b, n_e^e\right)}, \overrightarrow{\left(n_e^d, n_e^e\right)} \right\}$.

2.3 Properties and Measure

In graph theory, the properties of the graph are essentially used for characterizing the graphs according to the structure of the graph. In this section, the elementary properties of the graph are discussed in more detail.

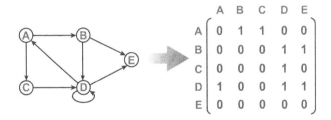

FIGURE 2.2
Illustration of adjacency matrix for directed graph.

2.3.1 Degree

As stated previously, the graph consists of a set of nodes. Each node in the graph, $G = \{\mathcal{N}, \mathcal{E}\}$, is adjacent to some nodes and non-adjacent to someone. In graph theory, the set of adjacent nodes is referred to as **neighbors**. The neighborhood of a node n_i in a graph, $G = \{\mathcal{N}, \mathcal{E}\}$, is written as $N(n_i)$.

Definition. Neighbors. *Given a graph $G = \{\mathcal{N}, \mathcal{E}\}$, the neighbors of each node, $N(n_i)$, are a suitable **subset** of nodes that are adjacent to the node, n_i.*

In graph representation, each node can be characterized with degree property, which defines the number of nodes to which this node is connected. In other words, the degree of the node represents the number of its adjacent nodes. The degree property is very straightforward in the case of the undirected graph; however, this may vary a little in the case of a directed graph. Specifically, each node in the directed graph has an in-degree and an out-degree. The in-degree of a node n_i represents the number of edges it receives, while the out-degree of node n_i is the number of edges going out from it.

Definition. Degree. *Given a graph $G = \{\mathcal{N}, \mathcal{E}\}$, the degree of a node n_i is the cardinality of the neighbors of the node n_i.*

$$D(n_i) = \sum_{n_j \in \mathcal{N}} adj_\mathcal{E}\left(\{n_i, n_j\}\right) = |N(n_i)|, \qquad (2.1)$$

where $adj_\mathcal{E}$ denotes an adjacency function formulated as follows:

$$adj_\mathcal{E}\left(\{n_i, n_j\}\right) = \begin{cases} 1 \text{ if } \left(n_e^i, n_e^j\right) \in \mathcal{E}, \\ 0 \text{ if } \left(n_e^i, n_e^j\right) \notin \mathcal{E}. \end{cases} \qquad (2.2)$$

Following the above definition, one can calculate the degree of each node n_i from the adjacency matrix. More precisely, one can compute the degree of a node n_y as follows:

$$D(n_i) = \sum_{j=0}^{N-1} A_{i,j}, \qquad (2.3)$$

Given the above definition, one could conclude that the sum of degrees of all nodes is twice the number of edges, $|\mathcal{E}|$, in the graph. To prove that, we advise the reader to refer to Ma and Tang (2021).

In Figure 2.3, connected graph $G = \{\mathcal{N}, \mathcal{E}\}$ is given, where $\mathcal{N} = \{n_1, n_2, n_3, n_4\}$ and $\mathcal{E} = \left\{\left(n_e^1, n_e^4\right), \left(n_e^1, n_e^2\right), \left(n_e^1, n_e^3\right), \left(n_e^2, n_e^4\right)\right\}$. The degree of nodes can be computed as follows D $(n_1) = 3$, D $(n_2) = 2$, D $(n_3) = 1$, and D $(n_4) = 2$.

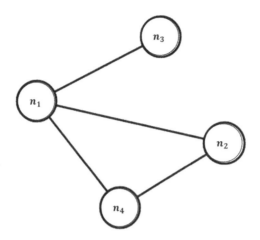

FIGURE 2.3
Illustration of undirected graph.

2.3.2 Connectivity

When it comes to the traversal of the graph from one node to another, it is essential to determine how the graph is connected. In graph theory, connectivity is a rudimentary property that characterizes if the graph is connected or not connected.

A graph can be declared, $G = \{\mathcal{N}, \mathcal{E}\}$, as **connected if it contains a path between every pair of nodes** $\{n_i, n_j\}$. From each node in the graph, there is a path to navigate to reach another node. This can be referred to as graph connectivity. On the other hand, a graph, $G = \{\mathcal{N}, \mathcal{E}\}$, with many disconnected nodes and edges is said to be disconnected. Figure 2.4 provides smart illustration of different forms of walks in graph.

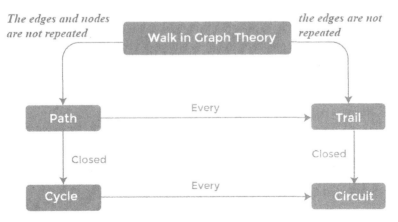

FIGURE 2.4
Illustration of kinds of walks in graph theory.

The traverse or walk of the graph can be declared as a series of nodes and edges of a graph $G = \{\mathcal{N}, \mathcal{E}\}$. In the traverse, the traverse will be known as a walk. In a walk, there can be repeated edges and vertices. The number of edges which is covered in a walk will be known as the length of the walk. In a graph, there can be more than one walk.

Definition. *traverse/walk. A series of nodes and edges refer to a traverse that start with a node and end with a node wherever each edge is occurrence of the nodes directly before and after it.*

It is worth mentioning that there are two categories of the traverse/walk. First, an open walk refers to a kind of walk in which the node at which the transverse begins differs from the nodes from the node at the end of the traverse. In simple words, the starting node differs from the ending node. Typically, the length of the open walk has to be more than 0. Second, the closed walk is a kind of walk in which the starting node of the walk is the same as the node at the end. In this context, we explore some common terms characterizing the walk/traverse in the graph theory.

A trail could be thought of as an open traverse without repeating edges, while the nodes are allowed to be repeated. Similarly, when closed walk/traverse is not allowed to repeat edges, it can be called the circuit. As with trail, the circuit allows repeating nodes. Speaking about the open walk, the term "path" is a sort of walk/traverse in which both nodes and edges are not permitted to repeat. It is possible for a path to just have the same node at the beginning and end. In an open stroll, the distance must be greater than 0. In graph theory, a closed path is often referred to as a cycle. A closed walk that forbids the repetition of edges or nodes is known as a cycle. In a cycle, just the beginning and finishing vertices may be the same.

Definition. *Subgraph. A graph $G' = \{\mathcal{N}', \mathcal{E}'\}$ is defined as a subgraph of graph $G = \{\mathcal{N}, \mathcal{E}\}$ if and only if the nodes $\mathcal{N}'$ are a subset of nodes $\mathcal{N}$, that is, $\mathcal{N}' \subset \mathcal{N}$, and $\mathcal{E}'$ is a subset of edges $\mathcal{E}$, that is, $\mathcal{E}' \subset \mathcal{E}$.*

Definition. *Connected component is defined as a subgraph, $G' = \{\mathcal{N}', \mathcal{E}'\}$, wherein there is always a path connecting pair of nodes.*

To make things simpler, a group of nodes constitute a connected component in an undirected graph, $G = \{\mathcal{N}, \mathcal{E}\}$, if and only if all nodes are reachable from any node, n_i, in this group. The chief focus here lies in node reachability. An example of a graph with the connected component and a graph with many connected components is presented in Figure 2.5.

Definition. *Connected graph is defined as a graph $G = \{\mathcal{N}, \mathcal{E}\}$ that contains one or more connected components.*

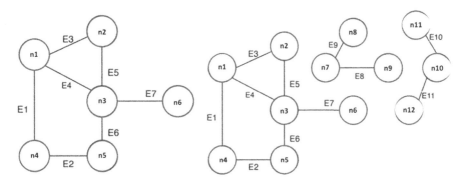

FIGURE 2.5
Illustration of connected graphs: (left) one connected graph and (right) three connected graphs.

Definition. *Shortest Path. For each pair of nodes $n_i, n_j \in \mathcal{N}$ in graph $G = \{\mathcal{N}, \mathcal{E}\}$, there is set P_{ij} containing all paths between node n_i and node n_j, where the shortest path in P_{ij} is defined as follows:*

$$p_{ij}^{sp} = \arg\min_{p \in P_{ij}} |p|, \tag{2.4}$$

where p refers to a path in P_{ij} with $|p|$ its length and p_{ij}^{sp} refers to the shortest path. It is worth mentioning that a pair of nodes could have one or more of the shortest paths. The crucial information that passes between two nodes is described by the shortest path. The total information of the shortest pathways between any two nodes in a graph reveals key details about the graph. The length of the longest and shortest path within a graph is referred to as the diameter of the graph.

Definition. *The diameter of a connected graph $G = \{\mathcal{N}, \mathcal{E}\}$ is defined as follows:*

$$diameter(G) = \max_{n_i, n_j \in \mathcal{N}} \min_{p \in P_{ij}} |p|. \tag{2.5}$$

2.3.3 Centrality

The importance of the node can be measured by the centrality of a node in the graph. In this section, we discuss the importance of the node by introducing a different way to measure node centrality.

2.3.3.1 Degree Centrality

The importance of the node is related to the other nodes connected to it. So, we use the degree of the node to measure the node centrality. For node n_i, the degree of node centrality can be defined as follow:

$$c_t(n_i) = t(n_i) = \sum_{j=1}^{|\mathcal{N}|} A_{ij}. \tag{2.6}$$

The following code snippet shows python implementation for calculating degree centrality `networkx` Library

```
1.  #. . . . . . . . . .class imports. . . . . . . . . . . . . .
2.  import networkx as nx
3.  #. . . . . . . Build Graph Gr: Graph of Karate Club. . . . . . . .
4.  Gr = nx.karate_club_graph()
5.  #. . . . . . . . . . . . Calculate Centrality. . . . . . . .
6.  deg_centrality = nx.degree_centrality(Gr)
7.  print(deg_centrality)
```

The in-degree centrality for a node n_i is the portion of nodes to which the input edges are linked. Hence, the following code snippet shows python implementation for calculating in-degree centrality using `networkx` Library

```
1.  #. . . . . . . . . .class imports. . . . . . . . . . . . . .
2.  import networkx as nx
3.  #. . . . . . . . Build Graph Gr: Graph of Karate Club. . . . . . .
4.  Gr = nx.karate_club_graph()
5.  #. . . . . . . . . . . Calculate Centrality. . . . . . . .
6.  in_deg_centrality = nx.in_degree_centrality(Gr)
7.  print(in_deg_centrality)
```

The out-degree centrality for a node n_i is the portion of nodes to which the output edges are linked. Hence, the following code snippet shows python implementation for calculating out-degree centrality using `networkx` Library

```
1.  #. . . . . . . . . . . class imports. . . . . . . . . . . . .
2.  import networkx as nx
3.  #. . . . . . . . Build Graph Gr: Graph of Karate Club. . . . . . .
4.  Gr = nx.karate_club_graph()
5.  #. . . . . . . . . . . Calculate Centrality. . . . . . . .
6.  deg_centrality = nx.degree_centrality(Gr)
7.  print(deg_centrality)
```

2.3.3.2 Eigenvector Centrality

An approach that gauges the transitive effect of nodes is called eigenvector centrality. A node's rating is increased more by interconnections coming from high-rated nodes than by interconnections coming from nodes with low ratings. A node that has a high eigenvector score is linked to numerous other nodes that also have high scores. The greatest absolute eigenvalue's corresponding eigenvector is calculated by the procedure.

The neighbor's nodes are important to a centrality degree and manipulate all of it equally. The neighbor's nodes are of different importance, so centrality's importance is different. We can manage this by using the score of the centrality of a node by giving the neighbor's nodes the score centrality, this is defined by the concept of the centrality of eigenvector (Ruhnau, 2000):

$$c_e(n_i) = \frac{1}{\lambda} \sum_{j=1}^{|\mathcal{N}|} A_{ij} \cdot c_e(n_j), \tag{2.7}$$

where $c_e \in \mathbb{R}^{|\mathcal{N}|}$ is a vector comprising the scores of centralities for all nodes. This can take the form of a matrix as follows:

$$c_e = \frac{1}{\lambda} A \cdot c_d, \tag{2.8}$$

where $c_e \in \mathbb{R}^{|\mathcal{N}|}$ represents the eigenvector of adjacency matrix A of the graph. λ represents the eigenvalue of adjacency matrix A. When given adjacency matrix A, there are many pairs of eigenvalues and eigenvectors and the centrality need to be positive. Hence, an eigenvector is carefully selected to have all elements with positive scores. Based on Perron-Frobenius theorem (Friedland, Gaubert and Han, 2013), there is a unique largest eigenvalue, and all positive elements for the eigenvector are based on a squared matrix. So, the λ can be selected as the biggest eigenvector and eigenvalue as the centrality score vector.

The following code snippet shows python implementation for calculating eigenvector centrality with `networkx` Library

```
1.  #. . . . . . . . . . . class imports. . . . . . . . .
2.  import networkx as nx
3.  #. . . . . . . . . Build Graph Gr: Graph of Karate Club. . . . . . .
4.  Gr = nx.karate_club_graph()
5.  #. . . . . . . . . . . Calculate Centrality. . . . . . . . .
6.  eg_centrality = nx. eigenvector_centrality (Gr)
7.  egn_centrality = nx. eigenvector_centrality_numpy (Gr)
8.  print (eg_centrality)
9.  print (egn_centrality)
```

2.3.3.3 Katz Centrality

The Katz centrality is a special case of the eigenvector centrality, which deliberates two important factor scores of the centrality of the neighbor's nodes and a small constant for the central node. Katz centrality can be computed as

$$c_k(n_i) = \alpha \sum_{j=1}^{N} A_{i,j}\, c_k(n_i) + \beta, \tag{2.9}$$

where β represents a predefined constant. A matrix representation can be derived from the scores of Katz centrality all nodes, as follows:

$$c_k = \alpha A c_k + \beta \tag{2.10}$$

$$(N - \alpha \cdot A)c_k = \beta \tag{2.11}$$

where $c_k \in \mathbb{R}^{|\mathcal{N}|}$ represents the centrality score of Katz. The c_k can be computed as

$$c_k = (Y - \alpha \cdot A)^{-1}\beta \tag{2.12}$$

The following code snippet shows python implementation for calculating the Katz centrality networkx Library

```
1.  #. . . . . . . . . . . class imports. . . . . . . . . . .
2.  import networkx as nx
3.  #. . . . . . . . Build Graph G: Graph of Karate Club. . . . . . . .
4.  G = nx.karate_club_graph()
5.  #. . . . . . . . . . . . Calculate Centrality. . . . . . . . . .
6.  k_centrality = nx. katz_centrality(G)
7.  print(k_centrality)
```

2.3.3.4 Betweenness Centrality

The measure of a node's power across a graph's data flows known as betweenness centrality can be used to identify this influence. It is frequently employed to identify nodes that connect two distinct regions of a graph. Unweighted shortest routes are determined between every couple of nodes in a network by the procedure. According to the number of shortest paths that travel throughout a node, each node is given a ranking. Higher betweenness centrality ratings will be achieved by nodes that regularly sit on the shortest paths between other nodes.

The aforementioned centrality scores are based on connections to neighboring nodes. The betweenness can be computed as

$$c_b(n_j) = \sum_{n_i \neq n_j \neq n_k} \frac{\sigma_{s,t}(n_j)}{\sigma_{s,t}} \tag{2.13}$$

where σ_{st} refers to the total number of the shortest paths from the node n_s to node n_t, while $\sigma_{s,t}(n_j)$ refers to the total paths stepping into the node n_j. The normalized betweenness centrality can be computed as

$$c_{nb}(n_j) = \frac{2 \sum_{n_i \neq n_j \neq n_t} \frac{\sigma_{st}(n_j)}{\sigma_{st}}}{(|\mathcal{N}|-1)(|\mathcal{N}|-2)} \tag{2.14}$$

The following code snippet shows python implementation for calculating **Betweenness** centrality using networkx Library

```
1.  #. . . . . . . . . . class imports. . . . . . . . . . . .
2.  import networkx as nx
```

```
3.  #. . . . . . . . . Build Graph Gr: Graph of Karate Club. . . . . . .
4.  Gr = nx.karate_club_graph()
5.  #. . . . . . . . . . . . . Calculate Centrality. . . . . . . . .
6.  b_centrality = nx. betweenness_centrality(Gr)
7.  print(b_centrality)
```

The above calculation can be performed on the subset of node instead of whole graph; hence, the above calculation is updated as follows:

$$c_b(n_j) = \sum_{s \in S, t \in T, n_i \neq n_j \neq n_k} \frac{\sigma_{s,t}(n_j)}{\sigma_{s,t}} \qquad (2.15)$$

where S and T denote the set of sources and targets, respectively. The implementation of subset betweenness centrality is updated as follows:

```
1.  #. . . . . . . . . . . class imports. . . . . . . . . . . . .
2.  import networkx as nx
3.  #. . . . . . . . . Build Graph Gr: Graph of Karate Club. . . . . . .
4.  Gr = nx.karate_club_graph()
5.  #. . . . . . . . . . . . Calculate Centrality. . . . . . . . .
6.  sources = {1,2,3,5}
7.  targets = {8,9,7,10}
8.  bs_centrality = nx. betweenness_centrality_subset(Gr, sources, targets)
9.  print(bs_centrality)
```

In a similar way, the betweenness centrality can be calculated for edge e as the number of all shortest paths passing through it. This can be formulated as follows:

$$c_b(e_i) = \sum_{s,t \in \mathcal{N}} \frac{\sigma_{s,t}(e_i)}{\sigma_{s,t}} \qquad (2.16)$$

For a subset of nodes, the edge **Betweenness** centrality can be calculated as follows:

$$c_b(e_i) = \sum_{s \in S, t \in T} \frac{\sigma_{s,t}(e_i)}{\sigma_{s,t}} \qquad (2.17)$$

The following code snippet shows python implementation for calculating the edge **Betweenness** centrality using networkx Library

```
1.  #. . . . . . . . . . class imports. . . . . . . . . . . . .
2.  import networkx as nx
3.  #. . . . . . . . Build Graph Gr: Graph of Karate Club. . . . . . .
4.  Gr = nx.karate_club_graph()
5.  #. . . . . . . . . . . Calculate Centrality. . . . . . . . .
6.  eb_centrality = nx. edge_betweenness_centrality (Gr)
7.  sources = {1,2,3,5}
```

```
8.   targets = {8,9,7,10}
9.   ebs_centrality = nx. edge_betweenness_centrality_subset
     (Gr,sources, targets)
10.  print(eb_centrality)
11.  print(ebs_centrality)
```

Another extension to the betweenness centrality is the group betweenness centrality that measures the betweenness centrality for a group of nodes, C, as the number of all-pairs shortest paths passes over any node belonging to that group. This can be formulated as follows:

$$c_b(C) = \sum_{s,t \in \mathcal{N}} \frac{\sigma_{s,t}(C)}{\sigma_{s,t}}. \tag{2.18}$$

The following code snippet shows python implementation for calculating the current-flow betweenness centrality using networkx Library

```
1.   #. . . . . . . . . . . class imports.. . . . . . . . . . . . . .
2.   import networkx as nx
3.   #. . . . . . . . . Build Graph Gr: Graph of Karate Club. . . . . . .
4.   Gr = nx.karate_club_graph()
5.   #. . . . . . . . . . . Calculate Centrality. . . . . . . . . . . .
6.   gb_centrality = nx. group_betweenness_centrality(Gr)
7.   print(gb_centrality)
```

Current-flow betweenness centrality is an extension betweenness centrality that makes use the electrical current paradigm for propagating information rather than using the shortest paths. This kind of centrality measure is also recognized as random-walk betweenness centrality (Newman, 2005).

The following code snippet shows python implementation for calculating the current-flow betweenness centrality using networkx Library

```
1.   #. . . . . . . . . . . class imports. . . . . . . . . . . . . . .
2.   import networkx as nx
3.   #. . . . . . . . . Build Graph Gr: Graph of Karate Club. . . . . .
4.   Gr = nx.karate_club_graph()
5.   #. . . . . . . . . . . alculate Centrality.. . . . . . . . . . . .
6.   cfb_centrality = nx.current_flow_betweenness_centrality(Gr)
7.   ecfb_centrality = nx.edge_current_flow_betweenness_centrality(Gr)
8.   acfb_centrality =
     nx.approximate_current_flow_betweenness_centrality(Gr)
9.   edge = (31, 33)
10.  sources = {1,2,3,5}
11.  targets = {8,9,7,10}
12.
13.  cfbs_centrality = nx.current_flow_betweenness_centrality_
     subset(Gr, sources, targets)
14.  ecfbs_centrality = nx.edge_current_flow_betweenness_centrality_
     subset(Gr, sources, targets)
15.
16.  print(cfb_centrality)
```

```
17.  print(ecfb_centrality)
18.  print(acfb_centrality)
19.  print(cfbs_centrality)
20.  print(ecfbs_centrality)
```

Communicability betweenness centrality (Estrada, Higham and Hatano, 2009) is another extension to the standard betweenness centrality and is measured as the number of walks that relates each couple of nodes. $G\{\mathcal{N}, \mathcal{E}\}$, composed of a set of nodes $\mathcal{N} = \{n_1,\ldots,n_N\}$, interconnected with a set of edge $\mathcal{E} = \{e_1,\ldots,e_E\}$, and A denotes the adjacency matrix of G. Let $G(r) = G\{\mathcal{N}, \mathcal{E}(r)\}$ be the graph created from eliminating all edges linked to node r, while keeping the node itself. The adjacency matrix of $G(r)$ is $A + \mathcal{E}(r)$, where $\mathcal{E}(r)$ contains nonzero elements at the row and column of r. The subgraph betweenness of a node r is formulated as follows:

$$\omega_r = \frac{1}{C}\sum_p \sum_q \frac{G_{prq}}{G_{pq}}, p \neq q, q \neq r, \tag{2.19}$$

where G_{prq} denotes the number of walks involving node r, G_{pq} denotes the number of closed walks beginning at node n_i and ending at node n_j, and C denotes the normalization factor equaling the number of elements in the sum. The resultant ω_r takes values between 0 and 1. A linked graph precludes the possibility of reaching the lower bound, while the star graph makes it possible to reach the upper bound.

The following code snippet shows python implementation for calculating the current-flow betweenness centrality using networkx Library

```
1.  #. . . . . . . . . . . class imports. . . . . . . . . . . . .
2.  import networkx as nx
3.  #. . . . . . . . . Build Graph G: Graph of Karate Club. . . . . . .
4.  G = nx.karate_club_graph()
5.  #. . . . . . . . . . . Calculate Centrality. . . . . . . . . . . .
6.  cb_centrality = nx.communicability_betweenness_centrality(G)
7.  print(cb_centrality)
```

2.3.3.5 Closeness Centrality

Given a node n_i, the closeness centrality of it is defined as the reciprocal of the mean of distances of shortest paths to n_i over all $n-1$ accessible nodes. An approach to identifying nodes that can effectively disseminate information throughout a graph is through their closeness centrality (Freeman, 1978). The average distance of a node from all other reachable nodes is measured by its closeness centrality:

$$c_c(n_i) = \frac{n-1}{\sum_{j=1}^{n-1} d(n_j, n_i)}. \tag{2.20}$$

The distances between nodes that receive a higher proximity score are the shortest. Depending on determining the shortest pathways between all pairs of nodes, the closeness centrality algorithm determines the total of each node's distances to all other nodes for each node n_i. To estimate the closeness centrality score for that node, the resultant total is then reversed. Moreover, closeness centrality can be calculated for nodes using level-based work filtering as described in incremental algorithms for closeness centrality (Sariyuce *et al.*, 2013), which identifies needless updates to the closeness centrality and cleans them out.

The following code snippet shows python implementation for calculating closeness centrality networkx Library

```
1.   #. . . . . . . . . . class imports. . . . . . . . . . . . .
2.   import networkx as nx
3.   #. . . . . . . . . Build Graph Gr: Graph of Karate Club . . . . . .
4.   Gr = nx.karate_club_graph()
5.   #. . . . . . . . . . Calculate Centrality . . . . . . . . . .
6.   c_centrality = nx. closeness_centrality(Gr)
7.   edge = (31, 33)
8.   ic_centrality = nx. incremental_closeness_centrality(Gr, edge)
9.   print(c_centrality)
10.  print(ic_centrality)
```

Further, compute current-flow centrality of node is an extended edition of closeness centrality depend on the active struggle between nodes in a network (Brandes and Fleischer, 2005). This metric is identified as information centrality (Stephenson and Zelen, 1989), which is a centrality measure that depends on the "information" enclosed in all potential paths between couples of nodes. Information centrality did not involve path enumeration and is not restricted to the geodesies or shortest paths.

```
1.   #. . . . . . . . . . class imports. . . . . . . . . . . . .
2.   import networkx as nx
3.   #. . . . . . . . . Build Graph Gr: Graph of Karate Club . . . . . .
4.   Gr = nx.karate_club_graph()
5.   #. . . . . . . . . . Calculate Centrality. . . . . . . . . .
6.   cfc_centrality = nx. current_flow_closeness_centrality(Gr)
7.   i_centrality = nx. information_centrality(Gr)
8.
9.   print(cfc_centrality)
10.  print(i_centrality)
```

2.3.3.6 Harmonic Centrality

A variation of closeness centrality called harmonic centrality, also referred to as valued centrality (Marchiori and Latora, 2000), was developed to address the issue that the initial calculation was faced with interconnected graphs. It comes from the discipline of social network analysis, like so many centrality algorithms. It offered an alternative method for determining the average distance than the Closeness Centrality algorithm. The harmonic centrality approach accumulates the inverse of a node's distances from all other nodes instead of adding up their actual distances. It can now handle unlimited values thanks to this.

The following code snippet shows python implementation for calculating the harmonic centrality `networkx` Library:

```
1. #. . . . . . . . . . class imports. . . . . . . . . . . .
2. import networkx as nx
3. #. . . . . . . . . Build Graph Gr: Graph of Karate Club. . . . . . .
4. Gr = nx.karate_club_graph()
5. #. . . . . . . . . . Calculate Centrality. . . . . . . . . .
6. h_centrality = nx. harmonic_centrality(Gr)
7. print(h_centrality)
```

2.4 Spectral Graph Analysis

Spectral graph analysis makes use of common matrices of eigenvalues representing the graph structure (e.g., adjacency or Laplacian matrix) for interpreting the inherent characteristics of underlying graphs. This field of science offers a rich set of algorithmic and statistical theories, counting networks with random walks, extrapolation, and expanders, which are valuable for different graph intelligence tasks. This section discusses the fundamental topics in the underlying conceptual theory and hypothetical facets of approaches that are practically suitable for improving graph intelligence solutions.

2.4.1 Laplacian Matrix

A matrix known as the graph Laplacian is at the core of the area of spectral graph analysis in addition to a number of significant graph intelligence algorithms, i.e., spectral graph networks.

Definition. *Given the adjacency matrix, A, of graph $G = \{\mathcal{N}, \mathcal{E}\}$, the Laplacian matrix, L, can be defined as follows:*

$$L = D - A \tag{2.21}$$

where D denotes diagonal degree matrix $D = diag\left(D(n_1),\ldots,D(n_N)\right)$.

```
import networkx as nx

# create a graph of 100 nodes with expected degrees of 25
n = 100   # n nodes
p = 0.25
```

```
# w = p*n for all nodes
w = [p * n for i in range(n)]
# configuration model
G1 = nx.expected_degree_graph(w)
# calculate laplacian matrix
lap1=nx.linalg.laplacian_matrix(G1)

G2 = nx.karate_club_graph()
# calculate laplacian matrix
lap2=nx.linalg.laplacian_matrix(G2)

G3 = nx.karate_club_graph()
# calculate laplacian matrix
lap3=nx.linalg.laplacian_matrix(G3)
```

By normalizing the Laplacian matrix, we can obtain the normalized Laplacian matrix as follows:

$$L = D^{-\frac{1}{2}}(D-A)D^{-\frac{1}{2}} = Y - D^{-\frac{1}{2}}AD^{-\frac{1}{2}} \qquad (2.22)$$

Both L and A are symmetric. Given f as a vector where its ith values $f[i]$ are associated with the node n_i. Multiplication of L by f, we can get a new vector h as follows:

$$h = Lf = (D-A)f = Df - Bf \qquad (2.23)$$

The element $h[i]$ is calculated as follows:

$$h[i] = D(n_i).q[i] - \sum_{j=1}^{|\mathcal{N}|} A_{i,j}.q[j] = D(n_i) \cdot q[i] - \sum_{n_j \in N(n_i)} A_{i,j}.q[j] = \sum_{n_j \in N(n_i)} (q[i] - q[j]).$$

$$(2.24)$$

To this point, $h[i]$ is the sum of the variances between node n_i and the relevant neighboring nodes $N(n_i)$. We can compute $q^T Lq$ as follows:

$$\begin{aligned}
q^T Lq &= \sum_{n_i \in \mathcal{N}} f[i] \sum_{n_j \in N(n_i)} (q[i] - q[j]) \\
&= \sum_{n_i \in \mathcal{N}} \sum_{n_j \in N(n_i)} (q[i] \cdot q[i] - q[i] \cdot q[j]) \\
&= \sum_{n_i \in \mathcal{N}} \sum_{n_j \in N(n_i)} \left(\frac{1}{2} q[i] \cdot q[i] - q[i] \cdot q[j] + \frac{1}{2} q[j] \cdot q[j] \right) \\
&= \frac{1}{2} \sum_{n_i \in \mathcal{N}} \sum_{n_j \in N(n_i)} (q[i] - q[j])^2.
\end{aligned} \qquad (2.25)$$

Then, the output of the above formula is the summation of the squares of the divergences between neighboring nodes. It calculates how much the values of nearby nodes vary from one another. It is simple to check that output is often positive for any real vector q that might be selected, proving that the Laplacian matrix is nonnegative and semi-certain:

```
import networkx as nx

# create a graph of 100 nodes with expected degrees of 25
n = 100   # n nodes
p = 0.25
# w = p*n for all nodes
w = [p * n for i in range(n)]
# configuration model
G1 = nx.expected_degree_graph(w)
# calculate laplacian matrix
lap1=nx.linalg.normalized_laplacian_matrix(G1)

G2 = nx.karate_club_graph()
# calculate laplacian matrix
lap2=nx.linalg.normalized_laplacian_matrix(G2)

G3 = nx.grid_2d_graph(10,10)
# calculate laplacian matrix
lap3=nx.linalg.normalized_laplacian_matrix(G3)
```

2.4.2 Graph Laplacian Matrix: On Eigenvalues

Another important topic of spectral graph analysis is introducing the eigenvalues for the graph Laplacian matrix.

Given a graph $G = \{\mathcal{N}, \mathcal{E}\}$, the eigenvalues of its Laplacian matrix L are nonnegatives.

For the Laplacian matrix L, λ represents an eigenvalue, and w represents the normalized eigenvector. So $\lambda w = Lw$, and u is a unit nonzero vector and $w^T w = 1$. Then,

$$\lambda = \lambda w^T w = w^T \lambda w = w^T L w \geq 0. \qquad (2.26)$$

For graph $G = \{\mathcal{N}, \mathcal{E}\}$, there are $|\mathcal{N}|$ eigenvalues/eigenvectors. All eigenvalues are positives or 0. Let $w_1 = \frac{1}{\sqrt{G = \{\mathcal{N}, \mathcal{E}\}}}(1,\ldots,1)$. We can verify $Lw_1 = 0 = 0w_1$, w_1 refers to an eigenvector with an eigenvalue equal to 0. The non-decreasing eigenvalue is $0 = \lambda_1 \leq \lambda_2 \leq,\ldots \ldots \leq \lambda_{|\mathcal{N}|}$. The normalized eigenvectors are represented as $w_1,\ldots,w_{|\mathcal{N}|}$.

The number of connected elements in graph $G = \{\mathcal{N}, \mathcal{E}\}$ is equal to the number of eigenvalues of its Laplacian matrix L (the multiplicity of the eigenvalue). Suggesting that there are K connected elements in the graph. We can divide the group of nodes $\mathcal{N}$ into K disjoint subsets $n_1, \ldots, n_K$. The first one presents at least K orthogonal eigenvectors matching to the eigenvalue 0. After that, K vectors $w_1, \ldots, w_K$ are built such *that* $w_y[z] = \frac{1}{\sqrt{n_i}}$ *if* $n_i \in \mathcal{N}$, and 0 otherwise. Then, it can be found that $Lw_i = 0$ for $i = 1, \ldots, K$, which justifies that all the K vectors are the eigenvectors of L matching to eigen-value 0. Also, we test the validation of $w_i^T w_j = 0$ if $i \neq j$, which represents that K eigenvectors are orthogonal to each other. Thus, the multiplicity of 0 eigenvalues shows at least K. The second one represents that K orthogo-nal eigenvectors matching the eigenvalue 0. Another eigenvector w^* is found matching the eigenvalue 0, which is orthogonal to all K eigenvectors. As w^* is nonzero, there should exist an element in w^* that is nonzero. Suppose, the component is $u^*[T]$ related to node $n_T \in n_i$:

$$w^{*T} L w^* = \frac{1}{2} \sum_{n_i \in \mathcal{N}} \sum_{n_j \in N(n_i)} (w^*[i] - w^*[j])^2. \tag{2.27}$$

To confirm $w^{*T} L w^* = 0$, the values of nodes in the same element must be the same. It establishes that every node in n_i has the same value $w^*[T]$ as a node n_T. Thus, $w^{*T} L w^* > 0$ stands. It means that w^* is not orthogonal to w_i, which is contradictory. So, there is no additional eigenvector matching the eigenvalue 0 outside the K vectors that we have built.

2.5 Graph Signal Analysis

Graph signal depicts a graph with attributes of features related to its nodes. It attracts attributes (data) and connectivity among nodes (information), which includes nodes, edges, and a function that maps the nodes to actual values. We can refer to a function of mapping with a graph $G = \{\mathcal{N}, \mathcal{E}\}$:

$$f : N \rightarrow \mathbb{R}^{|\mathcal{N}| \times T} \tag{2.28}$$

where T refers to the length of the vector (value) related to every node. Without any loss of generality, herein, one can set $T = 1$ and represent the mapped values for all nodes as $q \in \mathbb{R}^{|\mathcal{N}|}$ with $q[i]$ corresponding to node n_i.

2.5.1 Graph Fourier Transform

The classical Fourier transform (FT) (Gazi, 2018; Domingos and Moura, 2020)

$$f(E) = \langle f(t), \exp(-2\pi y t E) \rangle = \int_{-\infty}^{\infty} f(t) \exp(-2\pi y t E) dt, \tag{2.29}$$

divides a signal $f(t)$ into a sequence of compound exponentials $\exp(-2\pi y t E)$ for any real number E, where E can be observed as the frequency of the matching exponential. These exponentials are the eigenfunctions of the one-dimensional Laplace operator (or another command disparity operator) as:

$$\nabla(\exp(-2\pi ytE)) = \frac{\vartheta^2}{\vartheta t^2}\exp(-2\pi ytE) = \frac{\vartheta}{\vartheta t}(-2\pi ytE)\exp(-2\pi ytE) \quad (2.30)$$
$$= (-2\pi ytE)^2\exp(-2\pi ytE).$$

Analogously, the graph FT for a graph signal f on graph G can be denoted as

$$f[l] = \langle f, w_l \rangle = \sum_{y=1}^{I} f[y]w_l[y], \quad (2.31)$$

where w_l is the lth eigenvector of the Laplacian matrix L of the graph. The matching eigenvalue λ_l denotes the frequency or the softness of the eigenvector w_l. The vector f with $f[l]$ as its lth component is the Graph FT of f. The eigenvectors are the graph Fourier basis of the graph $G = \{\mathcal{N}, \mathcal{E}\}$, and f contains the graph Fourier coefficients matching to this basis for a signal f. The Graph FT of f can be also represented in the matrix form as follows:

$$f = W^T f, \quad (2.32)$$

where the lth column of the matrix W is w_l. As proposed by the following equation,

$$w_l^T L w_l = \lambda_l \cdot w_l^T w_l = \lambda_l, \quad (2.33)$$

the eigenvalue λ_l measures the smoothness of the matching eigenvector w_l. Precisely, the eigenvectors related to small eigenvalues differ slowly through the graph. In other words, the values of such eigenvectors at connected nodes are similar. Thus, through the graph, the eigenvector changes with low frequency. But on two nodes, the big eigenvalues with the eigenvectors may have various values, even if connected.

An additional example is the first eigenvector w_l related to the eigenvalue 0—it is constant over all the nodes, which indicates that its value does not change through the graph. Thus, it is very smooth and has a very low frequency of 0. These eigenvectors are the graph Fourier basis for graph $G = \{\mathcal{N}, \mathcal{E}\}$, and their matching eigenvalues refer to their frequencies. The Graph FT, as shown in Eq. (2.12), can be used as a process to change an input signal f into a graph Fourier basis with different frequencies. The attained coefficient f represents how much the matching graph Fourier basis contributes to the input signal.

2.6 Complex Graphs

In the previous sections, we discuss the simple graph and its features. In this section, we discuss the complex graphs.

2.6.1 Bipartite Graphs

A bipartite graph, abbreviated as **Bi-graph**, is a type of graph, the constituting nodes of which are decomposed into two independent sets (i.e., with no shared elements), while each edge only connects nodes from different sets. Bipartite graphs are broadly adopted to capture interactions between different objects.

Definition. *A bipartite graph is a graph $G = \{\mathcal{N}, \mathcal{E}\}$ whose nodes, $\mathcal{N}$, are divided into two disjoint sets, $\mathcal{N}^1$ and $\mathcal{N}^2$, such that $\mathcal{N} = \mathcal{N}^1 \cup \mathcal{N}^2$ and $\mathcal{N}^1 \cap \mathcal{N}^2 = \varnothing$, while each edge, $\mathcal{E}_i$, connects a node from $\mathcal{N}^1$ to another node from $\mathcal{N}^2$, such that $n_e^1 \in \mathcal{N}^1$, while $n_d^2 \in \mathcal{N}^2$ for all $e = \left(n_e^1, n_e^2\right) \in \mathcal{E}$.*

The bipartite graph is complete if and only if each node in $\mathcal{N}^1$ is connected to all nodes in $\mathcal{N}^2$. The bipartite graph is balanced if and only if $\mathcal{N}^1$ and $\mathcal{N}^2$ share the same cardinality, $\left|\mathcal{N}^1\right| = \left|\mathcal{N}^2\right|$.

The following code snippet shows how to create a bipartite graph using DGL:

```
import dgl

dgl.rand_bipartite('client', 'product', 'game', 25, 50, 5)
```

In another way, one can create a custom bipartite graph from the network using the following code snippet:

```
import dgl
import networkx as nx
import numpy as np

# Build two-edge unidirectional bipartite graph.
nx_g = nx.DiGraph()
# Include nodes for the source type
nx_g.add_nodes_from([1, 3], bipartite=0, feat1=np.zeros((2, 1)),
feat2=np.ones((2, 1)))
# Include nodes for the destination type
nx_g.add_nodes_from([2, 4, 5], bipartite=1, feat3=np.zeros((3, 1)))

nx_g.add_edge(1, 4, weight=np.ones((1, 1)), eid=np.array([1]))
nx_g.add_edge(3, 5, weight=np.ones((1, 1)), eid=np.array([0]))

# Change it into a DGLGraph with construction only.
g = dgl.bipartite_from_networkx(nx_g, utype='_U', etype='_E',
vtype='_V')
g
```

Moreover, one can build a custom bipartite graph from an existing dataset using a SciPy matrix as shown in the following code snippet:

```
import dgl
import numpy as np
from scipy.sparse import coo_matrix

# Source nodes for edges (2, 1), (4, 3), (6, 5)
source_ids = np.array([2, 4, 6])
# Destination nodes for edges (2, 1), (4, 3), (6, 5)
distenation_ids = np.array([1, 3, 5])
# Weight for edges (2, 1), (4, 3), (6, 5)
w = np.array([0.2, 0.4, 0.3])
sp_mat = coo_matrix((w, (src_ids, dst_ids)))
g = dgl.bipartite_from_scipy(sp_mat, utype='_U', etype='_E',
vtype='_V')
g
```

2.6.2 Heterogeneous Graphs

Heterogeneous graphs, or simply *heterographs*, are a type of graphs that consist of different categories of nodes and edges. These variations in the categories of nodes and edges enforce them to have diverse forms of features that are planned to model the characteristics of each type of node and edge. The nodes and edges of *heterographs* are attached with a diversity of information. Therefore, one feature tensor could not encode overall features of the entire *heterographs* because of the variability in types and dimensionalities of nodes and/or edges. In *heterographs*, a group of types should be defined for edges and nodes, correspondingly, each shares its own tensors. Because of the dissimilar data structure, the design of message passing differs, enabling the update function and message passing to be constrained on either node type or edge type.

Definition. *A Graph $G = \{\mathcal{N}, \mathcal{E}\}$ is called heterogeneous, if each node in $\mathcal{N} = \{n_1, \ldots n_N\}$ and/or each edge in $\mathcal{E} = \{e_1, \ldots e_E\}$ belongs to a type. Given $T_{\mathcal{N}}$ as the set types of nodes per graph and $T_{\mathcal{E}}$ as the set of types of edges, two mapping functions $\varphi_{\mathcal{N}} : \mathcal{N} \to T_{\mathcal{N}}$ and $\varphi_{\mathcal{E}} : \mathcal{E} \to T_{\mathcal{E}}$ could be applied to map nodes and edges to their types, respectively.*

For example, the data in movie recommendation system usually includes interactions between audience and movies in terms of rating operations. These interactions could be represented as heterogeneous graphs, where two kinds of nodes are available, namely "movies" and "individuals," while the interaction between individuals and movies corresponds to the edges of the graph. Moreover, if an interaction is marked with a rating, each rating value could correspond to a different edge type. Figure 2.6 illustrates an example of a heterogeneous graph of user-movie ratings.

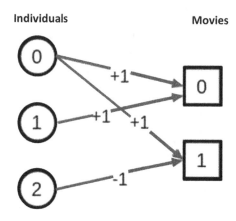

Individuals   **Movies**

FIGURE 2.6
Illustration of example on heterogeneous graphs.

To build a heterogeneous graph using DGL, the *dgl.heterograph()* can be used with a dictionary argument. The keys of this dictionary take the form of tuples (*srctype, edgetype, dsttype*) stipulating the name of the relation and the pair of elements it connects. These tuples are canonical edge types. The values of this dictionary initialize the graph topology, namely, the nodes and the connecting edges. The following code snippets show how to build heterogeneous graphs, for the above example, using DGL:

```
import dgl
import torch

data_dict = {
    ('person', 'follows', 'person'): (torch.tensor([0, 1]), torch.
    tensor([1, 2])),
    ('person', 'follows', 'page'): (torch.tensor([1, 1]), torch.
    tensor([1, 2])),
    ('person', 'buys', 'product'): (torch.tensor([0, 3]), torch.
    tensor([3, 4]))
}
g = dgl.heterograph(data_dict)
g
```

For a more realistic example, let's create a heterogeneous graph for the ACM citation dataset (Shi *et al.*, 2017). To do so, let's begin downloading the dataset as the SciPy matrix, then converting it into a heterogeneous graph using the following code snippets:

```
import scipy.io
import urllib.request

data_url = 'https://data.dgl.ai/dataset/ACM.mat'
data_file_path = '/tmp/ACM.mat'
```

```
urllib.request.urlretrieve(data_url, data_file_path)
data = scipy.io.loadmat(data_file_path)
print(list(data.keys()))
pa_g = dgl.heterograph({('paper', 'written-by', 'author') :
data['PvsA'].nonzero()})
```

Now, you can easily print out the structural information of the created heterogeneous graph using the following code snippets:

```
print('Node types:', pa_g.ntypes)
print('Edge types:', pa_g.etypes)
print('Canonical edge types:', pa_g.canonical_etypes)

# To differentiate the nodes of dissimilar types, stipulate the kind name.
print(pa_g.number_of_nodes('paper'))
print(pa_g.number_of_edges(('paper', 'written-by', 'author')))
print(pa_g.number_of_edges('written-by'))
print(pa_g.successors(1, etype='written-by'))

# Type name argument could be omitted whenever the conduct is definite.
print(pa_g.number_of_edges())
```

Now, you can create a subgraph of the ACM heterogeneous graph making use of paper-subject, paper-paper, and paper-author interactions. In the meantime, the reverse relationship can also be added to prepare for relation graph operations (discussed in Chapter 5):

```
import dgl
G = dgl.heterograph({
        ('paper', 'written-by', 'author') : data['PvsA'].nonzero(),
        ('author', 'writing', 'paper') : data['PvsA'].transpose().
        nonzero(),
        ('paper', 'citing', 'paper') : data['PvsP'].nonzero(),
        ('paper', 'cited', 'paper') : data['PvsP'].transpose().
        nonzero(),
        ('paper', 'is-about', 'subject') : data['PvsL'].nonzero(),
        ('subject', 'has', 'paper') : data['PvsL'].transpose().
        nonzero(),
    })

print(G)
```

Metagraph, also termed network schema, is a valuable summary of a heterogeneous graph informing about the number of objects available in the network, together with the probable links between them. Access to the metagraph enables one to visualize the graph using any respective tools. Given the metagraph of the heterogeneous one, you can easily visualize the created heterogeneous graph using the following code snippets:

```
import dgl
import torch
```

```
g = dgl.heterograph({
    ('person', 'follows', 'person'): (torch.tensor([0, 1]), torch.
    tensor([1, 2])),
    ('person', 'follows', 'page'): (torch.tensor([0, 1, 2]), torch.
    tensor([1, 2, 3])),
    ('person', 'plays', 'game'): (torch.tensor([1, 3]), torch.
    tensor([2, 3]))
})
meta_g = g.metagraph()
meta_g
```

2.6.3 Multi-dimensional Graphs

The real-world applications contain complex relationships between different objects such that any pair of objects could have multiple relations at the same time. This form of relationship can be represented by multi-dimensional graphs. For example, multi-dimensional relations can be created on popular social media sites such as Facebook, in which users are regarded as nodes. The users of Facebook can follow each other, which is regarded as a single relation. At the same time, the same users could be linked through other relations such as "liking" or "commenting" posts of others. This form of interactions comprising multiple simultaneous relationships can be certainly learnt as multi-dimensional graphs, whereas each dimension corresponds to a distinct type of relation.

Definition. *A multi-dimensional graph $G = \{\mathcal{N}, \mathcal{E}\}$ is a form that contains a group of N nodes $\mathcal{N} = \{n_1, \ldots, n_N\}$ and the number of E groups of edges $\mathcal{E} = \{\mathcal{E}_1, \ldots, \mathcal{E}_E\}$. Each edge set $\mathcal{E}_e$ outlines the eth sort of relations among the nodes lying within the conforming eth dimension. Those E kinds of relationships could also be interconnected by E adjacency matrices $A^1, \ldots, A^D$. For the dimension d, the relative adjacency matrix $A^e \in R^{N \times N}$ describes the interconnected edges $\mathcal{E}_d$ among nodes, $\mathcal{N}$.*

Practically speaking, you can easily build a multi-dimensional directed graph using the following python code snippets:

```
1.  #. . . . . . . . . . class imports. . . . . . . . . . . . .
2.  import dgl
3.  import networkx as nx
4.  #. . . . . . . . Build Graph G. . . . . . . . . . . . . . .
5.  G = nx.MultiDiGraph()
6.  #. . . . . . . . . Append one node at a time. . . . . . . .
7.  G.add_node(1)
8.  #. . . . . . . . Append the nodes. . . . . . . . . . . . . .
9.  G.add_nodes_from([2, 3], feat1=np.ones((2, 1)), feat2=np.ones((2, 1)))
10. G.add_nodes_from(range(50, 70), feat3=np.ones((2, 1)))
11. #. . . . . . . . . Append the nodes from another Graph. . . . . .
12. H = nx.path_graph(10)
13. G.add_nodes_from(H)
14.
15. #. . . . . . . . . . . . Append an edge. . . . . . . . . . .
16. key = G.add_edge(1, 2)
```

```
17.  #. . . . . . . . . . . . Append a set of edges. . . . . . . . .
18.  keys = G.add_edges_from([(1, 2), (1, 3)])
19.  #. . . . . . . . . . . Append a set of edges.. . . . . . . . .
20.  keys = G.add_edges_from(H.edges)
21.  G.graph
22.  g = dgl.from_networkx(G)

23.  g
```

2.6.4 Signed Graphs

Signed graphs refer to a type of graph consisting of nodes interconnected with edges that are classified as positive and negative ones. They have been accepted widely and increased popularity in many applications. For example, in social networks (Twitter, Facebook, etc.), the concept of signed relations can be easily observed in the interactions between users, i.e., "following vs blocking" and "friending vs unfriending." In the signed graph of these relations, the conduct of "unfriending" could be regarded as negative edges between users. In the meantime, the activity of "block" could also be regarded as negative edges. A formal definition of signed graphs is given as follows:

Definition. *A signed graph $G = \{\mathcal{N}, \mathcal{E}^+, \mathcal{E}^-\}$ is a special type of graph composed of a group N of nodes, $\mathcal{N} = \{n_1, \ldots, n_N\}$, a group of $\mathcal{E}^+$ edges, $\mathcal{E}^+ = \{e_1^+, \ldots, e_{E^+}^+\}$, and a group of $\mathcal{E}^-$ edges, $\mathcal{E}^- = \{e_1^-, \ldots, e_{E^-}^-\}$. The edge in G can just be either positive or negative, such that, $\mathcal{E}^+ \cap \mathcal{E}^- = \varnothing$.*

According to the above definition, it could be noted that each edge in the signed graph is given either a negative or positive sign, also known as *valence*. The edge with positive valence often denotes the circumstance that the relation it models exhibits some optimistic quality, such as gentleness, friendship, or faith. Similarly, the edge with negative valence embodies provoking spirits between nodes, like hate, aversion, or disbelief. If the edges missed the directional information, the relation is regarded as symmetric. In contrast, if the edges are directional, the graph can be referred to as a *signed digraph*.

2.6.5 Hypergraphs

Till this point, all the introduced categories of the graphs use the edges to encode pairwise relationships between objects. Nevertheless, real-life applications contain more complex relations between more than two objects. For example, in paper citation data, any definite author could publish three or more papers. Hence, the author could be regarded as a hyperedge linking manifold papers (represented as nodes). Contrasted with the edges in standard graphs, the hyperedges could represent high-level and complicated relations. Hypergraphs refer to the type of graphs built with hyperedges. A formal definition of hypergraphs is given as follows:

Definition. *A hypergraph $G = \{\mathcal{N}, \mathcal{E}, \mathcal{W}\}$ is a special type of graphs composed of a group N of nodes, $\mathcal{N} = \{n_1, \ldots, n_N\}$, a group of E hyperedges, $\mathcal{E} = \{e_1, \ldots, e_E\}$, and a diagonal matrix $\mathcal{W} \in \mathbb{R}^{|\mathcal{E}| \times |\mathcal{E}|}$ encoding the weight, $w_{i,i}$, of the hyperedge e_i. An occurrence matrix $H \in R^{N \times E}$ can be used to represent the hypergraph with $H_{i,j} = 1$ only if a node n_i occurs to the edge e_j.*

According to the above definition, the degree of node n_i could be calculated as $d(n_i) = \sum_{j=1}^{E} H_{i,j}$, while the hyperedge's degree is calculated as $d(e_j) = \sum_{i=1}^{N} H_{i,j}$.

2.6.6 Dynamic Graphs

Despite the differences between the above-mentioned categories of graphs, they have a common property of static structure, referring to the fixed edges or hyper-edges between nodes Nevertheless, in real-life problems, graphs are continually developing by adding new nodes and edges according to the change in the data they represent. For instance, the users of social networks are continuously build friendships with the users joining the social network lately. These types of developing graphs would be represented as dynamic graphs in which every node or edge is related to a timestamp. A formal definition of a dynamic graph is given as follows:

Definition. *A dynamic graph $G = \{\mathcal{N}, \mathcal{E}\}$ consists of a group of timestamped nodes $\mathcal{N} = \{n_1^t, \ldots, n_N^t\}$ and a group of timestamped edges $\mathcal{E} = \{e_1^t, \ldots, e_E^t\}$ where t denotes the time of presence of edge or node.*

In this context, two mapping functions $\varphi_{\mathcal{N}}$ and $\varphi_{\mathcal{E}}$ map each node and edge to the corresponding emergence timestamps.

In fact, it is not possible to record every timestamp of all nodes and edges of the graph. As a substitute, it could be feasible to examine the graph periodically to monitor its evolution. In each timestamp t, the existing edition of the graph G_t is recorded, and the process is repeated from time to time. By using this process, the dynamic graphs can be identified as discrete consisting of many graph snapshots. A formal definition of a dynamic graph is given as follows:

Definition. *A discrete dynamic graph, G_d, is a special case of a dynamic graph, $G = \{\mathcal{N}, \mathcal{E}\}$, consists of T editions of the original graph recorded along with the growth of a dynamic graph. Indeed, the number of T editions of the graphs is defined as $G_d = \{G_0, \ldots, G_T\}$ where G_t is the graph detected at timestep t.*

2.7 Graph Intelligence Tasks

This section provides in-depth overview of different types of graph intelligence tasks including graph-oriented task and node-oriented tasks, the former treats the data as a group of graphs and every instance is denoted as a single graph, while the later categories treat the data as a graph and each instance is denoted as a node.

2.7.1 Graph-Oriented Tasks

There is a connection between the tasks and the entire graph. A demonstrative example on graph-oriented tasks includes graph matching, graph categorization, and graph synthesis. In graph intelligence, the concept of inductive learning is often encountered in this family of tasks.

2.7.1.1 Graph Classification

There are many real-world contexts for the graph classification problem. When faced with this challenge, the standard approach is to compute a set of graph statistical data (i.e., graph features) that can be used to distinguish between distinct types of graphs. Current methods typically process the entire graph while computing such features. For example, in a graphlet-based method, the whole graph determines a number of unique graphlets (or subgraphs) exist. Nevertheless, in several practical contexts, graphs are noisy, with racist and discriminatory patterns localized to subsets of the graph. Assigning labels to previously unlabeled nodes in a graph is the goal of node classification. Each data point can be displayed as a graph in certain contexts. In the field of computational biology, for instance, molecules can be represented by graphs with atoms as nodes and ionic bonds as edges. Attributes like solubility and toxicity could be thought of as labels for these complex compounds. In practice, however, it is possible that we would like to instantaneously forecast these characteristics for recently found complex compounds. Graph classification, which seeks to determine the labels for unlabeled graphs, is one way to accomplish this (Wu *et al.*, 2021). The sophistication of graph constructions precludes the use of conventional classification methods for their organization.

Definition. *Graph classification is a graph intelligence task that shows the mapping function to correctly map a set of Z annotated graphs, $G_A = \left\{(G_i, b_i)\right\}_{i=1}^{Z}$, to the corresponding labels $\left\{(b_i)\right\}_{i=1}^{Z}$.*

However, the remaining details could be connected to the graphs in the preceding definition. In certain cases, for instance, it may be useful to classify graphs based on the attributes that are related to each node.

2.7.2 Node-Oriented Tasks

In this subsection, we introduce two node-focused tasks: node classification and link prediction. There are many studies on node-focused tasks like community detection and node raking.

2.7.2.1 Node Classification

The graph contains the node which is denoted as information that refers to the labels of these nodes. For instance, in social graphs, the users' information can be defined as age, name, and interests, which is treated as labels. On Instagram, there is much information that aids manger to classify their events and news. But less than 1% of Instagram users provide their full information. So, the graph is built based on these labels.

Definition. *Given a graph $G = \{\mathcal{N}, \mathcal{E}\}$ composed of a set of nodes in $\mathcal{N} = \{n_1, \ldots n_N\}$ and a set of edges $\mathcal{E} = \{e_1, \ldots e_E\}$, where labeled nodes are defined, $\mathcal{N}^l \subset \mathcal{N}$, and unlabeled nodes are denoted as $\mathcal{N}^u \subset \mathcal{N}$, such that $\mathcal{N}^l \cup \mathcal{N}^u = N$ && $\mathcal{N}^l \cap \mathcal{N}^u = \varnothing$. The node classification is a graph intelligence task that seeks to exploit labeled nodes to learn mapping function that could correctly predict the map the unlabeled nodes N_l.*

2.7.2.2 Link Prediction

Graphs often used in practical terms are incomplete, as they lack necessary edges. Those ties do, in fact, exist to some extent. Edges in the demonstrated graphs are missing because they are not noted or documented. However, a number of graphs are advancing on their own. It is easy to make new friends in social media platforms like Facebook. With the use of scholarly cooperation graphs, an author can establish new interactions of cooperation with other scholars. Apps like friend suggestion, knowledge graph finalization, and criminal investigative analysis can all profit from insinuating or making predictions of absent edges (Ji *et al.*, 2022). The link prediction dilemma is then formally defined.

Definition. *Given a graph $G = \{\mathcal{N}, \mathcal{E}\}$ composed of a set of nodes in $\mathcal{N} = \{n_1, \ldots n_N\}$ and a set of edges $\mathcal{E} = \{e_1, \ldots e_E\}$, where $\mathcal{E}^-$ is the set of all possible edges between nodes, where $\mathcal{E}'$ represents the complementary set of $\mathcal{E}$ such that $\mathcal{E}^- = \mathcal{E} \cap \mathcal{E}'$. The node classification is a graph intelligence task that estimates the likelihood of the existence of edges. More precisely, each edge in $\mathcal{E}'$ holds a score that represents similarities to the edge that currently exists or will appear in the future.*

It is important to keep in mind that while the definition is described in terms of simple graphs, it can be appropriately applied to the complex graphs discussed in the previous section. As such, in the case of signed graphs, it's not enough to simply know whether or not an edge exists; we also need to be capable of predicting its sign. It is of interest to infer hyperedges that characterize the connections between sets of nodes in hypergraphs.

2.8 Case Study

The expansive growth of internet technologies brings the cyber security solutions with a more complex form of data. The dynamicity and complexity of relationships between different entities in such digital world necessitate using different forms of graphs to these relationships. In view of this, it may be interesting for security audiences to discover and practically explore how to encode the security-related data into different forms of graph data discussed in the above sections. Being motivated by that, the supplementary materials are designated to provide an implementation of different functions to create different types of graphs using some realistic data as a case study of this chapter. The supplementary materials also provide the readers with recommendations for further reading about the content of this chapter.

The repository of supplementary materials is given in this link: https://github.com/DEEPOLOGY-AI/Book-Graph-Neural-Network/tree/main/Chapter%202.

References

Brandes, U. and Fleischer, D. (2005) 'Centrality Measures Based on Current Flow', in *Lecture Notes in Computer Science*. doi: 10.1007/978-3-540-31856-9_44.

Domingos, J. and Moura, J. M. F. (2020) 'Graph Fourier Transform: A Stable Approximation', *IEEE Transactions on Signal Processing*. doi: 10.1109/TSP.2020.3009645.

Estrada, E., Higham, D. J. and Hatano, N. (2009) 'Communicability Betweenness in Complex Networks', *Physica A: Statistical Mechanics and its Applications*. doi: 10.1016/j.physa.2008.11.011.

Friedland, S., Gaubert, S. and Han, L. (2013) 'Perron-Frobenius Theorem for Nonnegative Multilinear Forms and Extensions', *Linear Algebra and its Applications*. doi: 10.1016/j.laa.2011.02.042.

Gazi, O. (2018) 'Discrete Fourier Transform', in *Springer Topics in Signal Processing*. doi: 10.1007/978-981-10-4962-0_3.

Ji, S. *et al.* (2022) 'A Survey on Knowledge Graphs: Representation, Acquisition, and Applications', *IEEE Transactions on Neural Networks and Learning Systems*. doi: 10.1109/TNNLS.2021.3070843.

Freeman, L. C. (1978) 'Centrality in Social Networks Conceptual Clarification', *Social Networks*.

Freeman, L. C. (2002). Centrality in social networks: Conceptual clarification. Social network: critical concepts in sociology. Londres: Routledge, 1, 238–263.

Ma, Y. and Tang, J. (2021) *Deep Learning on Graphs, Deep Learning on Graphs*. doi: 10.1017/9781108924184.

Marchiori, M. and Latora, V. (2000) 'Harmony in the Small-World', *Physica A: Statistical Mechanics and its Applications*. doi: 10.1016/S0378-4371(00)00311-3.

Newman, M. E. J. (2005) 'A Measure of Betweenness Centrality Based on Random Walks', *Social Networks*. doi: 10.1016/j.socnet.2004.11.009.

Ruhnau, B. (2000) 'Eigenvector-Centrality – A Node-Centrality', *Social Networks*. doi: 10.1016/S0378-8733(00)00031-9.

Sariyuce, A. E. *et al.* (2013) 'Incremental Algorithms for Closeness Centrality', in *Proceedings – 2013 IEEE International Conference on Big Data, Big Data 2013*. doi: 10.1109/BigData.2013.6691611.

Shi, C. *et al.* (2017) 'A Survey of Heterogeneous Information Network Analysis', *IEEE Transactions on Knowledge and Data Engineering*. doi: 10.1109/TKDE.2016.2598561.

Stephenson, K. and Zelen, M. (1989) 'Rethinking Centrality: Methods and Examples', *Social Networks*. doi: 10.1016/0378-8733(89)90016-6.

Wu, Z. *et al.* (2021) 'A Comprehensive Survey on Graph Neural Networks', *IEEE Transactions on Neural Networks and Learning Systems*. doi: 10.1109/TNNLS.2020.2978386.

3

Graph Embedding: Methods, Taxonomies, and Applications

3.1 Introduction

The analysis of graph data is critical to provide valuable intuitions about how to better exploit the hidden graph representations that are widely spread across different graph intelligence applications such as social analysis, knowledge graph, and bioinformatics. Despite the importance and usefulness of graph analytics, modern graph analytics techniques are prohibitively expensive in terms of both computational resources and storage space.

Graph embedding is an additional method that can be used to solve the graph analytics challenge in a cost-effective and accurate manner. Graph embedding, in particular, is a method for preserving the structure of a graph while transforming it into a lower dimensional space. A convenient technique to calculate graph algorithms is to portray them as a group of low-dimensional vectors. Since the categories of graphs vary (as was covered in the preceding chapters), so does the information needed as input for graph embedding. The result of a graph embedding operation is a vector of low dimensionality that represents either some part of the graph or entire graph. To make things simpler, Figure 3.1 shows the embedding of toy sample from graph domains to a different two-dimensional space, that is, node, edge, subgraph, and graph embedding.

Graph analytics (Wang *et al.*, 2020) and representation learning (Yan, Hamilton and Blanchette, 2021) are two well-established fields of study that are related to the graph embedding dilemma. In specific, the goal of graph embedding is to retain the graph's structure while representing it as a set of low-dimensional vectors. To begin with, the purpose of graph analytics is to glean actionable insights from graph data. By contrast, representation learning receives representations of data that simplify the process of extracting relevant information to develop a classification or prediction model. Graph embedding concentrates on low-dimensional representation learning and can be thought of as a hybrid of the two issues. In this chapter, we implicitly highlight the differences between graph representation learning and graph embedding. To learn graph representations, it is not necessary for them to be high dimensional. As stated in Mahmood *et al.* (2017), each node is

DOI: 10.1201/9781003329701-3

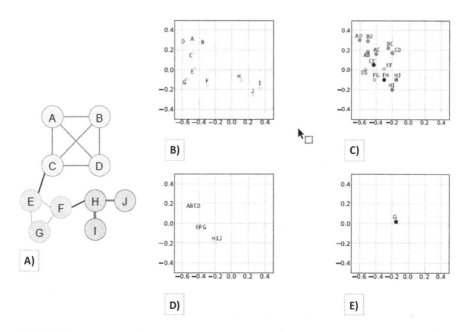

FIGURE 3.1
Illustration of embeddings of a toy graph into two-dimensional spaces. (A) Graph. (B) Node embedding. (C) Edge embedding. (D) Subgraph embedding. (E) Graph embedding.

represented by a vector whose dimension is the same as the number of nodes in the input graph. The geometric distance between any two nodes in a graph is represented by the size of that node's corresponding vector.

It is not easy to embed graphs in two- or three-dimensional spaces. The difficulties of graph embedding are context-specific, involving both input and output embedding. The input graph was segmented into various classes in this chapter. The dilemma of graph embedding is complicated by the fact that various kinds of embedding inputs have diverse information that must be retained in the embedded space. Only when structural information is used to embed a graph, for instance, the goal is to maintain the connectivity between nodes. Auxiliary information offers graph estate from other viewpoints, and thus it could also be regarded throughout the embedding for a graph with node label or features. In contrast to the predetermined nature of the embedding input, the embedded result is determined by the tasks that need to be completed. In particular, node embedding, which depicts neighboring nodes as similar vectors, is the most frequently encountered form of embedding output. The process of node embedding can improve node-related tasks like node classification and node clustering. However, there are situations where the tasks are more closely associated with a coarser level of the graph (e.g., a set of nodes, a subgraph, or the entire graph). Finding a correct form of embedding outputs for the target application is, therefore, the primary difficulty in this area. We classify the results of graph embedding as either node, edge, hybrid, or entire-graph embeddings. The difficulties and requirements of creating a "good" embedding vary depending on the output granularity. An excellent node embedding, for instance, keeps the node's commonality to the corresponding embedded-space neighbors intact. Conversely, the commonality at the graph stage is maintained by an excellent entire graph embedding, which symbolizes the graph as a vector (Ma and Tang, 2021).

3.2 Homogeneous Graph Embedding

In this section, we discuss various algorithms of graph embedding for various kinds of simple homogenous graphs unsigned, static, and undirected. The section debates the graph embedding methods according to the information they seek to reserve, such as node co-occurrence, topological role, node state, and community building.

3.2.1 Node Co-occurrence

Random walks are frequently used to retrieve node co-occurrence in a graph. If two nodes show correlated behavior within those random walks, we say that they are comparable. To ensure that the "commonality" derived from random walks could be reconstructed by the learned node perceptions, the mapping function is optimized. In order to preserve node co-occurrence, DeepWalk is a network embedding technique. First, we provide a high-level overview of the framework in which the DeepWalk method rests, outlining its mapping operator, extraction operator, reconstruction operator, and goal. We also discuss and implement state-of-the-art-demonstrative embedding algorithms, namely large-scale information network embedding (LINE) (Tang *et al.*, 2015) and node2vec (Grover and Leskovec, 2016).

In terms of mapping operator, a look-up table is a simple manner to define the mapping operator $f(n_i)$, which implies retrieving the embedding, em_i, of node n_i. This can be designated as follows:

$$f(n_i) = em_i = e_i^T M, \tag{3.1}$$

where, for node n_i, the corresponding one-hot encoding is denoted as $e_i \in \{0,1\}^N$, given $N = |\mathcal{N}|$. Specifically, e_i includes a single item $e_i[y] = 1$ and the remaining items are set to zero. $M \in \mathbb{R}^{N \times d}$ denote the learnable parameters of embedding with d referring to the embedding dimension. The *i*th row in matrix M refers to the embedding of node n_i. Thus, $N \times d$ refer to the number of parameters of mapping operator.

In terms of extraction operator, given $n^{(0)}$ as the starting node of graph G, we want to arbitrarily walk from starting node to one of the neighbor's nodes. This process continues repeating till T node is visited. This way, the number of randomly visited nodes during random walk can describe the length of the random. In the next, a formal definition is provided for the random walk.

Definition. *Given a connected graph $G = \{\mathcal{N}, \mathcal{E}\}$, and a random walk beginning at node $n^{(0)} \in \mathcal{N}$, where tth random walk corresponds to the node $n^{(t)} \in \mathcal{N}$, then, the random walk can continue to the following node based on some probability calculated as follows:*

$$p\left(n^{(t+1)} \mid n^{(t)}\right) = \begin{cases} \dfrac{1}{D\left(n^{(t)}\right)}, & \text{if } n^{(t+1)} \in N\left(n^{(t)}\right) \\ 0, & \text{otherwise} \end{cases}, \tag{3.2}$$

where $D\left(n^{(t)}\right)$ and $N\left(n^{(t)}\right)$ denote the degree and neighbors of node $n^{(t)}$. In brief, the random selection of the next node is derived from the uniform distribution. To recap the above operation, the generation of random walk with length T can be defined as follows:

$$\mathcal{W} = RW\left(G, n^{(t)}, T\right), \tag{3.3}$$

where $\mathcal{W} = \left(n^{(0)}, \ldots \ldots, n^{(T-1)}\right)$ and $n^{(0)}$ refers to the beginning node in random walk.

In many applications, including product suggestion and social analysis, random walks have been used to quantify degrees of commonality between entities. DeepWalk generates a sequence of short random walks on a given graph and uses the co-occurrence of nodes to draw conclusions. After that, we break down how we came up with the random walks and how we got the correlations out of them. Each node is treated as a potential beginning point for generating γ random walks, allowing for the generation of random walks that are capable of gathering information from the whole graph. As a result, the total number of possible random walks is $\gamma \cdot N$.

The random walks could be thought of as phrases in an "artificial language" with a lexicon defined by the set of all possible nodes $\mathcal{N}$. In these sentences, the model of the language attempts to keep information by taking the co-occurrence among the words according to the Skip-gram algorithm (McCormick, 2016). The "context" of the statement was determined by how far the words were from the word's center. The co-occurrence frequency of each word is then calculated based on the position of the words' centers within the contexts in which they first appear. The Skip-gram algorithm is able to preserve co-occurrence data. Thus, these hypotheses attempted to model co-occurrence interactions between nodes in random walks. A Tuple is adopted to represent the two nodes of co-occurrence $\left(n_{foc}, n_{con}\right)$, which are the focus node and context node, respectively.

Given the mapping operator and co-occurrence info, it is essential to argue the procedure of information reconstruction in the embedding domain. The reconstruction operator seeks to rebuild the co-occurrence features by deducing the probability of perceiving the tuples in the extracted information, O, i.e., $\left(n_{foc}, n_{con}\right) \in O$. As a result, two mapping operators are utilized in order to construct two representations, each of which corresponds to one of the node's two tasks. Each operator can be designed as follows:

$$f_{foc}\left(n_i\right) = w_y = e_i^T W_{foc}, \tag{3.4}$$

$$f_{con}\left(n_i\right) = n_i = e_i^T W_{con}. \tag{3.5}$$

In a pair $\left(n_{foc}, n_{con}\right)$, the co-occurrence relationships could be described as detecting n_{con} within the scope of focus node n_{foc}. Given the abovementioned mapping operators, the probability of perceiving n_{foc} within the scope of n_{foc} could be calculated via SoftMax operation:

$$p(n_{con} \mid n_{foc}) = \frac{\exp\left(f_{con}\left(n_{con}\right)^T f_{foc}\left(n_{foc}\right)\right)}{\sum_{n \in \mathcal{N}} \exp\left(f_{con}\left(n\right) f_{foc}^T\left(n_{foc}\right)\right)}. \tag{3.6}$$

For the tuple $\left(n_{foc}, n_{con}\right)$, this can be viewed as the reconstruction data in the embedding space. For any given tuple $\left(n_{foc}, n_{con}\right)$, the rebuilder *Reb* could compute the probability in the above formula as follows:

$$Reb\left(n_{con} \mid n_{foc}\right) = p\left(n_{con} \mid n_{foc}\right). \tag{3.7}$$

The reconstruction can be interpreted as capturing information in the original graph There are two ranks of probabilities to get the objective, high for *Reb* function in captured tuples and low for randomly generated tuples. In the co-occurrence, in the Skip-gram algorithm (McCormick, 2016), these tuples are not dependent to each other. So, the reconstructing O probability can be presented as:

$$O' = Reb(O) = \prod_{\left(n_{con}, n_{foc}\right) \in O} p\left(n_{con} \mid n_{foc}\right). \tag{3.8}$$

It is possible that O contains duplicated tuples. In order to get rid of these duplications in the above formula, we re-formulate it as:

$$O' = Reb(O) = \prod_{\left(n_{con}, n_{foc}\right) \in set(O)} p\left(n_{con} \mid n_{foc}\right)^{\#(n_{foc}, n_{con})}, \tag{3.9}$$

where $set(O)$ represents the group of single tuples in tuples in input without copies and $\#\left(n_{foc}, n_{con}\right)$ is the occurrence of tuples $\left(n_{foc}, n_{con}\right)$ in O. Thus, the tuples that are additional regular in O donate additional to the total probability in the above formula. To safeguard improved rebuilding, the parameters, (W_{foc}, W_{con}), of mapping operators need to be updated in such a way that maximizes the above formula by minimizing the following loss:

$$\mathcal{L}\left(W_{foc}, W_{con}\right) = - \sum_{\left(n_{con}, n_{foc}\right) \in\; set(O)} \#\left(n_{con} \mid n_{foc}\right) \cdot \log p\left(n_{con} \mid n_{foc}\right). \qquad (3.10)$$

In the denominator, the adding total nodes is a computationally impracticable in computing the probability. Two approaches have been adopted to represent this test: first, negative sampling and second, hierarchical SoftMax. The negative sample is a very common technique to speed up the learning process. It is adopted from noise-contrastive estimation (NCE) to increase the SoftMax log probability. So that, our objective isn't increasing the probabilities instead of study high-quality node illustrations. It is practical to simplify NCE providing the educated node illustrations preserve better quality. Thus, the next alterations are made to NCE, and negative sampling is distinct as follows. To create the negative sample tuples, a number of k nodes are sampled in such a way that they do not appear within the scope of focus node of each tuple $\left(n_{con}, n_{foc}\right)$ in O. The generated negative tuples can be used to define the objective of negative sampling for $\left(n_{con}, n_{foc}\right)$ as follows:

$$\log \sigma\left(f_{con}\left(n_{con}\right)^T f_{foc}\left(n_{foc}\right)\right) + \sum_{i=1}^{k} X_{N_i \sim P_i(N)}\left[\log \sigma\left(-f_{con}\left(n_{con}\right)^T f_{foc}\left(n_{foc}\right)\right)\right], \quad (3.11)$$

whereas the negative tuples are driven from the probability distribution $P_i(N)$ such that $P_i(N) \sim a(n)^{3/4}$. By optimizing the above formula, the probability between the sample nodes in the negative tuples has the lowest possible value, the possibilities between the sampling nodes in the truthful tuples have the highest possible value. As a result, it has a tendency to guarantee that the learnt node representations continue to keep the information regarding the co-occurrence. This way, the loss function can be written as follows:

$$\mathcal{L}\left(W_{foc}, W_{con}\right)$$

$$= \sum_{\left(n_{con}, n_{foc}\right) \in set(O)} \#(n_{con}, n_{foc}) \cdot \log \sigma\left(f_{con}\left(n_{con}\right)^T f_{foc}\left(n_{foc}\right)\right)$$

$$(3.12)$$

$$+ \sum_{i=1}^{k} X_{N_i \sim P_i(N)}\left[\log \sigma\left(- f_{con}\left(n_{con}\right)^T f_{foc}\left(n_{foc}\right)\right)\right].$$

The usage of negative sampling rather than the conservative SoftMax leads the computing complexity to be decreased from $O(|\mathcal{N}|)$ to $O(k)$. In this context, the node2vec and LINE are common approaches, which are proposed to maintain co-occurrence information. They differ somewhat from DeepWalk, but they still fit into the fundamental structure. Following that, we'll go through the distinctions between these approaches and DeepWalk.

Node2Vec: Through the biased-random walk, node2vec presents a more flexible technique to investigate the neighborhood of a given node, which is utilized to substitute the random walk in DeepWalk to produce O. A second-order random walk with two parameters, p *and* q, is presented particularly. This is how it's demarcated.

Definition. *A linked graph is denoted by* $G = \{\mathcal{N}, \mathcal{E}\}$. *In the graph G, we assume a random walk beginning at node* $n^{(0)} \in \mathcal{N}$. *Assume that the random walk has just completed a journey from node* $n^{(t-1)}$ *to node* $n^{(t)}$ *and is currently at noden*$^{(t)}$. *For the following step, the stroll must determine which node to visit. Instead of randomly selecting* $n^{(t+1)}$ *from among* $n^{(t)}$ *neighbors, a probability to sample is calculated based on both* $n^{(t)}$ *and* $n^{(t-1)}$. *The following is a definition of an unnormalized "probability" to pick the next node:*

$$\alpha_{pq}\left(n^{(t+1)} \mid n^{(t-1)}, n^{(t)}\right) = \begin{cases} 1 & \text{if } dis\left(n^{(t-1)}, n^{(t+1)}\right) = 1 \\ \dfrac{1}{q} & \text{if } dis\left(n^{(t-1)}, n^{(t+1)}\right) = 2, \\ \dfrac{1}{p} & \text{if } dis\left(n^{(t-1)}, n^{(t+1)}\right) = 0 \end{cases} \tag{3.13}$$

where $dis\left(n^{(t-1)}, n^{(t+1)}\right)$ estimates the size of the shortest path between node $n^{(t-1)}$ and $n^{(t+1)}$. To select the following node, $n^{(t+1)}$ can be selected by normalizing the abovementioned unnormalized probability. Notice that the second-order random walk depending on this normalized probability includes both the prior node $n^{(t-1)}$ and the present node $n^{(t)}$ at what time defining the following node $n^{(t+1)}$. The parameter p controls the chance of returning to node $n^{(t-1)}$ after moving from node $n^{(t-1)}$ to node $n^{(t)}$. A smaller p promotes the random walk to return, whereas a greater p ensures that the walk will less likely return to previously visited nodes. The walk uses the parameter q to distinguish between "inward" and "outward" nodes. When $q > 1$, the walk is skewed toward nodes near node $n^{(t-1)}$, and when $q < 1$, the walk is biased toward nodes far from node $n^{(t-1)}$, and when $q < 1$. As a result, we may produce random walks with varied focuses by varying the variables p and q. The remaining phases of node2vec are the same as DeepWalk after producing the random walks based on the normalized form of the probability.

```
import torch
import torch.nn as nn
```

```python
from torch.utils.data import DataLoader
from sklearn.linear_model import LogisticRegression
from dgl.sampling import node2vec_random_walk


class Node2vec(nn.Module):

    def __init__(self, g, embedding_dim, walk_length, p, q,
num_walks=14, window_size=7, num_negatives=7,
                 use_sparse=True, weight_name=None):
        super(Node2vec, self).__init__()

        assert walk_length >= window_size

        self.g = g
        self.embedding_dim = embedding_dim
        self.walk_length = walk_length
        self.p = p
        self.q = q
        self.num_walks = num_walks
        self.window_size = window_size
        self.num_negatives = num_negatives
        self.N = self.g.num_nodes()
        if weight_name is not None:
            self.prob = weight_name
        else:
            self.prob = None

        self.embedding = nn.Embedding(self.N, embedding_dim,
sparse=use_sparse)

    def reset_parameters(self):
        self.embedding.reset_parameters()

    def sample(self, batch):
        if not isinstance(batch, torch.Tensor):
            batch = torch.tensor(batch)
        batch = batch.repeat(self.num_walks)
        # positive
        pos_traces = node2vec_random_walk(self.g, batch, self.p,
self.q, self.walk_length, self.prob)
        pos_traces = pos_traces.unfold(1, self.window_size, 1)  #
rolling window
        pos_traces = pos_traces.contiguous().view(-1, self.
window_size)

        # negative
        neg_batch = batch.repeat(self.num_negatives)
        neg_traces = torch.randint(self.N, (neg_batch.size(0), self.
walk_length))
        neg_traces = torch.cat([neg_batch.view(-1, 1), neg_traces],
dim=-1)
        neg_traces = neg_traces.unfold(1, self.window_size, 1)  #
rolling window
        neg_traces = neg_traces.contiguous().view(-1, self.
window_size)
```

```
        return pos_traces, neg_traces

    def forward(self, nodes=None):

        emb = self.embedding.weight
        if nodes is None:
            return emb
        else:
            return emb[nodes]

    def loss(self, pos_trace, neg_trace):
        e = 1e-15

        # Positive
        pos_start, pos_rest = pos_trace[:, 0], pos_trace[:, 1:].
contiguous()  # start node and following trace
        w_start = self.embedding(pos_start).unsqueeze(dim=1)
        w_rest = self.embedding(pos_rest)
        pos_out = (w_start * w_rest).sum(dim=-1).view(-1)

        # Negative
        neg_start, neg_rest = neg_trace[:, 0], neg_trace[:,
1:].contiguous()
        w_start = self.embedding(neg_start).unsqueeze(dim=1)
        w_rest = self.embedding(neg_rest)
        neg_out = (w_start * w_rest).sum(dim=-1).view(-1)

        # compute loss
        pos_loss = -torch.log(torch.sigmoid(pos_out) + e).mean()
        neg_loss = -torch.log(1 - torch.sigmoid(neg_out) + e).mean()

        return pos_loss + neg_loss

    def loader(self, batch_size):

        return DataLoader(torch.arange(self.N), batch_size=batch_size,
shuffle=True, collate_fn=self.sample)

    @torch.no_grad()
    def evaluate(self, x_train, y_train, x_val, y_val):
        """
        Evaluate the quality of embedding vector via a downstream
classification task with logistic regression.
        """
        x_train = self.forward(x_train)
        x_val = self.forward(x_val)

        x_train, y_train = x_train.cpu().numpy(),
y_train.cpu().numpy()
        x_val, y_val = x_val.cpu().numpy(), y_val.cpu().numpy()
        lr = LogisticRegression(solver='lbfgs', multi_class='auto',
max_iter=150).fit(x_train, y_train)

        return lr.score(x_val, y_val)
```

LINE: the second order proximity aim of LINE can be stated as follows:

$$- \sum_{(n_{con}, n_{foc}) \in \mathcal{E}} \log \sigma \Big(f_{con}(n_{con})^T f_{foc}(n_{foc}) \Big)$$

$$+ \sum_{i=1}^{k} X_{N_i \sim P_i(N)} \Big[\log \sigma \Big(f_{con}(n_{con})^T f_{foc}(n_{foc}) \Big) \Big],$$

(3.14)

where $\mathcal{E}$ denotes the edges of graph G. It could be noted that the most distinct is that LINE used $\mathcal{E}$ for information to be reconstruction instead of O. Actually, $\mathcal{E}$ could be regarded as a distinct instance of O with 1 as the random walk length. Practically speaking, the implementation of LINE techniques is given in the following code snippets.

```python
import torch
import torch.nn as nn
import torch.nn.functional as F

class LINE(nn.Module):
    def __init__(self, size, embedding_dim=128, order=1):
        super(LINE, self).__init__()

        assert order in [1, 2], print("Order should either be int(1) or int(2)")

        self.embedding_dim = embedding_dim
        self.order = order
        self.nodes_embeddings = nn.Embedding(size, embedding_dim)

        if order == 2:
            self.contextnodes_embeddings = nn.Embedding(size, embedding_dim)
            # Initialization
            self.contextnodes_embeddings.weight.data = self.contextnodes_embeddings.weight.data.uniform_(
                -.5, .5) / embedding_dim

        # Initialization
        self.nodes_embeddings.weight.data = self.nodes_embeddings.weight.data.uniform_(
            -.5, .5) / embedding_dim

    def forward(self, v_i, v_j, neg_samples, device):

        v_i = self.nodes_embeddings(v_i).to(device)

        if self.order == 2:
            v_j = self.contextnodes_embeddings(v_j).to(device)
            neg_nodes = -self.contextnodes_embeddings(neg_samples).to(device)
        else:
```

```
        v_j = self.nodes_embeddings(v_j).to(device)
        neg_nodes = -self.nodes_embeddings(neg_samples).to(device)

    mulpositivebatch = torch.mul(v_i, v_j)
    positivebatch = F.logsigmoid(torch.sum(mulpositivebatch,
dim=1))

    mulnegativebatch = torch.mul(v_i.view(len(v_i), 1,
self.embedding_dim), neg_nodes)
    negativebatch = torch.sum(
        F.logsigmoid(
            torch.sum(mulnegativebatch, dim=2)
        ),
        dim=1)
    loss = positivebatch + negativebatch
    return -torch.mean(loss)
```

These aforementioned network embedding approaches may be seen from a matrix factorization viewpoint in Ma and Tang (2021). For DeepWalk, for instance, we have the given theorem.

Theorem DeepWalk with negative selection for a specified graph G is equal to factoring the given matrix in matrix form:

$$\log\left(\frac{vol(G)}{T}\left(\sum_{r=1}^{T} P^r\right)A^{-1}\right) - \log(k), \tag{3.15}$$

where $P = A^{-1}B$ with B, the adjacency matrix of graph G and A its corresponding degree matrix, T is the length of random walk, $vol(G) = \sum_{y=1}^{|N|} \sum^{|N|} B_{y,z}$, and k is the number of negative samples.

Therefore, the DeepWalk matrix factorization form may be included in the abovementioned generic architecture. The information extractor, in particular, is

$$\log\left(\frac{vol(G)}{T}\left(\sum_{r=1}^{T} P^r\right)A^{-1}\right). \tag{3.16}$$

The mapping function is similar to the ones presented for DeepWalk, where two mapping functions, $f_{ter}()$ and $f_{tet}()$, are available (). S_{ter} and S_{tet} are the parameters for these two mapping functions and are also the two groups of node descriptions for the graph G. In this scenario, the re-constructor can be expressed as $S_{tet}S_{ter}^{\mathsf{T}}$. As a result, the objective function may be expressed as follows:

$$\mathcal{L}(S_{tet}, S_{ter}) = \left\|\log\left(\frac{vol(G)}{T}\left(\sum_{r=1}^{T} P^r\right)A^{-1}\right) - \log(b) - S_{tet}S_{ter}^{\mathsf{T}}\right\|_F^2. \tag{3.17}$$

By reducing this goal, the embeddings S_{tet} and S_{ter} may be learnt. In the same way, LINE and node2vec may be expressed as a matrix.

The degree of nodes, essentially, might suggest their architectural role resemblance. In other words, two nodes with the same degree of structural similarity might be termed structurally similar. Furthermore, these nodes might be even more equivalent if their neighbors have comparable degrees. Based on this notion, a hierarchical architectural similarity measure is presented (Ma and Tang, 2021). The collection of nodes that are k-hops distant from node n is denoted by $R_k(n)$. We organize the nodes in $R_k(n)$ in the degree sequence $(R_k(n))$ based on their degree. Then, given their k-hop neighbors, the architectural distance $g_k(n_1, n_2)$ between two nodes n_1 and n_1 may be recursively determined as follows:

$$g_k(n_1, n_2) = g_{k-1}(n_1, n_2) + dis(v(R_k(n_1)), v(R_k(n_2)), \tag{3.18}$$

where $dis(v(R_k(n_1)), v(R_k(n_2))) \geq 0$ assists the distance among the ordered degree orders of n_1 and n_2. On the other side, it represents the degree of similarity between n_1 and n_2's k-hop neighbors. It's worth noting that $g_{-1}(\cdot, \cdot)$ is set to 0. $dis(\cdot, \cdot)$ and $g_k(\cdot, \cdot)$ are both distance measurements. As a result, the bigger they are, the more different the two inputs are. The sequences $v(R_k(n_1))$ and $v(R_k(n_1))$ can be of varied lengths, with any numbers as their members. As a result, the distance function dis($\cdot$,) is chosen as dynamic time warping (DTW) since it can handle sequences of various widths. The DTW method determines the best matching among two sequences by minimizing the sum of the distances between the aligned elements. The distance among two items a *and* b is calculated using the formula:

$$d(a,b) = \frac{\max(a,b)}{\min(a,b)} - 1. \tag{3.19}$$

Observe that this distance is determined by the ratio of the two components' greatest and minimum values; hence, it might view $d(1,2)$ as very distinct from $d(100,101)$, which is desirable when assessing degree differences.

We can create a multi-layered weighted graph that encodes the architectural resemblance between the nodes after collecting the pairwise structural distance. With k^* as the diameter of the initial graph G, we may construct a k^* layered graph in which the k-th layer is based on the following weights:

$$s_k(w,n) = \exp(-g_k(w,n)).$$

The weight of the edge connecting nodes w and n in the k-th layer of the graph is denoted by $s_k(w,n)$d. When the distance $g_k(w,n)$ among nodes w and n is lower, the link between them is greater. We then use directed edges to connect the graph's multiple levels. Each node v in layer k is linked to its matching node in layers $k - 1$ and $k + 1$ in particular. The edge weights among layers are explained as follows:

$$s\left(n^{(k)}, n^{(k+1)}\right) = \log(\Gamma_k(n) + x), k = 0, \ldots k^* - 1, \ s\left(n^{(k)}, n^{(k+1)}\right) = 1, k = 0, \ldots k^*, \quad (3.20)$$

where $n^{(k)}$ denotes the node n in the k-th layer.

$$\Gamma_k(n) = \sum_{n_z \in N} \mathbb{I}\left(s_k(n, n_z)\right) > \bar{s}_k). \quad (3.21)$$

In the layer k, $\bar{s}_k = \sum_{(w,n) \in E_k} s_k(w, n) / \left(\frac{1}{2}\right)$ is the mean edge weight of the whole graph (E_k is its collection of edges). As a result, $\Gamma_k(n)$ quantifies how similar node n is to other nodes in layer k. If a node is nearly identical to other nodes in the recent layer, its design assures that it has a strong link to the next layer. As a result, it's probable to direct the random walk to the up layer in order to gather additional data.

A biased random walk approach is described for generating a series of random walks that can then be used to reconstruct co-occurrence tuples. Assume the random walk is now at node w in layer k; in the following step, the random walk stays in the same layer with probability q and hops to a different layer with probability $1 - q$, where q is a hyperparameter. The chance of walking from the recent node u to some other node n is determined as follows if the random walk remains simultaneously layer:

$$P_k(n| w) = \frac{\exp\left(-g_k(n, w)\right)}{M_k(w)}, \quad (3.22)$$

where $M_k(w)$ is a normalization feature for the node u in the layer k, which is distinct as follows:

$$M_k(w) = \sum_{(n,w) \in E_k} \exp\left(-g_k(n, w)\right), \quad (3.23)$$

If the walk chooses to walk to additional layer, the probabilities to the layer $k + 1$ and to the layer $k - 1$ are computed as follows:

$$P_k\left(w^{(k)}, w^{(k+1)}\right) = \frac{s\left(w^{(k)}, w^{(k+1)}\right)}{s\left(w^{(k)}, w^{(k+1)}\right) + s\left(w^{(k)}, w^{(k-1)}\right)}, \quad (3.24)$$

$$P_k\left(w^{(k)}, w^{(k-1)}\right) = 1 - P_k\left(w^{(k)}, w^{(k+1)}\right). \quad (3.25)$$

This biased random walk may be used to produce a series of random walks from which the co-occurrence links among nodes can be extracted. It's worth noting that the co-occurrence associations are only recovered between nodes from different levels, not between nodes from the same layer. To put it another way, co-occurrence links are only produced when the random walk uses the same layer for each step. These co-occurrence associations may be used to recreate information from the embedding area using DeepWalk.

3.2.2 Node State

One sort of essential information in graphs is the global state of nodes, like the centrality scores presented in Section 3.3.3. A network embedding approach is suggested to maintain node co-occurrence knowledge and node global state simultaneously. The approach is made up of two parts: (1) a component that keeps track of co-occurrence information, and (2) a component that keeps track of the global state. DeepWalk, which was introduced in Section 3.2.1, has the same component for preserving co-occurrence information. As a result, we'll concentrate on the component that keeps track of global status information in this part. The suggested strategy, rather than conserving global status scores for nodes in the graph, tries to preserve their global status ranking. As a result, the extractor produces global status scores before ranking the nodes based on those values. To recover the ranking information, the re-constructor is used. The extractor and re-constructor are described next.

The extraction operator determines the global status scores before determining the nodes' global rank. To compute the global status scores, any of the centrality metrics mentioned in Section 3.3.3 can be used. The nodes can be reconfigured in decreasing order based on the scores after getting the global status scores. The rearranged nodes are denoted as $\left(n_{(1)}, \ldots, n_{(I)}\right)$ where the subscript indicates the node's rank.

The reconstruction operator job is to retrieve the ranking information collected from the node embeddings by the extractor. The re-constructor seeks to retain ranking order of all pairs of nodes in $\left(n_{(1)}, \ldots, n_{(I)}\right)$ to reconstruct the global ranking. Assuming that the order of nodes in $\left(n_{(1)}, \ldots, n_{(I)}\right)$ is unrelated of other pairings, the likelihood of the global ranking being retained may be described using the node embedding as follows:

$$P_{global} = \prod_{1 \leq y < z \leq I} P\left(n_{(y)}, n_{(z)}\right). \tag{3.26}$$

The chance that node $n_{(y)}$ is ranked before node $n_{(z)}$ according to their node embeddings is $P\left(n_{(y)}, n_{(z)}\right)$. It is modeled as follows:

$$P\left(n_{(y)}, n_{(z)}\right) = \sigma\left(S^T\left(w_{(y)} - w_{(z)}\right)\right), \tag{3.27}$$

where $w_{(y)}$ and $w_{(z)}$ are the node embeddings for nodes $n_{(y)}$ and $n_{(z)}$ (or the mapping function outputs for $(n_{(y)}, n_{(z)})$), respectively, and S is a vector of variables to be learnt. We predict that each ordered pair $((n_{(y)}, n_{(z)})$ will have a high likelihood of being generated from the embedding in order to retain the order information. This may be accomplished by reducing the goal function in the following:

$$\mathcal{L}_{global} = -\log P_{global},\qquad(3.28)$$

It's worth noting that this $\mathcal{L}_{global}$ global may be paired with the goal of preserving co-occurrence information, allowing the learnt embeddings to keep both the co-occurrence information and the global status.

3.2.3 Community Topology

The development of embedding approaches to maintain such crucial information has been prompted by one of the most notable properties of graphs. The preservation of both component architecture, like relationships and co-occurrence, and community architecture is advocated using a matrix factorization-based technique. Then, we'll utilize the generic framework to explain its element for preserving node-oriented architecture information then provide the component for preserving community architecture information with flexibility maximization, and then talk about the overall goal.

The pairwise connection information and the similarity of node neighbors are two forms of node-oriented structural information that are retained. Both forms of information may be retrieved and represented as matrices from a particular graph.

The adjacency matrix B can be used to represent the judgment connection information retrieved from the graph. The re-constructor's purpose is to rebuild the graph's pairwise link information (or adjacency matrix). The neighborhood similarity metric determines how similar two nodes' neighbors are. The pairwise neighborhood similarity of nodes n_y and n_z is obtained as follows:

$$v_{y,z} = \frac{B_y B_z^{\mathsf{T}}}{\left\|B_y\right\|\left\|B_z\right\|},\qquad(3.29)$$

where B_y is the yth row of the adjacency matrix, denoting the node $n\,y$'s neighborhood information. When nodes n_y and n_z have more common neighbors, $v_y,\ z$ is greater, and when nodes $n\,y$ and $n\,z$ do not share any neighbors, $v\,y,z$ is zero. Intuitively, if $n\,y$ and $n\,z$ have a lot of common neighbors, that is, $v\,y,$ z is big, they're more probable in DeepWalk's random walks. As a result, this data has an implied link to the co-occurrence. These pairwise neighborhood similarity connections may be summed up in a matrix v, with $v\_$ as the y, zth element is $v_{y,z}$. In summary, two matrices, B and V, may be used to represent the extracted data.

The goal of reconstruction operator is to retrieve these two kinds of extracted data as B and V. To recreate them all at once, it first joins them linearly as follows:

$$P = B + \eta.V, \tag{3.30}$$

where the relevance of neighborhood similarity is controlled by $\eta > 0$. The matrix P is then rebuilt from the embedding domain as $S_{tet}S_{ter}^T$, where S_{tet} and $S_{ter}r$ are variables of two mapping functions $f\,tet$ and $f\,ter$, respectively. They are designed in the same way as DeepWalk. The goal may be expressed as follows:

$$\mathcal{L}(S_{tet}, S_{ter}) = \left\| P - S_{tet}S_{ter}^T \right\|_F^2, \tag{3.31}$$

where $\|.\|_F$ denotes the Frobenius norm of a matrix. The Frobenius standard of a matrix is denoted by $\|.\|_F$.

A community in a graph is made up of a group of tightly linked nodes. In a graph, there are frequently several communities. The goal of community discovery is to categorize nodes in a network into distinct groups. Modularity maximization is a prominent community detection approach. In particular, given a network with two communities and a given node-community allocation, the modularity may be defined as follows:

$$K = \frac{1}{2 \cdot vol(G)} \sum_{y,z} \left(B_{y,z} - \frac{a(n_y)a(n_z)}{vol(G)} \right) f_y f_z, \tag{3.32}$$

where $a(n_y)$ is the degree of node n_y, $f_y = 1$ if node is the degree of node $f_y = -1$ and $vol(G) = \sum_{n_y \in N} a(n_y)$ if node n_y belongs to the first community. In a randomly generated graph, $\frac{a(n_y)a(n_z)}{vol(G)}$ approximates the anticipated number of edges between nodes n_y and n_z. The randomly produced graph contains the same number of nodes, node degrees, and edges as G; however, the edges are randomly arranged between nodes. As a result, the modularity K is determined by the difference between the proportion of observed edges in the original graph that fall into communities and the predicted fraction in the randomly generated graph.

A positive modularity K implies the presence of community structure, and a bigger modularity K frequently signifies the discovery of superior community structures. As a result, we may maximize the modularity K by identifying the appropriate community assignments to discover excellent communities. In addition, the modularity K may be expressed as a matrix:

$$K = \frac{1}{2 \cdot vol(G)} f^T C f, \tag{3.33}$$

where $f \in \{-1, 1\}^I$ is the community assignment vector with the yth element $f[y] = f_y$ and $C \in \mathbb{R}^{I \times I}$ is distinct as follows:

$$C_{y,z} = B_{y,z} - \frac{a(n_y)a(n_z)}{vol(G)}. \tag{3.34}$$

The definition of the modularity can be extended to $j > 2$ communities. In detail, the community assignment vector f can be generalized as a matrix $F \in \{0, 1\}^{I \times j}$ where each column of F represents a community. The yth row of the matrix F is a one-hot vector indicating the community of node n_y, where only one element of this row is 1 and the others are 0. Therefore, we have $ac(F^T F) = I$, where $ac(X)$ denotes the trace of a matrix X. After discarding some constants, the modularity for a graph with m communities can be defined as follows: $K = ac(F^T C F)$. The assignment matrix F can be learned by maximizing the modularity K as follows:

$$\max_F J = ac(F^T C F), \text{ s.t. } ac(F^T F) = I. \tag{3.35}$$

Note that F is a discrete matrix that is often relaxed to be a continuous matrix during the optimization process.

To jointly preserve the node-oriented structure information and the community structure information, another matrix A is introduced to reconstruct the indicator matrix F together with S_{ter}. As a result, the objective of the entire framework is as:

$$\min_{S_{ter}, tet} \left\| P - S_{tet} S_{ter}^T \right\|_M^2 + \alpha \left\| F - S_{ter} A^T \right\|_M^2$$
$$- \beta.ac(F^T C F), \text{ s.t. } S_{tet} \geq 0, S_{ter} \geq 0, A \geq 0, ac(F^T F) = I, \tag{3.36}$$

where the term $\left\| F - S_{ter} A^T \right\|_M^2$ connects the community structure information with the node representations, the nonnegative constraints are added as nonnegative matrix factorization is adopted by Ma and Tang (2021) and the hyperparameters α *and* β control the balance among three terms.

3.3 Heterogeneous Graph Embedding

In the previous chapter, we learnt that heterogeneous graphs are composition of diverse types of nodes and edges and turned to be pervasive robust graphs a roust tools for embracing insightful relations and topological in real-world applications such as social networks, biological networks, citation networks, and cyber-security.

Owing to the omnipresence of heterogeneous graphs, learning the embedding of heterogeneous graphs becomes an important challenge for wide verity of graph analysis tasks, for example, link prediction, graph classification, and node classification. Conventional embedding methods (e.g., matrix factorization) were used to create low-dimensional representations heterogeneous graphs. Nevertheless, the computational complexity of disintegrating a big matrix is typically highly expensive, and their performance also exhibits some statistical limitations (Wang *et al.*, 2020). As a remedy, heterogeneous graph embedding was introduced to enable efficient mapping from input space to embedding while retaining the semantics and the structural heterogeneity of the graph. In general, the heterogeneity of nodes and edges in the heterogeneous graph prevented the use of the homogeneous embedding methods discussed in the previous sections. In particular, the following aspects shape barriers in face of homogeneous embedding, when it comes to be applied to the graph.

i. The construction in heterogeneous graphs is typically reliant on semantics (i.e., meta-path structure), which means that the local assembly of single node in heterogeneous graph could be very dissimilar when encountering various kinds of relationships.

ii. **Heterogeneous features:** The diverse kinds of edges and nodes possess a dissimilar set of features typically belonging to a diverse feature space, which necessitate developing the heterogeneous graph embedding techniques (such as heterogeneous GNNs) to be able to handle the heterogeneousness of features to better extract information (Wang *et al.*, 2020).

iii. **Application based:** The heterogeneous graph is typically application reliant, where the elementary construction of heterogeneous graph regularly could seized be via graph- or meta-path, nevertheless, choosing meta-path selection remains a challenging task in realism as it necessitates satisfactory amount of domain knowledge.

Numerous heterogeneous graphs embedding strategies have been developed to address the aforementioned problems, and a number of them have already shown efficiency when used in real-world applications such cyber-security, malware detection, and Internet of Things (IoT). In this context, heterogeneous graphs embedding methods are classified, according to the information they use, into four categories, namely application-based heterogeneous graph embedding, attribute-based method graph embedding, dynamic heterogeneous graph embedding, and structure-retaining heterogeneous graph embedding. The following subsections dive into details of each of these categories.

3.3.1 Application-Based Heterogeneous Graph Embedding

When the foregoing data, such as characteristics, is insufficient, heterogeneous graph embedding has been tightly integrated with certain applications. In these situations, it is important to think about two things in particular: how to build a heterogeneous graph for a certain application, and what data, that is, subject knowledge, must be integrated into heterogeneous graph embedding to maximize the utility of the heterogeneous graph for that application. A variety of applications can be figured out in this regard such as recommendations, recognition, and nearby searches (Zhang *et al.*, 2021).

The relationship between the customer and the object in a recommendation system may be easily represented as a heterogeneous graph with two kinds of nodes. Therefore, recommendations are a common setting that heavily employs heterogeneous graph. Applying heterogeneous network embedding to suggestion applications is a growing area of study since it allows for the easy incorporation of new forms of information, such as social interactions. In this regard, the goal of HERec (Shi *et al.*, 2019) is to discover client and object embeddings under many meta-paths and then combine them into a single suggestion. Using meta-path-guided random walks on user-item heterogeneous graph, it first locates instances when users and objects appear together. Next, it takes the client and object occurrence patterns and applies node2vec (Grover and Leskovec, 2016) to generate tentative embeddings. HERec provides a fusion function to combine the many embeddings since the embeddings under distinct meta-paths include diverse semantics, leading to improved recommending efficiency:

$$g\left(h_u^m\right) = \frac{1}{|P|} \sum_{m=1}^{M} W_m h_u^m + b_m, \tag{3.37}$$

where h_u^m denotes the embedding of the node of client u under meta-path m. M represents the set of meta-paths.

User experience is quite close to the fusing of object embeddings. The final step is a projection layer, which is used to guess which products people would like most. HERec simultaneously optimizes the graph embedding and recommendations objectives. On the other hand, the vicinity searching uses the topological and semantic information of heterogeneous graph to locate nodes that are nearest to a particular node. Previous research has tackled this issue in homogenous graphs, such as online search. The use of heterogeneous graph in proximity search has been attempted recently (Ji *et al.*, 2022). Nevertheless, these approaches are rigid since they rely solely on statistics, such as the amount of linked meta-paths, to determine how close two nodes are in heterogeneous graph. Some embedding approaches have been suggested as machine learning has progressed such as Prox (Liu *et al.*, 2017), Distance-aware DAG Embedding (D2AGE) (Liu *et al.*, 2018). When deciding how to use heterogeneous graph embedding in practice, domain expertise is often an important factor to take into account. Meta-paths are used in proximity search methods to capture the semantic relationships between nodes, improving performance. This means that for application-wise heterogeneous graph embedding, capturing the domain knowledge unique to the application through the use of heterogeneous graph is crucial.

3.3.2 Feature-Based Heterogeneous Graph Embedding

Heterogeneous graph embedding relies on both the graph architecture and the rich properties. In order to extract node embeddings from such complicated structures and a wide variety of properties, attribute-assisted heterogeneous graph embedding algorithms have been developed. Because of the various types of nodes and edges, heterogeneous GNNs face additional difficulties in utilizing the neighborhood information, as they must resolve the heterogeneity of characteristics and develop efficient fusion techniques. In contrast, GNNs can straightforwardly fuse the characteristics of neighbors to upgrade node embeddings. Heterogeneous GNNs are classified into unsupervised and semi-supervised categories, and the benefits and drawbacks of each are discussed next.

The goal of unsupervised heterogeneous GNNs is to discover generalizable node embeddings. They do this by constantly drawing on the synergies among various attribute classes in order to identify any hidden patterns. As far as unsupervised heterogeneous GNNs go, HetGNN (Zhang *et al.*, 2019) is the gold standard. Content aggregation, neighbor aggregation, and genre aggregation are its constituent components. The goal of content aggregation is to master integrated embeddings derived from the contents of various nodes, which may include images, text, or characteristics:

$$f_1(n) = \frac{\sum_{i \in C_n} \left[\overrightarrow{LSTM}\{FC(h_i)\} \oplus \overleftarrow{LSTM}\{FC(h_i)\} \right]}{|C_n|}, \tag{3.38}$$

where C_n denotes the kind of features of node n. h_i represents ith features of node n. A bi-directional LSTM (Imrana *et al.*, 2021) was applied to capture the embeddings learned via manifold features encoder FC. The aggregation of neighbors seeks to combine the nodes sharing the same category by means of a Bi-LSTM to learn the positional representation:

$$f_2^t(n) = \frac{\sum_{n' \in N_t(n)} \left[\overrightarrow{LSTM}\{f_1(n')\} \oplus \overleftarrow{LSTM}\{f_1(n')\} \right]}{|N_t(n)|}, \tag{3.39}$$

where $N_t(n)$ denotes the first-level nodes that are neighboring to node n with category t. Category aggregation adopts attention mechanism to combine the embeddings of diverse categories and generates the ultimate node embeddings, h_n, that is calculated as follows:

$$h_n = \propto^{n,n} \cdot f_1(n) + \sum_{t \in O_n} \propto^{n,t} \cdot f_2^t(n), \qquad (3.40)$$

where O_n represents the group of node kinds. Lastly, a varied skip-gram loss was leveraged to act as non-supervised loss for optimizing the node embeddings. The three aggregate techniques allow HetGNN to maintain the diversity of graph topologies and node characteristics. In contrast to unsupervised heterogeneous GNNs, semi-supervised heterogeneous GNNs are designed to acquire comprehensive knowledge of node embeddings relevant to a given job. To get the best results, they focus on what matters most for the work at hand, both in terms of structure and attributes. Using a hierarchical attention mechanism, a heterogeneous graph attention network (HAN) was proposed to account for node and semantic relevance. There are three components: focusing on individual nodes, focusing on the meaning of individual words, and making predictions. In order to understand the significance of nodes along a given meta-path, node-level attention employs the self-attention mechanism.

3.3.3 Topology-Retained Heterogeneous Graph Embedding

The appropriate preservation of the graph topologies is one of the fundamental requirements of graph embedding. As a result, complex graph topologies, such as second-order topologies, high-order structures, and community topologies, are given more attention by the homogeneous graph embedding. The fact that a heterogeneous graph typically comprises various relationships between its nodes, nevertheless, necessitates taking graph heterogeneity into account. Learning contextual features from the graph topologies is thus an essential focus of heterogeneous graph embedding.

This section examines common topology-based methods of heterogeneous graph embedding under three classes of approaches: edge-, meta-path-, and subgraph-based approaches. An edge is an observable relationship between pairs of nodes, a meta-path is a collection of several edge types, and a subgraph is a very small subsection of a graph. The three components are the heterogeneous graph's core components since they allow it to gather semantic data from many angles. The standard topology-retaining heterogeneous graph embedding techniques in each of the abovementioned three categories of topologies will be discussed in the following sections, and their advantages and disadvantages will be discussed.

3.3.3.1 Edge-Based Embedding

Link represents one of the most fundamental pieces of information that heterogeneous graph embedding must maintain. Unlike homogeneous graph, edges of heterogeneous graph have dissimilar forms and comprise a diversity of semantics. To distinguish various types of links, one classical idea is to deal with them in different metric spaces, rather than a unified metric space. The projected metric embedding (PME) was proposed in Chen *et al.* (2018) to deal with each edge type as a relationship and adopt a relationship-related matrix to transmute the nodes into dissimilar metric domains. Thus, the nodes linked with various types of edges could be adjacent to each other in diverse metric domains, therefore, enable gathering the graph's heterogeneity. In this setting, the distance is estimate with the following metric learning function:

$$S_r\left(n_i;\,n_j\right) = w_{ij}\left\|M_r h_i - M_r h_j\right\|_2,\tag{3.41}$$

where w_{ij} denotes the weights of the edge connecting node i with node j, h_i and h_j represent the node embeddings of the node i and node j, correspondingly; M_r denotes the projection matrix of, r, relationship. PME deliberates the relationships between nodes during the minimization of distance between them, therefore catching the heterogeneity of graph. By making use of relationship-related matrix to gather the heterogeneity of edge, unlike PME, extra embedding techniques were presented to maximize the resemblance of pair of nodes interconnected with particular relationships. Common examples on those methods are embedding of embedding (EOE) (Xu *et al.*, 2017) and HeGAN (Hu, Fang and Shi, 2019), which use the relationship-oriented matrix M_r to compute the resemblance between pair of nodes as follows:

$$S_r\left(n_i;\,n_j\right) = \frac{1}{1 + \exp\left(-h_i^T M_r h_j\right)},\tag{3.42}$$

In particular, EOE was developed to learn embeddings of joined heterogeneous graphs consisting of pair of diverse but interrelated subgraphs. EOE divided the edge in heterogeneous graphs into inter- and intra-graph edges. Intra-graph edges link pair of nodes sharing the same type, while inter-graph edges link pair of nodes belonging to dissimilar types. For gathering the heterogeneity in inter-graph edge, EOE leverages the previous formula to estimate the similarity between nodes. In a different way, HeGAN integrated generative adversarial networks (GAN) (Goodfellow *et al.*, 2014) to capture heterogeneous node embeddings, by using the above formula to act as a discriminator to determine if the node embeddings are generated by the generator.

The aforementioned embedding techniques chiefly reserve the edge topology according to the distance or resemblance estimation on node embeddings, while AspEM (Shi, Gui, *et al.*, 2018) and HEER (Shi, Zhu, *et al.*, 2018) seek to enlarge the likelihood of standing edges. In these cases, the heterogeneous similarity can be estimated as follows:

$$S_r\left(n_i; n_j\right) = \frac{\exp\left(\mu_r^T \cdot g_{ij}\right)}{\sum_{\tilde{i} \in E^-} \exp\left(\mu_r^T \cdot g_{\tilde{i}j}\right) + \sum_{\tilde{j} \in E^-} \exp\left(\mu_r^T \cdot g_{i\tilde{j}}\right)}, \qquad (3.43)$$

where E^- represents the set of negative edges indicating no linkage between node $\tilde{i}$ and node j, $g_{ij} = h_i \odot h_j$, where $\odot$ represents Hadamard product. μ_r denotes the embedding of relationship r.

To sum up, the edge-based heterogeneous embedding techniques can crudely be divided into two main categories. First, the embedding techniques for explicit preservation of the edges' proximity. Second, the embedding techniques for preserving the node's proximity by implicitly exploiting the edge information. For both categories of techniques, the first-order information of heterogeneous graph is exploited.

3.3.3.2 Path-Based Embedding

Unfortunately, the abovementioned edge-based embedding techniques are able to learn the local constructions of heterogeneous graph, which is the first-level relationship. Actually, the high-level relationships characterize more composite semantic representations that are essential for heterogeneous graph embedding. For instance, given heterogeneous citation graph in Figure 3.2,

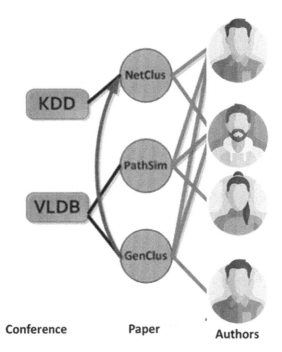

FIGURE 3.2
Illustration of heterogeneous citation graph.

the author-publication and publication-venue relations represent first-level relation. At the same time, the relations of publication-publication, author-conference, and author-author could not be well seized. Thus, the high-level relationships are presented to estimate more composite relationships. Because there are so many high-order relationships, the standard practice that we follow in order to cut down on complication is to pick the high-level relationships that have rich semantics. These are referred to as meta-paths. In this section, we will discuss several typical meta-path-founded heterogeneous graph embedding techniques. These approaches fall into one of two types, namely random walk-based techniques or hybrid relation-based techniques.

Random walk-based techniques typically make use of a meta-path to direct random walk on heterogeneous graphs. As a result, the resulting node sequence might include a large amount of semantic data. Node embedding has the capability of keeping both first- and high-level closeness since it keeps the topology of the node sequence intact.

A metapath2vec (Dong, Chawla and Swami, 2017) provides a demonstrative method on that, which primarily make use of meta-path directed arbitrary walk to produce diverse node sequences with valuable semantics; and next it develops non-homogeneous skip-gram method for retaining the closeness between node n_i and the corresponding contextual neighboring nodes in the sequences of random walk:

$$\arg \max_{\theta} \sum_{n \in \mathcal{N}} \sum_{t \in A} \sum_{c_t \in C_t(n)} \log p(c_t \mid n, \theta), \tag{3.44}$$

where $C_t(n)$ denotes the nodes sharing the context with node n belonging to type t. $p(c_t \mid n, \theta)$ represents distance function for node n as well as contextual neighbors c_t, and it calculates as follows:

$$p(c_t \mid n, \theta) = \frac{e^{h_{c_t} \cdot h_n}}{\sum_{n \in \mathcal{N}} e^{h_0 \cdot h_n}}. \tag{3.45}$$

The above formula should compute the comparison between center node and its neighboring nodes. Next, a negative sampling approach was proposed to decrease the computing costs. Thus, the above formula could be approached as:

$$\log(h_{c_t} \cdot h_n) + \sum_{q=1}^{Q} \mathbb{E}_{\tilde{n}^q \sim P(\tilde{n})} \left[\log Sigmoid(-h_{\tilde{n}^q} \cdot h_n) \right], \tag{3.46}$$

where n^q denotes the negative node sampled form the distribution $P(\tilde{n})$ for Q times. With the use of negative sampling, the computing complexity is significantly decreased. Nevertheless, during the selection of negative samples, the metapath2vec did not take into account the sorts of nodes in the same distribution $P(\tilde{n})$. To address that, the metapath2vec++ was developed for sampling the negative nodes with identical type like the chief node, such that. This can be formulated as follows:

$$\log\left(h_{c_t} \cdot h_n\right) + \sum_{q=1}^{Q} \mathbb{E}_{\tilde{n}_t^q \cdot P(\tilde{n}_t)}\left[\log Sigmoid(-h_{\tilde{n}_t^q} \cdot h_n)\right]. \tag{3.47}$$

With the minimization of objective function, metapath2vec and metapath-2vec++ are able to professionally and effectually gather organizational and semantic representations. Several variations on the original metapath2vec were proposed. For example, heterogeneous randomness walk is generated by Spacey (Ji *et al.*, 2022) to combine multiple high-order meta-paths into one through modulating the rate at which diverse types of nodes can change states. Random walk methods without meta-paths aren't common. The work (Hussein, Yang and Cudré-Mauroux, 2018) developed Jump and Stay strategies (JUST) for random walk, which allow for selectively switching or maintaining the type of the next node. To strike a middle ground among the different relationships, Balanced Heterogeneous Information Network to Vector (BHIN2vec) (Lee, Park and Yu, 2019) was suggested as an extension to skip-gram method. By changing the rate of training between tasks, BHIN2vec considers the heterogeneous graph embedding as a multi-relationship-dependent task and stabilizes the impact of diverse relationships on node embeddings. In hyperbolic spaces (Barros *et al.*, 2023), where similarity between nodes can be measured using hyperbolic distance, Hyperbolic Heterogeneous Network Embedding (HHNE) (Wang, Zhang and Shi, 2019) performs a meta-path-guided random walk. This allows for the emergence of heterogeneous graph possessions such as ordered and power-law constructions, which is reflected in the resulting node embeddings.

Unlike the techniques that depend on the random walks, there are some approaches that leverage the mixture of first- and high-level relationships (i.e., meta-path) to learn the heterogeneity characteristics of heterogeneous graph. This family of embedding methods is known as a hybrid relation-wise embedding. A representative method of this family is Heterogeneous Information Networks to vector (HIN2vec) (Fu, Lee and Lei, 2017), which perform the cooperative prediction of multiple relationships to capture both node and meta-path embeddings. The goal of the HIN2vec algorithm is to determine whether or not two nodes are connected together by a meta-path, which functions as a multilabel and connects a job involving classification. Given pair of nodes n_i and n_j, HIN2vec calculates the resemblance in the hybrid relationship r as follows:

$$S_r\left(n_i; n_j\right) = sigmoid\left(\sum W_{Ii} \odot W_{Jj} \odot f_{01}\left(W_{R\tilde{r}}\right)\right). \tag{3.48}$$

The one-hot vectors of nodes and relation are denoted as $\vec{i}$, $\vec{j}$, and $\vec{r}$, correspondingly. f_{01} denotes a regularization method constraining the embedding values in range [0,1]. W denotes mapping matrix. HIN2vec has the ability to learn the embedding of various nodes and connections between them (metapaths). In addition to this, regarding the relation set R, it encompasses more than just the first-order structures (e.g., author-publication relationships), as well as the higher order structures. Because of this, the node embeddings are able to capture different semantics.

Relation structure-aware heterogeneous information network embedding model (RHINE) (Lu *et al.*, 2019) is another relation-based hybrid approach that uses relation-specific distance metric to increase the expressiveness of node embeddings. There are two types of relationships identified here: affiliation relations (ARs) and interaction relationships (IRs). RHINE presents a translation-dependent distance measure for IRs, while the Euclidean distance function is introduced for ARs. RHINE is capable of learning heterogeneity of node embeddings that take into account the underlying relational structure by combining the two-distance measure.

Overall, it turns out that random walk-based methods primarily use a meta-path guided tactic for heterogeneous graph embedding, whereas hybrid relation-based techniques view a meta-path as a high-order relation and learn meta-path-centered embeddings concurrently. Random walk-based techniques aren't as flexible as hybrid relation-based methods when it comes to putting together different meta-paths in a heterogeneous graph embedding.

3.3.3.3 Subgraph Embedding

A subgraph in the graph a more intricate topology that can considerably improve the capacity to capture complicated structural information linkages by integrating subgraphs into graph embedding. Two common forms of subgraph can be found in this regard, namely the metagraph for signifying the high-order similarity between node; and the hyperedge, which joins a number of nodes that are intimately connected while maintaining their indestructibility.

It was proposed that metagraph2vec (Zhang *et al.*, 2018) employs a metagraph-guided random walk to build a heterogeneous node series. Node embeddings are instead learned using the heterogeneous skip-gram method (McCormick, 2016). The high-level similarities and topological representations between nodes are effectively captured by metagraph2vec using this method. Mg2vec (Zhang *et al.*, 2022) seeks to learn the embeddings for metagraphs and nodes concurrently, unlike metagraph2vec, which only utilizes metagraphs in the preparation stage. It begins with an enumeration of all metagraphs and continues by maintaining the closeness of all nodes and metagraphs. This can be formulated as follows:

$$P\left(M_i \mid n\right) = \frac{exp\left(M_i \cdot h_n\right)}{\sum_{M_j \in M} exp\left(M_i \cdot h_n\right)}, \tag{3.49}$$

where M_i denotes the ith metagraph embedding, while $\mathcal{M}$ represents the group of metagraphs. Obviously, $P(M_i \mid n)$ signifies the first-level interaction between the nodes and their subgraphs. More, mg2vec conserves the immediacy between node couples and their subgraph to model the second-level representations as follows:

$$P(M_i \mid u, n) = \frac{exp(M_i \cdot f(h_u, h_n))}{\sum_{M_{j \in \mathcal{M}}} exp(M_i \cdot f(h_u, h_n))}, \tag{3.50}$$

where $f()$ denotes a deep or shallow network to model the embeddings of pair of nodes. By conserving the low- and high-level immediacy between nodes and metagraphs, mg2vec enables capturing the topological representations and the resemblance between nodes and metagraphs.

Subgraphs (represented by metagraphs and hyperedges, respectively) typically hold far more advanced structural and semantic information than do edge and meta-path constructions. However, the great complexity of subgraphs is a challenge for heterogeneous graph embedding methods that rely on subgraphs. It is worthwhile to investigate how to strike a compromise between effectiveness and efficiency when developing subgraph-based heterogeneous graph embedding algorithms for real-world applications.

3.3.4 Dynamic Heterogeneous Graph Embedding

At the outset of this section, we point out that prior heterogeneous graph studies (Cai, Zheng and Chang, 2018) only provide a synthesis of static approaches while largely ignoring dynamic ones. To bridge this gap and account for the fact that graphs in the actual world are inherently dynamic over time, we provide a synopsis of dynamic heterogeneous graph embedding approaches here. In particular, we can classify them as either incremental updating techniques or retrained updating techniques. The first retrains the models at every time step, whereas the latter uses current node embeddings to learn the embedding of a node at the following time step. Both have advantages and disadvantages that will be weighed in the final analysis.

As an example of an incremental updating method, dynamic HIN embedding model (DyHNE) (Wang *et al.*, 2022) was developed using matrix disruption theory; it learns node embeddings with heterogeneous graph's diversity and development in mind. DyHNE maintains the first- and second-order proximities depending on the meta-path to guarantee performance. The first-level closeness criterion calls for nodes that are linked via by meta-path m to share a similar embedding. Additionally, the second-level closeness implies that the node embedding ought to be near to the weighted combination of its neighbor embeddings. On the other hand, retrained updating techniques initially adopt GNNs to learn the timestamped embeddings of node or edge and then develop some kind of recurrent or attention network, to learn and extract the temporal information of heterogeneous graph.

3.4 Bipartite Graph Embedding

The interaction between two different kinds of nodes can be modeled using a general structure known as a bipartite graph. It has been broadly implemented in a variety of real-world applications, including information extraction, medicinal chemistry, and recommendation engines. For example, in recommender systems, the user and the item each represent a different kind of node. The relationships that take place between users and items are represented as a bipartite graph, and the demonstrated edges of this graph record users' historical purchasing behaviors. In addition, as opposed to heterogeneous graphs, bipartite graphs have distinguishable structural features, such as the absence of immediate connections between nodes of a similar category. This is in contrast to the presence of such links in heterogeneous graphs. A problem that has been around for a long time is trying to master meaningful node representations for bipartite graphs. The graph embedding paradigm has seen a sizeable amount of development in recent times, which is cause for celebration. The majority of these models are not suited for the modeling of bipartite graphs, despite the fact that they perform admirably in the contexts of homogeneous and heterogeneous graphs, respectively. As a direct consequence of this, they are not ideal for the process of learning bipartite graph embeddings. In order to find a solution to this issue, a number of studies that are focused on the modeling of bipartite graphs have been proposed. They could be approximately broken down into two categories: methods that are centered on random walks and techniques that are centered on rebuilding. The first approach is based on designing the heuristics of random walks in order to create a variety of various node sequences. Following that, they learn node representations by making predictions regarding context nodes while operating within a sliding window. The restructuring works are very closely connected to the cooperative filtering process. They educate themselves on a variety of encoding systems in an effort to recreate the adjacency matrix. GNNs are trained in some functions, in specific, to learn node characterizations by iteratively collating attributes of adjacent nodes (Cao *et al.*, 2021).

3.5 Case Study

The graph embedding is critical topic in the field of graph intelligence leading with significant applications and opportunities in the era of cybersecurity, that is, fraud detection and anomaly detection malware analysis. With the emergence of the new families of unknown threats (i.e., zero-day attacks), the research focus has moved toward exploiting the embedding methods, discussed earlier, to provide a solution to these threats real world.

In view of this, it seems interesting for the graph intelligence audiences to discover and practically explore how to apply graph embedding techniques (discussed in the previous sections) in different domains of the security-related applications. Motivated by that, the supplementary materials of this chapter are designated to provide an implementation of the different embedding techniques (graph embedding, node embedding, edge embedding, and subgraph embedding) to different types of graph data representing realistic data from different real-world case studies. The supplementary materials of this chapter also provide the readers with recommendations for further reading about the content of this chapter. The repository of supplementary materials is given in this link: https://github.com/DEEPOLOGY-AI/ Book-Graph-Neural-Network/tree/main/Chapter%203.

References

Barros, C. D. T. *et al.* (2023) 'A Survey on Embedding Dynamic Graphs', *ACM Computing Surveys*. doi: 10.1145/3483595.

Cai, H., Zheng, V. W. and Chang, K. C. C. (2018) 'A Comprehensive Survey of Graph Embedding: Problems, Techniques, and Applications', *IEEE Transactions on Knowledge and Data Engineering*. doi: 10.1109/TKDE.2018.2807452.

Cao, J. *et al.* (2021) 'Bipartite Graph Embedding via Mutual Information Maximization', in *WSDM 2021 – Proceedings of the 14th ACM International Conference on Web Search and Data Mining*. doi: 10.1145/3437963.3441783.

Chen, H. *et al.* (2018) 'PME: Projected Metric Embedding on Heterogeneous Networks for Link Prediction', in *Proceedings of the ACM SIGKDD International Conference on Knowledge Discovery and Data Mining*. doi: 10.1145/3219819.3219986.

Dong, Y., Chawla, N. V. and Swami, A. (2017) 'Metapath2vec: Scalable Representation Learning for Heterogeneous Networks', in *Proceedings of the ACM SIGKDD International Conference on Knowledge Discovery and Data Mining*. doi: 10.1145/ 3097983.3098036.

Fu, T. Y., Lee, W. C. and Lei, Z. (2017) 'HIN2Vec: Explore Meta-paths in Heterogeneous Information Networks for Representation Learning', in *International Conference on Information and Knowledge Management, Proceedings*. doi: 10.1145/3132847.3132953.

Goodfellow, I. J. *et al.* (2014) 'Generative Adversarial Nets', in *Advances in Neural Information Processing Systems*.doi: 10.3156/jsoft.29.5_177_2.

Grover, A. and Leskovec, J. (2016) 'Node2vec: Scalable Feature Learning for Networks', in *Proceedings of the ACM SIGKDD International Conference on Knowledge Discovery and Data Mining*. doi: 10.1145/2939672.2939754.

Hu, B., Fang, Y. and Shi, C. (2019) 'Adversarial Learning on Heterogeneous Information Networks', in *Proceedings of the ACM SIGKDD International Conference on Knowledge Discovery and Data Mining*. doi: 10.1145/3292500.3330970.

Hussein, R., Yang, D., & Cudré-Mauroux, P. (2018, October) 'Are Meta-paths Necessary? Revisiting Heterogeneous Graph Embeddings', in *Proceedings of the 27th ACM International Conference on Information and Knowledge Management* (pp. 437–446). doi: 10.1145/3269206.3271777.

Imrana, Y. *et al.* (2021) 'A Bidirectional LSTM Deep Learning Approach for Intrusion Detection', *Expert Systems with Applications*. doi: 10.1016/j.eswa.2021.115524.

Ji, S. *et al.* (2022) 'A Survey on Knowledge Graphs: Representation, Acquisition, and Applications', *IEEE Transactions on Neural Networks and Learning Systems*. doi: 10.1109/TNNLS.2021.3070843.

Lee, S., Park, C. and Yu, H. (2019) 'Bhin2vec: Balancing the Type of Relation in Heterogeneous Information Network', in *International Conference on Information and Knowledge Management, Proceedings*. doi: 10.1145/3357384.3357893.

Liu, Z. *et al.* (2017) 'Semantic Proximity Search on Heterogeneous Graph by Proximity Embedding', in *31st AAAI Conference on Artificial Intelligence, AAAI 2017*. doi: 10.1609/aaai.v31i1.10486.

Liu, Z. *et al.* (2018) 'Distance-sware DAG Embedding for Proximity Search on Heterogeneous Graphs', in *32nd AAAI Conference on Artificial Intelligence, AAAI 2018*. doi: 10.1609/aaai.v32i1.11885.

Lu, Y. *et al.* (2019) 'Relation Structure-aware Heterogeneous Information Network Embedding', in *33rd AAAI Conference on Artificial Intelligence, AAAI 2019, 31st Innovative Applications of Artificial Intelligence Conference, IAAI 2019 and the 9th AAAI Symposium on Educational Advances in Artificial Intelligence, EAAI 2019*. doi: 10.1609/aaai.v33i01.33014456.

Ma, Y. and Tang, J. (2021) *Deep Learning on Graphs*. doi: 10.1017/9781108924184.

Mahmood, A. *et al.* (2017) 'Using Geodesic Space Density Gradients for Network Community Detection', *IEEE Transactions on Knowledge and Data Engineering*. doi: 10.1109/TKDE.2016.2632716.

McCormick, C. (2016) 'Word2Vec Tutorial – The Skip-Gram Model', *Chris McCormick's Blog*.

Shi, C. *et al.* (2019) 'Heterogeneous Information Network Embedding for Recommendation', *IEEE Transactions on Knowledge and Data Engineering*. doi: 10.1109/TKDE.2018.2833443.

Shi, Y., Gui, H. *et al.* (2018) 'ASPEM: Embedding Learning by Aspects in Heterogeneous Information Networks', in *SIAM International Conference on Data Mining, SDM 2018*. doi: 10.1137/1.9781611975321.16.

Shi, Y., Zhu, Q. *et al.* (2018) 'Easing Embedding Learning by Comprehensive Transcription of Heterogeneous Information Networks', in *Proceedings of the ACM SIGKDD International Conference on Knowledge Discovery and Data Mining*. doi: 10.1145/3219819.3220006.

Tang, J. *et al.* (2015) 'LINE: Large-scale Information Network Embedding', in *WWW 2015 – Proceedings of the 24th International Conference on World Wide Web*. doi: 10.1145/2736277.2741093.

Wang, F. *et al.* (2020) 'Recent Advances on Graph Analytics and Its Applications in Healthcare', in *Proceedings of the ACM SIGKDD International Conference on Knowledge Discovery and Data Mining*. doi: 10.1145/3394486.3406469.

Wang, X. *et al.* (2020) 'A Survey on Heterogeneous Graph Embedding: Methods, Techniques, Applications and Sources'. Available at: http://arxiv.org/abs/2011.14867.

Wang, X. *et al.* (2022) 'Dynamic Heterogeneous Information Network Embedding with Meta-Path Based Proximity', *IEEE Transactions on Knowledge and Data Engineering*. doi: 10.1109/TKDE.2020.2993870.

Wang, X., Zhang, Y. and Shi, C. (2019) 'Hyperbolic Heterogeneous Information Network Embedding', in *33rd AAAI Conference on Artificial Intelligence, AAAI*

2019, 31st Innovative Applications of Artificial Intelligence Conference, IAAI 2019 and the 9th AAAI Symposium on Educational Advances in Artificial Intelligence, EAAI 2019. doi: 10.1609/aaai.v33i01.33015337.

Xu, L. *et al.* (2017) 'Embedding of Embedding (EOE) : Joint Embedding for Coupled Heterogeneous Networks', in *WSDM 2017 – Proceedings of the 10th ACM International Conference on Web Search and Data Mining.* doi: 10.1145/3018661.3018723.

Yan, Z., Hamilton, W. L. and Blanchette, M. (2021) 'Graph Neural Representational Learning of RNA Secondary Structures for Predicting RNA-Protein Interactions', *Bioinformatics.* doi: 10.1093/BIOINFORMATICS/BTAA456.

Zhang, C. *et al.* (2019) 'Heterogeneous Graph Neural Network', in *Proceedings of the ACM SIGKDD International Conference on Knowledge Discovery and Data Mining.* doi: 10.1145/3292500.3330961.

Zhang, D. *et al.* (2018) 'MetaGraph2Vec: Complex Semantic Path Augmented Heterogeneous Network Embedding', in *Lecture Notes in Computer Science (including subseries Lecture Notes in Artificial Intelligence and Lecture Notes in Bioinformatics).* doi: 10.1007/978-3-319-93037-4_16.

Zhang, W. *et al.* (2022) 'Mg2vec: Learning Relationship-Preserving Heterogeneous Graph Representations via Metagraph Embedding', *IEEE Transactions on Knowledge and Data Engineering.* doi: 10.1109/TKDE.2020.2992500.

Zhang, Y. *et al.* (2021) 'IGE+: A Framework for Learning Node Embeddings in Interaction Graphs', *IEEE Transactions on Knowledge and Data Engineering.* doi: 10.1109/TKDE.2019.2940459.

4

Toward Graph Neural Networks: Essentials and Pillars

4.1 Introduction

Graph neural networks (GNNs) can be defined as a family of approaches that seek to extend and adapt the deep learning models to be able to train and learn from graph-structured data. Generally speaking, we designate the term "Graph Intelligence" to denote a branch of AI-concerning methods for learning from graph data. The traditional deep learning models could not be straightforwardly generalized to graph-organized datasets as the graph topology is not a consistent grid. The research in the field of graph intelligence could date back to the beginning of the 21st century, when the first GNN was developed for both graph- and node-oriented tasks. With the prominent success of deep learning in different application domains, the research community devoted a lot of effort to developing and advancing graph intelligence tasks and applications. Thus, without doubt, deep learning is regarded as the cornerstone of graph intelligence.

This chapter emphasizes providing an entry point for understanding and developing a simple GNN from scratch either for both node- and graph-oriented tasks. Thus, the main content of this chapter revolves around discovering the main building blocks of graph networks, such as graph filters, pooling operators, and aggregators.

In this chapter, we discover the concept of graph filters and different standpoints for designing graph filters, which could be crudely divided into two types, namely, spatial- and spectral-dependent graph filters. Then, we dive into the details of the concept of graph normalization and explore the state-of-the-art normalization layer from both theoretical and practical perspectives. Following that, the graph pooling operators are discussed as a robust layer for performing downsampling operations to fuse the graph representations to high-level feature space. The discussion explores both legacy and standard pooling operators and the state-of-the-art pooling operator with topology-preservation capability. Moreover, the graph aggregation operators are also explained as an essential component of graph networks that enable aggregating the final representation knowledge by

DOI: 10.1201/9781003329701-4

collapsing the nodes into a static number of features, irrespective of the size of the input graph.

4.2 Graph Filters

Different approaches to designing graph filters can be loosely divided into two types: (1) graph filters with a spatial focus and (2) graph filters with a spectral focus. In order to carry out the feature refinement process in the graph domain, the spatial-based graph filters directly make use of the graph representation (i.e., edges). On the other hand, the filtration process in the spectral domain is designed using spectral graph theory for the spectral-dependent graph filters, in contrast. Those two types of graph filters are highly tied to one another. Particularly, some of the graph filters that are spectral-dependent could be viewed as spatial-dependent filters. In the following sections, we present spectral-dependent graph filters and describe how a few of them might be seen from a spatial standpoint. We then go through additional spatial graph filters.

4.2.1 Spatial-Dependent Graph Filters

Spatial-based approaches define graph convolutions based on a node's semantic relationship, similar to how a standard convolution neural networks (CNNs) does its convolutional filter on an image. Each pixel in an image can be thought of as a node, making them a unique type of graph. The adjacent pixels are physically related to one another. By averaging the pixel values of the core node and its neighbors over all channels, a filter is applied to a patch. Similar to this, the spatial-dependent graph filters learn the features of a certain node with the representations of its neighbors to get the current representation for the underlying node. Graph networks as general constructions with interactive inductive bias offer a sophisticated interface for learning objects, relationships, and topological representations. Graph networks are built up with graph filters in a consecutive, encode-process-decode, or recurring way. Non-local neural networks (NLNNs), message passing neural networks (Gilmer *et al.*, 2017), and GraphSAGE (Hamilton, Ying and Leskovec, 2017) are common examples of spatial filters.

Hint: For more information about spatial graph filters, you can refer to the supplementary materials of this chapter.

4.2.2 Spectral-Dependent Graph Filters

The spectral space of graph inputs is used to create the spectral-dependent graph filters. Before describing how it might be used to create spectrum-based graph filters, the discussion begins by explaining the spectral filtering in the graph. The wavelengths of a graph signal are modulated in the graph spectral filtering process such that certain of its frequency content is retained and enhanced, while the remainder is subtracted and decreased. Therefore, in order to rebuild graph information in the spatial space, a graph Fourier transform must first apply to it in order to extract its graph Fourier coefficients. Later, the extracted coefficients are modulated prior to rebuilding the signal in the spatial space. The graph spectral filtration operation, which can be employed to filter particular wavelengths in the input signal, has been introduced. For instance, we can create a low-pass filter if we want the filtered signal to be clean. As a result, the filtered signal that is produced is seamless because it primarily preserves the low-frequency component of the input signal. We frequently are unsure of which wavelengths are more crucial when using the spectral-based filter as a graph filter in GNNs. Consequently, the graph filters could also be trained using data-driven learning, exactly such as the traditional neural networks. In particular, we can model using a few algorithms and then supervise the learning of the parameters from the data.

4.3 Graph Normalization

Normally, normalization is used to prepare the data before training the model. To provide a standard scale for numerical values is the main goal of normalization. The learning process will be skewed if the graph dataset contains numerical features that vary widely, which will result in inconsistent model training. The distribution of the inputs to layers may vary after the mini-batch settings have been updated, which could be one explanation for this conundrum. This might force the learning algorithm to keep pursuing a moving goal, which would prevent the network's convergence. "Internal covariate shift" refers to this variance in the network's layer input distribution. In this context, normalization has long been a hot topic for research in graph intelligence due to its potential to drastically cut training time for a variety of reasons. First, normalizing the node features can retain the contribution of each feature, as some features have higher numerical values than others, which can make the network unbiased to high-valued node/edge features. In doing so, it gets rid of the internal covariate shift. Second, it can also smear the lost surface. Third, as it limits weights to a certain range and prevents them from exploding out of control, it may improve the convergence of GNNs. Fourth, normalization can unintentionally assist regularizing the GNN that is a win. When it comes to optimizing neural networks, normalization has been proved to be beneficial since 1998 (LeCun *et al.*, 2012). After the release of batch normalization (Ioffe and Szegedy, 2015), this study direction has been widely investigated by researchers. Since then, a wide range of normalization techniques have been developed. Modern normalization layers are widespread and effective methods for reliably accelerating the convergence of deep networks, which we investigate in this section.

4.3.1 Batch Normalization

Batch normalization is a layer for normalizing a batch of node features as follows:

$$x_i' = \frac{x - E[x]}{\sqrt{Var[x] + \epsilon}} \odot \gamma + \beta, \tag{4.1}$$

where the mean, $E[x]$, and variance, $Var[x]$, are computed for each node's dimensions within the mini-batch.

4.3.2 Instance Normalization

Instance normalization (Huang and Belongie, 2017) is a layer for normalizing each individual instance of a batch of node features as follows:

$$x_i' = \frac{x - E[x]}{\sqrt{Var[x] + \epsilon}} \odot \gamma + \beta, \tag{4.2}$$

where the mean, $E[x]$, and variance, $Var[x]$, are computed for each dimension distinctly for each object in a training batch.

4.3.3 Layer Normalization

Layer normalization (Ba, Kiros and Hinton, 2016) is similar to the previously mentioned layers, but the mean, $E[x]$, and variance, $Var[x]$, are computed across all nodes and all node channels separately for each object in a training batch.

4.3.4 Graph Normalization

Graph normalization (Cai *et al.*, 2020) for normalizing individual graphs is as follows:

$$x_i' = \frac{x - \sigma \odot E[x]}{\sqrt{Var[x - \sigma \odot E[x]] + \epsilon}} \odot \gamma + \beta, \tag{4.3}$$

where σ symbolizes parameters that regulate the amount of information to preserve in the mean.

4.3.5 Graph Size Normalization

Graph size normalization (Dwivedi *et al.*, 2020) was proposed for normalizing each individual graph in a training batch of node features as follows:

$$x_i' = \frac{x_i}{\sqrt{|\mathcal{N}|}}. \tag{4.4}$$

4.3.6 Pair Normalization

A normalization layer (Zhao and Akoglu, 2019) was proposed and founded on a cautious investigation of graph filters that avoid similarity between all node embeddings; thus, it is fast and fit for implementing without any modification to the network:

$$x_i^c = x_i - \frac{1}{n}\sum_{i=1}^{n} x_i, \tag{4.5}$$

$$x_i' = s \cdot \frac{x_i^c}{\sqrt{\frac{1}{n}\sum_{i=1}^{n}\left\|x_i^c\right\|_2^2}}. \tag{4.6}$$

4.3.7 Mean Subtraction Normalization

Mean subtraction layer (Yang *et al.*, 2020) was proposed for normalization by subtracting the mean from the inputs as follows:

$$x_i^c = x_i - \frac{1}{|\mathcal{N}|}\sum_{j\in\mathcal{N}} x_j. \tag{4.7}$$

4.3.8 Message Normalization

Message normalization (Li *et al.*, 2020) was proposed for normalizing the aggregated messages as follows:

$$x_i' = MLP\left(x_i + s \cdot \left\|x_i\right\|_2 \cdot \frac{m_i}{\left\|m_i\right\|_2} \right). \tag{4.8}$$

4.3.9 Differentiable Group Normalization

Group normalization layer (Zhou *et al.*, 2020) was proposed for normalizing node features in a group-wise manner using a trainable soft cluster assignment.

$$S = SoftMax(XW), \tag{4.9}$$

where $W \in \mathbb{R}^{F \times G}$ signifies a trainable parameter matrix mapping each node into proper G clusters. Then, group-wise normalization is then achieved as follows:

$$X' = X + \lambda \sum_{i=1}^{G} BatcNorm(S[:, i] \odot X). \tag{4.10}$$

4.4 Graph Pooling

The graph filters process the features of the node while maintaining the graph topology unchanged. Hence, each node comes up with a new set of features. Some graph intelligence tasks need to capture the representation of the whole graph. Capturing such representation necessitates summarizing the node representations. Two primary forms of information are essential to generate rich graph representation: (1) graph topology and (2) node features. In this regard, graph pooling operators were presented to capture and generate the graph-level representation directly from the graph node representations. In graph intelligence tasks, pooling is typically adopted for two purposes: first, hierarchical learning; and second, reducing dimensionality. The number of nodes and, therefore, the number of model parameters that must be learned is typically reduced via graph pooling methods. In order for the graph networks to learn broad-scale and universal patterns in the data, several pooling methods additionally require a hierarchical representation of the data. In this section, we explore the state-of-the-art graph pooling operators.

4.4.1 Global Add Pooling

Global add pooling or sum pooling calculates batch-wise graph-level-outputs by addition of node features across the node dimension, so as to calculate the output of a single-graph G_i as follows:

$$r_i = \sum_{n=1}^{N_i} x_n. \tag{4.11}$$

The computation of sum pooling is given in the following code snippet:

```
import dgl
import torch as th
from dgl.nn import SumPooling
# create a random graph with 4 nodes and 5 edges
g1 = dgl.rand_graph(4, 5)
g1_n_features = th.rand(3, 5)
g1_n_features
# create a random graph with 3 nodes and 5 edges
```

```
g2 = dgl.rand_graph(3, 6)
g2_n_features = th.rand(4, 5)
g2_n_features

# Apply sum pooling layer
sumpool = SumPooling()

batch_g = dgl.batch([g1, g2])

batch_f = th.cat([g1_n_features, g2_n_features])
sumpool(batch_g, batch_f)
```

4.4.2 Global Mean Pooling

Global mean pooling calculates batch-wise graph-level-outputs by averaging the features of nodes across the node dimension, so as to calculate the output of a single-graph G_i as follows:

$$r_i = \frac{1}{N_i} \sum_{n=1}^{N_i} x_n. \tag{4.12}$$

The computation of mean pooling is given in the following code snippet:

```
import dgl
import torch as th
from dgl.nn import AvgPooling
# create a random graph with 4 nodes and 5 edges
g1 = dgl.rand_graph(4, 5)
g1_n_features = th.rand(3, 5)
g1_n_features

# create a random graph with 3 nodes and 5 edges
g2 = dgl.rand_graph(3, 6)
g2_n_features = th.rand(4, 5)
g2_n_features

# Apply Avgerage Pooling layer
avgpool = AvgPooling()

batch_g = dgl.batch([g1, g2])

batch_f = th.cat([g1_n_features, g2_n_features])
avgpool(batch_g, batch_f)
```

4.4.3 Global Max Pooling

Global max pooling calculates batch-wise graph-level-outputs by taking the maximum of node features across the node dimension, by calculating the output of a single-graph G_i as follows:

$$r_i = max_{n=1}^{N_i}. \tag{4.13}$$

The computation of max pooling is given in the following code snippet:

```
import dgl
import torch as th
from dgl.nn import MaxPooling
# create a random graph with 4 nodes and 5 edges
g1 = dgl.rand_graph(4, 5)
g1_n_features = th.rand(3, 5)
g1_n_features

# create a random graph with 3 nodes and 5 edges
g2 = dgl.rand_graph(3, 6)
g2_n_features = th.rand(4, 5)
g2_n_features

# Apply MaxPooling layer
maxpool = MaxPooling()

batch_g = dgl.batch([g1, g2])

batch_f = th.cat([g1_n_features, g2_n_features])
maxpool(batch_g, batch_f)
```

4.4.4 top_k Pooling

top_k pooling was proposed by Gao and Ji (2021) and Knyazev, Taylor and Amer (2019) to adaptively choose some nodes to designate a minor graph according to the relative scalar projection elements on a trainable projection vector:

$$y = \frac{X_P}{\|p\|}, \tag{4.14}$$

$$i = top_k(y), \tag{4.15}$$

$$X' = (X \odot \tanh(y))_i, \tag{4.16}$$

$$A' = A_{i,i}, \tag{4.17}$$

where $\|p\|$ represents the L2 norm, top_k operation chooses the top_k indices from particular input vector, $\odot$ denotes elementwise multiplication, while i denotes indexing function receiving slices at indices stated through i. The nodes to drop are selected according to the projection weight over learnable vector, p. To promote the flow of gradients into p, the projection weights are also adopted as gating values, which means that retaining nodes with lower weights can experience less important feature retaining.

when the min *weight* $\tilde{\alpha}$ is a value in [0, 1], the top_k pooling can be formulated as follows:

$$y = SoftMax(X_P), \tag{4.18}$$

$$i = y_i > \tilde{\alpha}, \tag{4.19}$$

$$X' = (X \odot y)_i, \tag{4.20}$$

$$A' = A_{i,i}, \tag{4.21}$$

where nodes are dropped depending on a learnable projection score p.

4.4.5 Self-Attention (SA) Graph Pooling

The self-attention (SA) pooling proposed by Lee, Lee and Kang (2019) as a generalization of the SA mechanism for graph downsampling/pooling operator allows learning hierarchical representations in an endwise manner by means of comparatively insufficient parameters. The SA mechanism was adopted to differentiate the nodes to be dropped from those to be reserved. The SA makes use of graph convolution filter to compute attention weights, node features of node, as well as graph topology, are taken into account. As with top_k pooling, the projection weights are obtained by the dot product between p and the nodes' features.

$$y = GNN(X, A), \tag{4.22}$$

$$i = top_k(y), \tag{4.23}$$

$$X' = (X \odot tanh(y))_i, \tag{4.24}$$

$$A' = A_{i,i}, \tag{4.25}$$

when the min *weight* $\tilde{\alpha}$ is a value in [0, 1], the top_k pooling can be formulated as follows:

$$y = SoftMax\,(GNN(X, A)), \tag{4.26}$$

$$i = y_i > \tilde{\alpha}, \tag{4.27}$$

$$X' = \left(X \odot tanh\left(y\right)\right)_i, \tag{4.28}$$

$$A' = A_{i,i}. \tag{4.29}$$

4.4.6 Sort Pooling

Sort aggregation is a pooling operator proposed by Zhang *et al.* (2018), where the features of a node are arranged in descendant order according to their latter feature channel. Then, it selects the ordered features of top_k nodes arranged according to the highest value of each node.

```
import dgl
import torch as th
```

```
from dgl.nn import SortPooling
# create a random graph with 4 nodes and 5 edges
g1 = dgl.rand_graph(4, 5)
g1_n_features = th.rand(3, 5)
g1_n_features

# create a random graph with 3 nodes and 5 edges
g2 = dgl.rand_graph(3, 6)
g2_n_features = th.rand(4, 5)
g2_n_features

# Apply SortPooling layer
sortpool = SortPooling(2)

batch_g = dgl.batch([g1, g2])

batch_f = th.cat([g1_n_features, g2_n_features])
sortpool(batch_g, batch_f)
```

4.4.7 Edge Pooling

A pooling operator is proposed by Diehl (2019) and Diehl *et al.* (2019) to select a group of edges and then adopted edge contractions, and a node features a combination mechanism for generating the new graph. It calculates a score value of each edge as a straightforward linear combination of the features of concatenated nodes. Given the edge connecting node i with node j, the edge score can be calculated as:

$$r\left(e_{ij}\right) = W\left(n_i \,\|\, n_j\right) + b,\tag{4.30}$$

$$s_{ij} = \tanh\left(r\left(e_{ij}\right)\right), \; s_{ij} = \text{SoftMax}\left(r\left(e_{ij}\right)\right),\tag{4.31}$$

where W and b are the learning parameters. To integrate the features of the nodes, the sum operation was applied, then a gating mechanism is applied to multiply the edge score with the integrated node features.

$$n_{ij} = s_{ij} \cdot \left(n_i \,\|\, n_j\right).\tag{4.32}$$

4.4.8 Adaptive Structure Aware Pooling (ASAP)

Adaptive Structure Aware Pooling (ASAP) was proposed by Ranjan, Sanyal and Talukdar (2020) as a differentiable and sparse pooling operator for addressing the limits of other pooling operators. ASAP made use of adapted GNN and SA mechanism for capturing the node importance in the particular graph. Moreover, it enables learning sparse soft cluster assignments for nodes for efficient pooling of graphs.

4.4.9 PAN Pooling

Path integral-based GNNs (PAN) was proposed by Ma *et al.* (2020) to perform adaptive top_k pooling where global node importance is measured based on node features and the maximal entropy transition matrix:

$$score = \beta_1 X \cdot p + \beta_2 \cdot deg(M). \tag{4.33}$$

4.4.10 Memory Pooling

Memory pooling (Khasahmadi *et al.*, 2020) was proposed as a memory layer consisting of a multi-head collection of memory keys and a convolution filter for aggregating the soft cluster assignments from different heads to learn both graphs coarsening and joint graph representation learning:

$$S_{i,j}^h = \frac{\left(1 + \frac{\left\|x_i - k_j^{h2}\right\|}{\tau}\right)^{-\frac{1+r}{2}}}{\sum_{k=1}^{K}\left(1 + \frac{\left\|x_i - k_j^{h2}\right\|}{\tau}\right)^{-\frac{1+r}{2}}}, \tag{4.34}$$

$$S = SoftMax\left(Conv2D\left(\big\|_{h=1}^{H}\right)\right), \tag{4.35}$$

$$X' = S^T XW, \tag{4.36}$$

where H and K represent the number of heads and clusters, respectively.

4.4.11 Differentiable Pooling

The differentiable pooling operator was proposed by Ying *et al.* (2018) to create the super nodes in a differentiable manner. In other words, a soft assignment matrix from the nodes in the input graph to the super-nodes is learned using one or more graph filters. The columns of the assignment matrix are viewed as super-nodes, while the SoftMax function is applied in a row-wise fashion; therefore, each row is normalized, to sum up to 1. According to the dense learned assignment matrix $S \in \mathbb{R}^{B \times N \times C}$, the differentiable pooling operator returns the coarsened adjacency matrix, A', and, similarly, returns the super-nodes features linearly combining the node features of the input graph according to the assignment S:

$$X' = SoftMax(S)^T \cdot X, \tag{4.37}$$

$$A' = SoftMax(S)^T \cdot A \cdot SoftMax(X). \tag{4.38}$$

Two auxiliary objectives were involved in the design of a differentiable pooling operator.

First, the link prediction loss

$$L_{lp} = \left\| A - SoftMax(X) \cdot SoftMax(S)^T \right\|_F .$$

(4.39)

Second, the entropy regularization,

$$L_{lp} = \frac{1}{N} \sum_{n=1}^{N} H(s_n).$$

(4.40)

4.4.12 MinCut Pooling

Similar to the MinCut pooling operator was proposed by Bianchi, Grattarola and Alippi (2020) to aggregate node embeddings, X, according to the cluster assignments S, also takes the adjacency matrix A to generate a coarsened adjacency matrix A' representing the power of connectivity between each pair of clusters:

$$X' = SoftMax(S)^T \cdot X,$$

(4.41)

$$A' = SoftMax(S)^T \cdot A \cdot SoftMax(X).$$

(4.42)

Two auxiliary objectives are used to optimize the graph filter and *SoftMax* layer of MinCut pooling operator. First, the MinCut loss is defined as follows:

$$L_c = \frac{Tr(S^T AS)}{Tr(S^T DS)},$$

(4.43)

where D denotes the degree matrix.

Second, the orthogonality loss is defined as follows:

$$L_o = \left\| \frac{S^T S}{\left\| S^T S \right\|_F} - \frac{I_c}{\sqrt{C}} \right\|_F ,$$

(4.44)

where C is the number of clusters, where $\|\cdot\|_F$ denotes the Frobenius norm.

4.4.13 Spectral Modularity Pooling

The spectral modularity pooling operator was proposed (Tsitsulin *et al.*, 2020) to use the learnt assignment matrix $S \in \mathbb{R}^{B \times N \times C}$, to generate the coarsened symmetrically normalized adjacency matrix, the learnt cluster assignment matrix, the feature matrix of the pooled node:

$$X' = SoftMax(S)^T \cdot X,$$

(4.45)

$$A' = SoftMax(S)^T \cdot A \cdot SoftMax(X). \tag{4.46}$$

However, it integrated a relaxed modularity maximization objective to enable recovery of the challenging clustering construction of the real and random graph.

Three auxiliary objectives have been investigated to optimize the cluster assignment. First, the spectral loss is defined as follows:

$$L_s = \frac{1}{2m} Tr(S^T BS), \tag{4.47}$$

where B is the modularity matrix. Second, the orthogonality loss is defined as shown in the previous section. Third, the cluster loss is defined as follows:

$$L_c = \frac{\sqrt{C}}{n} \left\| \sum_i C_i \right\|_F - 1. \tag{4.48}$$

4.5 Graph Aggregation

Unlike pooling operation, the graph aggregation could receive graphs of possibly variable sizes and generate static-length demonstrative vectors. To further interpret the difference between aggregation and pooling, you can look at Figure 4.1, adapted from Cheung *et al.* (2020).

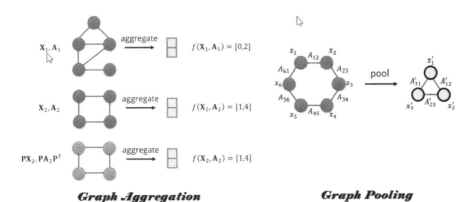

Graph Aggregation   **Graph Pooling**

FIGURE 4.1
Graph aggregation vs graph pooling.

```
import torch
import torch.nn as nn
import torch.nn.functional as F

class Aggregator(nn.Module):
    """
    Base Aggregator class. Adapting
    from PR# 403
    This class is not supposed to be called
    """

    def __init__(self):
        super(Aggregator, self).__init__()

    def forward(self, node):
        neighbour = node.mailbox["m"]
        c = self.aggregate(neighbour)
        return {"c": c}

    def aggregate(self, neighbour):
        # N x F
        raise NotImplementedError
```

4.5.1 Sum Aggregation

As the name implies, the sum aggregation is performed by summing up the features from a group of entities. This can be defined as:

$$\mathcal{A}_{sum}(X) = \sum_{x_i \in X} x_i. \tag{4.49}$$

4.5.2 Mean Aggregation

The mean aggregation operator is similar to the sum aggregation, but it performs aggregation by averaging the features from a group of entities. This can be defined as:

$$\mathcal{A}_{mean}(X) = \frac{1}{|X|} \sum_{x_i \in X} x_i. \tag{4.50}$$

```
class MeanAggregator(Aggregator):
    """
    Mean Aggregator
    """

    def __init__(self):
        super(MeanAggregator, self).__init__()

    def aggregate(self, neighbour):
        mean_neighbour = torch.mean(neighbour, dim=1)
        return mean_neighbour
```

4.5.3 Max Aggregation

As the name suggests, the max aggregation operator takes the maximum of messages across a group of entities. This can be defined as:

$$\mathcal{A}_{max}(X) = \max_{x_i \in X} x_i. \tag{4.51}$$

```
class MaxAggregator(Aggregator):
    """
    Max aggregator
    """

    def __init__(self, in_feats, out_feats, activation, bias):
        super(MaxAggregator, self).__init__()
        self.linear = nn.Linear(in_feats, out_feats, bias=bias)
        self.activation = activation
        # Xavier initialization of weight
        nn.init.xavier_uniform_(
            self.linear.weight, gain=nn.init.calculate_gain("relu")
        )

    def aggregate(self, neighbour):
        neighbour = self.linear(neighbour)
        if self.activation:
            neighbour = self.activation(neighbour)
        maxpool_neighbour = torch.max(neighbour, dim=1)[0]
        return maxpool_neighbour
```

4.5.4 Min Aggregation

Min aggregation operator acts as a contradiction of the max aggregation operator by taking the minimum of messages across a group of entities:

$$\mathcal{A}_{min}(X) = \min_{x_i \in X} x_i. \tag{4.52}$$

4.5.5 Multiple Aggregation

As the name indicates, the multiply operator performs aggregation by multiplying the features from a group of entities. This can be defined as:

$$\mathcal{A}_{mul}(X) = \prod_{x_i \in X} x_i. \tag{4.53}$$

4.5.6 Variance Aggregation

As the name indicates, the variance operator performs aggregation by calculating the variance of features from a group of entities. This can be defined as:

$$\mathcal{A}_{var}(X) = mean\left(\left\{x_i^2 : x_i \in X\right\}\right) - mean(X). \tag{4.54}$$

4.5.7 Standard Deviation (STD) Aggregation

The standard deviation (STD) aggregation operator is an extension to $\mathcal{A}_{var}(X)$, which performs aggregation by calculating the STD of features from a group of entities. This can be defined as:

$$\mathcal{A}_{std}(X) = \sqrt{variance(X)}. \tag{4.55}$$

4.5.8 SoftMax Aggregation

The work (Guohao, Chenxin and Ali, 2020) presented the concept of generalized mean-max aggregation for providing a kind of permutation invariant aggregation by interpolating between two messages x_1 and x_2 to bargain a more improved aggregator than $\mathcal{A}_{mean}(X)$ and $\mathcal{A}_{max}(X)$. The SoftMax Aggregation operators implemented this concept as follows:

$$\mathcal{A}_{softmax}(X) = \sum_{x_j \in X} \frac{\exp(t \cdot x_i)}{\sum_{x_j \in X} \exp(t \cdot x_j)} \cdot x_i, \tag{4.56}$$

where t is known as the inverse temperature variable controlling the softness of the SoftMax when aggregating over a set of messages X. The low value of t makes $\mathcal{A}_{softmax}(X)$ perform like $\mathcal{A}_{mean}(X)$, while the high value of makes $\mathcal{A}_{softmax}(X)$ perform like $\mathcal{A}_{max}(X)$.

4.5.9 Power Mean Aggregation

In the work (Guohao, Chenxin and Ali, 2020), the power mean aggregation is introduced as generalized mean-max aggregation, which is calculated as follows:

$$\mathcal{A}_{powermean}(X \mid p) = \left(\frac{1}{|X|} \sum_{x_i \in X} x_i^p \right)^{1/p}, \tag{4.57}$$

where p regulates the power during aggregation.

4.5.10 Long Short-term Memory (LSTM) Aggregation

The work (Hamilton, Ying and Leskovec, 2017) presented a complex aggregation operator that depends on a long short-term memory (LSTM), because of its expressiveness ability. Nevertheless, it is worth mentioning that LSTM is not characteristically symmetric (which means it is not permutation invariant), as it processes the messages in a sequential fashion. In this setting, the

LSTM was adapted to deal with an unordered set by basically running LSTM on arbitrary permutation of the neighbors of the node. For more information about LSTM, refer to Chapter 1.

```python
class LSTMAggregator(Aggregator):
    """
    LSTM aggregator for graphsage
    """

    def __init__(self, in_feats, hidden_feats):
        super(LSTMAggregator, self).__init__()
        self.lstm = nn.LSTM(in_feats, hidden_feats, batch_first=True)
        self.hidden_dim = hidden_feats
        self.hidden = self.init_hidden()

        nn.init.xavier_uniform_(
            self.lstm.weight, gain=nn.init.calculate_gain("relu")
        )

    def init_hidden(self):
        """
        Defaulted to initialite all zero
        """
        return (
            torch.zeros(1, 1, self.hidden_dim),
            torch.zeros(1, 1, self.hidden_dim),
        )

    def aggregate(self, neighbours):
        """
        aggregation function
        """
        # N X F
        rand_order = torch.randperm(neighbours.size()[1])
        neighbours = neighbours[:, rand_order, :]

        (lstm_out, self.hidden) = self.lstm(
            neighbours.view(neighbours.size()[0], neighbours.size()
            [1], -1)
        )
        return lstm_out[:, -1, :]

    def forward(self, node):
        neighbour = node.mailbox["m"]
        c = self.aggre(neighbour)
        return {"c": c}
```

4.5.11 Set2Set

The Set2Set aggregation operator was proposed by Vinyals, Bengio and Kudlur (2016), which integrated "content"-centered attention to act as associative memory. This memory enables generating the same output vector if the memory is randomly shuffled. The Set2Set aggregation can be formulated as follows:

$$q_t = LSTM\left(q_{t-1}^*\right), \tag{4.58}$$

$$\alpha_{i,t} = SoftMax\left(x_i \cdot q_t\right), \tag{4.59}$$

$$r_t = \sum_{i=1}^{N} \alpha_{i,t} \cdot x_i, \tag{4.60}$$

$$q_t^* = q_t \| r_t, \tag{4.61}$$

where q_t^* describes the output of the layer with double the dimensionality as the input.

From a practical standpoint, the implementation of set2set aggregation is straightforward as shown in the following code snippet.

```
import dgl
import torch as th
from dgl.nn import Set2Set
# create a random graph with 4 nodes and 5 edges
g1 = dgl.rand_graph(4, 5)
g1_n_features = th.rand(3, 5)
g1_n_features

# create a random graph with 3 nodes and 6 edges
g2 = dgl.rand_graph(3, 6)
g2_n_features = th.rand(4, 5)
g2_n_features

# Apply Set2Set layer
s2spool = Set2Set(4, 3, 1)

batch_g = dgl.batch([g1, g2])

batch_f = th.cat([g1_n_features, g2_n_features])
s2spool(batch_g, batch_f)
```

4.5.12 Degree Scaler Aggregation

Degree Scaler Aggregation was proposed by Corso *et al.* (2020) to combine multiple aggregation operators (i.e., $\mathcal{A}_{min}(X)$, $\mathcal{A}_{max}(X)$, $\mathcal{A}_{std}(X)$, and $\mathcal{A}_{var}(X)$) then transforms their output with amplification scaler.

$$S_{amp}(d) = \frac{log(d+1)}{\delta}, \delta = \frac{1}{|train|} \sum_{i \in train} log(d_i + 1), \tag{4.62}$$

where δ represents the normalization parameter calculated over the training graphs, while d denotes the degree of the node accepting the message.

The scaler is further generalized by including the negative α parameter for attenuation purposes, such that it has zero for no scaling and positive for amplification. The attenuation scaler can be defined as follows:

$$S_{atten}(d,\alpha) = \left(\frac{log(d+1)}{\delta}\right)^{\alpha}, \; d > 0, \; -1 \le \alpha \le 1. \tag{4.63}$$

4.5.13 Graph Multiset Transformer

The Graph multiset transformer pooling operator was proposed by Baek, Kang and Hwang (2021), which acts by clustering nodes of the whole input graph throughout the attention-dependent pooling task, while a multi-head SA mechanism is adopted to compute the interaction between nodes as stated by its structural dependences.

4.5.14 Attentional Aggregation

The soft attention aggregation operator was proposed by Li *et al.* (2016) to aggregate the messages from nodes as follows:

$$r_i = \sum_{n=1}^{N_i} SoftMax\left(h_{gate}(x_n)\right) \odot h_{\varphi}(x_n). \tag{4.64}$$

4.6 Case Study

GNNs represent the cornerstone for graph intelligence methods. Despite the previous section covering both mathematical concepts and practical implementation of different components of GNNs, it may be difficult for non-practitioners and beginners to fully implement the graph intelligence model in an end-to-end fashion. The infancy role of graph intelligence in the era of cyber-security (i.e., fraud detection and anomaly detection malware analysis) increased making it interesting to discover by the cyber-security community, especially from a practical standpoint. With the emergence of the new families of unknown threats (i.e., zero-day attacks) increases the curiosity of the community toward exploring the opportunity of GNNs in developing a solution to these threats in real world. Motivated by that, the supplementary materials of this chapter are designated to provide a holistic in-lab tutorial for implementing simple GNN for different graph tasks. To make things simpler, the material uses graph data from real-world case studies to train and test the model. Also, the supplementary materials provide the readers with extra knowledge and tricks for building efficient GNN, that is, creating graph datasets, augmenting graph data, hyperparameter selection, and other development tricks. The supplementary materials of this chapter also provide the readers with recommendations for further reading about the content of this chapter. The repository of supplementary materials is given in this link: https://github.com/DEEPOLOGY-AI/Book-Graph-Neural-Network/tree/main/Chapter%204.

References

Ba, J. L., Kiros, J. R. and Hinton, G. E. (2016) 'Layer Normalization'. Available at: http://arxiv.org/abs/1607.06450.

Baek, J., Kang, M. and Hwang, S. J. (2021) 'Accurate Learning of Graph Representations with Graph Multiset Pooling'. Available at: http://arxiv.org/abs/2102.11533.

Bianchi, F. M., Grattarola, D. and Alippi, C. (2020) 'Spectral Clustering with Graph Neural Networks for Graph Pooling', in *37th International Conference on Machine Learning, ICML 2020.*

Cai, T. *et al.* (2020) 'GraphNorm: A Principled Approach to Accelerating Graph Neural Network Training'. Available at: http://arxiv.org/abs/2009.03294.

Cheung, M. *et al.* (2020) 'Graph Signal Processing and Deep Learning: Convolution, Pooling, and Topology', *IEEE Signal Processing Magazine.* doi: 10.1109/MSP.2020.3014594.

Corso, G. *et al.* (2020) 'Principal Neighbourhood Aggregation for Graph Nets', in *Advances in Neural Information Processing Systems 33 (NeurIPS 2020).* https://proceedings.neurips.cc/paper/2020/hash/99cad265a1768cc2dd013f0e740300ae-Abstract.html

Diehl, F. (2019) 'Edge Contraction Pooling for Graph Neural Networks'. Available at: http://arxiv.org/abs/1905.10990.

Diehl, F. *et al.* (2019) 'Towards Graph Pooling by Edge Contraction', in *ICML 2019 Workshop: Learning and Reasoning with Graph-Structured Representations.*

Dwivedi, V. P. *et al.* (2020) 'Benchmarking Graph Neural Networks'. Available at: http://arxiv.org/abs/2003.00982.

Gao, H. and Ji, S. (2021) 'Graph U-Nets', *IEEE Transactions on Pattern Analysis and Machine Intelligence.* doi: 10.1109/TPAMI.2021.3081010.

Gilmer, J. *et al.* (2017) 'Neural Message Passing for Quantum Chemistry', in *34th International Conference on Machine Learning, ICML 2017.*

Guohao, L., Chenxin, X., Ali, T. and Bernard, G. (2020) 'DeeperGCN: All You Need to Train Deeper GCNs'. Available at: https://arxiv.org.

Hamilton, W. L., Ying, R. and Leskovec, J. (2017) 'Inductive Representation Learning on Large Graphs', in Advances in Neural Information Processing Systems 30 (NIPS 2017). https://proceedings.neurips.cc/paper/2017/hash/5dd9db5e033da9c6fb5ba83c7a7ebea9-Abstract.html

Huang, X. and Belongie, S. (2017) 'Arbitrary Style Transfer in Real-time with Adaptive Instance Normalization', in *Proceedings of the IEEE international conference on computer vision*, pp. 1501–1510.

Ioffe, S. and Szegedy, C. (2015) 'Batch Normalization: Accelerating Deep Network Training by Reducing Internal Covariate Shift', in *32nd International Conference on Machine Learning, ICML 2015*, pp. 448–456.

Khasahmadi, A. H. *et al.* (2020) 'Memory-Based Graph Networks'. Available at: http://arxiv.org/abs/2002.09518.

Knyazev, B., Taylor, G. W. and Amer, M. R. (2019) 'Understanding Attention and Generalization in Graph Neural Networks', in Advances in Neural Information Processing Systems 32 (NeurIPS 2019). https://proceedings.neurips.cc/paper/2019/hash/4c5bcfec8584af0d967f1ab10179ca4b-Abstract.html

LeCun, Y. A. *et al.* (2012) 'Efficient Backprop', in *Lecture Notes in Computer Science (Including Subseries Lecture Notes in Artificial Intelligence and Lecture Notes in Bioinformatics)*. Springer, pp. 9–48. doi: 10.1007/978-3-642-35289-8_3.

Lee, J., Lee, I. and Kang, J. (2019) 'Self-attention Graph Pooling', in *36th International Conference on Machine Learning, ICML 2019*.

Li, Y. *et al.* (2016) 'Gated Graph Sequence Neural Networks', in *4th International Conference on Learning Representations, ICLR 2016 – Conference Track Proceedings*.

Li, G. *et al.* (2020) 'DeeperGCN: All You Need to Train Deeper GCNs'. Available at: http://arxiv.org/abs/2006.07739.

Ma, Z. *et al.* (2020) 'Path Integral Based Convolution and Pooling for Graph Neural Networks', in *Advances in Neural Information Processing Systems*. doi: 10.1088/1742-5468/ac3ae4.

Ranjan, E., Sanyal, S. and Talukdar, P. (2020) 'ASAP: Adaptive Structure Aware Pooling for Learning Hierarchical Graph Representations', in *AAAI 2020 – 34th AAAI Conference on Artificial Intelligence*. doi: 10.1609/aaai.v34i04.5997.

Tsitsulin, A. *et al.* (2020) 'Graph Clustering with Graph Neural Networks'. Available at: http://arxiv.org/abs/2006.16904.

Vinyals, O., Bengio, S. and Kudlur, M. (2016) 'Order Matters: Sequence to Sequence for Sets', in *4th International Conference on Learning Representations, ICLR 2016 – Conference Track Proceedings*. arXiv: 1511.06391

Yang, C. *et al.* (2020) 'Revisiting Over-Smoothing in Deep GCNs'. Available at: http://arxiv.org/abs/2003.13663.

Ying, R. *et al.* (2018) 'Hierarchical Graph Representation Learning with Differentiable Pooling', in *Advances in Neural Information Processing Systems*. https://dl.acm.org/doi/abs/10.5555/3327345.3327389

Zhang, M. *et al.* (2018) 'An End-to-End Deep Learning Architecture for Graph Classification', in *32nd AAAI Conference on Artificial Intelligence, AAAI 2018*. doi: 10.1609/aaai.v32i1.11782.

Zhao, L. and Akoglu, L. (2019) 'PairNorm: Tackling Oversmoothing in GNNs'. Available at: http://arxiv.org/abs/1909.12223.

Zhou, K. *et al.* (2020) 'Towards Deeper Graph Neural Networks with Differentiable Group Normalization'. Available at: http://arxiv.org/abs/2006.06972.

5

Graph Convolution Networks: A Journey from Start to End

5.1 Introduction

The convolutional operation has been serving as the foundation of the majority of deep learning models since convolutional neural networks (CNNs) have shown to be highly able to capture and learn complex representations even when dealing with data of high dimensionality. CNN's capacity to learn a series of filters in order to extract more complicated patterns is what makes it so powerful. These same concepts can be used to analyze graph data if we use a little creativity. The generalization of the convolution operator to be better suited to the graph domain brings a new family of graph neural networks (GNNs) with some necessary attributes described as follows. (1) Localization: weights for learned feature extraction should be localized. They should be relevant across the whole input graph and should only take into account the data in a certain region. (2) Scalability: these feature extractors' learning processes must be extensible, meaning that the number of trainable parameters ought to be unaffected by the size of the graph. (3) Interpretability: the convolutional operator ought to (ideally) be based on a theoretical or physical explanation, and its workings ought to be clear-cut (Ward *et al.*, 2022).

As stated in the previous chapter, convolutional GNNs can be taxonomized into two classes of approaches, namely, spectral and spatial. On one hand, spectral approaches are concerned with defining graph convolutions by presenting filters from the standpoint of graph signal analysis in which the operation of graph convolutions is regarded as denoising graph signals. It applies an eigen decomposition to the graph Laplacian matrix to empower the interpretation of the graph structural relations that might recognize clusters of this graph (see Figure 5.1). On the other hand, spatial-based approaches act in a similar way as the vision-based convolutional layers by designing graph convolutional layers according to the spatial relationships of nodes in the graph. Without a doubt, images could be regarded as a distinct case of the graph in which each pixel denotes a certain node in the input graph and is unswervingly linked to its neighboring pixels. Applying a convolutional filter means calculating the weighted mean of pixel values of the chief pixel

DOI: 10.1201/9781003329701-5

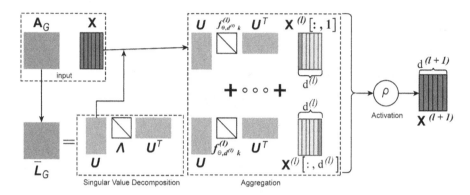

FIGURE 5.1
Systematic diagram of generic framework of spectral graph convolution networks.

(Adapted from Zhou *et al.*, 2022.)

and adjacent pixels in every channel. Likewise, the spatial graph convolutions convolve the representations of the dominant node and its adjacency nodes to capture and fuse the efficient representation for the dominant node and from a different angle, spatial convolutional GNNs. The main idea of the convolutional GNNs revolves around passing the messages and node information across the edges of the graphs. Compared to spectral graph convolution, the spatial graph is presently more commonly used because of its gorgeous efficiency, elasticity, scalability, and generalizability.

This chapter explores popular families of GNNs known as convolution graph networks (GCNs) by exploring their basic notion, and design criteria. Following that, we dive into details of state-of-the-art graph convolutional networks (GCNs) algorithms by describing their mathematical background followed by their python implementation.

5.2 Graph Convolutional Network

GCN was proposed in the work of Kipf and Welling (2017) as a straightforward and efficient layer-wise information propagation rule for graph intelligence networks that can operate explicitly on graphs.

In its simplest form, the layer-wise propagation rule can be designated as follows:

$$f\left(H^{<l>}, A\right) = \sigma\left(A H^{<l>} w^{<l>}\right),\tag{5.1}$$

where $w^{<l>}$ denotes the weight parameters of the l-th layer of the model, while $\sigma(\cdot)$ denotes a nonlinearity function, for example, rectified linear units (ReLU).

In spite of its straightforwardness, this propagation rule is quite robust. However, this model encountered two primary limitations. First, multiplying with A implies that the feature vectors of all neighbors are summed up for each node without containing feature vectors of the node itself. As a remedy, an identity matrix, I, can be added to A for imposing self-loops in the graph, such that

$$\tilde{A} = A + I. \tag{5.2}$$

Second, the matrix A is characteristically non-normalized and hence the multiplying A would totally adjust the magnitude of the feature vectors. This could easily be interpreted by examining the eigenvalues of A. In GCN, a diagonal matrix of node degree D^{-1} can be applied to normalize matrix A so as to have all rows sum to one:

$$A_{norm} = D^{-1}A. \tag{5.3}$$

The previous normalization refers to calculating the average of feature vectors of neighbors of each node. In actual fact, dynamics are always favoring the symmetrical normalization; hence, GNS normalizes the A as follows:

$$A = D^{-\frac{1}{2}}AD^{-\frac{1}{2}}. \tag{5.4}$$

This no longer sums to the direct average of neighbors' features. The combination of the previous two tricks fundamentally drives the propagation rule of GCN (Kipf and Welling, 2017):

$$f\left(H^{<l>}, A\right) = \sigma\left(\tilde{D}^{-\frac{1}{2}}\tilde{A}\tilde{D}^{-\frac{1}{2}}H^{<l>}w^{<l>}\right), \tag{5.5}$$

where $\tilde{D}$ denotes the diagonal matrix of $\tilde{A}$. It is worth mentioning that the GCN could be interpreted as a generalization of a differentiable variant of the eminent graph-based Weisfeiler-Lehman algorithm that operates as follows: for every node, n_i in the input graph G does the following. First, extract feature vector $\left\{h_{n_j}\right\}$ of neighbors $\left\{n_j\right\}$, then, the node feature is updated as follows:

$$h_{n_j} \leftarrow hash\left(\sum_j h_{v_j}\right), \tag{5.6}$$

where $hash$ $(\cdot)$ denotes injective hash function. These two steps are repeated interchangeably till convergence. To sum up, the layer-wise propagation rule of graph convolutions can be delivered into the vectorized formulation:

$$h_i^{l+1} = \sigma\left(\sum_j \frac{1}{c_{ij}} W^{(l)}h_{n_j}^l\right), \tag{5.7}$$

where j denotes the index of neighbors of the node n_i, c_{ij} denotes the normalization factor for the edge (n_i, n_j) driven from the proportionally normalized adjacency matrix.

Let's define the graph convolutional layer by implementing the abovementioned concepts into PyTorch code.

```
import torch
from torch import nn
from dgl.base import import DGLError

class GraphConvolutionalLayer(nn.Module):

    def __init__(self, in_feats, out_feats, norm='both', weight=True,
bias=True, activation=None, allow_zero_in_degree=False):
        super(GraphConvolutionalLayer, self).__init__()
        if norm not in ('none', 'both', 'right', 'left'):
            raise DGLError('Invalid norm value. Must be either "none",
"both", "right" or "left".'
                            ' But got "{}".'.format(norm))
        self._in_feats = in_feats
        self._out_feats = out_feats
        self._norm = norm
        self._allow_zero_in_degree = allow_zero_in_degree

        if weight:
            self.weight = nn.Parameter(torch.Tensor(in_feats,
out_feats))
        else:
            self.register_parameter('weight', None)

        if bias:
            self.bias = nn.Parameter(torch.Tensor(out_feats))
        else:
            self.register_parameter('bias', None)

        self.reset_parameters()

        self._activation = activation

    def reset_parameters(self):
        r"""

        Hint: Reset to the initial training parameters.

        """
        if self.weight is not None:
            init.xavier_uniform_(self.weight)
        if self.bias is not None:
            init.zeros_(self.bias)

    def forward(self, graph, feat, weight=None, edge_weight=None):
        r"""

        Hint: Here, calculate the graph convolution.
```

```
        """
        with graph.local_scope():
            if not self._allow_zero_in_degree:
                if (graph.in_degrees() == 0).any():
                    raise DGLError('The graph contain 0-in-degree nodes,'
                                    'invalid node output')
            aggregate_fn = fn.copy_src('h', 'm')
            if edge_weight is not None:
                assert edge_weight.shape[0] == graph.number_of_edges()
                graph.edata['_edge_weight'] = edge_weight
                aggregate_fn = fn.u_mul_e('h', '_edge_weight', 'm')

            feat_src, feat_dst = expand_as_pair(feat, graph)
            if self._norm in ['left', 'both']:
                degs = graph.out_degrees().float().clamp(min=1)
                if self._norm == 'both':
                    norm = torch.pow(degs, -0.5)
                else:
                    norm = 1.0 / degs
                shp = norm.shape + (1,) * (feat_src.dim() - 1)
                norm = torch.reshape(norm, shp)
                feat_src = feat_src * norm

            if weight is not None:
                if self.weight is not None:
                    raise DGLError('External weight is provided while
at the same time the'
                                        ' module has defined its own weight
                                        parameter. Please'
                                        ' create the module with flag
                                        weight=False.')
            else:
                weight = self.weight

            if self._in_feats > self._out_feats:
                # mult W first to reduce the feature size for aggregation.
                if weight is not None:
                    feat_src = torch.matmul(feat_src, weight)
                graph.srcdata['h'] = feat_src
                graph.update_all(aggregate_fn, fn.sum(msg='m', out='h'))
                rst = graph.dstdata['h']
            else:
                # aggregate first then mult W
                graph.srcdata['h'] = feat_src
                graph.update_all(aggregate_fn, fn.sum(msg='m', out='h'))
                rst = graph.dstdata['h']
                if weight is not None:
                    rst = torch.matmul(rst, weight)

            if self._norm in ['right', 'both']:
                degs = graph.in_degrees().float().clamp(min=1)
                if self._norm == 'both':
                    norm = torch.pow(degs, -0.5)
                else:
                    norm = 1.0 / degs
                shp = norm.shape + (1,) * (feat_dst.dim() - 1)
```

```
        norm = torch.reshape(norm, shp)
        rst = rst * norm

    if self.bias is not None:
        rst = rst + self.bias

    if self._activation is not None:
        rst = self._activation(rst)

    return rst
```

Since we already implemented the graph convolutions, it is time to explore the implementation of the final three-layered GCN as shown by the following code snippets:

```
import torch
import torch.nn as nn
import torch.nn.functional as F
import dgl

class GraphConvolutionalNet(nn.Module):
    def __init__(self, in_size, hid_size, out_size):
        super().__init__()
        self.layers = nn.ModuleList()
        # Multiple Graph convolution layers
        self.layers.append(
            GraphConvolutionalLayer(in_size, hid_size, activation=F.relu)
        )
        self.layers.append(GraphConvolutionalLayer(hid_size, out_size))
        self.dropout = nn.Dropout(0.5)

    def forward(self, g, features):
        h = features
        for i, layer in enumerate(self.layers):
            if i != 0:
                h = self.dropout(h)
            h = layer(g, h)
        return h
```

5.3 Deeper Graph Convolution Network

In Li, Xiong and Thabet (2020), the performance of graph convolutions was improved by adding generalized aggregation function (see the previous chapter) that can overcome the existing aggregation methods. The generalized aggregation method (SoftMax, Power Mean) presented is completely differentiable and could be optimized during the training. In addition, the DeeperGCN investigating the way by which adapting the existing GCN skips connectivity and presents another layer of graph normalization.

To begin implementing DeeperGCN, let's define some building modules, namely, multi-layered perceptron (MLP) and message normalization layer.

```python
import torch
import torch.nn as nn
import torch.nn.functional as F

class MLP(nn.Sequential):

    def __init__(self,
                 channels,
                 act='relu',
                 dropout=0.,
                 bias=True):
        layers = []

        for i in range(1, len(channels)):
            layers.append(nn.Linear(channels[i - 1], channels[i], bias))
            if i < len(channels) - 1:
                layers.append(nn.BatchNorm1d(channels[i], affine=True))
                layers.append(nn.ReLU())
                layers.append(nn.Dropout(dropout))

        super(MLP, self).__init__(*layers)

class MessageNorm(nn.Module):
    def __init__(self, learn_scale=False):
        super(MessageNorm, self).__init__()
        self.scale = nn.Parameter(torch.FloatTensor([1.0]),
        requires_grad=learn_scale)

    def forward(self, feats, msg, p=2):
        msg = F.normalize(msg, p=2, dim=-1)
        feats_norm = feats.norm(p=p, dim=-1, keepdim=True)
        return msg * feats_norm * self.scale
```

Now, let's define the generalized graph convolutional layer as follows:

```python
import torch
import torch.nn as nn
import torch.nn.functional as F
import dgl.function as fn

from ogb.graphproppred.mol_encoder import BondEncoder
from dgl.nn.functional import edge_softmax

class GeneralizedGraphConvolution(nn.Module):

    def __init__(self,
                 in_dim,
                 out_dim,
                 aggregator='softmax',
                 beta=1.0,
                 learn_beta=False,
                 p=1.0,
```

```
                    learn_p=False,
                    msg_norm=False,
                    learn_msg_scale=False,
                    mlp_layers=1,
                    eps=1e-7):
        super(GeneralizedGraphConvolution, self).__init__()

        self.aggr = aggregator
        self.eps = eps

        channels = [in_dim]
        for _ in range(mlp_layers - 1):
            channels.append(in_dim * 2)
        channels.append(out_dim)

        self.mlp = MLP(channels)
        self.msg_norm = MessageNormalization(learn_msg_scale) if
msg_norm else None

        self.beta = nn.Parameter(torch.Tensor([beta]), requires_
grad=True) if learn_beta and self.aggr == 'softmax' else beta
        self.p = nn.Parameter(torch.Tensor([p]), requires_grad=True)
if learn_p else p

        self.edge_encoder = BondEncoder(in_dim)

    def forward(self, g, node_feats, edge_feats):
        with g.local_scope():
            # Node and edge feature size need to match.
            g.ndata['h'] = node_feats
            g.edata['h'] = self.edge_encoder(edge_feats)
            g.apply_edges(fn.u_add_e('h', 'h', 'm'))

            if self.aggr == 'softmax':
                g.edata['m'] = F.relu(g.edata['m']) + self.eps
                g.edata['a'] = edge_softmax(g, g.edata['m'] * self.beta)
                g.update_all(lambda edge: {'x': edge.data['m'] * edge.
data['a']},
                             fn.sum('x', 'm'))

            elif self.aggr == 'power':
                minv, maxv = 1e-7, 1e1
                torch.clamp_(g.edata['m'], minv, maxv)
                g.update_all(lambda edge: {'x': torch.pow(edge.
data['m'], self.p)},
                             fn.mean('x', 'm'))
                torch.clamp_(g.ndata['m'], minv, maxv)
                g.ndata['m'] = torch.pow(g.ndata['m'], self.p)

            else:
                raise NotImplementedError(f'Aggregator {self.aggr} is
not supported.')

            if self.msg_norm is not None:
                g.ndata['m'] = self.msg_norm(node_feats, g.ndata['m'])
```

```
feats = node_feats + g.ndata['m']

return self.mlp(feats)
```

5.4 GCN with Initial Residual and Identity Mapping (GCNII)

On real-world datasets, GCNs and later variations have demonstrated higher performance in a number of application domains. Notwithstanding their popularity, the over-smoothing issue makes the majority of the current GCN models shallow. The difficulty of creating and evaluating deep GCNs is examined in this research. The work of Chen *et al.* (2020) proposed GCNII, as another edition of the GCN model that is empowered with the initial residual and identity mapping method. The purpose of these two methods is to truly extend GCN by enabling it to express a K-order polynomial filter via random constants. This can be formulated as follows:

$$f\left(H^{<l>}, A\right) = \sigma\left(\left(\left(1-\alpha_{<l>}\right)\left(\tilde{D}^{-\frac{1}{2}}\tilde{A}\tilde{D}^{-\frac{1}{2}}\right)H^{<l>} + \alpha_{<l>}H^{<0>}\right)\left(1-\beta_l\right)I_n + \beta_l W^{<l>}\right).$$

(5.8)

This implies two updates, one is applying residual connection to combine the smoothed representation, $\left(\tilde{D}^{-\frac{1}{2}}\tilde{A}\tilde{D}^{-\frac{1}{2}}\right)H^{<l>}$, which is demonstrated to incompletely resolve the over-smoothing problem. The other is combining the identity mapping with the weight parameters.

Let's begin our implementation by defining a class for normalizing the positive scalar edge weights on a graph.

```python
import torch

from torch import nn
from torch.nn import init
import dgl.function as fn
import math
from dgl.base import DGLError
from dgl.transforms import reverse
from dgl.convert import block_to_graph
from dgl.heterograph import DGLBlock

class EdgeWeightNorm(nn.Module):

    def __init__(self, norm='both', eps=0.):
        super(EdgeWeightNorm, self).__init__()
        self._norm = norm
        self._eps = eps
```

```
    def forward(self, graph, edge_weight):

        with graph.local_scope():
            if isinstance(graph, DGLBlock):
                graph = block_to_graph(graph)
            if len(edge_weight.shape) > 1:
                raise DGLError('Error messages.')
            if self._norm == 'both' and torch.any(edge_weight <=
0).item():
                raise DGLError('Error messages.')

            dev = graph.device
            graph.srcdata['_src_out_w'] = torch.ones((graph.number_of_
src_nodes())).float().to(dev)
            graph.dstdata['_dst_in_w'] = torch.ones((graph.number_of_
dst_nodes())).float().to(dev)
            graph.edata['_edge_w'] = edge_weight

            if self._norm == 'both':
                reversed_g = reverse(graph)
                reversed_g.edata['_edge_w'] = edge_weight
                reversed_g.update_all(fn.copy_edge('_edge_w', 'm'),
fn.sum('m', 'out_weight'))
                degs = reversed_g.dstdata['out_weight'] + self._eps
                norm = torch.pow(degs, -0.5)
                graph.srcdata['_src_out_w'] = norm

            if self._norm != 'none':
                graph.update_all(fn.copy_edge('_edge_w', 'm'),
fn.sum('m', 'in_weight'))

                degs = graph.dstdata['in_weight'] + self._eps
                if self._norm == 'both':
                    norm = torch.pow(degs, -0.5)
                else:
                    norm = 1.0 / degs
                graph.dstdata['_dst_in_w'] = norm

            graph.apply_edges(lambda e: {'_norm_edge_weights':
                                          e.src['_src_out_w'] * \
                                          e.dst['_dst_in_w'] * \
                                          e.data['_edge_w']})
            return graph.edata['_norm_edge_weights']
```

According to the previous formulas, we can implement the GCNII layer (with identity mapping and initial residuals distillation) as follows:

```
class GCNIILayer(nn.Module):

    def __init__(self,
                 in_feats,
                 layer,
                 alpha=0.1,
                 lambda_=1,
                 project_initial_features=True,
```

```
                    allow_zero_in_degree=False,
                    bias=True,
                    activation=None):
        super().__init__()

        self._in_feats = in_feats
        self._project_initial_features = project_initial_features

        self.alpha = alpha
        self.beta = math.log(lambda_ / layer + 1)

        self._bias = bias
        self._activation = activation
        self._allow_zero_in_degree = allow_zero_in_degree

        self.weight1 = nn.Parameter(torch.Tensor(self._in_feats,
self._in_feats))

        if self._project_initial_features:
            self.register_parameter("weight2", None)
        else:
            self.weight2 = nn.Parameter(
                torch.Tensor(self._in_feats, self._in_feats))

        if self._bias:
            self.bias = nn.Parameter(th.Tensor(self._in_feats))
        else:
            self.register_parameter("bias", None)

        self.reset_parameters()

    def reset_parameters(self):
        r"""
        Description
        -----------
        Reset to the initial training parameters.
        """
        nn.init.normal_(self.weight1)
        if not self._project_initial_features:
            nn.init.normal_(self.weight2)
        if self._bias:
            nn.init.zeros_(self.bias)

    def forward(self, graph, feat, feat_0, edge_weight=None):

        with graph.local_scope():
            if not self._allow_zero_in_degree:
                if (graph.in_degrees() == 0).any():
                    raise DGLError(
                        "Error Messages."
                    )

            # normalize to get smoothed representation
            if edge_weight is None:
                degs = graph.in_degrees().float().clamp(min=1)
                norm = torch.pow(degs, -0.5)
```

```
            norm = norm.to(feat.device).unsqueeze(1)
        else:
            edge_weight = EdgeWeightNorm('both')(graph, edge_weight)

        if edge_weight is None:
            feat = feat * norm
        graph.ndata["h"] = feat
        msg_func = fn.copy_u("h", "m")
        if edge_weight is not None:
            graph.edata["_edge_weight"] = edge_weight
            msg_func = fn.u_mul_e("h", "_edge_weight", "m")
        graph.update_all(msg_func, fn.sum("m", "h"))
        feat = graph.ndata.pop("h")
        if edge_weight is None:
            feat = feat * norm
        # scale
        feat = feat * (1 - self.alpha)

        # initial residual connection to the first layer
        feat_0 = feat_0[: feat.size(0)] * self.alpha

        if self._project_initial_features:
            rst = feat.add_(feat_0)
            rst = torch.addmm(
                feat, feat, self.weight1, beta=(1 - self.beta),
alpha=self.beta
            )
        else:
            rst = torch.addmm(
                feat, feat, self.weight1, beta=(1 - self.beta),
alpha=self.beta
            )
            rst += torch.addmm(
                feat_0, feat_0, self.weight2, beta=(1 - self.
beta), alpha=self.beta
            )

        if self._bias:
            rst = rst + self.bias

        if self._activation is not None:
            rst = self._activation(rst)

        return rst
```

5.5 Topology Adaptive Graph Convolutional Networks

The work of Du *et al.* (2017) presented topology adaptive GCN (TAGCN) as a spectral network for applying convolutions on the node domain. The TAGCN introduced a methodical technique to develop a group of static-size trainable filters to convolve over graphs. The topographic anatomy of these filters matches up and adjusts the graph structure of the graph once they convolve the graph. The TAGCN is compatible with convolution as established in graph signal analysis in addition to inheriting the characteristics of convolutions in CNN for matrix data. TAGCN substitutes the static square filters in standard convolutions for the grid-planned data volumes in conventional CNNs. Therefore, the node-based convolution of TAGCN is dependable with convolution in standard convolutions. TAGCN performs better than previous spectrum CNNs on a variety of datasets and is operationally lighter than other recent advancements because no estimate to the convolution is required.

To define the topology adaptive convolutional layer, let's see the next code snippet:

```
import torch
import torch.nn as nn

class TAGraphConvolution(nn.Module):

    def __init__(self, in_feats, out_feats, k=2, bias=True,
activation=None):
        super(TAGConv, self).__init__()
        self._in_feats = in_feats
        self._out_feats = out_feats
        self._k = k
        self._activation = activation
        self.lin = nn.Linear(in_feats * (self._k + 1), out_feats,
bias=bias)

        self.reset_parameters()

    def reset_parameters(self):
        r"""
        Description
        Reset to the initial training parameters.

        """
        gain = nn.init.calculate_gain('relu')
        nn.init.xavier_normal_(self.lin.weight, gain=gain)

    def forward(self, graph, feat, edge_weight=None):

        with graph.local_scope():
            assert graph.is_homogeneous, 'Graph is not homogeneous'
            if edge_weight is None:
                norm = th.pow(graph.in_degrees().float().clamp(min=1),
-0.5)
                shp = norm.shape + (1,) * (feat.dim() - 1)
                norm = th.reshape(norm, shp).to(feat.device)

            msg_func = fn.copy_u("h", "m")
            if edge_weight is not None:
                graph.edata["_edge_weight"] = EdgeWeightNorm(
                    'both')(graph, edge_weight)
```

```
            msg_func = fn.u_mul_e("h", "_edge_weight", "m")
        # D-1/2 A D -1/2 X
        fstack = [feat]
        for _ in range(self._k):
            if edge_weight is None:
                rst = fstack[-1] * norm
            else:
                rst = fstack[-1]
            graph.ndata['h'] = rst

            graph.update_all(msg_func,
                             fn.sum(msg='m', out='h'))
            rst = graph.ndata['h']
            if edge_weight is None:
                rst = rst * norm
            fstack.append(rst)

        rst = self.lin(th.cat(fstack, dim=-1))

        if self._activation is not None:
            rst = self._activation(rst)

        return rst
```

Now, you can implement the TAGCN as follows:

```
import torch
import torch.nn as nn

class TAGraphConvolutionNetwork(nn.Module):
    def __init__(self, g, in_feats, n_hidden, n_classes, n_layers,
activation, dropout):
        super(TAGraphConvolutionNetwork, self).__init__()
        self.g = g
        self.layers = nn.ModuleList()
        # input layer
        self.layers.append(TAGraphConvolution(in_feats, n_hidden,
activation=activation))
        # hidden layers
        for i in range(n_layers - 1):
            self.layers.append(TAGraphConvolution(n_hidden, n_hidden,
activation=activation))
        # output layer
        self.layers.append(TAGraphConvolution(n_hidden, n_classes))
#activation=None
        self.dropout = nn.Dropout(p=dropout)

    def forward(self, features):
        h = features
        for i, layer in enumerate(self.layers):
            if i != 0:
                h = self.dropout(h)
            h = layer(self.g, h)
        return h
```

5.6 Relational Graph Convolutional Network

Relational GCN (RGCN) was proposed (Schlichtkrull *et al.*, 2018) as a special case of spatial graph convolutional intelligence model that is specifically developed to operate and learn high-level graph representation from extremely multi-relational graph data. RGCN presented a parameter-sharing method to impose sparsity restraints that are leveraged to enable the network to learn from multigraphs possessing a big number of relationships. Further, the RGCN-integrated factorization models, DistMult, empower the model to perform multi-step information propagation that could meaningfully improve the performance of different downstream tasks on the relational graph (see Figure 5.2).

Recall that in GCN, the hidden representation for each node i of the $(l + 1)$th layer is defined in Equation (5.6).

The main distinction between RGCN lies in that the edges encapsulate dissimilar relationships. In the standard GCN, the weight parameter $W^{(l)}$ is

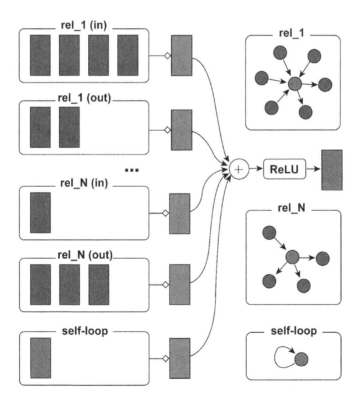

FIGURE 5.2
Illustration of relation graph convolution network.

(Adapted from Schlichtkrull *et al.*, 2018.)

common between all edges in layer l. On the other hand, the RGCN enables diverse kinds of edges to have diverse weights parameters, while the edges sharing the same kind of relationships, r, are related to the same projection parameters $W_r^{(l)}$. Thus, the hidden representation of node i in the $(l+1)$th the layer could be articulated as follows:

$$h_i^{l+1} = \sigma \left(W_0^{(l)} h_j^{(l)} + \sum_{r \in R} \sum_{j \in N_r(i)} \frac{1}{c_{i,j}^r} W_r^{(l)} h_j^{(l)} \right), \qquad (5.9)$$

where $N_r(i)$ represents the group of indices of neighboring nodes of node i with relation $r \in R$, while $c_{i,j}^r$ denotes the normalization factor. The RGCN adopted $c_{i,j}^r = |N_i^r|$. However, the challenge in directly applying the previous formula is the fast growth in the number of training parameters, especially in the case of complex multi-relational data. To tackle this issue and avoid potential overfitting, the RGCN introduced adopted basis decomposition.

$$W_r^{(l)} = \sum_{b+1}^{B} a_{rb}^{(l)} n_b^{(l)}. \qquad (5.10)$$

Thus, the parameter $W_r^{(l)}$ is defined as the linear recipe of basis transformation $v_b^{(l)}$ with coefficients $a_{rb}^{(l)}$. The number of bases BB is much smaller than the number of relations in the knowledge base.

To sum up, the workflow of RGCN involves calculating the departing message of each node by means of node representation and weight parameters related to a particular type of edge. Then, the arriving messages to create new node representations are aggregated.

The following code is the definition of an R-GCN hidden layer.

```
import torch
import dgl
import torch.nn as nn
import torch.nn.functional as F
from dgl import DGLGraph
import dgl.function as fn
from functools import partial
import torch as th
from torch import nn
from dgl.nn import TypedLinear
from torchmetrics.functional import accuracy

class RelationGraphConvolutionLayer(nn.Module):

    def __init__(self, input_feat, output_feat, num_rels,
regularizer=None, num_bases=None,
                 bias=True, activation=None, self_loop=True,
dropout=0.0, layer_norm=False):
        super(RelationGraphConvolutionLayer, self).__init__()
```

```
        self.linear_r = TypedLinear(input_feat, output_feat, num_rels,
regularizer, num_bases)
        self.bias = bias
        self.activation = activation
        self.self_loop = self_loop
        self.layer_norm = layer_norm

        # bias
        if self.bias:
            self.h_bias = nn.Parameter(th.Tensor(output_feat))
            nn.init.zeros_(self.h_bias)

        # TODO: consider remove those options in the future to make
        #    the module only about graph convolution.
        # layer norm
        if self.layer_norm:
            self.layer_norm_weight = nn.LayerNorm(output_feat,
elementwise_affine=True)

        # weight for self loop
        if self.self_loop:
            self.loop_weight = nn.Parameter(th.Tensor(input_feat,
output_feat))
            nn.init.xavier_uniform_(self.loop_weight, gain=nn.init.
calculate_gain('relu'))

        self.dropout = nn.Dropout(dropout)

    def message(self, edges):
        """Message function."""
        m = self.linear_r(edges.src['h'], edges.data['etype'], self.
presorted)
        if 'norm' in edges.data:
            m = m * edges.data['norm']
        return {'m' : m}

    def forward(self, g, feat, etypes, norm=None, *, presorted=False):

        self.presorted = presorted
        with g.local_scope():
            g.srcdata['h'] = feat
            if norm is not None:
                g.edata['norm'] = norm
            g.edata['etype'] = etypes
            # message passing
            g.update_all(self.message, fn.sum('m', 'h'))
            # apply bias and activation
            h = g.dstdata['h']
            if self.layer_norm:
                h = self.layer_norm_weight(h)
            if self.bias:
                h = h + self.h_bias
            if self.self_loop:
                h = h + feat[:g.num_dst_nodes()] @ self.loop_weight
            if self.activation:
                h = self.activation(h)
```

```
        h = self.dropout(h)
        return h
```

At this point, we are ready to build our RCGN as shown in the following code snippet.

```
import torch
import dgl
import torch.nn as nn

class RelationGraphConvolutionNet(nn.Module):
    def __init__(self, num_nodes, h_dim, out_dim, num_rels,
                 regularizer="basis", num_bases=-1, dropout=0.,
                 self_loop=False,
                 ns_mode=False):
        super(RelationGraphConvolutionNet, self).__init__()

        if num_bases == -1:
            num_bases = num_rels
        self.emb = nn.Embedding(num_nodes, h_dim)
        self.conv1 = RelationGraphConvolutionLayer(h_dim, h_dim,
num_rels, regularizer, num_bases, self_loop=self_loop)
        self.conv2 = RelationGraphConvolutionLayer(h_dim, out_dim,
num_rels, regularizer, num_bases, self_loop=self_loop)
        self.dropout = nn.Dropout(dropout)
        self.ns_mode = ns_mode

    def forward(self, g, nids=None):
        if self.ns_mode:
            # forward for neighbor sampling
            x = self.emb(g[0].srcdata[dgl.NID])
            h = self.conv1(g[0], x, g[0].edata[dgl.ETYPE], g[0].
edata['norm'])
            h = self.dropout(F.relu(h))
            h = self.conv2(g[1], h, g[1].edata[dgl.ETYPE], g[1].
edata['norm'])
            return h
        else:
            x = self.emb.weight if nids is None else self.emb(nids)
            h = self.conv1(g, x, g.edata[dgl.ETYPE], g.edata['norm'])
            h = self.dropout(F.relu(h))
            h = self.conv2(g, h, g.edata[dgl.ETYPE], g.edata['norm'])
            return h
```

5.7 Case Study

GCNs are an extremely important family of graph intelligence methods that show great achievements in a broad range of graph analysis tasks. However, the role of GCNs in the era of cyber-security (i.e., fraud detection and anomaly detection malware analysis) is still in its infancy. This, in turn, increased the interest of the community in discovering the potential of GCNs in addressing the current cyber threats from a practical standpoint. Motivated by that, the supplementary materials of this chapter are designated to provide a holistic in-lab tutorial for implementing full working experiments (training and testing) of the abovementioned GNNs for different graph tasks. Moreover, the material provides a practical discussion of more advanced GCNs. In supplementary materials, the performance of the GCNs was experimentally evaluated in real-world case studies with the main emphasis on security-related ones. The supplementary materials of this chapter also provide the readers with recommendations for further reading about the content of this chapter. The repository of supplementary materials is given in this link: https://github.com/DEEPOLOGY-AI/Book-Graph-Neural-Network/tree/main/Chapter%205.

References

Chen, M. *et al.* (2020) 'Simple and Deep Graph Convolutional Networks', in *37th International Conference on Machine Learning, ICML*.

Du, J. *et al.* (2017) 'Topology Adaptive Graph Convolutional Networks'. doi: http://arxiv.org/abs/1710.10370.

Kipf, T. N. and Welling, M. (2017) 'Semi-supervised Classification with Graph Convolutional Networks', in *5th International Conference on Learning Representations, ICLR 2017 – Conference Track Proceedings*. doi: 10.48550/arXiv.1609.02907

Li, G., Xiong, C., Thabet, A., Ghanem, B. (2020) 'DeeperGCN: All You Need to Train Deeper GCNs'. doi: 10.48550/arXiv.2006.07739.

Schlichtkrull, M. *et al.* (2018) 'Modeling Relational Data with Graph Convolutional Networks', in *Lecture Notes in Computer Science (Including Subseries Lecture Notes in Artificial Intelligence and Lecture Notes in Bioinformatics)*. doi: 10.1007/978-3-319-93417-4_38.

Ward, I. R. *et al.* (2022) 'A Practical Tutorial on Graph Neural Networks', in *ACM Computing Surveys*. doi: 10.1145/3503043.

Zhou, Y. *et al.* (2022). 'Graph Neural Networks: Taxonomy, Advances, and Trends', *ACM Transactions on Intelligent Systems and Technology*. doi: 10.1145/3495161.

6

Graph Attention Networks:
A Journey from Start to End

6.1 Introduction

In this chapter, the readers are going to learn about the family of graph neural networks (GNNs) that are based on attention mechanisms. In particular, we would learn about graph attention networks (GATs) by visualizing and interpreting their composition as well as the underlying attention mechanism. In the previous chapter about graph convolutional networks (GCNs), it is demonstrated that compounding the local graph construction and node-level features resulted in a respectable performance on the tasks of node classification. Nevertheless, the strategy in which GCNs perform aggregations mainly depends on the structure of the graph, which, in turn, negatively impacts the generalizability of the modes. A common solution to this issue is to basically average the features of all neighbor nodes. In different types, GATs are designed to promote a different category of aggregation.

To sum up, this chapter theoretically and practically explains the following state-of-the-art GATs:

- GAT
- GAT version 2 (GATv2)
- Graph transformer (GT)
- GT network (GTN)

6.2 Graph Attention Network

GAT (Veličković *et al.*, 2018) is a special form of graph network that can function on graph representations of data by using a masked self-attention mechanism to address the limitations of GCNs, as discussed in the earlier chapter. In particular, GAT stacks multiple layers, whereby the per-layer nodes are capable of attending the features of their neighborhoods. This way, the GAT can empower the network to implicitly calculate a variety of weights for diverse nodes in a neighborhood, with no need for any form of exhaustive matrix computations, while alleviating the reliance on pre-knowledge of the structure of the graph representation upfront. With this capability, GAT can tackle many main challenges of spectral-founded GNN instantaneously, enabling the model willingly to solve inductive and transductive dilemmas. The analysis and visualization of the learned attention parameters are also beneficial to empower the interpretability of the model in terms of the importance of neighbors.

Before diving into the details of the GAT, one may need to be aware and thorough with the attention mechanisms, that is, self-attention and multi-head attention (MHA) (Vaswani *et al.*, 2017), which act as the backbone of the building of all GATs.

In the previous chapters, we have learned that GCNs combine node-wise features and local graph construction to achieve satisfactory performance on the tasks related to node classification. Nevertheless, the structure-founded nature of message aggregation in GCNs makes them unable to generalize well. Specifically, the GCN, a graph convolution operation, produces the normalized sum of neighbors' node features as follows:

$$h_i^{l+1} = Relu\left(\sum_{j \in \mathcal{N}(i)} \frac{1}{c_{i,j}} W^{(l)} h_j^{(l)}\right) \qquad (6.1)$$

where $\mathcal{N}(i)$ represents the group of one-hop neighbors, $c_{i,j} = \left(\sqrt{|\mathcal{N}(i)| \cdot \mathcal{N}(j)|}\right)$ denotes the normalization factor depending on the topological structure of the graph, *ReLU* symbolizes the rectified linear units, and $W^{(l)}$ represents the joint weight matrix designed for node-specific feature transformation. To incorporate v_i in the neighbors, the network merely integrates a self-loop in each node.

The central originality that GAT conveys to the board is in what way the information from the one-hop neighborhood is aggregated. GAT presented the attention mechanism to replace the statically normalized convolutional layer. The main difference between the design of GCN and GAT is given in Figure 6.1.

The design of attentional operations in GAT strictly follows the additive attention (Bahdanau, Cho and Bengio, 2015); nonetheless, the model is agnostic to the specific selection of attention mechanism (see Figure 6.2). The input of each layer is consisting of a group of features, $h = \vec{h}_1, \vec{h}_2, \ldots, \vec{h}_N$, where $\vec{h}_i \in \mathbb{R}^F$, N and F denote the number of nodes and per-node features. The GAT layer generates an output consisting of a group of node features (with possibly dissimilar cardinality F') as its output, $h = \vec{h'}_1, \vec{h'}_2, \ldots, \vec{h'}_N$, where $\vec{h'}_i \in \mathbb{R}^{F'}$.

In GAT, the design of the attentional layer can be decomposed into four distinct stages, described as follows: First, linear transformation—to attain

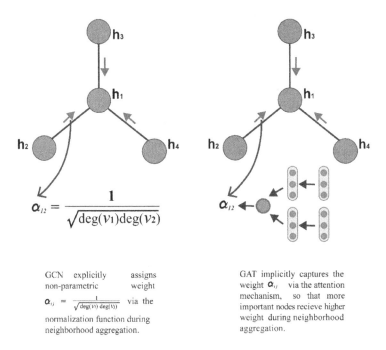

GCN explicitly assigns non-parametric weight $\alpha_{ij} = \frac{1}{\sqrt{\deg(v_i)\,\deg(v_j)}}$ via the normalization function during neighborhood aggregation.

GAT implicitly captures the weight α_{ij} via the attention mechanism, so that more important nodes recieve higher weight during neighborhood aggregation.

FIGURE 6.1
Graph attention network vs graph convolutional network.

satisfactory communicative power to transmute the graph data from input space to high-level feature spaces, a set of one or more learnable linear transformation is essential. To achieve that, the first step in the GAT layer is to apply a joint linear transformation to each node together with a parameter matrix of weights, $W \in \mathbb{R}^{F \times F'}$ to every node:

$$z_i^{(l)} = W^{(l)} h_i^{(l)}. \tag{6.2}$$

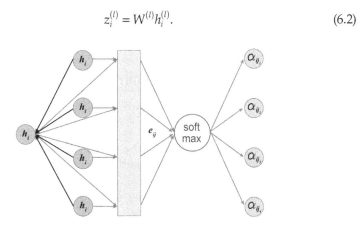

FIGURE 6.2
Illustration of attention mechanism.

Second, the attention coefficients are calculated as a pair-wise non-normalized attention weight between a couple of neighbors. In this phase, z embeddings of the two nodes are concatenated, and the output undergoes dot product with a learnable weight vector $\vec{a}_i^{(l)}$, then, *LeakyReLU* activation is applied to introduce nonlinearity. Such kind of attention is generally known as additive attention, different from the dot-product attention presented in the Transformer model (Vaswani *et al.*, 2017). Next, self-attention is applied to the nodes, where a joint attentional mechanism $a: \mathbb{R}^{F'} \times \mathbb{R}^{F'} \to \mathbb{R}$ is used to calculate the attention coefficients as follows:

$$e_{i,j}^{(l)} = LeakyReLU\left(\vec{a}^{(l)^T}{}_i \cdot \left(z_i^{(l)} \| z_j^{(l)}\right)\right). \tag{6.3}$$

This phase is regarded as the most significant step as it indicates the reputation of node *j*th features with respect to node *i*. This step enables every node to concentrate on every other node, dipping all organizational information:

```
def edge_attention(self, edges):

    z2 = torch.cat([edges.src['z'], edges.dst['z']], dim=1)
    a = self.attn_fc(z2)
    return {'e' : F.leaky_relu(a)}
```

It is worth noting that the graph structure is added to the mechanism by conducting *masked attention*, in which the coefficient $e_{i,j}^{(l)}$ is computed for all nodes $j \in N_i$, where N_i represents the first-order neighborhood of *i*th node in the graph.

The third stage, normalization, seeks to make coefficients straightforwardly equivalent across diverse nodes by normalizing them across all choices of *j* using the SoftMax function as:

$$\alpha_{i,j}^{(l)} = \frac{\exp\left(e_{i,j}^{(l)}\right)}{\sum_{k \in \mathcal{N}(i)} \exp\left(e_{i,k}^{(l)}\right)}. \tag{6.4}$$

Fourth, in the aggregation stage, just as with GCN, the embeddings from different neighbors are combined together, while being mounted by the attention weights:

$$h_i^{(l)} = \sigma\left(\sum_{j \in \mathcal{N}(i)} \alpha_{i,j}^{(l)} \cdot z_j^{(l)}\right). \tag{6.5}$$

In the following, we provide the python implementation of the SoftMax and aggregation operations:

```
def reduce_func(self, nodes):

    alpha = F.softmax(nodes.mailbox['e'], dim=1)
    h = torch.sum(alpha * nodes.mailbox['z'], dim=1)

    return {'h' : h}
```

To obtain a complete practical interpretation of the GAT layer, the python implementation of the GAT layer is given as follows:

```
import torch
import torch.nn as nn
import torch.nn.functional as F

class GraphAttentionLayer(nn.Module):
    def __init__(self, g, in_dim, out_dim):
        super(GraphAttenitonLayer, self).__init__()
        self.g = g
        # equation (1)
        self.fc = nn.Linear(in_dim, out_dim, bias=False)
        # equation (2)
        self.attn_fc = nn.Linear(2 * out_dim, 1, bias=False)
        self.reset_parameters()

    def reset_parameters(self):
        """Reinitialize learnable parameters."""
        gain = nn.init.calculate_gain('relu')
        nn.init.xavier_normal_(self.fc.weight, gain=gain)
        nn.init.xavier_normal_(self.attn_fc.weight, gain=gain)

    def edge_attention(self, edges):
        # edge UDF for equation (2)
        z2 = torch.cat([edges.src['z'], edges.dst['z']], dim=1)
        a = self.attn_fc(z2)
        return {'e': F.leaky_relu(a)}

    def message_func(self, edges):
        # message UDF for equation (3) & (4)
        return {'z': edges.src['z'], 'e': edges.data['e']}

    def reduce_func(self, nodes):
        # reduce UDF for equation (3) & (4)
        # equation (3)
        alpha = F.softmax(nodes.mailbox['e'], dim=1)
        # equation (4)
        h = torch.sum(alpha * nodes.mailbox['z'], dim=1)
        return {'h': h}
    def forward(self, h):
        # equation (1)
        z = self.fc(h)
        self.g.ndata['z'] = z
        # equation (2)
```

```
self.g.apply_edges(self.edge_attention)
# equation (3) & (4)
self.g.update_all(self.message_func, self.reduce_func)
return self.g.ndata.pop('h')
```

MHA: Similar to the concept of multi-channel convolutions in GCN, the GAT presented MHA to empowering the model capability as well as stability of the learning process. In this case, multiple attention heads are developed, and each has its own set of parameters. Simultaneously, each head can calculate its output, and the final output is computed by either concatenating or averaging the head's output (see Figure 6.3).

In the case of concatenation, the output is calculated as follows:

$$h_i^{(l+1)} = \|_{k=1}^{K} \sigma\left(\sum_{j \in \mathcal{N}(i)} \alpha_{i,j}^{(k)} V^k \cdot h_j^{(l)} \right).$$
(6.6)

In the case of average, the output is calculated as follows:

$$h_i^{(l+1)} = \sigma\left(\sum_{k=1}^{K} \sum_{j \in \mathcal{N}(i)} \alpha_{i,j}^{(k)} W^k \cdot h_j^{(l)} \right),$$
(6.7)

where $\|$ denotes the concatenation layer, K represents the number of heads. Concatenation is commonly used for intermediary layers, while the average is usually used at the final layer. To obtain a complete practical interpretation of multi-head GAT, the python implementation of the multi-head GAT layer is given as follows:

```
import torch
import torch.nn as nn
```

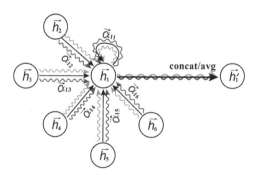

FIGURE 6.3
Illustration of multi-head attention mechanism.

(Adapted from Veličković *et al.*, 2018.)

```
import torch.nn.functional as F

class MultiHeadGraphAttenitonLayer(nn.Module):
    def __init__(self, g, in_dim, out_dim, num_heads, merge='cat'):
        super(MultiHeadGraphAttenitonLayer, self).__init__()
        self.heads = nn.ModuleList()
        for i in range(num_heads):
            self.heads.append(GraphAttenitonLayer(g, in_dim, out_dim))
        self.merge = merge

    def forward(self, h):
        head_outs = [attn_head(h) for attn_head in self.heads]
        if self.merge == 'cat':
            # concat on the output feature dimension (dim=1)
            return torch.cat(head_outs, dim=1)
        else:
            # merge using average
            return torch.mean(torch.stack(head_outs))
```

Now, it's time to bring the above layers together to build a simple two-layered GAT:

```
import torch
import torch.nn as nn
import torch.nn.functional as F

class GraphAttenitonNet(nn.Module):
    def __init__(self, g, in_dim, hidden_dim, out_dim, num_heads):
        super(GraphAttenitonNet, self).__init__()
        self.layer1 = MultiHeadGraphAttentionLayer(g, in_dim, hidden_
dim, num_heads)
        self.layer2 = MultiHeadGraphAttenitonLayer(g, hidden_dim *
num_heads, out_dim, 1)

    def forward(self, h):
        h = self.layer1(h)
        h = F.elu(h)
        h = self.layer2(h)
        return h
```

6.3 Graph Attention Network version 2(GATv2)

GATv2s (Brody, Alon and Yahav, 2021) is an extension to the GAT that solves the problem of static attention problem encountered in the GAT (see Section 6.2). In particular, static attention refers to a scenario in which attention to the main nodes has the identical rank for any query node. The calculation of attention in GAT is defined according to Equation (6.3). It is worth noting that the query node i, the attention order of keys just relies on the learnable weight vector $\vec{a}^{(l)}{}_i$ of node j. Consequently, all queries sharer the same keys' attention order; hence, they are static. To address that, GATv2 enables dynamic attention by updating the attention mechanism as follows:

$$e_{i,j}^{(l)} = \vec{a}^{(l)^T}{}_i \cdot LeakyReLU\left(\left(z_i^{(l)} \| z_j^{(l)}\right)\right). \tag{6.8}$$

The findings demonstrate that the static nature of standard GATs makes them unable to fit the training data in some graph learning tasks such as tasks based on a fully connected bipartite graph. In contrast, the dynamic nature of GATv2 allows an efficient modeling of graph representation in such tasks.

To obtain a complete practical interpretation of how the GATv2 layer differs from the GAT layer, the python implementation of the GATv2 layer is given as follows:

```python
import torch as th
from torch import nn

from dgl import function as fn
from dgl.base import DGLError
from dgl.utils import expand_as_pair
from dgl.nn.functional import edge_softmax
from dgl.nn.pytorch.utils import Identity

class GraphAttentionv2Layer(nn.Module):

    def __init__(
        self,
        in_feats,
        out_feats,
        num_heads,
        feat_drop=0.0,
        attn_drop=0.0,
        negative_slope=0.2,
        residual=False,
        activation=None,
        allow_zero_in_degree=False,
        bias=True,
        share_weights=False,
    ):
        super(GraphAttentionv2Layer, self).__init__()
        self._num_heads = num_heads
        self._in_src_feats, self._in_dst_feats = expand_as_pair(in_feats)
        self._out_feats = out_feats
        self._allow_zero_in_degree = allow_zero_in_degree
        if isinstance(in_feats, tuple):
            self.fc_src = nn.Linear(
                self._in_src_feats, out_feats * num_heads, bias=bias
            )
            self.fc_dst = nn.Linear(
                self._in_dst_feats, out_feats * num_heads, bias=bias
            )
```

```
        else:
            self.fc_src = nn.Linear(
                self._in_src_feats, out_feats * num_heads, bias=bias
            )
            if share_weights:
                self.fc_dst = self.fc_src
            else:
                self.fc_dst = nn.Linear(
                    self._in_src_feats, out_feats * num_heads, bias=bias
                )
        self.attn = nn.Parameter(th.FloatTensor(size=(1, num_heads,
out_feats)))
        self.feat_drop = nn.Dropout(feat_drop)
        self.attn_drop = nn.Dropout(attn_drop)
        self.leaky_relu = nn.LeakyReLU(negative_slope)
        if residual:
            if self._in_dst_feats != out_feats * num_heads:
                self.res_fc = nn.Linear(
                    self._in_dst_feats, num_heads * out_feats, bias=bias
                )
            else:
                self.res_fc = Identity()
        else:
            self.register_buffer("res_fc", None)
        self.activation = activation
        self.share_weights = share_weights
        self.bias = bias
        self.reset_parameters()

    def reset_parameters(self):

        gain = nn.init.calculate_gain("relu")
        nn.init.xavier_normal_(self.fc_src.weight, gain=gain)
        if self.bias:
            nn.init.constant_(self.fc_src.bias, 0)
        if not self.share_weights:
            nn.init.xavier_normal_(self.fc_dst.weight, gain=gain)
            if self.bias:
                nn.init.constant_(self.fc_dst.bias, 0)
        nn.init.xavier_normal_(self.attn, gain=gain)
        if isinstance(self.res_fc, nn.Linear):
            nn.init.xavier_normal_(self.res_fc.weight, gain=gain)
            if self.bias:
                nn.init.constant_(self.res_fc.bias, 0)


    def forward(self, graph, feat, get_attention=False):

        with graph.local_scope():
            if not self._allow_zero_in_degree:
                if (graph.in_degrees() == 0).any():
                    raise DGLError("Error Message")
            if isinstance(feat, tuple):
                h_src = self.feat_drop(feat[0])
                h_dst = self.feat_drop(feat[1])
                feat_src = self.fc_src(h_src).view(
```

```
                -1, self._num_heads, self._out_feats
            )
            feat_dst = self.fc_dst(h_dst).view(
                -1, self._num_heads, self._out_feats
            )
        else:
            h_src = h_dst = self.feat_drop(feat)
            feat_src = self.fc_src(h_src).view(
                -1, self._num_heads, self._out_feats
            )
            if self.share_weights:
                feat_dst = feat_src
            else:
                feat_dst = self.fc_dst(h_dst).view(
                    -1, self._num_heads, self._out_feats
                )
            if graph.is_block:
                feat_dst = feat_dst[: graph.number_of_dst_nodes()]
                h_dst = h_dst[: graph.number_of_dst_nodes()]
        graph.srcdata.update(
            {"el": feat_src}
        )  # (num_src_edge, num_heads, out_dim)
        graph.dstdata.update({"er": feat_dst})
        graph.apply_edges(fn.u_add_v("el", "er", "e"))
        e = self.leaky_relu(
            graph.edata.pop("e")
        )  # (num_src_edge, num_heads, out_dim)
        e = (
            (e * self.attn).sum(dim=-1).unsqueeze(dim=2)
        )  # (num_edge, num_heads, 1)
        # compute softmax
        graph.edata["a"] = self.attn_drop(
            edge_softmax(graph, e)
        )  # (num_edge, num_heads)
        # message passing
        graph.update_all(fn.u_mul_e("el", "a", "m"), fn.sum("m",
"ft"))
        rst = graph.dstdata["ft"]
        # residual
        if self.res_fc is not None:
            resval = self.res_fc(h_dst).view(
                h_dst.shape[0], -1, self._out_feats
            )
            rst = rst + resval
        # activation
        if self.activation:
            rst = self.activation(rst)

        if get_attention:
            return rst, graph.edata["a"]
        else:
            return
```

At this point, we are ready to create the GATV2 architecture as follows:

```
import torch
import torch.nn as nn
```

```python
class GraphAttentionNetv2(nn.Module):
    def __init__(
        self,
        no_layers,
        in_dim,
        no_hidden,
        no_classes,
        heads,
        activation,
        feat_drop,
        attn_drop,
        negative_slope,
        residual,
    ):
        super(GraphAttentionNetv2, self).__init__()
        self.no_layers = no_layers
        self.gatv2_layers = nn.ModuleList()
        self.activation = activation
        # input projection (no residual)
        self.gatv2_layers.append(
            GraphAttentionv2Layer(
                in_dim,
                no_hidden,
                heads[0],
                feat_drop,
                attn_drop,
                negative_slope,
                False,
                self.activation,
                bias=False,
                share_weights=True,
            )
        )
        # hidden layers
        for l in range(1, no_layers):

            self.gatv2_layers.append(
                GraphAttentionv2Layer(
                    no_hidden * heads[l - 1],
                    no_hidden,
                    heads[l],
                    feat_drop,
                    attn_drop,
                    negative_slope,
                    residual,
                    self.activation,
                    bias=False,
                    share_weights=True,
                )
            )
        # output projection
        self.gatv2_layers.append(
            GraphAttentionv2Layer(
                no_hidden * heads[-2],
                no_classes,
                heads[-1],
```

```
                feat_drop,
                attn_drop,
                negative_slope,
                residual,
                None,
                bias=False,
                share_weights=True,
            )
        )

    def forward(self, g, inputs):
        h = inputs
        for l in range(self.no_layers):
            h = self.gatv2_layers[l](g, h).flatten(1)
        # output projection
        logits = self.gatv2_layers[-1](g, h).mean(1)
        return logits
```

6.4 Generalized Graph Transformer Network

Generalized GT (Dwivedi and Bresson, 2020) was proposed as a generalization of a standard transformer network on graph data. Two variants of GT
layers were proposed, one with edge features and the other without edge
features. To make things simpler, Figure 6.4 displays a schematic diagram
of both layers that are composed of three key building blocks, namely, the
Laplacian Positional Encodings (LPEs) of input graphs, the MHA layer with
attention constrained to confined neighbors, and the feed-forward network.

Unlike the traditional transformer (Vaswani *et al.*, 2017), the main distinctions of the generalized GT can be summarized as follows. First, the positional encoding is calculated with the Laplacian mechanism that computes
the eigenvectors of graph Laplacian for each graph prior to the training,
where *k*-lowest non-trivial eigenvectors of a particular node were settled as
the positional embedding of this node. Given input graph G, in which each
node has a set of features $\alpha_i \in \mathbb{R}^{d_n \times 1}$, and each edge has a set of features edge
features $\beta_{i,j} \in \mathbb{R}^{d_e \times 1}$, both node's and edge's features are fed into a linear projection to be embedded into d-dimensional features h_i^0 and e_{ij}^0. It is worth noting that the LPEs are included into the node features only in the input layer.

Second, the attention method acts as a function of the node's neighborhood
linking designated as follows:

$$h_i^{(l+1)} = O_h^l \,\|_{k=1}^{H} \left(\sum_{j \in \mathcal{N}(i)} w_{i,j}^{(k,l)} \cdot V^{k,l} \cdot h_j^{(l)} \right), \tag{6.9}$$

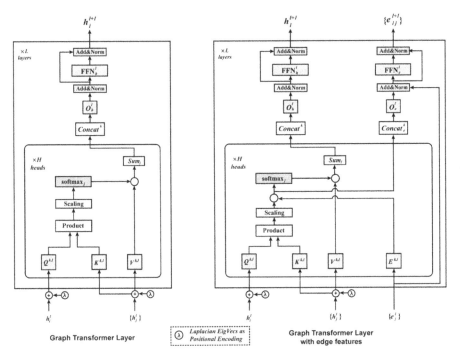

FIGURE 6.4
Illustration of generalized graph transformer.

(Adapted from Dwivedi and Bresson, 2020.)

where

$$w_{i,j}^{(k,l)} = SoftMax\left(\frac{Q^{k,l}h_j^{(l)} \cdot K^{k,l}h_j^{(l)}}{\sqrt{d_k}}\right), \qquad (6.10)$$

where $Q^{k,l}, Q^{k,l}, Q^{k,l} \in \mathbb{R}^{d_k \times d}$, and $O_h^l \in \mathbb{R}^{d \times d}$.

Third, the FFN module replaces the layer normalization with batch normalization (normalization layers are discussed in the chapter, to achieve higher performance).

Beyond, another variant of the version generalized GT was introduced by including the *edge representation* in the architecture shown in Figure 6.4. This edition of variants GT is highly useful for modeling graph representation from graphs with irritating relations (edge information) between nodes, that is, knowledge graphs and molecular graphs. In this context, two important aspects are worth mentioning about edge-aware GT: first, each layer contains a nominated pipeline edge feature and second, the edge features are bonded to the matching pairwise implied attention weights. Mathematically speaking, the calculation of the edge-aware GT layer can be formulated as follows:

$$h_i^{(l+1)} = O_h^l \parallel_{k=1}^H \left(\sum_{j \in \mathcal{N}(i)} w_{i,j}^{(k,l)} \cdot V^k \cdot h_j^{(l)} \right),$$ (6.11)

$$\hat{e}_i^{(l+1)} = O_e^l \parallel_{k=1}^H \left(\hat{w}_{i,j}^{(k,l)} \right),$$ (6.12)

$$\hat{w}_{i,j}^{(k,l)} = \left(\frac{Q^{k,l} h_j^{(l)} \cdot K^k h_j^{(l)}}{\sqrt{d_k}} \right) \cdot E^k \cdot e_{i,j},$$ (6.13)

$$w_{i,j}^{(k,l)} = SoftMax\left(\hat{w}_{i,j}^{(k,l)} \right).$$ (6.14)

Now, let's begin building the generalized GT by defining some utility methods as follows:

```
import torch
import torch.nn as nn
import torch.nn.functional as F

import dgl
import dgl.function as fn
import numpy as np

"""
    Graph Transformer Layer with node features only.

"""

"""
    Util functions
"""
def scaled_exp(field, scale_constant):
    def func(edges):
        # clamp for softmax numerical stability
        return {field: torch.exp((edges.data[field] / scale_constant).
clamp(-5, 5))}

    return func
```

Then, let's start defining the MHA layer using the following code snippet:

```
class MultiHeadAttentionLayer(nn.Module):
    def __init__(self, in_dim, out_dim, num_heads, use_bias):
        super().__init__()

        self.out_dim = out_dim
```

```
        self.num_heads = num_heads

        if use_bias:
            self.Q = nn.Linear(in_dim, out_dim * num_heads, bias=True)
            self.K = nn.Linear(in_dim, out_dim * num_heads, bias=True)
            self.V = nn.Linear(in_dim, out_dim * num_heads, bias=True)
        else:
            self.Q = nn.Linear(in_dim, out_dim * num_heads, bias=False)
            self.K = nn.Linear(in_dim, out_dim * num_heads, bias=False)
            self.V = nn.Linear(in_dim, out_dim * num_heads, bias=False)


    def propagate_attention(self, g):
        # Compute attention score
        g.apply_edges(src_dot_dst('K_h', 'Q_h', 'score')) #, edges)
        g.apply_edges(scaled_exp('score', np.sqrt(self.out_dim)))

        # Send weighted values to target nodes
        eids = g.edges()
        g.send_and_recv(eids, fn.src_mul_edge('V_h', 'score', 'V_h'),
fn.sum('V_h', 'wV'))
        g.send_and_recv(eids, fn.copy_edge('score', 'score'),
fn.sum('score', 'z'))

    def forward(self, g, h):

        Q_h = self.Q(h)
        K_h = self.K(h)
        V_h = self.V(h)

        # Reshaping into [num_nodes, num_heads, feat_dim] to
        # get projections for multi-head attention
        g.ndata['Q_h'] = Q_h.view(-1, self.num_heads, self.out_dim)
        g.ndata['K_h'] = K_h.view(-1, self.num_heads, self.out_dim)
        g.ndata['V_h'] = V_h.view(-1, self.num_heads, self.out_dim)

        self.propagate_attention(g)

        head_out = g.ndata['wV']/g.ndata['z']

        return head_out
```

At this point, we can implement the generalized GT layer (without edge information) using the following code snippet:

```
class GraphTransformerLayer(nn.Module):
    """
        Param:
    """
    def __init__(self, in_dim, out_dim, num_heads, dropout=0.0,
layer_norm=False, batch_norm=True, residual=True, use_bias=False):
        super().__init__()

        self.in_channels = in_dim
        self.out_channels = out_dim
```

```
        self.num_heads = num_heads
        self.dropout = dropout
        self.residual = residual
        self.layer_norm = layer_norm
        self.batch_norm = batch_norm

        self.attention = MultiHeadAttentionLayer(in_dim, out_dim//
num_heads, num_heads, use_bias)

        self.O = nn.Linear(out_dim, out_dim)

        if self.layer_norm:
            self.layer_norm1 = nn.LayerNorm(out_dim)

        if self.batch_norm:
            self.batch_norm1 = nn.BatchNorm1d(out_dim)

        # FFN
        self.FFN_layer1 = nn.Linear(out_dim, out_dim*2)
        self.FFN_layer2 = nn.Linear(out_dim*2, out_dim)

        if self.layer_norm:
            self.layer_norm2 = nn.LayerNorm(out_dim)

        if self.batch_norm:
            self.batch_norm2 = nn.BatchNorm1d(out_dim)

    def forward(self, g, h):
        h_in1 = h # for first residual connection

        # multi-head attention out
        attn_out = self.attention(g, h)
        h = attn_out.view(-1, self.out_channels)

        h = F.dropout(h, self.dropout, training=self.training)

        h = self.O(h)

        if self.residual:
            h = h_in1 + h # residual connection

        if self.layer_norm:
            h = self.layer_norm1(h)

        if self.batch_norm:
            h = self.batch_norm1(h)

        h_in2 = h # for second residual connection

        # FFN
        h = self.FFN_layer1(h)
        h = F.relu(h)
        h = F.dropout(h, self.dropout, training=self.training)
        h = self.FFN_layer2(h)

        if self.residual:
```

```
        h = h_in2 + h # residual connection

    if self.layer_norm:
        h = self.layer_norm2(h)

    if self.batch_norm:
        h = self.batch_norm2(h)

    return h
```

Moving forward, we can implement the edge-aware generalized GT layer by, first, developing MLP process–vectorized graph representation using the following code snippet:

```
import torch
import torch.nn as nn
import torch.nn.functional as F

"""
    Dense layers after graph vector representation
"""

class MLPReadout(nn.Module):

    def __init__(self, input_dim, output_dim, L=2): #L=nb_hidden_layers
        super().__init__()
        list_dense_layers = [ nn.Linear( input_dim//2**l , input_
dim//2**(l+1) , bias=True ) for l in range(L) ]
        list_dense_layers.append(nn.Linear( input_dim//2**L , output_
dim , bias=True ))
        self.dense_layers = nn.ModuleList(list_dense_layers)
        self.L = L

    def forward(self, x):
        y = x
        for l in range(self.L):
            y = self.dense_layers[l](y)
            y = F.relu(y)
        y = self.dense_layers[self.L](y)
        return y
```

Here, we implement some utility functions related to edge features:

```
import torch
import torch.nn as nn
import torch.nn.functional as F

import dgl
import dgl.function as fn
import numpy as np

"""
    Graph Transformer Layer with node and edge features
```

```
"""

def src_map_dst(src_field, dst_field, out_field):
    def func(edges):
        return {out_field: (edges.src[src_field] * edges.
dst[dst_field])}
    return func

def scaleit(field, scale_constant):
    def func(edges):
        return {field: ((edges.data[field]) / scale_constant)}
    return func

# Improving implicit attention scores with explicit edge features, if
available
def enh_exp_atten(implicit_attn, explicit_edge):
    """
        implicit_attn: the output of K Q
        explicit_edge: the explicit edge features
    """
    def func(edges):
        return {implicit_attn: (edges.data[implicit_attn] * edges.
data[explicit_edge])}
    return func

# To copy edge features to be passed to FFN_e
def out_edge_feats(edge_feat):
    def func(edges):
        return {'e_out': edges.data[edge_feat]}
    return func

def exp(field):
    def func(edges):
        # clamp for softmax numerical stability
        return {field: torch.exp((edges.data[field].sum(-1,
keepdim=True)).clamp(-5, 5))}
    return func
```

Typically, the MHA is reimplemented to consider edge information as follows:

```
class MultiHeadAttentionLayer(nn.Module):
    def __init__(self, in_dim, out_dim, num_heads, use_bias):
        super().__init__()

        self.out_dim = out_dim
        self.num_heads = num_heads

        if use_bias:
            self.Q = nn.Linear(in_dim, out_dim * num_heads, bias=True)
            self.K = nn.Linear(in_dim, out_dim * num_heads, bias=True)
            self.V = nn.Linear(in_dim, out_dim * num_heads, bias=True)
            self.proj_e = nn.Linear(in_dim, out_dim * num_heads, bias=True)
        else:
```

```
            self.Q = nn.Linear(in_dim, out_dim * num_heads, bias=False)
            self.K = nn.Linear(in_dim, out_dim * num_heads, bias=False)
            self.V = nn.Linear(in_dim, out_dim * num_heads, bias=False)
            self.proj_e = nn.Linear(in_dim, out_dim * num_heads, bias=False)

    def propagate_attention(self, g):
        # Compute attention score
        g.apply_edges(src_map_dst('K_h', 'Q_h', 'score')) #, edges)

        # scaling
        g.apply_edges(scalit('score', np.sqrt(self.out_dim)))

        # Use available edge features to modify the scores
        g.apply_edges(enh_exp_atten('score', 'proj_e'))

        # Copy edge features as e_out to be passed to FFN_e
        g.apply_edges(out_edge_features('score'))

        # softmax
        g.apply_edges(exp('score'))

        # Send weighted values to target nodes
        eids = g.edges()
        g.send_and_recv(eids, fn.src_mul_edge('V_h', 'score', 'V_h'),
fn.sum('V_h', 'wV'))
        g.send_and_recv(eids, fn.copy_edge('score', 'score'),
fn.sum('score', 'z'))
    def forward(self, g, h, e):

        Q_h = self.Q(h)
        K_h = self.K(h)
        V_h = self.V(h)
        proj_e = self.proj_e(e)

        # Reshaping into [num_nodes, num_heads, feat_dim] to
        # get projections for multi-head attention
        g.ndata['Q_h'] = Q_h.view(-1, self.num_heads, self.out_dim)
        g.ndata['K_h'] = K_h.view(-1, self.num_heads, self.out_dim)
        g.ndata['V_h'] = V_h.view(-1, self.num_heads, self.out_dim)
        g.edata['proj_e'] = proj_e.view(-1, self.num_heads, self.out_dim)

        self.propagate_attention(g)

        h_out = g.ndata['wV'] / (g.ndata['z'] + torch.full_like
(g.ndata['z'], 1e-6)) # adding eps to all values here
        e_out = g.edata['e_out']

        return h_out, e_out
```

Using the above functions, the generalized GT layer can be implemented as follows:

```
class GraphTransformerLayer(nn.Module):
    """
        Param:
```

```
        """
    def __init__(self, in_dim, out_dim, num_heads, dropout=0.0,
layer_norm=False, batch_norm=True, residual=True, use_bias=False):
        super().__init__()

        self.in_channels = in_dim
        self.out_channels = out_dim
        self.num_heads = num_heads
        self.dropout = dropout
        self.residual = residual
        self.layer_norm = layer_norm
        self.batch_norm = batch_norm

        self.attention = MultiHeadAttentionLayer(in_dim, out_dim//
num_heads, num_heads, use_bias)

        self.O_h = nn.Linear(out_dim, out_dim)
        self.O_e = nn.Linear(out_dim, out_dim)

        if self.layer_norm:
            self.layer_norm1_h = nn.LayerNorm(out_dim)
            self.layer_norm1_e = nn.LayerNorm(out_dim)
        if self.batch_norm:
            self.batch_norm1_h = nn.BatchNorm1d(out_dim)
            self.batch_norm1_e = nn.BatchNorm1d(out_dim)

        # FFN for h
        self.FFN_h_layer1 = nn.Linear(out_dim, out_dim*2)
        self.FFN_h_layer2 = nn.Linear(out_dim*2, out_dim)

        # FFN for e
        self.FFN_e_layer1 = nn.Linear(out_dim, out_dim*2)
        self.FFN_e_layer2 = nn.Linear(out_dim*2, out_dim)

        if self.layer_norm:
            self.layer_norm2_h = nn.LayerNorm(out_dim)
            self.layer_norm2_e = nn.LayerNorm(out_dim)

        if self.batch_norm:
            self.batch_norm2_h = nn.BatchNorm1d(out_dim)
            self.batch_norm2_e = nn.BatchNorm1d(out_dim)

    def forward(self, g, h, e):
        h_in1 = h # for first residual connection
        e_in1 = e # for first residual connection

        # multi-head attention out
        h_attn_out, e_attn_out = self.attention(g, h, e)

        h = h_attn_out.view(-1, self.out_channels)
        e = e_attn_out.view(-1, self.out_channels)

        h = F.dropout(h, self.dropout, training=self.training)
        e = F.dropout(e, self.dropout, training=self.training)

        h = self.O_h(h)
```

```
e = self.O_e(e)

if self.residual:
    h = h_in1 + h # residual connection
    e = e_in1 + e # residual connection

if self.layer_norm:
    h = self.layer_norm1_h(h)
    e = self.layer_norm1_e(e)

if self.batch_norm:
    h = self.batch_norm1_h(h)
    e = self.batch_norm1_e(e)

h_in2 = h # for second residual connection
e_in2 = e # for second residual connection
# FFN for h
h = self.FFN_h_layer1(h)
h = F.relu(h)
h = F.dropout(h, self.dropout, training=self.training)
h = self.FFN_h_layer2(h)

# FFN for e
e = self.FFN_e_layer1(e)
e = F.relu(e)
e = F.dropout(e, self.dropout, training=self.training)
e = self.FFN_e_layer2(e)

if self.residual:
    h = h_in2 + h # residual connection
    e = e_in2 + e # residual connection

if self.layer_norm:
    h = self.layer_norm2_h(h)
    e = self.layer_norm2_e(e)

if self.batch_norm:
    h = self.batch_norm2_h(h)
    e = self.batch_norm2_e(e)

return h, e
```

Finally, the above layers can be used to implement the generalized transformer network as follows:

6.5 Graph Transformer Network (GTN)

Recently, graph networks have been extensively adopted in numerous graph representation learning tasks by performing convolution or attention operations explicitly on graphs, making use of the features of nodes and neighbors in the spectral domain. However, a key problem of these networks is the

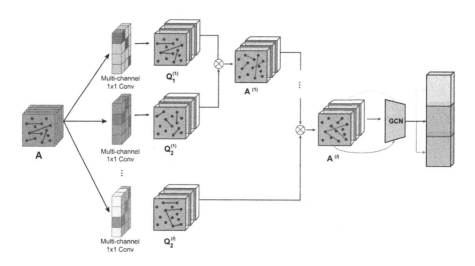

FIGURE 6.5
Illustrated of GTN.

(Adapted from Yun *et al.*, 2019.)

operation on the assumption that the underlying graph structure is static and homogeneous. Meanwhile, the GATs debated in the previous sections are accepted as the static graph structure, a noisy graph containing missing edges leads to ineffective modeling with incorrect neighbors on the graph. Many types of tasks consist of different kinds of nodes and connecting edges thereby termed a heterogeneous graph. An inexperienced method is to disregard the node/edge kinds and regard them as a homogeneous graph. However, this is still suboptimal since models could not exploit the underlying information. GTN (Yun *et al.*, 2019) was proposed to learn to transmute a heterogeneous graph into valuable meta-path graph reorientation and fully capture node representation on the graphs. GTINs could be regarded as a graph similar to spatial transformer networks (Mehta and Rastegari, 2021) that obviously proposed to model the spatial renovations of input features.

In the GTN, graph convolutions were adopted to effectively model valuable representations for node classification. The implementation of the graph convolution layer (GTConv) is given as follows:

```
import torch
import numpy as np
import torch.nn as nn
import torch.nn.functional as F
import math
from torch_scatter import scatter_add
import torch_sparse

class GraphTransformerConv(nn.Module):
```

```
def __init__(self, in_channels, out_channels, softmax_flag=True):
    super(GraphTansformerConv, self).__init__()
    self.in_channels = in_channels
    self.out_channels = out_channels
    self.weight = nn.Parameter(th.Tensor(out_channels, in_channels))
    self.softmax_flag = softmax_flag
    self.reset_parameters()

def reset_parameters(self):
    nn.init.normal_(self.weight, std=0.01)

def forward(self, A):
    if self.softmax_flag:
        Filter = F.softmax(self.weight, dim=1)
    else:
        Filter = self.weight
    num_channels = Filter.shape[0]
    results = []
    for i in range(num_channels):
        for j, g in enumerate(A):
            A[j].edata['w_sum'] = g.edata['w'] * Filter[i][j]
        sum_g = dgl.adj_sum_graph(A, 'w_sum')
        results.append(sum_g)
    return results
```

The GTN could learn meta-paths for prearranged graph representation by integrating graph convolution to learn from meta-path graphs. This enables the model to learn more valuable meta-paths and result in practically numerous graph convolutions by means of manifold meta-path graph representations. The GT layer was designed to generate a meta-path graph, as shown in Figure 6.5. It consists of two mechanisms. First, the GT layer delicately chooses two graph constructions from entrant adjacency matrices. Second, the GT layer learns a new graph construction by the conformation of two relationships. In particular, the SoftMax function is applied to calculate the convex mixture of adjacency matrices by 1×1 convolutions as depicted in Figure 6.5. From practical viewpoint, the implementation of the GT layer is given as follows:

```
class GraphTansformer(nn.Module):

    def __init__(self, in_channels, out_channels, num_nodes, first=True):
        super(GTLayer, self).__init__()
        self.in_channels = in_channels
        self.out_channels = out_channels
        self.first = first
        self.num_nodes = num_nodes
        if self.first == True:
            self.conv1 = GraphTansformerConv(in_channels, out_channels,
num_nodes)
            self.conv2 = GraphTansformerConv(in_channels, out_channels,
num_nodes)
        else:
```

```
            self.conv1 = GraphTransformerConv(in_channels, out_channels,
num_nodes)

    def forward(self, A, num_nodes, H_=None, eval=False):
        if self.first == True:
            result_A = self.conv1(A, num_nodes, eval=eval)
            result_B = self.conv2(A, num_nodes, eval=eval)
            W = [(F.softmax(self.conv1.weight, dim=1)),(F.softmax
(self.conv2.weight, dim=1))]
        else:
            result_A = H_
            result_B = self.conv1(A, num_nodes, eval=eval)
            W = [(F.softmax(self.conv1.weight, dim=1))]
        H = []
        for i in range(len(result_A)):
            a_edge, a_value = result_A[i]
            b_edge, b_value = result_B[i]
            mat_a = torch.sparse_coo_tensor(a_edge, a_value, (num_
nodes, num_nodes)).to(a_edge.device)
            mat_b = torch.sparse_coo_tensor(b_edge, b_value, (num_
nodes, num_nodes)).to(a_edge.device)
            mat = torch.sparse.mm(mat_a, mat_b).coalesce()
            edges, values = mat.indices(), mat.values()
            H.append((edges, values))
        return H, W
```

At this point, we are ready to create the GTN architecture as follows:

```
class GraphTansformerNetwork(nn.Module):

    def __init__(self, num_edge, num_channels, w_in, w_out, num_class,
num_nodes, num_layers):
        super(GraphTansformerNetwork, self).__init__()
        self.num_edge = num_edge
        self.num_channels = num_channels
        self.num_nodes = num_nodes
        self.w_in = w_in
        self.w_out = w_out
        self.num_class = num_class
        self.num_layers = num_layers

        layers = []
        for i in range(num_layers):
            if i == 0:
                layers.append(GraphTansformer(num_edge, num_channels,
num_nodes, first=True))
            else:
                layers.append(GraphTansformer(num_edge, num_channels,
num_nodes, first=False))
        self.layers = nn.ModuleList(layers)

        self.gcl = GraphConvolutionalLayer(in_channels=self.w_in,
out_channels=w_out)
        self.linear = nn.Linear(self.w_out*self.num_channels, self.
num_class)
```

```python
    def normalization(self, H, num_nodes):
        norm_H = []
        for i in range(self.num_channels):
            edge, value=H[i]
            deg_row, deg_col = self.norm(edge.detach(),
num_nodes, value)
            value = (deg_row) * value
            norm_H.append((edge, value))
        return norm_H

    def norm(self, edge_index, num_nodes, edge_weight, improved=False,
dtype=None):
        if edge_weight is None:
            edge_weight = torch.ones((edge_index.size(1), ),
                                     dtype=dtype,
                                     device=edge_index.device)
        edge_weight = edge_weight.view(-1)
        assert edge_weight.size(0) == edge_index.size(1)
        row, col = edge_index
        deg = scatter_add(edge_weight.clone(), row, dim=0,
dim_size=num_nodes)
        deg_inv_sqrt = deg.pow(-1)
        deg_inv_sqrt[deg_inv_sqrt == float('inf')] = 0

        return deg_inv_sqrt[row], deg_inv_sqrt[col]

    def forward(self, A, X, target_x, target, num_nodes=None,
eval=False, node_labels=None):
        if num_nodes is None:
            num_nodes = self.num_nodes
        Ws = []
        for i in range(self.num_layers):
            if i == 0:
                H, W = self.layers[i](A, num_nodes, eval=eval)
            else:
                H, W = self.layers[i](A, num_nodes, H, eval=eval)
            H = self.normalization(H, num_nodes)
            Ws.append(W)
        for i in range(self.num_channels):
            edge_index, edge_weight = H[i][0], H[i][1]
            if i==0:
                X_ = self.gcl(X,edge_index=edge_index.detach(),
edge_weight=edge_weight)
                X_ = F.relu(X_)
            else:
                X_tmp = F.relu(self.gcl(X,edge_index=edge_index.
detach(), edge_weight=edge_weight))
                X_ = torch.cat((X_,X_tmp), dim=1)

        y = self.linear(X_[target_x])

        return y
```

6.6 Case Study

It is estimated that attack campaigns by criminal gangs and nation-states cost the United States economy up to $109 billion annually (Fanning, 2015). Governments and huge corporations are the primary targets of these complex cyber-attacks, which aim to disrupt key services and steal intellectual property (Reddy, Kolli and Balakrishnan, 2021). Deterring these attacks necessitates the creation of powerful antivirus software that can quickly detect new forms of malicious software before they can spread over a network and infect other computers. Because most newly discovered malware is polymorphic (Tajoddin and Jalili, 2018), signature-centered malware detection is no longer effective (Scott, 2017). Instead, researchers are turning to other methods of malware detection that do not rely on signatures. To deal with these challenges, the field of cyber-security has recently moved toward graph representations of complex malware as they are able to model the complex interactions, necessitate no feature engineering, retain structural information, and are strong to public mystification methods. In this regard, MALNET (Freitas *et al.*, 2020) was presented as the first huge-scale ontology of malware function call graphs (FCGs), whereby each FGC characterizes calling relations among functionalities in a software program, where functions act as the nodes of the graph and inter-procedural calls act as the edges of the graph. MALNET comprises a total of 1.2 million graphs, averaging over 35,000 edges and 15,000 nodes per graph, across a topology of 47 classes and 696 families of malware. Given the GATs discussed in the previous sections, we use the MALNET as the case study to evaluate the potential of these networks in detecting different types of malware. The detailed implementation of different GATs on the MALNET is given in the supplementary materials of this chapter. The supplementary materials of this chapter also provide the readers with recommendations for further reading about the content of this chapter. The repository of supplementary materials is given in https://github.com/DEEPOLOGY-AI/Book-Graph-Neural-Network/tree/main/Chapter%206.

References

Bahdanau, D., Cho, K. H. and Bengio, Y. (2015) 'Neural Machine Translation by Jointly Learning to Align and Translate', in *3rd International Conference on Learning Representations, ICLR 2015 – Conference Track Proceedings*.

Brody, S., Alon, U. and Yahav, E. (2021) 'How Attentive are Graph Attention Networks?' doi: http://arxiv.org/abs/2105.14491.

Dwivedi, V. P. and Bresson, X. (2020) 'A Generalization of Transformer Networks to Graphs'. doi: http://arxiv.org/abs/2012.09699.

Fanning, K. (2015) 'Minimizing the Cost of Malware', *Journal of Corporate Accounting and Finance*. doi: 10.1002/jcaf.22029.

Freitas, S. *et al.* (2020) 'A Large-Scale Database for Graph Representation Learning'. doi: http://arxiv.org/abs/2011.07682.

Mehta, S. and Rastegari, M. (2021) 'MobileViT: Light-Weight, General-Purpose, and Mobile-Friendly Vision Transformer'. doi: http://arxiv.org/abs/2110.02178.

Reddy, V., Kolli, N. and Balakrishnan, N. (2021) 'Malware Detection and Classification Using Community Detection and Social Network Analysis', *Journal of Computer Virology and Hacking Techniques*. doi: 10.1007/s11416-021-00387-x.

Scott, J. (2017) 'Signature Based Malware Detection is Dead', in *Cybersecurity Think Tank, Institute for Critical Infrastructure Technology*.

Tajoddin, A. and Jalili, S. (2018) 'HM3alD: Polymorphic Malware Detection using Program Behavior-aware Hidden Markov Model', *Applied Sciences (Switzerland)*. doi: 10.3390/app8071044.

Vaswani, A. *et al.* (2017) 'Attention is All You Need', in *Advances in Neural Information Processing Systems*, pp. 5999–6009.

Veličković, P. *et al.* (2018) 'Graph Attention Networks', in *6th International Conference on Learning Representations, ICLR 2018 – Conference Track Proceedings*. doi: 10.1007/978-3-031-01587-8_7.

Yun, S. *et al.* (2019) 'Graph Transformer Networks', in *Advances in Neural Information Processing Systems*.

7

Recurrent Graph Neural Networks:
A Journey from Start to End

7.1 Introduction

In a conventional deep network, higher-level representations are extracted from input data through subsequent layers of learning parameters. In the context of vision-based deep networks, the early layers identify the existence of low-level representations such as short curves and lines, while the latter layers identify the existence of high-level representations such as compound patterns. The high-level characteristics generated by these successive layers could then be given to a SoftMax layer or a single neuron for generating the final decision. In sequential or temporal data, recurrent neural networks (RNNs), such as long-short-term memory (LSTM) and gated recurrent units (GRUs), show great achievements because of its ability to model the hidden representation based on the historical information rather than instance information.

Likewise, the early graph neural networks (GNNs) learn high-level representations from the input graphs by means of consecutive abstraction of node and edge features, which then are directed to some kind of output operations. In simple words, GNNs transform input graphs into convenient embeddings, which are manipulated through the network to obtain correct outcomes. Unfortunately, some GNNs might only deal with directed acyclic graphs, and some of them necessitate the received graphs to contain "supersource" nodes, and others necessitate heuristic methods to manipulate the cyclical structure of particular graphs. Characteristically, the legacy recursive approaches depend on "unfolding" distinct snapshot of graphs to a determinate set of trees, as recursive counterparts that could, in the sequel, be transformed valuable embeddings by recurrent networks.

In this chapter, we study the recurrent GNNs as an extension to the standard GNNs that deliver solution that can be functional to general graphs. Given that the node features are normally adopted as the initial input, the standard graph layers (convolutional, attention, transformer) are combined with recurrent nets to model the evolution of their weights or propagate the learned topological representations from one timestep to the next timestep. Instead of generating embedding for the entire input graph through recurrent

DOI: 10.1201/9781003329701-7

encoding operation, the recurrent GNNs generate embeddings at node level via message passing scheme for elastic information proliferation. In the following sections, we explore the state-of-the-art recurrent graph networks from both theoretical and technical perspectives.

7.2 Tree-Long Short-Term Memory

The primary downside of the conventional LSTM models described in Chapter 1 depends on the fact that they just for severely sequential information broadcast. Thus, Tree-LSTM was proposed to extend the traditional LSTM by allowing richer networking topologies whereby each LSTM cell is capable of handling information in a form of topological tree of nodes. The Tree-LSTM model early introduced in Tai, Socher and Manning (2015) based on the notion of presenting syntactical information of language modeling operations by replacing the traditional chain-based LSTM with tree-based LSTM. The challenge in training Tree-LSTMs is batching—a typical practice for accelerating the training deep learning to systems. Nevertheless, the inherent diversity of shapes of trees makes the parallelization a more challenging task. A possible remedy to this issue is to combine overall trees in a one graph in which the message passing can have induced them under guidance from the assembly of constituting tree. Before diving into more details, we should note that there exist two kinds of Tree-LSTM, namely, Child-Sum Tree-LSTMs, and *N-ary* Tree-LSTMs. In the following subsections, we explore the design of both types of Tree-LSTMs for constituency trees.

7.2.1 Child-Sum Tree-LSTMs

Child-Sum Tree-LSTMs calculate over the hidden representations of a node based on representation from all children without any restriction on the number or order children. This implies that Child-Sum Tree-LSTMs share the learning parameters between children. In particular, given the tree structure with $C(j)$ denoting the group of children of node j. The transition calculations of Child-Sum Tree-LSTM cells can be given as follows:

$$\tilde{h}_j = \sum_{k \in C(j)} h_k, \tag{7.1}$$

where h_k represents the hidden representation of the chilled k of node j.

First, the input gate is calculated as follows:

$$i_j = \sigma\left(W^{(i)}x_j + U^{(i)}\tilde{h}_j + b^{(i)}\right). \tag{7.2}$$

Second, the forget gate is calculated as follows:

$$f_{jk} = \sigma\left(W^{\langle f\rangle}x_j + U^{\langle f\rangle}h_k + b^{\langle f\rangle}\right).$$ (7.3)

Third, the forget gate is calculated as follows:

$$o_j = \sigma\left(W^{\langle o\rangle}x_j + U^{\langle o\rangle}\tilde{h}_j + b^{\langle o\rangle}\right).$$ (7.4)

Fourth, apply pointwise nonlinearity using hyperbolic tangent function then calculate the memory cell state as follows:

$$u_j = \tanh\left(W^{\langle u\rangle}x_j + U^{\langle u\rangle}\tilde{h}_j + b^{\langle u\rangle}\right),$$ (7.5)

$$c_j = i_j \odot u_j + \sum_{k\in C(j)} f_{jk} \odot c_k.$$ (7.6)

Finally, the hidden sate of the node j is calculated as follows:

$$h_j = o_j \cdot \tanh\left(c_j\right).$$ (7.7)

Instinctively, the parameter matrices in the above formulas can be interpreted as encoding relationships between the constituent trajectories of the Tree-LSTM. Given that the Child-Sum Tree-LSTM node builds its representation according to the summation of the child-hidden states h_k, it is appropriate for trees with unordered children with a great branching factor. This way, Child-Sum Tree-LSTM is an appropriate option for dealing with dependency trees, where the number of children of a node could be extremely inconstant. Child-Sum Tree-LSTMs applied to a dependency tree can be referred to as Dependency Tree-LSTM. The following code snippets show the PyTorch implementation of Child-Sum Tree-LSTMs:

```
class ChildSumTreeLSTMCell(nn.Module):
    def __init__(self, x_size, h_size):
        super(ChildSumTreeLSTMCell, self).__init__()
        self.W_iou = nn.Linear(x_size, 3 * h_size, bias=False)
        self.U_iou = nn.Linear(h_size, 3 * h_size, bias=False)
        self.b_iou = nn.Parameter(th.zeros(1, 3 * h_size))
        self.U_f = nn.Linear(h_size, h_size)

    def message_func(self, edges):
        return {'h': edges.src['h'], 'c': edges.src['c']}

    def reduce_func(self, nodes):
        h_tild = th.sum(nodes.mailbox['h'], 1)
        f = th.sigmoid(self.U_f(nodes.mailbox['h']))
```

```
c = th.sum(f * nodes.mailbox['c'], 1)
return {'iou': self.U_iou(h_tild), 'c': c}

def apply_node_func(self, nodes):
    iou = nodes.data['iou'] + self.b_iou
    i, o, u = th.chunk(iou, 3, 1)
    i, o, u = th.sigmoid(i), th.sigmoid(o), th.tanh(u)
    c = i * u + nodes.data['c']
    h = o * th.tanh(c)
    return {'h': h, 'c': c}
```

7.2.2 *N-ary* Tree-LSTMs

Being different from the Child-Sum Tree-LSTMs, the *N-ary* Tree-LSTMs differentiate between positions of children nodes and require a fixed branching threshold (i.e., it operates with a predefined max number of children $(1 \leq ch \leq N)$, each of them has a different set of parameters. In this form of Tree-LSTMs, a memory cell c_j and hidden representation h_j are kept for each node j. The node j receives, as inputs the data vector x_j as well as hidden representations of the child nodes and later calculates the output of gates, as with standard LSTM, to update memory cell c_j and hidden representation h_j as follows:

First, the input gate is calculated as follows:

$$i_j = \sigma \left(W^{\langle i \rangle} x_j + \sum_{q=1}^{N} U_q^{\langle i \rangle} h_j^q + b^{\langle i \rangle} \right). \tag{7.8}$$

Second, the forget gate is calculated as follows:

$$f_{jk} = \sigma \left(W^{\langle f \rangle} x_j + \sum_{q=1}^{N} U_{kq}^{\langle f \rangle} h_j^q + b^{\langle f \rangle} \right). \tag{7.9}$$

Third, the forget gate is calculated as follows:

$$o_j = \sigma \left(W^{\langle o \rangle} x_j + \sum_{q=1}^{N} U_{kq}^{\langle o \rangle} h_j^q + b^{\langle o \rangle} \right). \tag{7.10}$$

Fourth, update the cell state of node j as follows:

$$u_j = \tanh \left(W^{\langle u \rangle} x_j + \sum_{q=1}^{N} U_q^{\langle u \rangle} h_j^q + b^{\langle u \rangle} \right), \tag{7.11}$$

$$c_j = i_j \odot u_j + \sum_{q=1}^{N} f_j^q \odot c_j^q, \tag{7.12}$$

$$h_j = o_j \cdot \tanh\left(c_j\right), \tag{7.13}$$

where h_j^k and c_j^k denote the hidden and cell state of the child k of node j. In Eq. (7.9), $k = 1, 2, \dots, N$.

The adoption of distinct parameter matrices for each child k results in *N-ary* Tree-LSTM cell to model more high-level acclimatization on the states of children of node j, compared to Child-Sum Tree-LSTM cells. Again, Eq. (7.9) describes a parameterization of the forget gate of the kth child node containing "off-diagonal" parameter matrices $U_{kq}^{<f>}$, conditioned on $k! = q$, to enable a better control of information proliferation from children to the parent node. When it comes to applying binary *N-ary* Tree-LSTM cells to binarized constituency trees, it could be called Constituency Tree-LSTM. The following code snippets show the PyTorch implementation of *N-ary* Tree-LSTM:

```
import torch as th
import torch.nn as nn

class TreeLSTMCell(nn.Module):
    def __init__(self, x_size, h_size):
        super(TreeLSTMCell, self).__init__()
        self.W_iou = nn.Linear(x_size, 3 * h_size, bias=False)
        self.U_iou = nn.Linear(2 * h_size, 3 * h_size, bias=False)
        self.b_iou = nn.Parameter(th.zeros(1, 3 * h_size))
        self.U_f = nn.Linear(2 * h_size, 2 * h_size)

    def message_func(self, edges):
        return {'h': edges.src['h'], 'c': edges.src['c']}

    def reduce_func(self, nodes):
        # concatenate h_jl for equation (1), (2), (3), (4)
        h_cat = nodes.mailbox['h'].view(nodes.mailbox['h'].size(0), -1)
        # equation (2)
        f = th.sigmoid(self.U_f(h_cat)).view(*nodes.mailbox['h'].size())
        # second term of equation (5)
        c = th.sum(f * nodes.mailbox['c'], 1)
        return {'iou': self.U_iou(h_cat), 'c': c}

    def apply_node_func(self, nodes):
        # equation (1), (3), (4)
        iou = nodes.data['iou'] + self.b_iou
        i, o, u = th.chunk(iou, 3, 1)
        i, o, u = th.sigmoid(i), th.sigmoid(o), th.tanh(u)
        # equation (5)
        c = i * u + nodes.data['c']
        # equation (6)
        h = o * th.tanh(c)
        return {'h' : h, 'c' : c}
```

Now, we can build the Tree-LSTM model using either Child-Sum Tree-LSTM cell or *N-ary* Tree-LSTM using the following code snippets:

```
class TreeLSTM(nn.Module):
    def __init__(self,
                 num_vocabs,
                 x_size,
                 h_size,
                 num_classes,
                 dropout,
                 pretrained_emb=None):
        super(TreeLSTM, self).__init__()
        self.x_size = x_size
        self.embedding = nn.Embedding(num_vocabs, x_size)
        if pretrained_emb is not None:
            print('Using glove')
            self.embedding.weight.data.copy_(pretrained_emb)
            self.embedding.weight.requires_grad = True
        self.dropout = nn.Dropout(dropout)
        self.linear = nn.Linear(h_size, num_classes)
        self.cell = TreeLSTMCell(x_size, h_size)

    def forward(self, batch, h, c):

        g = batch.graph
        # to heterogenous graph
        g = dgl.graph(g.edges())
        # feed embedding
        embeds = self.embedding(batch.wordid * batch.mask)
        g.ndata['iou'] = self.cell.W_iou(self.dropout(embeds)) *
batch.mask.float().unsqueeze(-1)
        g.ndata['h'] = h
        g.ndata['c'] = c
        # propagate
        dgl.prop_nodes_topo(g,
                        message_func=self.cell.message_func,
                        reduce_func=self.cell.reduce_func,
                        apply_node_func=self.cell.apply_node_func)
        # compute logits
        h = self.dropout(g.ndata.pop('h'))
        logits = self.linear(h)
        return logits
```

7.3 Gated Graph Sequence Neural Networks

To recap, the conventional graph networks are operated by mapping input graphs into outputs through two processing phases, first, the model propagation phase, in which the network is calculated, which extracted the representations of nodes. Second, an output function generates an output by mapping the extracted node representations to the corresponding class-labels. The model is fully differentiable; hence, the learning parameters can be updated and optimized via the gradient-optimizer. In particular, Almeida-Pineda algorithm (Almeida, 1987; Pineda, 1987) is used for learning, which alleviates the need to save the middle states for computing the gradients. However, the main shortcoming of the Almeida-Pineda algorithm is the need to constrain the parameters to make propagation phase as a reduction map, which is essential to guarantee convergence, but it could bind the expressivity of the network. The gated GNN (Li *et al.*, 2016) was proposed as an adaptation to standard GNNs to better suit sequential data. The major adjustment of GNNs lies in the adoption of GRUs (Cho *et al.*, 2014) to redesign the propagation model in such a way that enables taking into account the input vectors from preceding node sequences. Thus, the rudimentary recurrence of the propagation model can be defined as follows:

First, perform initialization by coping the node annotations into the first components of the elements of state and set the remaining to zeros:

$$h_n^1 = \left[x_n^T, 0 \right]^T. \tag{7.14}$$

Second, the information flow between various nodes of the graph through receiving and leaving edges with parameters reliant on the type and direction of edge:

$$a_n^t = A_n^T \left[h_1^{t-1}, \ldots, h_{|\mathcal{N}|}^{t-1} \right]. \tag{7.15}$$

The residual part operates like GRU by integrating historical information from different nodes and from the earlier timesteps to calculate the hidden state of each node.

The reset gate is calculated as follows:

$$r_n^t = \sigma \left(a_n^t \cdot W_r + h_n^{t-1} \cdot U_r + b_r \right). \tag{7.16}$$

The updated gate is calculated as follows:

$$z_n^t = \sigma \left(a_n^t \cdot W_z + h_n^{t-1} \cdot U_z + b_z \right). \tag{7.17}$$

The hidden state is calculated as follows:

$$\tilde{h}_n^t = \tanh \left(X_t \cdot W_{xh} + \left(R_t \odot H_{t-1} \right) \cdot U + b_h \right), \tag{7.18}$$

$$h_n^t = z_n^t \odot \tilde{h}_n^t + \left(1 - z_{nt}^t \right) \odot h_n^{t-1}. \tag{7.19}$$

Technically speaking, let's begin implementing the gated layer by importing necessary libraries and defining the gated GNN as follows:

```python
import torch as th
from torch import nn
from torch.nn import init
from dgl import function as fn
import dgl
from dgl.nn.pytorch import GlobalAttentionPooling
import torch

class GatedGraphConvolution(nn.Module):

    def __init__(self,
                 in_features,
                 out_features,
                 n_steps,
                 n_etypes,
                 bias=True):
        super(GatedGraphConvolution, self).__init__()
        self._in_features = in_features
        self._out_features = out_features
        self._n_steps = n_steps
        self._n_etypes = n_etypes
        self.linears = nn.ModuleList(
            [nn.Linear(out_features, out_features) for _ in range(n_etypes)]
        )
        self.gru = nn.GRUCell(out_features, out_features, bias=bias)
        self.reset_parameters()

    def reset_parameters(self):
        r"""

        Hint: Reinitialize the learning parmaters with Glorot uniform method.

        """
        gain = init.calculate_gain('relu')
        self.gru.reset_parameters()
        for linear in self.linears:
            init.xavier_normal_(linear.weight, gain=gain)
            init.zeros_(linear.bias)

    def set_allow_zero_in_degree(self, set_value):
        r"""

        Hint
        ----
        Set allow_zero_in_degree flag based on set_value paramters
        ----
        """
        self._allow_zero_in_degree = set_value

    def forward(self, graph, feature, etypes=None):
        with graph.local_scope():
            assert graph.is_homogeneous, \
                "not a homogeneous graph; convert it with to_homogeneous " \
                "and pass in the edge type as argument"
            if self._n_etypes != 1:
                assert etypes.min() >= 0 and etypes.max() < self._n_etypes, \
                    "edge type indices out of range [0, {})".format(
                        self._n_etypes)

            zero_pad = feature.new_zeros(
```

```
                    (feature.shape[0], self._out_features - feature.shape[1]))
            feature = torch.cat([feature, zero_pad], -1)

        for _ in range(self._n_steps):
            if self._n_etypes == 1 and etypes is None:
                # Fast path when graph has only one edge type
                graph.ndata['h'] = self.linears[0](feature)
                graph.update_all(fn.copy_u('h', 'm'), fn.sum('m', 'a'))
                a = graph.ndata.pop('a')  # (N, D)
            else:
                graph.ndata['h'] = feature
                for i in range(self._n_etypes):
                    eids = torch.nonzero(
                        etypes == i, as_tuple=False).view(-1).
type(graph.idtype)
                    if len(eids) > 0:
                        graph.apply_edges(
                            lambda edges: {
                                'W_e*h': self.linears[i](edges.
src['h'])},
                            eids
                        )
                graph.update_all(fn.copy_e('W_e*h', 'm'), fn.sum('m', 'a'))
                a = graph.ndata.pop('a')  # (N, D)
            feature = self.gru(a, feature)
        return feature
```

7.3.1 Graph Classification

In traditional GNNs (Scarselli *et al.*, 2009), there is no point in generating initial node representations for the reason that the reduction map restriction guarantees that the static point is autonomous of the initializations. The gated GNN no longer follows this setting as it allows the inclusion of the labels of node as supplementary inputs. To discriminate, these labels of nodes are adopted as inputs from the labels announced previously, and this is known as the node annotations. It is worth mentioning that the adoption of GRU model in the propagation model implies the use of backpropagation-through-time to calculate the gradients. Another distinct point about gated GCN lies in the fact that the recurrence is unrolled for T timesteps instead of unrolling up to convergence.

There are numerous categories of single-step outputs that could be generated by gated GNN for dissimilar circumstances. Among them, graph-level outputs are commonly encountered in graph classification tasks. Thus, the gated GNN can express the graph level representation as follows:

$$h_G = \tanh\left(\sum_{n \in \mathcal{N}} \sigma\left(i\left(h_n^t, x_n\right)\right) \odot \tanh\left(h_n^t\right)\right), \tag{7.20}$$

where $\sigma\left(i\left(h_n^t, x_n\right)\right)$ functions as a soft attention strategy for determining nodes that are pertinent to the existing graph-level job. $i\left(h_n^t, x_n\right)$ represents neural network receiving h_n^t and x_n as concatenated input, which is processed to generate output scores, that is, classification scores, where σ represents a sigmoid function and symbol ⊙ denotes the Hamdard product. Now, let's give a look on the PyTorch implementation of gated GNN for graph classification task:

```python
class GatedGraphConvolutionNet(nn.Module):
    def __init__(self,
                    annotation_size,
                    out_features,
                    n_steps,
                    n_etypes,
                    num_classes):
        super(GatedGraphConvolutionNet, self).__init__()

        self.annotation_size = annotation_size
        self.out_features = out_features

        self.ggnn = GatedGraphConvolution(in_features=out_features,
                                out_features=out_features,
                                n_steps=n_steps,
                                n_etypes=n_etypes)

        pooling_gate_nn = nn.Linear(annotation_size + out_features, 1)
        self.pooling = GlobalAttentionPooling(pooling_gate_nn)
        self.output_layer = nn.Linear(annotation_size + out_features,
num_classes)

        self.loss_fn = nn.CrossEntropyLoss()

    def forward(self, graph, labels=None):
        etypes = graph.edata.pop('type')
        annotation = graph.ndata.pop('annotation').float()

        assert annotation.size()[-1] == self.annotation_size

        node_num = graph.number_of_nodes()

        zero_pad = torch.zeros([node_num, self.out_features - self.
annotation_size],
                            dtype=torch.float, device=annotation.device)

        h1 = torch.cat([annotation, zero_pad], -1)
        out = self.ggnn(graph, h1, etypes)

        out = torch.cat([out, annotation], -1)

        out = self.pooling(graph, out)

        logits = self.output_layer(out)
        preds = torch.argmax(logits, -1)
        if labels is not None:
            loss = self.loss_fn(logits, labels)
            return loss, preds
        return preds
```

7.3.2 Node Section

Again, the gated GNNs support numerous categories of single-step outputs according to the underlying task. Among them, the node selection tasks are supported by gated GNNs as it enables each node to calculate node scores as outputs using SoftMax operation:

$$o_n = g\left(h_n^t, x_n\right), \text{ for } n \in \mathcal{N}. \tag{7.21}$$

Now, let's give a look on the PyTorch implementation of gated GNN for node selection task:

```
class NodeSelectGatedGraphConvolutionNet(nn.Module):
    def __init__(self, annotation_size,out_features, n_steps, n_etypes):
        super(NodeSelectGatedGraphConvolutionNet, self).__init__()

        self.annotation_size = annotation_size
        self.out_features = out_features

        self.ggnn = GatedGraphConvolution(in_features=out_features,
                                out_features=out_features,
                                n_steps=n_steps,
                                n_etypes=n_etypes)

        self.output_layer = nn.Linear(annotation_size + out_features, 1)
        self.loss_fn = nn.CrossEntropyLoss()

    def forward(self, graph, labels=None):
        etypes = graph.edata.pop('type')
        annotation = graph.ndata.pop('annotation').float()

        assert annotation.size()[-1] == self.annotation_size

        node_num = graph.number_of_nodes()

        zero_pad = 'torch.zeros([node_num, self.out_features - self.
annotation_size],
                                dtype=torch.float,
                                device=annotation.device)

        h1 = torch.cat([annotation, zero_pad], -1)
        out = self.ggnn(graph, h1, etypes)

        all_logits = self.output_layer(torch.cat([out, annotation],
-1)).squeeze(-1)
        graph.ndata['logits'] = all_logits

        batch_g = dgl.unbatch(graph)
        preds = []
        if labels is not None:
            loss = 0.0
```

```
for i, g in enumerate(batch_g):
    logits = g.ndata['logits']
    preds.append(torch.argmax(logits))
    if labels is not None:
        logits = logits.unsqueeze(0)
        y = labels[i].unsqueeze(0)
        loss += self.loss_fn(logits, y)

if labels is not None:
    loss /= float(len(batch_g))
    return loss, preds
return preds
```

7.3.3 Sequence Outputs

This section discusses how to adapt gated GNN to generate sequence of outputs by extending it to gated graph sequence neural networks (GGSNNs), where multiple gated GNNs are operating sequentially to generate a sequence of outputs.

In this setting, one of two sceneries can be followed to train GGSNNs, first, state all midway annotations $\mathcal{X}^k$; second, fully train the model using only graphs $\mathcal{X}^0$ and annotation sequences. The first setting could advance performance in the case of having domain knowledge about definite transitional information that ought to be characterized in the interior state of nodes, whereas the second is more a generic method.

To further understand sequential outputs based on experiential annotations, imagine having to make a series of forecasts for a graph, in which each forecast only pertains to a certain area of the graph. It is sufficient to have single bit in each node, signifying if the node has been "understood" thus far, in order to guarantee that we anticipate an output for each portion of the graph precisely once. In some circumstances, a few annotations are enough to fully describe the state-of-the-output function. In this situation, we could want to explicitly add this data to the model by using labels that denote the intended intermediary annotations. Those annotations might be adequate in some circumstances, allowing us to develop a model in which the gated GNNs are deemed conditionally autonomous.

Given the annotated data, $\mathcal{X}^k$, in this situation, the sequence classification problem could be divided into single-stride classification problems during training time and trained as independent gated GNNs. Estimated annotations through one stage would be utilized as inputs for the following stage during testing. Whenever data is completely viewed, this is comparable to learning from directed graphs.

On the other hand, in case of the unavailability of intermediary node annotations $\mathcal{X}^k$ throughout training, the annotation can be considered the hidden states of the models that train the entire GGSNN conjointly through the backward propagation of gradients through the complete sequence.

Now, let's give a look on the PyTorch implementation of GGSNN for a sequential output task:

```python
class SequenceGatedGraphConvolutionNet(nn.Module):
    def __init__(self, annotation_size, out_features, n_steps, n_
etypes, max_seq_length, num_cls):
        super(SequenceGatedGraphConvolutionNet, self).__init__()

        self.annotation_size = annotation_size
        self.out_features = out_features
        self.max_seq_length = max_seq_length

        self.ggnn = GatedGraphConv(in_features=out_features,
out_features=out_features,
                                   n_steps=n_steps,n_etypes=n_etypes)

        self.annotation_out_layer = nn.Linear(annotation_size +
out_features, annotation_size)

        pooling_gate_nn = nn.Linear(annotation_size + out_features, 1)
        self.pooling = GlobalAttentionPooling(pooling_gate_nn)

        self.output_layer = nn.Linear(annotation_size + out_features,
num_cls)
        self.loss_fn = nn.CrossEntropyLoss(reduction='none')

    def forward(self, graph, seq_lengths, ground_truth=None):
        etypes = graph.edata.pop('type')
        annotation = graph.ndata.pop('annotation').float()

        assert annotation.size()[-1] == self.annotation_size

        node_num = graph.number_of_nodes()

        all_logits = []
        for _ in range(self.max_seq_length):
            zero_pad = torch.zeros([node_num, self.out_features
- self.annotation_size],
                                   dtype=torch.float,
                                   device=annotation.device)

            h1 = torch.cat([annotation.detach(), zero_pad], -1)
            out = self.ggnn(graph, h1, etypes)
            out = torch.cat([out, annotation], -1)
            logits = self.pooling(graph, out)
            logits = self.output_layer(logits)
            all_logits.append(logits)

            annotation = self.annotation_out_layer(out)
            annotation = F.softmax(annotation, -1)

        all_logits = torch.stack(all_logits, 1)
        preds = torch.argmax(all_logits, -1)
        if ground_truth is not None:
            loss = sequence_loss(all_logits, ground_truth, seq_lengths)
```

```
    return loss, preds
  return preds
```

7.4 Graph-Gated Recurrent Units

A graph-GRU (GGRU) is a common form of recurrent GNN that has been proposed recently (Zhang *et al.*, 2018) as an extension to standard GRU to suit graph sequence data (see Figure 7.1). Let's figure out the implementation of GGRU using the following code snippets:

```
import numpy as np
import torch
import torch.nn as nn
import dgl
import dgl.nn as dglnn
from dgl.base import DGLError
import dgl.function as fn
from dgl.nn.functional import edge_softmax

class GraphGRUCell(nn.Module):
    '''Graph GRU could leverage any message passing net as an
alternative to the linear layer
    '''
```

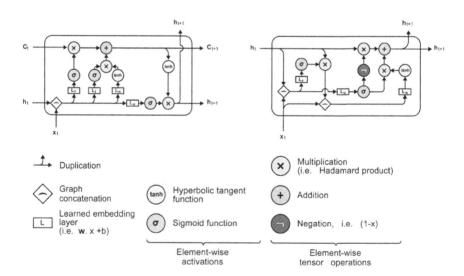

FIGURE 7.1

Illustration of graph LSTM cells (left) and graph GRU cells (right).

(Adapted from Ward, I. R., Joyner, J., Lickfold, C., Guo, Y., & Bennamoun, M. (2022). A practical tutorial on graph neural networks. ACM Computing Surveys (CSUR), 54(10s), 1-35. https://dl.acm.org/doi/full/10.1145/3503043)

```
def __init__(self, input_features, output_features, net):
    super(GraphGRUCell, self).__init__()
    self.input_features = input_features
    self.output_features = output_features
    self.dir = dir
    # net can be any GNN model
    self.r_net = net(input_features+output_features, output_features)
    self.u_net = net(input_features+output_features, output_features)
    self.c_net = net(input_features+output_features, output_features)
    # Manually add bias Bias
    self.r_bias = nn.Parameter(torch.rand(output_features))
    self.u_bias = nn.Parameter(torch.rand(output_features))
    self.c_bias = nn.Parameter(torch.rand(output_features))

def forward(self, g, x, h):
    r = torch.sigmoid(self.r_net(
        g, torch.cat([x, h], dim=1)) + self.r_bias)
    u = torch.sigmoid(self.u_net(
        g, torch.cat([x, h], dim=1)) + self.u_bias)
    h_ = r*h
    c = torch.sigmoid(self.c_net(
        g, torch.cat([x, h_], dim=1)) + self.c_bias)
    new_h = u*h + (1-u)*c
    return new_h
```

Now you are ready to build any GGRU-based network. Following the reference papers, let's build a GGRU-based encoder-decoder network. To do so, we first build the GGRU-based encoder as follows:

```
class GGRUEncoder(nn.Module):

    def __init__(self, input_features, output_features, num_layers, net):
        super(GGRUEncoder, self).__init__()
        self.input_features = input_features
        self.output_features = output_features
        self.num_layers = num_layers
        self.net = net
        self.layers = nn.ModuleList()
        if self.num_layers <= 0:
            raise DGLError("Layer Number must be greater than 0! ")
        self.layers.append(GraphGRUCell(
            self.input_features, self.output_features, self.net))
        for _ in range(self.num_layers-1):
            self.layers.append(GraphGRUCell(
                self.output_features, self.output_features, self.net))

    # hidden_states should be a list which for different layer
    def forward(self, g, x, hidden_states):
        hiddens = []
        for i, layer in enumerate(self.layers):
            x = layer(g, x, hidden_states[i])
            hiddens.append(x)
        return x, hiddens
```

Next, we build the GGRU-based decoder as follows:

```
class  GGRUDecoder(nn.Module):

    def __init__(self, input_features, hidden_features, output_
features, num_layers, net):
        super(GGRUDecoder, self).__init__()
        self.input_features = input_features
        self.hidden_features = hidden_features
        self.output_features = output_features
        self.num_layers = num_layers
        self.net = net
        self.out_layer = nn.Linear(self.hidden_features, self.
output_features)
        self.layers = nn.ModuleList()
        if self.num_layers <= 0:
            raise DGLError("Layer Number must be greater than 0!")
        self.layers.append(GraphGRUCell(self.input_features, self.
hidden_features, net))
        for _ in range(self.num_layers-1):
            self.layers.append(GraphGRUCell(self.hidden_features,
self.hidden_features, net))

    def forward(self, g, x, hidden_states):
        hiddens = []
        for i, layer in enumerate(self.layers):
            x = layer(g, x, hidden_states[i])
            hiddens.append(x)
        x = self.out_layer(x)
        return x, hiddens
```

Now, we can build the GGRU-based encoder-decoder network as follows:

```
class GraphRNN(nn.Module):

    def __init__(self, input_features,output_features, seq_len, num_layers,
net, decay_steps):

        super(GraphRNN, self).__init__()
        self.input_features = input_features
        self.output_features = output_features
        self.seq_len = seq_len
        self.num_layers = num_layers
        self.net = net
        self.decay_steps = decay_steps

        self.encoder = GGRUEncoder(self.input_features, self.output_features,
                                   self.num_layers, self.net)

        self.decoder = GGRUDecoder(self.input_features, self.output_
features, self.input_features, self.num_layers,
                                   self.net)
    # Threshold For Teacher Forcing
    def compute_thresh(self, batch_cnt):
        return self.decay_steps/(self.decay_steps + np.exp(batch_cnt /
self.decay_steps))
```

```
def encode(self, g, inputs, device):
    hidden_states = [torch.zeros(g.num_nodes(), self.output_features).to(
        device) for _ in range(self.num_layers)]
    for i in range(self.seq_len):
        _, hidden_states = self.encoder(g, inputs[i], hidden_states)

    return hidden_states

def decode(self, g, teacher_states, hidden_states, batch_cnt, device):
    outputs = []
    inputs = torch.zeros(g.num_nodes(), self.input_features).to(device)
    for i in range(self.seq_len):
        if np.random.random() < self.compute_thresh(batch_cnt) and
self.training:
            inputs, hidden_states = self.decoder(
                g, teacher_states[i], hidden_states)
        else:
            inputs, hidden_states = self.decoder(g, inputs, hidden_states)
        outputs.append(inputs)
    outputs = torch.stack(outputs)
    return outputs

def forward(self, g, inputs, teacher_states, batch_cnt, device):
    hidden = self.encode(g, inputs, device)
    outputs = self.decode(g, teacher_states, hidden, batch_cnt, device)
    return outputs
```

7.5 Case Study

Graph recurrent networks are a very important family of graph intelligence methods that show great achievements in a broad range of graph analysis tasks. However, the role of graph convolutional networks in the era of cyber-security (i.e., fraud detection and anomaly detection malware analysis) is still in its infancy. This, in turn, increased the interest of the community in discovering the potential of graph recurrent networks in addressing the current cyber threats from a practical standpoint. Motivated by that, the supplementary materials of this chapter are designated to provide a holistic in-lab tutorial for implementing full working experiments (training and testing) of the abovementioned model for different graph tasks. The supplementary materials also provide detailed explanation and implementation of recurrent GNNs such as recurrent relation networks (Palm, Paquet and Winther, 2018), recurrent event network (Jin *et al.*, 2020), and EvolveGCN (Pareja *et al.*, 2020). The supplementary materials of this chapter also provide the readers with recommendations for further reading about the content of this chapter. The repository of supplementary materials is given in https://github.com/DEEPOLOGY-AI/Book-Graph-Neural-Network/tree/main/Chapter%207.

References

Almeida, L. B. (1987) 'Learning Rule for Asynchronous Perceptrons with Feedback in a Combinatorial Environment', in *Proceedings of the IEEE First International Conference on Neural Networks (San Diego, CA), II, pp.* 609–618. *Piscataway, NJ: IEEE.*

Cho, K. *et al.* (2014) 'Learning Phrase Representations using RNN Encoder-Decoder for Statistical Machine Translation', in *EMNLP 2014–2014 Conference on Empirical Methods in Natural Language Processing, Proceedings of the Conference.* doi: 10.3115/v1/d14-1179.

Jin, W. *et al.* (2020) 'Recurrent Event Network: Autoregressive Structure Inference Over Temporal Knowledge Graphs', in *EMNLP 2020–2020 Conference on Empirical Methods in Natural Language Processing, Proceedings of the Conference.* doi: 10.18653/v1/2020.emnlp-main.541.

Li, Y. *et al.* (2016) 'Gated Graph Sequence Neural Networks', in *4th International Conference on Learning Representations, ICLR 2016 – Conference Track Proceedings.*

Palm, R. B., Paquet, U. and Winther, O. (2018) 'Recurrent Relational Networks', in Advances in Neural Information Processing Systems 31 (NeurIPS 2018. https://proceedings.neurips.cc/paper/2018/hash/b9f94c77652c9a76fc8a442748cd54bd-Abstract.html

Pareja, A. *et al.* (2020) 'EvolveGCN: Evolving Graph Convolutional Networks for Dynamic Graphs', in *AAAI 2020 – 34th AAAI Conference on Artificial Intelligence.* doi: 10.1609/aaai.v34i04.5984.

Pineda, F. J. (1987) 'Generalization of Back-Propagation to Recurrent Neural Networks', *Physical Review Letters.* doi: 10.1103/PhysRevLett.59.2229.

Scarselli, F. *et al.* (2009) 'The Graph Neural Network Model', *IEEE Transactions on Neural Networks.* doi: 10.1109/TNN.2008.2005605.

Tai, K. S., Socher, R. and Manning, C. D. (2015) 'Improved Semantic Representations from Tree-Structured Long Short-Term Memory Networks', in *ACL-IJCNLP 2015 – 53rd Annual Meeting of the Association for Computational Linguistics and the 7th International Joint Conference on Natural Language Processing of the Asian Federation of Natural Language Processing, Proceedings of the Conference.* doi: 10.3115/v1/p15-1150.

Zhang, J. *et al.* (2018) 'GaAN: Gated Attention Networks for Learning on Large and Spatiotemporal Graphs', in *34th Conference on Uncertainty in Artificial Intelligence 2018, UAI 2018.*

8

Graph Autoencoders: A Journey from Start to End

DOI: 10.1201/9781003329701-8

8.1 Introduction

In the previous chapters, we explored various families of graph intelligence approaches for supervisory learning of best mappings between graph samples and corresponding labels in different graph intelligence tasks. Three common families have been studied, namely, graph convolutional neural networks (GCNs), graph attention networks, and recurrent graph neural networks. Following the same strategy, this chapter explores one more family of graph intelligence methods called "graph autoencoders (GAEs)," which is a generalization of standard autoencoders on graph-structured data.

GAE is capable of capturing graph representations by executing valuable transformations that enable efficient encoding of the input graph. This makes GAE able to effectively tool for graph generation tasks and graph reasoning tasks. Nevertheless, this is not a straightforward task as it seems for someone, because of the high irregularity in the size and structure of graphs. We can no longer apply convolution explicitly since each network contains a broad range of unordered nodes and a varied number of neighbors for each node. It could be easy to understand the variance between AEs and GAEs by looking at and comparing Figures 8.1 and 8.2.

An annotated graph is no longer necessary in the case of GAEs because they can effectively encode the unlabeled graph data into high-level representational space. Consequently, GAEs show wide acceptance in a broad range of unsupervised and semi-supervised learning tasks, GAEs can enhance latent and condensed graph representations (called coding) from raw input graphs. These representations' dimensions are often smaller than the dimensions of the input data, making GAEs an effective tool for reducing the dimensionality in large-scale graph tasks. More specifically, GAEs are capable of serving as reliable feature detectors, making them suitable for use in the unsupervised pretraining of graph intelligence approaches.

This chapter starts looking into the fundamental ideas behind creating GAEs, including their primary parts, structural design, training, optimization, loss, and other factors. Then, we theoretically and practically investigate

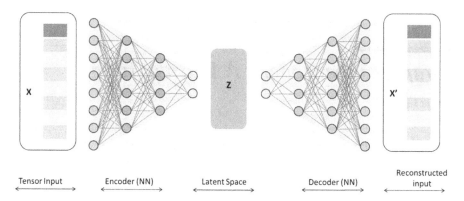

FIGURE 8.1
Systematic diagram of standard autoencoder.

the state-of-the-art GAEs methods such as variational GAEs (VGAE), regularized GAE (RGAE), regularized VGAE (RVGAE), and Dirichlet VGAE (DVGAE).

8.2　General Framework of Graph Autoencoders

GAEs characterize the task of applying the graph network to perform the autoencoding operation by projecting the feature of input graphs into a new representation (called the latent representation), which has more valuable attributes than the original input representation. These attributes involve (1) the data separability, which means that the latent information is more classifiable; (2) latent representation has low dimension than the input space; (3) the latent representation obfuscates the data for security or privacy objectives. GAEs consist of two building modules each with distinct functionality.

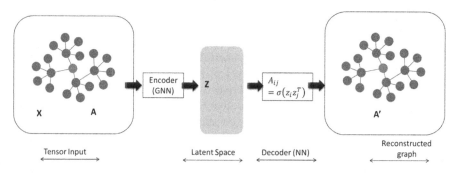

FIGURE 8.2
Systematic diagram of graph autoencoder.

In the early stage, the encoding module, $g_\varphi(\cdot)$, (shortened as encoder) receives the graph input in the form of the adjacency matrix and feature matrix then encodes this input into a latent representation using any graph network (graph convolution, graph attention, etc.).

In the following code snippet, we define graph convolution to be used to constitute the encoder part of GAE:

```python
import torch
from torch import nn
import torch.nn.functional as F
import numpy as np

class GraphConvolution(nn.Module):
    """Basic graph convolution layer for undirected graph without edge
labels."""
    def __init__(self, input_dim, output_dim, dropout, device):
        super(GraphConvolution, self).__init__()
        self.input_dim = input_dim
        self.output_dim = output_dim
        self.weights = nn.Parameter(torch.Tensor(input_dim, output_dim))
        self.dropout = dropout
        self.device = device
        self.reset_parameters()

    def reset_parameters(self):
        init_range = np.sqrt(6.0 / (self.input_dim + self.output_dim))
        nn.init.uniform_(self.weights, -init_range, init_range)

    def forward(self, inputs, adj, act=nn.ReLU()):
        x = inputs
        x = F.dropout(x, self.dropout, training=self.training)
        x = torch.matmul(x, self.weights)
        x = x.to(self.device)
        adj = torch.sparse_coo_tensor(indices=torch.from_numpy(adj[0].
transpose()), values=torch.from_numpy(adj[1]),
size=adj[2]).to(torch.float32).to_dense()
        adj = adj.to(self.device)
        x = torch.matmul(adj, x)
        outputs = act(x)
        return outputs
```

Moreover, the below code snippet defines a graph convolution layer for sparse input to be also used to constitute the encoder part of GAE:

```python
import torch
from torch import nn
import torch.nn.functional as F
import numpy as np

class GraphConvolutionSparse(nn.Module):
    """Graph convolution layer for sparse inputs."""
    def __init__(self, input_dim, output_dim, dropout, device):
        super(GraphConvolutionSparse, self).__init__()
        self.input_dim = input_dim
```

```
        self.output_dim = output_dim
        self.weights = nn.Parameter(torch.Tensor(input_dim, output_dim))
        self.dropout = dropout
        self.device = device
        self.reset_parameters()

    def reset_parameters(self):
        init_range = np.sqrt(6.0 / (self.input_dim + self.output_dim))
        nn.init.uniform_(self.weights, -init_range, init_range)

    def forward(self, inputs, adj, act=nn.ReLU()):
        x = inputs
        x = torch.sparse_coo_tensor(indices=torch.from_numpy(x[0].
transpose()), values=torch.from_numpy(x[1]), size=x[2]).to(torch.
float32)
        x = x.to(self.device)
        x = torch.matmul(x.to_dense(), self.weights)
        x = F.dropout(x, self.dropout, training=self.training)
        adj = torch.sparse_coo_tensor(indices=torch.from_numpy(adj[0].
transpose()), values=torch.from_numpy(adj[1]),
                                      size=adj[2]).to(torch.float32).to_dense()
        adj = adj.to(self.device)
        x = torch.matmul(adj, x)
        outputs = act(x)
        return outputs
```

Mathematically speaking, the encoder g_φ, consisting of one or more neural layers, receives some input X and returns the corresponding low-dimensional latent representation z. This can be mathematically represented as follows:

$$Z = g_\varphi(X, A), \tag{8.1}$$

where φ represents the set of parameters of the encoding module. Z denotes the obtained latent representation from the graph encoding layers.

Once the latent representation is obtained, the decoding module (shortened as a decoder), $f_\theta(\cdot)$, is integrated to reconstruct the original graph from that condensed representation, as shown in Figure 8.2. In particular, the latent representation Z is passed to the decoding module $f_\theta(\cdot)$, which is built with an inner product to generate X' by reconstructing the original input. This could be mathematically characterized as follows:

$$\tilde{x} = f_\theta(Z), \tag{8.2}$$

where θ represents the parameter of the decoder.

To train the GAE, the GAE has to learn the optimal parameters, θ and φ, for both encoding and decoding modules, correspondingly, by minimizing some loss function that estimates the difference between the received graphs and reconstructed counterparts, which is identified as reconstruction loss. In its easiest formula, such a loss is computed as mean square error:

$$L(\theta, \varphi) = \frac{1}{n} \sum_{i=1}^{n} \left(X - f_\theta\left(g_\varphi(X)\right)\right)^2. \tag{8.3}$$

With a well-defined loss function, we can perform end-to-end learning across this network to optimize the encoding and decoding in order to strike a balance between both sensitivity to inputs and generalizability—we do not want the network to overfit and "memorize" all training inputs. Rather, the goal is for the encoder network to represent repeating patterns within the input data in a more compressed and efficient format. One could do end-to-end training of the GAE using a carefully chosen loss function to optimize the decoding module and encoding module in order to balance the network's sympathy to inputs with generalizability—we don't wish it to overfit and "memorize" all training inputs. Instead, the encoding module is supposed to reflect recurring patterns in the input data in a more concise and effective way.

Similar to AEs, the GAEs can be divided into their constituent layers after training to carry out particular tasks. Encoding reliable embeddings for supervised downstream tasks (link prediction, graph classification, node classification, node clustering, embedding, etc.) is a common business use for the encoder while decoding new graph instances with attributes from the original dataset is a common usage scenario for the decoder. This makes it possible to create big artificial datasets. Now, let's define the decoding module as the inner product of vectorized latent representations. The following code snippets show the PyTorch implementation of the decoding module presented in Kipf and Welling (2016):

```python
import torch
from torch import nn
import torch.nn.functional as F

class InnerProductDecoder(nn.Module):
    """Decoder model layer for link prediction."""
    def __init__(self, dropout, device):
        super(InnerProductDecoder, self).__init__()
        self.dropout = dropout
        self.device = device

    def forward(self, inputs, act=nn.Sigmoid()):
        inputs = F.dropout(inputs, self.dropout, training=self.training)
        x = inputs.transpose(1,0)
        x = torch.matmul(inputs, x)
        x = torch.reshape(x, [-1])
        outputs = act(x)
        outputs = outputs.to(self.device)
        return outputs
```

At this point, we are ready to define GAE class using the following code snippets:

```
import torch
from torch import nn
import torch.nn.functional as F
import numpy as np

class GraphConvAutoEncoder(nn.Module):
    def __init__(self, args, num_features, num_nodes, features_
nonzero, dropout, pos_weight, device):
        super(GraphConvAutoEncoder, self).__init__()

        self.args = args
        self.device = device
        self.features_nonzero = features_nonzero
        self.input_dim = num_features
        self.pos_weight = pos_weight
        self.n_samples = num_nodes
        self.GCN = GraphConvolution(self.args.hidden1, self.args.
hidden2, dropout, self.device)
        self.GCN_sparse = GraphConvolutionSparse(self.input_dim, self.
args.hidden1, dropout, self.device)
        self.InpDecoder = InnerProductDecoder(dropout, self.device)

    def forward(self, features, adj, labels):
        hidden1 = self.GCN_sparse(features, adj)
        latent_mean = self.GCN(hidden1, adj, lambda x: x)
        decodings = self.InpDecoder(latent_mean, lambda x: x)

        labels = torch.sparse_coo_tensor(indices=torch.from_
numpy(labels[0].transpose()), values=labels[1],
                                    size=labels[2]).to(torch.float32)
        labels = torch.reshape(labels.to_dense(), [-1]).to(self.device)
        loss = torch.mean(nn.BCEWithLogitsLoss(pos_weight=torch.
tensor(self.pos_weight))(decodings, labels))
        accurate_prediction = torch.eq((torch.greater_equal(torch.
sigmoid(decodings), 0.5)).to(torch.int32),
                                    labels.to(torch.int32))
        accuracy = torch.mean(accurate_prediction.to(torch.float32))

        return loss, accuracy, latent_mean
```

It is worth noting that the design of encoding and decoding modules is not restricted to the above definition only. Thus, we provide a more generic and customizable implementation of GAE as follows:

```
from typing import Any
import torch
EPS = 1e-15
MAX_LOGSTD = 10

class GraphConvAutoEncoder(nn.Module):
    def __init__(self, encoder, decoder=None):
```

```
    super().__init__()
    self.encoder = encoder
    self.decoder = InnerProductDecoder() if decoder is None else decoder
    GraphConvAutoEncoder.reset_parameters(self)

  def reset_parameters(self):
    reset(self.encoder)
    reset(self.decoder)

  def encode(self, *args, **kwargs):
    r"""Operate the encoding module to computes node-specific latent
representation."""
    return self.encoder(*args, **kwargs)

  def decode(self, *args, **kwargs):
    r"""Operate the decoding module and computes edge probabilities."""
    return self.decoder(*args, **kwargs)

  def recon_loss(self, z, pos_edge_index, neg_edge_index=None):
    r"""
        Given the vectorized latent repesentations, we calculate
binary cross entropy loss between negative and positive edges.
      """
    pos_loss = -torch.log(self.decoder(z, pos_edge_index,
sigmoid=True) + EPS).mean()
    if neg_edge_index is None:
        neg_edge_index = negative_sampling(pos_edge_index, z.size(0))
    neg_loss = -torch.log(1-self.decoder(z, neg_edge_index,
sigmoid=True) +EPS).mean()

    return pos_loss + neg_loss

  def reset(value: Any):
    if hasattr(value, 'reset_parameters'):
      value.reset_parameters()
    else:
      for child in value.children() if hasattr(value, 'children') else []:
          reset(child)
```

8.3 Variational Graph Autoencoder

The VGAE (Kipf and Welling, 2016) was proposed as a simple customization of the standard variational autoencoder (VAE) (Kingma and Welling, 2014) to extract and learn representational patterns from graph data. The main objective here is to generate graphs based on the existing ones or perform reasoning about graphs. Nevertheless, it is not so straightforward to apply the traditional VAE for the reason that graph data is inherently inconsistent (see Figure 8.3).

The encoding module of VGAE was built up with graph convolutions (see Chapter 5), where feature matrix X and adjacency matrix A are received as

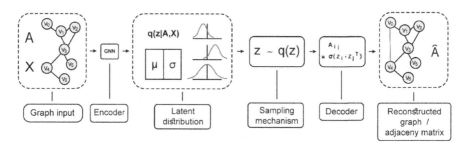

FIGURE 8.3
Illustration of variational autoencoders.

inputs to be processed to generate the latent representation Z. The first graph convolution generates a lower-dimensional feature matrix. It is defined as

$$X' = GraphConv(X, A) = RELU\left(\bar{A}XW_0\right), \tag{8.4}$$

where $\bar{A}$ is calculated as follows:

$$\bar{A} = D^{-\frac{1}{2}} - AD^{-\frac{1}{2}}. \tag{8.5}$$

Then, another graph convolution is applied to generate mean μ and log σ^2 statistics as follows:

$$\mu = GraphConv_\mu(X, A) = \bar{A}X'W_1, \tag{8.6}$$

$$\log \sigma^2 = GraphConv_\sigma(X, A) = \bar{A}X'W_1. \tag{8.7}$$

Following, the latent representation Z is calculated through the parameterization step to follow:

$$Z = \mu + \sigma * \epsilon, \tag{8.8}$$

where $\epsilon \sim N(0, 1)$.

The decoding module of VGAE is implemented as an inner product between latent representations Z, and the output of the decoding module is a recreated adjacency matrix A' defined as follows:

$$A' = \sigma\left(zz^T\right), \tag{8.9}$$

where $\sigma(\bullet)$ represents the sigmoid function.

To sum up, the encoding module of VGAE is as follows:

$$q\left(z_i \mid X, A\right) = N\left(z_i \mid u_i, diag\left(\sigma_i^2\right)\right), \tag{8.10}$$

while the decoding module of VGAE is as follows:

$$p\left(A_{ij} = 1 \mid z_i, z_j\right) = \sigma\left(z_i z_j^T\right). \tag{8.11}$$

Being different from GAE, the VGAE's loss function enforces an extra penalty that guarantees to normalize the latent distributions. The loss of VGAE consists of two main objective functions. First, the reconstruction loss measures the difference between the recreated adjacency matrix and the input adjacency matrix. In particular, it calculates binary cross-entropy between the input A and logits of output A'. Second, the Kulback-Leibler (KL) divergence to estimate how the $p(Z)$ is close to $q(Z \mid X, A)$, where $p(Z) = N(0, 1)$:

$$L = \mathbb{E}_{q(Z|X, A)}\left[\log p(A \mid Z)\right] - KL[q(Z \mid X, A) \| p(Z)]. \tag{8.12}$$

Once the latent representation is obtained, it could be easy to bargain a means to learn the similarity of each row (node-wise) in the latent representation for generating the decoding output (reconstructed adjacency matrix). The inner product can compute the cosine similarity of two vectorized representations, which is valuable for applying a distance metric (e.g., Wasserstein space distance and ranking loss) that is invariant to the scale of the vectors.

At this point, we are ready to define VGAE class using the following code snippets:

```python
import torch
from torch import nn
import torch.nn.functional as F
import numpy as np

class GraphConvVarAutoEncoder(nn.Module):
    def __init__(self, args, num_features, num_nodes, features_
nonzero, dropout, pos_weight, device):
        super(GraphConvVarAutoEncoder, self).__init__()

        self.args = args
        self.device = device
        self.input_dim = num_features # {int} 19
        self.features_nonzero = features_nonzero # {int} 19
        self.n_samples = num_nodes # {int} 19
        self.pos_weight = pos_weight # {float}
        self.GCN_sparse = GraphConvolutionSparse(self.input_dim, self.
args.hidden1, dropout, self.device)
        self.GCN = GraphConvolution(self.args.hidden1, self.args.
hidden2, dropout, self.device)
        self.GCN_std = GraphConvolution(self.args.hidden1, self.args.
hidden2, dropout, self.device)
        self.InpDecoder = InnerProductDecoder(dropout, self.device)

    def forward(self, features, adj, labels):
        hidden1 = self.GCN_sparse(features, adj)
        latent_mean = self.GCN(hidden1, adj, lambda x: x)
```

```
        latent_std = self.GCN_std(hidden1, adj, lambda x: x)
        latent = latent_mean + torch.randn([self.n_samples, self.args.
hidden2]).to(self.device) * torch.exp(latent_std)
        decodings = self.InpDecoder(z, lambda x: x)

        labels = torch.sparse_coo_tensor(indices=torch.from_
numpy(labels[0].transpose()), values=labels[1], size=labels[2]).
to(torch.float32)
        labels = torch.reshape(labels.to_dense(), [-1]).to(self.device)

        loss = torch.mean(nn.BCEWithLogitsLoss(pos_weight=torch.
tensor(self.pos_weight))(decodings,labels))
        log_like = loss
        kl = (0.5 / self.n_samples) * torch.mean(torch.sum(1 + 2 *
latent_std - torch.square(latent_mean) - torch.square(torch.
exp(latent_std)), 1))

        loss -= kl
        accurate_prediction = torch.eq((torch.greater_equal(torch.sigmoid
(decodings), 0.5)).to(torch.int32), labels.to(torch.int32))
        accuracy = torch.mean(accurate_prediction.to(torch.float32))

        return cost, accuracy, latent_mean, log_like

    def forward_val(self, features, adj, labels):
        hidden1 = self.GCN_sparse(features, adj)
        latent_mean = self.GCN(hidden1, adj, lambda x: x)
        latent_std = self.GCN_std(hidden1, adj, lambda x: x)
        latent = latent_mean + torch.randn([self.n_samples, self.args.
hidden2]).to(self.device) * torch.exp(latent_std)
        decodings = self.InpDecoder(z, lambda x: x)

        labels = torch.sparse_coo_tensor(indices=torch.from_
numpy(labels[0].transpose()), values=labels[1], size=labels[2]).
to(torch.float32)
        labels = torch.reshape(labels.to_dense(), [-1]).to(self.device)

        accurate_prediction = torch.eq((torch.greater_equal(torch.sigmoid
(decodings), 0.5)).to(torch.int32), labels.to(torch.int32))
        accuracy = torch.mean(accurate_prediction.to(torch.float32))

        loss = torch.mean(nn.BCEWithLogitsLoss(pos_weight=torch.
tensor(self.pos_weight))(decodings,labels))

        return cost, accuracy, latent_mean
```

It is worth mentioning that the design of encoding and decoding modules is not restricted to the above definition only. Thus, we provide a more generic and customizable implementation of VGAE as follows:

```
class GraphConvVarAutoEncoder(GraphConvAutoEncoder):
    def __init__(self, encoder, decoder=None):
        super().__init__(encoder, decoder)

    def reparameterize(self, mu, logstd):
```

```
    if self.training:
      return mu + torch.randn_like(logstd) * torch.exp(logstd)
    else:
      return mu

  def encode(self, *args, **kwargs):
    self.__mu__, self.__logstd__ = self.encoder(*args, **kwargs)
    self.__logstd__ = self.__logstd__.clamp(max=MAX_LOGSTD)
    z = self.reparametrize(self.__mu__, self.__logstd__)
    return z

  def kl_loss(self, mu=None, logstd=None):
    mu = self.__mu__ if mu is None else mu
    logstd = self.__logstd__ if logstd is None else logstd.clamp(
    max=MAX_LOGSTD)
    return -0.5 * torch.mean(torch.sum(1 + 2 * logstd - mu**2 -
logstd.exp()**2, dim=1))
```

8.4 Regularized Variational Graph Autoencoder

The aforementioned strategies are often irregular that prioritize maintaining the topological relations or reducing the reconstruction loss. Further, the distribution of data the latent space has largely gone unnoticed. When confronted with sparse and stochastic graphs in the real world, unregularized embedding algorithms frequently learn a defective inference mechanism leading to weak latent representations lacking structural information. Introducing some regularization to the latent codes and requiring them to adhere to a previous data distribution is one approach that is frequently used to address this issue. In this regard, two adversarial approaches were proposed to extend the above-stated GAE, namely the adversarially RGAE (ARGAE) and the adversarially regularized VGAE (ARVGAE) (Pan *et al.*, 2018).

These methods seek not only to minimize the reconstruction loss of the graph construction but also to impose the latent representation to contest a prior distribution. They encode the input graphs into the latent representation by integrating graph convolutions to take the advantage of both graph representation and node information within a network. The decoding module is updated to reconstruct topological information by integrating an adversarial learning method for regularizing the latent features to improve graph representational learning power. The added adversarial regularization seeks to differentiate the encoder-generated latent representations from those originated from a factual prior distribution. The adversarial regularization and graph encoding modules are conjointly optimized in an integrated approach with the intention of empowering each other to reach an improved graph embedding for different graph intelligence tasks.

```
class RegularizedGraphAE(GraphConvAutoEncoder):
  def __init__(self, encoder, discriminator, decoder=None):
```

```
    super().__init__(encoder, decoder)
    self.discriminator = discriminator
    reset(self.discriminator)

def reset_parameters(self):
    super().reset_parameters()
    reset(self.discriminator)

def reg_loss(self, z):
    real = torch.sigmoid(self.discriminator(z))
    real_loss = -torch.log(real + EPS).mean()
    return real_loss

def discriminator_loss(self, z):
    real = torch.sigmoid(self.discriminator(torch.randn_like(z)))
    fake = torch.sigmoid(self.discriminator(z.detach()))
    real_loss = -torch.log(real + EPS).mean()
    fake_loss = -torch.log(1 - fake + EPS).mean()
    return real_loss + fake_loss
```

The adversarial regularization is designed as an ordinary multilayered perceptron (MLP) with a sigmoid output layer, where adversarial MLP functions as a discriminator, $D(Z)$, to decide if the latent representation derive from prior p_z(positive) or from graph encoding module (negative) (see Figure 8.4). By optimizing the appropriate loss function (cross-entropy), the binary classifier can eventually regularize the network to improve the embedding during the training process. The discriminator loss can be formulated as follows:

$$-\frac{1}{2}\mathbb{E}_{z \sim p_z}[\log D(Z)] - \frac{1}{2}\mathbb{E}_X \log\big(1 - D\big(g_\varphi(X, A)\big)\big), \qquad (8.13)$$

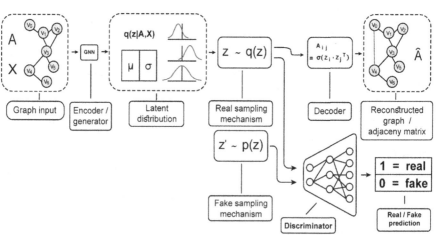

FIGURE 8.4
The architecture of adversarial regularized GVAEs.

(Adapted from Pan *et al.*, 2018.)

where p_z is designated as simple Gaussian distribution. The training of the encoding module using discriminator loss can be formulated as follows:

$$\min_{g_\varphi} \max_D \mathbb{E}_{z \sim p_z}[\log D(Z)] + \mathbb{E}_X \log\left(1 - D\left(g_\varphi(X, A)\right)\right) \qquad (8.14)$$

Now, let's implement the ARVGAE as shown in the following code snippet:

```
class RegularizedVarGraphAE(RegularizedGraphAE):
  def __init__(self, encoder, discriminator, decoder=None):
    super().__init__(encoder, discriminator, decoder)
    self.VGAE = VGAE(encoder, decoder)

  @property
  def __mu__(self):
    return self.VGAE.__mu__

  @property
  def __logstd__(self):
    return self.VGAE.__logstd__

  def reparametrize(self, mu, logstd):
    return self.VGAE.reparametrize(mu, logstd)

  def encode(self, *args, **kwargs):
    return self.VGAE.encode(*args, **kwargs)

  def kl_loss(self, mu=None, logstd=None):
      return self.VGAE.kl_loss(mu, logstd)
```

8.5 Graphite Variational Autoencoder

Graphite (Grover, Zweig and Ermon, 2019) was proposed as a generative approach to graphs explicitly learning a model articulating a combined distribution across the elements of input node-wise features and adjacency matrix of graphs. Similar to VGAEs, Graphite makes use of graph intelligence networks to implement encoding modules as well as decoding modules. In this context, the encoding operation is performed as discussed in the previous sections; however, the decoding of latent representations to recreate the input graphs is achieved via a multilayered iterative process. The process begins with a preliminary reconstruction according to the contingent latent representations and improves the recreated graph through message passing in an iterative fashion. The step-by-step enhancement could be competently applied using GNNs.

8.6 Dirichlet Graph Variational Autoencoder (DGVAE)

The DGVAE (Li *et al.*, 2020) was proposed as an extension to the existing VGAE by automatically encoding the cluster decomposition in latent space by using Dirichlet distributions to substitute the Gaussian distribution of nodes' features, whereas the latent representations could be regarded as the memberships of graph cluster. In DGVAE, the evidence lower bound (ELBO) was presented as a de facto reconstruction method that acts as a method of relaxed balanced graph cut based on a spectral clustering approach requiring the calculation of spectral low pass and/or K eigenvectors. In the DGVAE, the mean field approximation is adopted to outline the intimate variation in the encoding module as with VGAE and Graphite:

$$q(Z \mid X, A) = \prod_{i=1}^{N} q(z_i \mid X, A). \tag{8.15}$$

However, here, the variational marginals $q(z_i \mid X, A)$ are presumed to belong to Dirichlet distributions to facilitate interpreting the latent representations. Nevertheless, explicitly impending the Dirichlet distributions could complicate the application of the reparameterization trick strategy. Therefore, this problem is tackled in DVGAE by applying the Laplace approximation method to use the logistic normal distribution, $p(z_i) = \text{Dir}(\alpha)$, to estimate the Dirichlet distributions.

To begin our implementation journey, let's figure out how to develop the Dirichlet autoencoder using the following code snippet.

```python
import torch
from torch import nn
from torch.nn import Parameter
import torch.nn.functional as F
import numpy as np

class DirichletAutoEncoder(nn.Module):
    def __init__(self, args, num_features, num_nodes, features_
nonzero, dropout, pos_weight, device):
        super(DirichletAutoEncoder, self).__init__()

        self.args = args
        self.device = device
        self.input_dim = num_features # {int} 19
        self.features_nonzero = features_nonzero # {int} 19
        self.n_samples = num_nodes # {int} 19
        self.pos_weight = pos_weight # {float}
        self.GCN_sparse = GraphConvolutionSparse(self.input_dim, self.
args.hidden1, dropout, self.device)
        self.GCN = GraphConvolution(self.args.hidden1, self.args.
hidden2, dropout, self.device)
```

```
        self.InpDecoder = InnerProductDecoder(dropout, self.device)

    def forward(self, features, adj, labels):
        hidden1 = self.GCN_sparse(features, adj)
        latent_mean = self.GCN(hidden1, adj, lambda x: x)
        reconstructions = self.InpDecoder(latent_mean, lambda x: x)

        labels = torch.sparse_coo_tensor(indices=torch.from_
numpy(labels[0].transpose()), values=labels[1],
                                    size=labels[2]).to(torch.float32)
        labels = torch.reshape(labels.to_dense(), [-1]).to(self.device)
        correct_prediction = torch.eq((torch.greater_equal(torch.
sigmoid(reconstructions), 0.5)).to(torch.int32),
                                    labels.to(torch.int32))
        accuracy = torch.mean(correct_prediction.to(torch.float32))
        loss = torch.mean(nn.BCEWithLogitsLoss(pos_weight=torch.
tensor(self.pos_weight))(reconstructions, labels))


        return cost, latent_mean, loss
```

Then, let's figure out how to develop Dirichlet GAE using the following code snippet:

```
import torch
from torch import nn
import torch.nn.functional as F
import numpy as np


class DirichletVarAutoEncoder(nn.Module):
    def __init__(self, args, num_features, num_nodes, features_
nonzero, dropout, pos_weight, device):
        super(DirichletVarAutoEncoder, self).__init__()

        self.args = args
        self.device = device
        self.input_dim = num_features # {int} 19
        self.features_nonzero = features_nonzero # {int} 19
        self.n_samples = num_nodes # {int} 19
        self.pos_weight = pos_weight # {float}
        self.GCN_sparse = GraphConvolutionSparse(self.input_dim, self.
args.hidden1, dropout, self.device)
        self.GCN = GraphConvolution(self.args.hidden1, self.args.
hidden2, dropout, self.device)
        self.GCN_std = GraphConvolution(self.args.hidden1, self.args.
hidden2, dropout, self.device)
        self.InpDecoder = InnerProductDecoder(dropout, self.device)

    def forward(self, features, adj, labels):
        hidden1 = self.GCN_sparse(features, adj)
        latent_mean = self.GCN(hidden1, adj, lambda x: x)
        latent_std = self.GCN_std(hidden1, adj, lambda x: x)
        latent = latent_mean + torch.randn([self.n_samples, self.args.
hidden2]).to(self.device) * torch.sqrt(torch.exp(latent_std))
```

```
        reconstructions = self.IPDecoder(latent, lambda x: x)

        labels = torch.sparse_coo_tensor(indices=torch.from_
numpy(labels[0].transpose()), values=labels[1], size=labels[2]).
to(torch.float32)
        labels = torch.reshape(labels.to_dense(), [-1]).to(self.device)

        cost = torch.mean(nn.BCEWithLogitsLoss(pos_weight=torch.
tensor(self.pos_weight))(reconstructions,labels))

        a = 0.01 * np.ones((1, self.args.hidden2)).astype(np.float32)
        mu2 = torch.tensor((np.log(a).T - np.mean(np.log(a), -1)).T)
        var2 = torch.tensor(((((1.0 / a) * (1 - (2.0 / self.args.
hidden2)))).T +
                                (1.0 / (self.args.hidden2 * self.
                                args.hidden2)) * np.sum(1.0 / a,
                                -1)).T)
        mu2 = mu2.to(self.device)
        var2 = var2.to(self.device)
        ## the KL loss for the c
        latent_loss = 1 * (torch.sum(torch.div(torch.exp(latent_std),
var2), -1) + \
                        torch.sum(torch.multiply(torch.div((mu2
                        - latent_mean), var2),
                                    (mu2 - latent_mean)), -1)
                                    - self.args.hidden2 + \
                        torch.sum(torch.log(var2), -1) - torch.
                        sum(latent_std, -1))
        kl = 0.5 / self.n_samples * torch.mean(latent_loss)

        loss += 1 * kl
        correct_prediction = torch.eq((torch.greater_equal(torch.
sigmoid(reconstructions), 0.5)).to(torch.int32), labels.to(torch.
int32))
        accuracy = torch.mean(correct_prediction.to(torch.float32))

        return loss, accuracy, latent

    def forward_reconstruction(self, features, adj, labels):
        hidden1 = self.GCN_sparse(features, adj)
        latent_mean = self.GCN(hidden1, adj, lambda x: x)
        latent_std = self.GCN_std(hidden1, adj, lambda x: x)
        latent = latent_mean + torch.randn([self.n_samples, self.args.
hidden2]).to(self.device) * torch.sqrt(torch.exp(latent_std))
        reconstructions = self.InpDecoder(latent, lambda x: x)

        labels = torch.sparse_coo_tensor(indices=torch.from_
numpy(labels[0].transpose()), values=labels[1], size=labels[2]).
to(torch.float32)
        labels = torch.reshape(labels.to_dense(), [-1]).to(self.device)

        loss = torch.mean(nn.BCEWithLogitsLoss(pos_weight=torch.
tensor(self.pos_weight))(reconstructions,labels))
        correct_prediction = torch.eq((torch.greater_equal(torch.
sigmoid(reconstructions), 0.5)).to(torch.int32), labels.to(torch.
int32))
```

```
accuracy = torch.mean(correct_prediction.to(torch.float32))

return loss, accuracy, latent_mean
```

8.7 Case Study

The full working experiments (training and testing) of the previously mentioned algorithms are discussed in the supplementary materials of this chapter, which are available at this repository: https://github.com/DEEPOLOGY-AI/Book-Graph-Neural-Network/tree/main/Chapter8.

References

Grover, A., Zweig, A. and Ermon, S. (2019) 'Graphite: Iterative Generative Modeling of Graphs', in *36th International Conference on Machine Learning, ICML 2019*.

Kingma, D. P. and Welling, M. (2014) 'Auto-encoding Variational Bayes', in *2nd International Conference on Learning Representations, ICLR 2014 – Conference Track Proceedings*. doi: 10.48550/arXiv.1312.6114

Kipf, T. N. and Welling, M. (2016) 'Variational Graph Auto-Encoders'. doi: http://arxiv.org/abs/1611.07308.

Li, J. *et al.* (2020) 'Dirichlet Graph Variational Autoencoder', in *Advances in Neural Information Processing Systems*.

Pan, S. *et al.* (2018) 'Adversarially Regularized Graph Autoencoder for Graph Embedding', in *IJCAI International Joint Conference on Artificial Intelligence*. doi: 10.24963/ijcai.2018/362.

9

Interpretable Graph Intelligence: A Journey from Black to White Box

9.1 Introduction

The continual developments of graph intelligence or graph neural networks (GNNs) have been revolutionizing the graph intelligence in a broad range of research tasks, such as natural language processing (NLP), computer vision (CV), bioinformatics, and cybersecurity. Generally, deep learning models are known to be designed as black boxes without being interpretable for the users. The same concept applies to the graph intelligence. When it comes to critical applications, the human users cannot trust the decisions made by the model unless they understand the internal reasoning mechanisms behind these decisions. The lack of trust prevents the integration of graph intelligence into serious applications relating to fairness, confidentiality, and security. Specifically for users in interdisciplinary fields, precise forecasts and understandable explanations are required for the safe and reliable deployment of graph intelligence. These observations highlight the necessity of creating explanatory methods for the opaque graph networks.

Explainable artificial intelligence (XAI) is a rapidly evolving branch of AI, which emphasizes designing interpretability techniques explaining the behaviors of AI algorithms and the logic behind their generated decisions. Multiple categories of the XAI methods have been presented to improve the interpretability of deep learning models trained with image, tabular, and sequential data. The majority of the XAI methods could afford input-driven explanations, for example, assigning significance scores for the features of input or grasping the general behaviors of deep models. When it comes to graph intelligence, several graph-related tasks have been extensively researched (see the previous chapters), including graph classification, node classification, and link prediction. In the previous chapters, we could note the availability of different families (convolutional, recurrent, etc.) of graph networks has been proposed to improve the graph representation learning. Nevertheless, compared with visual, textual, and tabular data, the

DOI: 10.1201/9781003329701-9

interpretability of graph intelligence models is more challenging because the inherent unfamiliarity of novice users to such form of data. Therefore, the attention of XAI community has been positioned toward explaining graph intelligence models from different angles and at different levels of explanation.

When we talk about the explainability of graph intelligence model, we're referring to their propensity for making their forecasts easily digestible and transparent. If the reasoning behind graph intelligence models' predictions is unclear, people will be less likely to put their faith in them, reducing their usefulness in important domains like justice (e.g., credit risk prediction) and cyber security. As a result, there has been a rise in study into the interpretability and explainability of graph intelligence models so that developers may better understand the reasoning behind graph intelligence models' predictions. Researchers can use these features to capture causality in graph intelligence models or get insights for future exploration in applications; developers can use them to build more resilient graph intelligence model systems; and regulators can use them to guarantee that graph intelligence models are fair. Here, we provide a brief overview of recent developments, detailing how graph intelligence models arrive at their forecasts. When it comes to graph intelligence models' interpretability and explainability, we begin by introducing the fundamental notions and categories. We then present some common approaches and compare them to each other. Finally, we suggest some future study avenues. Ideas and classifications possibility of explanation and interpretation intrinsically interpretable models and post hoc explanation methods are two types of approaches that aim to increase interpretability in machine learning. Graph intelligence models' interpretability makes the use of naturally interpretable designs in graph intelligence model architectures to provide light on graph intelligence model predictions. However, when graph intelligence models have been trained, the goal of explainability is to offer some sort of post hoc explanation. The former are referred to as interpretable graph intelligence models in this survey, whereas the latter are referred to as explanations for graph intelligence models. Modalities of clarification feature summary statistics, feature summary visualization, internal parameters, data points, and inherently interpretable (surrogate) models are all examples of the types of explanation outcomes that can be obtained from general machine learning models. To what extent particular edges, nodes, or features contribute most to the final outputs is a common question among the many different approaches developed for graph intelligence models at present. As a result, graph intelligence models typically produce explanations in the form of graphs, with particular components (i.e., edges, nodes, or features) marked as explanations for the given sample. Since subgraphs with specified patterns (i.e., motifs) are the building blocks of certain more complicated networks, explanations of graph intelligence models are sometimes presented in this form.

9.2 Interpretability Methods for Graph Intelligence

In recent times, a number of different strategies have been suggested in order to explain the predictions made by deep graph models. These strategies concentrate on various facets of the graph models and offer a variety of perspectives on them in order to better facilitate comprehension. In most cases, they provide answers to a few questions; one example of such a question is "which input edges are more significant?" Which input nodes are more significant than others? Which characteristics of the node are prioritized the most? What kinds of graph patterns will result in the most accurate prediction of a particular class? A taxonomy of the many approaches to graph intelligence model explanation is provided here so that the various ways can be understood in greater depth. Figure 9.1 presents an illustration of the hierarchy that underpins our taxonomy. The many approaches are separated into two primary categories, known as instance- and model-level methods, according to the nature of the explanations that are offered for each one.

In general, these two groups of methodologies each provide an explanation of deep graph models from a unique perspective. While techniques at the model level offer high-level observations and more general knowledge, instance-level methodologies explain things in a manner that is specific to a certain instance. It is necessary to have human supervision in order to review the interpretations of deep graph models in order to verify and trust them. More human supervision is required for systems that operate at the

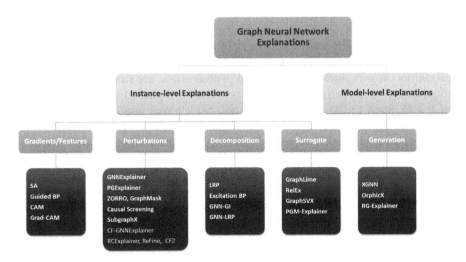

FIGURE 9.1
Taxonomy of explainable graph intelligence methods.

instance level since specialists are required to investigate the interpretations for a variety of input graphs. Because the interpretations for model-level approaches are on a higher level, there is less need for human oversight of these procedures. In addition, the descriptions of instance-level procedures are derived from actual input cases in order to make them simpler and more straightforward to comprehend. Nevertheless, it is possible that the interpretations for model-level procedures are not human-intelligible. This is due to the fact that the derived graph topologies might not even occur in the physical world. In general, these two categories of approaches can be blended into one another to produce a more comprehensive comprehension of deep graph models; for this reason, it is essential to look into both of them in the following sections.

9.3 Instance-Level Interpretability

The interpretations for each input graph are determined by the inputs through the use of instance-level techniques. These approaches explain deep models by determining the most essential input attributes for its prediction. They do this by starting with an input graph. We divide the approaches into four distinct categories according to the numerous ways in which the important scores can be obtained: techniques that depend on gradients or attributes, techniques that depend on perturbations, techniques that depend on decomposition, and techniques that depend on surrogates. To be more specific, the gradients- and features-dependent approaches make use of the gradients or the feature values to highlight the importance of various input features. In addition, perturbation-dependent algorithms examine the change in forecasting that occurs in response to a variety of input perturbations in order to determine the significance scores of the inputs. The prediction scores, such as anticipated probabilities, are first decomposed by the decomposition algorithms, and then they are passed on to the neurons in the deepest hidden layer. After that, they make use of the scores that have been deconstructed as the importance scores and back propagate such scores layer by layer till they reach the input space. In the meantime, surrogate-based approaches begin by drawing samples from a dataset consisting of the examples that are geographically close to the given example. After that, these techniques apply a straightforward and easily comprehensible model, such as a decision tree, to the dataset that has been sampled. Next, the interpretations provided by the surrogate model are utilized in order to provide an interpretation for the initial predictions. This section begins by describing the instance-level approaches for graph intelligence model explanations and then proceeds to analyze the motives, approaches, capabilities, and limits of each type in turn.

9.3.1 Gradients-Dependent Explanations

This subsection emphasizes discussing the gradient-dependent approaches and the features-dependent approaches for explaining the graph intelligence solutions.

9.3.1.1 Conceptual View

The most easy technique, which is extensively utilized in both image and text jobs, is to use gradients or features to describe deep models. The most important thing to keep in mind is to use the gradients or the values of hidden features on the map as estimations of the relevance of the input. In particular, gradients-based approaches use back-propagation to calculate the gradients of target prediction with regard to the input characteristics. In the meantime, feature-based approaches use approximation to map the concealed information to the input space in order to evaluate the relevance of the features. In such systems, it is a common practice to interpret larger gradients or feature values as signifying greater relevance. It is important to keep in mind that the model parameters are strongly associated with both the gradients and the hidden properties; hence, such interpretations could represent the data that is included in the model. Because these approaches are straightforward and generic, it is not difficult to adapt them for use in the graph realm.

Recently, several methods have been applied to explain graph intelligence models, including sensitivity analysis (SA) (Baldassarre and Azizpour, 2019), guided back-propagation (GBP) (Baldassarre and Azizpour, 2019), class activation maps (CAM) (Pope *et al.*, 2019a), and gradient CAM (Grad-CAM) (Pope *et al.*, 2019a). The key difference among these methods lies in the procedure of gradient back-propagation and how different hidden feature maps are combined.

9.3.1.2 Methods

Feature-dependent explanation techniques mostly make use of the mappings from embedding space to input space to estimate the donation caried out by elements from the input instances. The most important differences between feature-dependent explanation techniques lies in mechanisms of creating the mapping.

CAM (Pope *et al.*, 2019a) was proposed to determine which nodes are significant by mapping the features of the nodes in the final layer to the input space. It is necessary for the graph intelligence model architecture to utilize both a fully connected (FC) layer and a global average pooling (GAP) layer as the final classifier in order to accomplish this. To be more specific, CAM starts with the final node embeddings and then combines various feature maps using weighted summations in order to derive relevance scores for input nodes. It is important to keep in mind that the weights are derived from the very last linear layer that is linked to the target prediction. This method, although likewise being relatively straightforward, does, however, suffer from a number of significant drawbacks. To begin, CAM has specific constraints that must be met by the graph intelligence model structure; this constrains the use and generalization of the algorithm. Second, it makes the heuristic assumption that the end-node embeddings can accurately reflect the relevance of the input data, which is not always the case. In addition, it is only capable of explaining graph classification models; it cannot be successfully applied to node classification jobs because it requires the final FC layer in order to map estimates to the various nodes.

In mathematical term, CAM can be used to explain the graph intelligence models possessing a GAP layer before the final decision layer by computing the heat map as follows:

$$L_{CAM}^{(c)} = ReLU\left(\sum_k w_k^{(c)} A_k \right) \tag{9.1}$$

whereas A_k denotes the activation of kth node in the targeted layer of the graph intelligence model. The $w_k^{(c)}$ represents the weight related to class-label c for node kth node in the linear layer.

The Grad-CAM algorithm (Pope *et al.*, 2019a) expands the capabilities of the CAM to generic graph classification models by eliminating the constraints imposed by the GAP layer. It combines the various feature maps through using gradients as the weights, as opposed to employing weights that are determined by the difference between the GAP outcome and the FC output. In more specific terms, it begins by computing the gradients of the goal predictions with regard to the ultimate node embeddings. Next, it takes such gradients and averages them in order to derive the weight for each feature map. Having said that, it is likewise founded on intuitive hypotheses and is unable to explain nodes categorization models.

In mathematical terms, the Grad-CAM computes the saliency map as follows:

$$L_{Grad-CAM}^{(c)} = ReLU\left(\sum_k w_k^{(c)} A_k \right), \tag{9.2}$$

where the parameter $w_k^{(c)}$ is calculated as follows:

$$w_k^{(c)} = \frac{1}{Z} \sum_{i=1}^{H} \sum_{j=1}^{W} \underbrace{\frac{\partial Y^{(c)}}{\partial A_k^{i,j}}}_{\text{gradients via backprop}}, \tag{9.3}$$

where A_k denotes the activation of kth node in the targeted layer of graph intelligence model. $Y^{(c)}$ represents the output of the model with respect to class c prior to the SoftMax layer.

The main step for generating Grad-CAM explanation:

1. The graph input is forward-propagate through the graph intelligence models.
2. A raw score is computed for the targeted class, which implies the activation of nodes prior to the SoftMax layer.
3. All activations were set to zero.
4. The gradient of the targeted class is back propagated to the last graph layer preceding the linear layers.
5. The gradient for the targeted class is used to weight each feature map.
6. The average of the feature maps is computed via ReLU activation.
7. Visualize the output.

```
1.    #. . . . . . . . . . . . Class imports. . . . . . . . .
2.    import torch
3.    import torch.nn.functional as F
4.    from torch.autograd import Variable
5.    import BaseExplainer
6.
7.    #. . . . . . . . . . . . Build explainer. . . . . . . .
8.    class Grad_CAM(BaseExplainer):
9.
10.       def __init__(self, device, path_GI_model):
11.           super(Grad_CAM, self).__init__(device, path_GI_model)
12.
13.           #. . . . . . . . . . . .Generate explanation. . . . . . . .
14.       def explain(self, graph,
15.                           model=None,
16.                           draw_graph=0,
17.                           vis_ratio=0.2):
18.
19.           if model == None:
20.               model = self.model
21.           #. . . . . . . . . . . . Graph copy. . . . . . . . .
22.           tmp_graph = graph.clone()
23.           tmp_graph.edge_attr = Variable(tmp_graph.edge_attr,
      requires_grad=True)
24.           pred = model(tmp_graph)
25.           pred[0, graph.y].backward()
26.           edge_grads = tmp_graph.edge_attr.grad
27.
28.           alpha = torch.mean(edge_grads, dim=1)
29.           edge_score = F.relu(torch.sum((graph.edge_attr.T *
      alpha).T, dim=1)).cpu().numpy()
30.           edge_score = self.norm_imp(edge_score)
31.
```

```
32.              if draw_graph:
33.                  self.visualize(graph, edge_score, self.name,
    vis_ratio=vis_ratio)
34.                  self.last_result = (graph, edge_score)
35.
36.              return edge_score
```

Gradient-driven explanation methods: In order to determine the relative importance of components in data points, gradient-based algorithms utilize a variety of gradient-processing techniques. By computing the gradients of graph intelligence models on input space, these approaches generate local interpretations for the present instances. In gradient-based approaches, input examples are used as variables of graph intelligence models in place of model parameters, and the back-propagation method is used to derive the gradients of graph intelligence models in the feature space.

SA: Squared gradient values are used directly in SA (Baldassarre and Azizpour, 2019) as significance ratings for various input attributes. Back-propagation, which is the same to network training except that the goal is input features rather than model parameters, can be used to immediately calculate it. Keep in mind that attributes of either edges or nodes in a graph could be used as input. It presumes that input features with larger absolute gradient values are more crucial. It's easy to use and effective, but it has a few drawbacks that prevent it from being ideal. To begin, SA can simply highlight the significance of the responsiveness between inputs and outputs. Saturation issues are another concern area (Baldassarre and Azizpour, 2019). To a large extent, gradients fail to capture the proportions of inputs in the model's concentration areas, where the output seldom shifts in response to variations in the inputs.

Guided BP: The concept behind Guided BP (Baldassarre and Azizpour, 2019) is comparable to that of SA, but the method of back-propagating gradients is handled differently. Due to the difficulty in justifying negative gradients, Guided when using BP, only favorable gradients are back propagated, while negative gradients are clipped to zero. The significance of various input attributes is then weighed exclusively using positive gradients. Keep in mind the Guided BP has the same restrictions as SA.

```
1.    #. . . . . . . . . Class imports. . . . . . . . . . . . . . .
2.    from torch.autograd import Variable
3.    import BaseExplainer
4.
5.    #. . . . . . . . Build explainer. . . . . . . . . . . . . . .
 .
6.    class Sensitivity_Analysis(BaseExplainer):
7.
8.
9.        def __init__(self, device, path_GI_model):
10.           super(Sensitivity_Analysis, self).__init__(device,
    path_GI_model)
11.
12.       #. . . . . . . . . . Generate explanation. . . . . . . . .
```

```
13.        def explain(self, graph,
14.                          model=None,
15.                          draw_graph=0,
16.                          vis_ratio=0.2):
17.
18.            if model == None:
19.                model = self.model
20.
21.            #. . . . . . Graph copy. . . . . . . . . . . . . . . .
22.            tmp_graph = graph.clone()
23.
24.            tmp_graph.edge_attr = Variable(tmp_graph.edge_attr,
       requires_grad=True)
25.            tmp_graph.x = Variable(tmp_graph.x, requires_grad=True)
26.            pred = model(tmp_graph)
27.            pred[0, tmp_graph.y].backward()
28.
29.            edge_grads = pow(tmp_graph.edge_attr.grad, 2).sum(dim=1).
       cpu().numpy()
30.            edge_imp = self.norm_imp(edge_grads)
31.
32.            if draw_graph:
33.                self.visualize(graph, edge_imp, self.name,
       vis_ratio=vis_ratio)
34.            self.last_result = (graph, edge_imp)
35.
36.            return edge_imp
```

9.3.2 Perturbation-Dependent Explanation Methods

Perturbation-based explanation methods are a class of interpretability techniques that involve systematically modifying inputs to a model to understand
how they affect the model's predictions. These methods involve introducing
small, controlled changes to the input features of a model and observing how
these changes affect the output of the model.

9.3.2.1 Conceptual View

Explanations of deep image models frequently make use of methods that
rely on perturbation. The primary reason for doing this is to investigate the
variants of the output as a function of the various perturbations of the input.
Intrinsically speaking, when important input information is kept, the estimations ought to be comparable to the predictions that were made in the
beginning. The currently available methods learn a generator to generate a
mask in order to select crucial input pixels for the purpose of explaining
deep image models. On the other hand, graph models do not lend themselves
well to the direct application of such methods. Graphs, in contrast to images,
are not defined by pixels but rather by nodes and edges, and their size cannot be changed while maintaining the same number of nodes and edges.
In addition, in contrast to images, compositional information is essential for

graphs and could help determining the features and functions they exhibit. The counterfactual explanation of causation describes it as "If X had not taken place, then Y would not have taken place." In the context of explainers for graph intelligence models, when one edge, node, or single node feature are deleted from the justification for the current output, graph intelligence models will start generating completely different results if the element that was deleted or altered is a counterfactual explanation for the current output. This is the case even if the taken-down or altered element is not a counterfactual explanation for the current output. Therefore, in contrast to technique that relies on gradients or features, techniques that are based on perturbations of elements of graphs make an effort to identify the counterfactual explanation or underlying cause for graph intelligence models. To be more specific, perturbation-dependent techniques include the application of masks to edges, nodes, or node features in order to filter out the elements that are the most important for providing explanations for graph intelligence models. It is to be anticipated that graph intelligence models will produce forecasts on explanations that are comparable to those produced on input data. In this context, a wide variety of perturbation-dependent methods have been presented to interpreting the graph intelligence models. These methods include Causal Screening (Gonzalgo, Stephenson and Thompson, 2011), PGExplainer (Luo *et al.*, 2020), GNNExplainer (Ying *et al.*, 2019), GraphMask (Schlichtkrull, De Cao and Titov, 2020), SubgraphX (Yuan *et al.*, 2021), ZORRO (Anonymous Authors, 2021).

They have the same high-level processing pipeline, which is illustrated in Figure 9.2. First, with the graph that serves as inputs, a variety of masks are constructed in order to highlight significant aspects of the graph. Take note that different masks, such as node masks, edge masks, and node feature masks, are generated depending on the explanation tasks that are performed. After that, the generated masks are merged with the graph that was provided

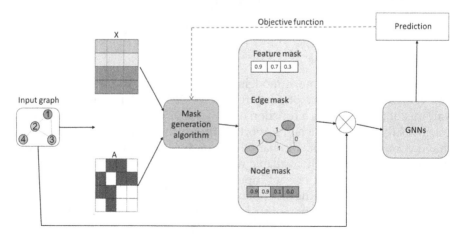

FIGURE 9.2
Generic workflow of perturbation-depended interpretability methods.

as inputs to produce a new graph that contains the essential information that was provided. In the final step, the newly constructed graph is introduced into the graph intelligence models that have been previously trained in order to evaluate the masks and update the algorithms that generate masks. Intuitively, the significant input features that are masked should be able to convey the primary semantic meaning, which will consequently result in a prediction that is comparable to the initial one. The primary distinction between these approaches can be drawn from three distinct aspects: the algorithm used to generate the masks, the types of masks used, and the objective function.

It is important to note that there are three distinct kinds of masks: approximated discrete masks, soft masks, and discrete masks. Figure 9.2 demonstrates estimated discrete masks for nodes, soft masks for node features, and discrete masks for edges. The soft masks have continuous variables that range from 0 *to* 1, and the algorithm that generates the mask could be straightforwardly updated using back propagation. Nevertheless, soft masks are afflicted with the "introduced evidence" problem (Dabkowski and Gal, 2017), which states that any nonzero or non-one value in the mask may add additional deeper information or new noise to the input graph, thereby influencing the outcomes of the interpretation. This problem causes soft masks to struggle from the "introduced evidence" issue. The discrete masks, on the other hand, only have the values 0 *and* 1 written on them. This allows one to circumvent the "introduced evidence" dilemma because there is no novel real number presented. Discrete masks, on the other hand, often entail non-differentiable processes, like sampling. The policy gradient method is a common approach that people take to solve this problem. In addition, recent research (Yuan *et al.*, 2022) suggests using reparameterization techniques to estimate the discrete masks. These techniques include Gumbel-Soft max assessment and sparse deregulations, to name a couple examples. It is important to keep in mind that the output mask is not purely discrete; rather, it offers a solid estimation. This not only facilitates back-propagation, yet it helps to relieve the "introduced evidence" problem to a great extent.

9.3.2.2 Explanation Methods

GNNExplainer was presented to learns soft masks related to the features of both nodes and edges with main aim to explain the outcomes of graph intelligence models through the mask optimization. For acquiring these masks, the GNNExplainer performs arbitrary initialization of soft masks, then considers them as a learnable parameter that can be optimized during the training. After that, GNNExplainer syndicates these masks into the input graph through Hamdard products. Following that, the optimization of masks is performed by enlarging the communal information between the estimates of the raw graph as well as the calculations derived from of the recently attained graph. Though the diversity of regularisation factors (like element-wise entropy) exploited to boost enhanced masks to stand discrete, the obtained masks remain soft, such that the GNNExplainer could not evade "Introduced evidence" problem. Furthermore, the masks are optimized for each input graph independently and therefore the interpretation might lack a comprehensive view.

The python implementation of the GNNExplainer is given in the following code snippets:

```
1.   #. . . . . . . . . . class imports. . . . . . . . .
2.   from math import sqrt
3.   import torch
4.   from torch import nn
5.   from tqdm import tqdm
6.   from dgl.base import NID, EID
7.   from dgl import khop_in_subgraph
8.   #. . . . . . . . Build explainer. . . . . . . . . .
9.   class GNNExplainer(nn.Module):
10.      r"""
11.         . . . .
12.      Parameters
13.         . . . . . . . . . . . . . . . . . . . . . . .
14.      * model: The GNN model to explain.
15.      * The are graph and node feature.
16.      * Optional edge weight argument
17.      * The forward function returns the logits for the estimated
18.             node/graph classes.
19.      """
20.
21.      def __init__(self,
22.                   model,
23.                   num_hops,
24.                   lr=0.01,
25.                   num_epochs=100,
26.                   *,
27.                   alpha1=0.005,
28.                   alpha2=1.0,
29.                   beta1=1.0,
30.                   beta2=0.1,
31.                   log=True):
32.          super(GNNExplainer, self).__init__()
33.          self.model = model
34.          self.num_hops = num_hops
35.          self.lr = lr
36.          self.num_epochs = num_epochs
37.          self.alpha1 = alpha1
38.          self.alpha2 = alpha2
39.          self.beta1 = beta1
40.          self.beta2 = beta2
41.          self.log = log
42.
43.      def _init_masks(self, graph, feature):
44.          r"""Initialization of trainable node feature and edge
     mask.
45.             . . . . . . . . . . . . . . . . . . . . . . .
46.          Parameters
47.             . . . . . . . . . . . . . . . . . . . . . . .
48.          * DGLGraph : graph -> Input graph.
```

```
49.            * Tensor : feature -> Input node features.
50.
51.            . . . . . . . . . . . . . . . . . . . . . . . . . .
52.            Returns
53.            . . . . . . . . . . . . . . . . . . . . . . . . . .
54.
55.            * Tensor: feature_mask -> mask with dimension D which
      denote the size of node features.
56.
57.            *Tensor: edge_mask -> Edge mask with dimension E,which
      represent the number of edges.
58.
59.            """
60.            num_nodes, feature_size = feature.size()
61.            num_edges = graph.num_edges()
62.            device = feature.device
63.
64.            std = 0.1
65.            feature_mask = nn.Parameter(torch.randn(1, feature_size,
      device=device) * std)
66.
67.            std = nn.init.calculate_gain('relu') * sqrt(2.0 / (2 *
      num_nodes))
68.            edge_mask = nn.Parameter(torch.randn(num_edges,
      device=device) * std)
69.
70.            return feature_mask, edge_mask
71.
72.     def _loss_regularize(self, loss, feature_mask, edge_mask):
73.            r"""Add regularization terms to the loss.
74.            . . . . . . . . . . . . . . . . . . . . . . . . . .
75.            Parameters
76.            . . . . . . . . . . . . . . . . . . . . . . . . . .
77.            * Tensor: loss ->  Loss value.
78.
79.            * Tensor: feature_mask -> Feature mask with dimension D
80.                       denoting the size of node features.
81.            * Tensor: edge_mask -> Edge mask wth dimension E, which
82.                       denote number of edges.
83.
84.            . . . . . . . . . . . . . . . . . . . . . . . . . .
85.            Returns
86.            . . . . . . . . . . . . . . . . . . . . . . . . . .
87.            * Tensor: Loss value with regularization terms added.
88.            """
89.            # Epsilon for numerical stability
90.            eps = 1e-15
91.
92.            edge_mask = edge_mask.sigmoid()
93.            # Edge mask sparsity regularization
94.            loss = loss + self.alpha1 * torch.sum(edge_mask)
95.            # Edge mask entropy regularization
96.            ent = - edge_mask * torch.log(edge_mask + eps) - \
97.                (1 - edge_mask) * torch.log(1 - edge_mask + eps)
98.            loss = loss + self.alpha2 * ent.mean()
99.
100.           feat_mask = feat_mask.sigmoid()
```

```
101.        # Feature mask sparsity regularization
102.        loss = loss + self.beta1 * torch.mean(feat_mask)
103.        # Feature mask entropy regularization
104.        ent = - feat_mask * torch.log(feat_mask + eps) - \
105.            (1 - feat_mask) * torch.log(1 - feat_mask + eps)
106.        loss = loss + self.beta2 * ent.mean()
107.
108.        return loss
109.
110.    def explain_node(self, node_id, graph, feat, **kwargs):
111.        r"""Learn and return a node feature mask and subgraph
    that play a
112.        crucial role to explain the prediction made by the GNN
    for node
113.        :attr:`node_id`.
114.        Parameters
115.        ----------
116.        node_id : int
117.            The node to explain.
118.        graph : DGLGraph
119.            A homogeneous graph.
120.        feat : Tensor
121.            The input feature of shape :math:`(N, D)`. :math:`N`
    is the
122.            number of nodes, and :math:`D` is the feature size.
123.        kwargs : dict
124.            Additional arguments passed to the GNN model.
    Tensors whose
125.            first dimension is the number of nodes or edges will be
126.            assumed to be node/edge features.
127.        Returns
128.        -------
129.        new_node_id : Tensor
130.            The new ID of the input center node.
131.        sg : DGLGraph
132.            The subgraph induced on the k-hop in-neighborhood of
    :attr:`node_id`.
133.        feat_mask : Tensor
134.            Learned feature importance mask of shape
    :math:`(D)`, where :math:`D` is the
135.            feature size. The values are within range :math:`(0, 1)`.
136.            The higher, the more important.
137.        edge_mask : Tensor
138.            Learned importance mask of the edges in the
    subgraph, which is a tensor
139.            of shape :math:`(E)`, where :math:`E` is the number
    of edges in the
140.            subgraph. The values are within range :math:`(0, 1)`.
141.            The higher, the more important.
142.        """
143.        self.model.eval()
144.        num_nodes = graph.num_nodes()
145.        num_edges = graph.num_edges()
146.
147.        # Extract node-centered k-hop subgraph and
148.        # its associated node and edge features.
```

```
149.          sg, inverse_indices = khop_in_subgraph(graph, node_id,
      self.num_hops)
150.          sg_nodes = sg.ndata[NID].long()
151.          sg_edges = sg.edata[EID].long()
152.          feature= feature[sg_nodes]
153.          for key, item in kwargs.items():
154.              if torch.is_tensor(item) and item.size(0) == num_nodes:
155.                  item = item[sg_nodes]
156.              elif torch.is_tensor(item) and item.size(0) == num_edges:
157.                  item = item[sg_edges]
158.              kwargs[key] = item
159.
160.          # Get the initial prediction.
161.          with torch.no_grad():
162.              logits = self.model(graph=sg, feature=feature, **kwargs)
163.              pred_label = logits.argmax(dim=-1)
164.
165.          feature_mask, edge_mask = self._init_masks(sg, feature)
166.
167.          params = [feature_mask, edge_mask]
168.          optimizer = torch.optim.Adam(params, lr=self.lr)
169.
170.          if self.log:
171.              pbar = tqdm(total=self.num_epochs)
172.              pbar.set_description(f'Explain node {node_id}')
173.
174.          for _ in range(self.num_epochs):
175.              optimizer.zero_grad()
176.              h = feature * feature_mask.sigmoid()
177.              logits = self.model(graph=sg, feature=h,
178.                          eweight=edge_mask.sigmoid(), **kwargs)
179.              log_probs = logits.log_softmax(dim=-1)
180.              loss = -log_probs[inverse_indices, pred_label
      [inverse_indices]]
181.              loss = self._loss_regularize(loss, feature_mask,
      edge_mask)
182.              loss.backward()
183.              optimizer.step()
184.
185.              if self.log:
186.                  pbar.update(1)
187.
188.          if self.log:
189.              pbar.close()
190.
191.          feature_mask = feature_mask.detach().sigmoid().squeeze()
192.          edge_mask = edge_mask.detach().sigmoid()
193.
194.          return inverse_indices, sg, feature_mask, edge_mask
195.
196.      def explain_graph(self, graph, feature, **kwargs):
197.          r"""Learn and return a node feature mask and an edge
      mask that play a
198.          crucial role to explain the prediction made by the GNN
      for a graph.
199.          Parameters
```

```
200.            ----------
201.            graph : DGLGraph
202.                A homogeneous graph.
203.            feature : Tensor
204.                The input feature of shape :math:`(N, D)`. :math:`N` is
      the
205.                number of nodes, and :math:`D` is the feature size.
206.            kwargs : dict
207.                Additional arguments passed to the GNN model.
      Tensors whose
208.                first dimension is the number of nodes or edges will be
209.                assumed to be node/edge features.
210.            Returns
211.            -------
212.            Tensor: feature_mask
213.                Learned feature importance mask of shape
      :math:`(D)`, where :math:`D` is the
214.                feature size. The values are within range :math:`(0, 1)`.
215.                The higher, the more important.
216.            Tensor: edge_mask
217.                Learned importance mask of the edges in the graph,
      which is a tensor
218.                of shape :math:`(E)`, where :math:`E` is the number
      of edges in the
219.                graph. The values are within range :math:`(0, 1)`.
      The higher,
220.                the more important.
221.
222.            """
223.            self.model.eval()
224.
225.            # Get the initial prediction.
226.            with torch.no_grad():
227.                logits = self.model(graph=graph, feature=feature,
      **kwargs)
228.                pred_label = logits.argmax(dim=-1)
229.
230.            feature_mask, edge_mask = self._init_masks(graph, feature)
231.
232.            params = [feature_mask, edge_mask]
233.            optimizer = torch.optim.Adam(params, lr=self.lr)
234.
235.            if self.log:
236.                pbar = tqdm(total=self.num_epochs)
237.                pbar.set_description('Explain graph')
238.
239.            for _ in range(self.num_epochs):
240.                optimizer.zero_grad()
241.                h = feature * feature_mask.sigmoid()
242.                logits = self.model(graph=graph, feature=h,
243.                                eweight=edge_mask.sigmoid(), **kwargs)
244.                log_probs = logits.log_softmax(dim=-1)
245.                loss = -log_probs[0, pred_label[0]]
246.                loss = self._loss_regularize(loss, feature_mask,
      edge_mask)
247.                loss.backward()
```

```
248.                optimizer.step()
249.
250.            if self.log:
251.                pbar.update(1)
252.
253.        if self.log:
254.            pbar.close()
255.
256.        feature_mask = feature_mask.detach().sigmoid().squeeze()
257.        edge_mask = edge_mask.detach().sigmoid()
258.
259.        return feature_mask, edge_mask
```

PGExplainer learns approximated discrete masks for edges to explain the predictions. To obtain edge masks, it trains a parameterized mask predictor to predict edge masks. Given an input graph, it first obtains the embeddings for each edge by concatenating the corresponding node embeddings. Then the predictor uses the edge embeddings to predict the probability of each edge being selected, which can be treated as the importance score. Next, the approximated discrete masks are sampled via the reparameterization trick. Finally, the mask predictor is trained by maximizing the mutual information between the original predictions and new predictions. Note that even though the reparameterization trick is employed, the obtained masks are not strictly discrete but can largely alleviate the "introduced evidence" problem. In addition, since all edges in the dataset share the same predictor, the explanations can provide a global understanding of the trained GNNs.

The python implementation of the PGExplainer is given in the following code snippets:

```
1.   #. . . . . . . . . . .Class imports. . . . . . . . . . .
2.   from typing import Optional
3.   from math import sqrt
4.
5.   import os
6.   import time
7.   import torch
8.   import numpy as np
9.   import torch.nn as nn
10.  from torch.optim import Adam
11.  from torch_geometric.data import Data, Batch
12.  from tqdm import tqdm
13.  import networkx as nx
14.  from torch_geometric.nn import MessagePassing
15.  from torch_geometric.utils import to_networkx
16.  mport model_args, data_args, explainer_args
17.
18.  EPS = 1e-6
19.
20.  #. . . . . . . . . Build explainer. . . . . . . . . . .
21.  class PGExplainer(nn.Module):
22.
23.      def __init__(self, model, epochs: int = 20, lr: float = 0.003,
```

```
24.                    top_k: int = 6, num_hops: Optional[int] = None):
25.          # lr=0.005, 0.003
26.          super(PGExplainer, self).__init__()
27.          self.model = model
28.          self.lr = lr
29.          self.epochs = epochs
30.          self.top_k = top_k
31.          self.__num_hops__ = num_hops
32.          self.device = model.device
33.
34.          self.coff_size = explainer_args.coff_size
35.          self.coff_ent = explainer_args.coff_ent
36.          self.init_bias = 0.0
37.          self.t0 = explainer_args.t0
38.          self.t1 = explainer_args.t1
39.
40.          self.elayers = nn.ModuleList()
41.          if model_args.model_name == 'gat':
42.              input_feature = model_args.gat_heads * model_args.
    gat_hidden * 2
43.          elif model_args.concate:
44.              input_feature = int(torch.Tensor(model_args.latent_
    dim).sum()) * 2
45.          else:
46.              input_feature = model_args.latent_dim[-1] * 2
47.          self.elayers.append(nn.Sequential(nn.Linear(input_
    feature, 64), nn.ReLU()))
48.          self.elayers.append(nn.Linear(64, 1))
49.          self.elayers.to(self.device)
50.          self.ckpt_path = os.path.join('./checkpoint', data_args.
    dataset_name,
51.  f'PGE_generator_{model_args.model_name}.pth')
52.
53.
54.
55.      @property
56.      def num_hops(self):
57.          """ return the number of layers of GNN model """
58.          if self.__num_hops__ is not None:
59.              return self.__num_hops__
60.
61.          k = 0
62.          for module in self.model.modules():
63.              if isinstance(module, MessagePassing):
64.                  k += 1
65.          return k
66.
67.
68.      def concrete_sample(self, log_alpha, beta=1.0,
    training=True):
69.          """ Sample from the instantiation of concrete
    distribution when training
70.          \epsilon \sim  U(0,1), \hat{e}_{ij} = \sigma (\frac{\log
    \epsilon-\log (1-\epsilon)+\omega_{i j}}{\tau})
71.          """
72.              if training:
```

```
73.                   random_noise = torch.rand(log_alpha.shape)
74.                   random_noise = torch.log(random_noise) - torch.
     log(1.0 - random_noise)
75.                   gate_inputs = (random_noise.to(log_alpha.device) +
     log_alpha) / beta
76.                   gate_inputs = gate_inputs.sigmoid()
77.              else:
78.                   gate_inputs = log_alpha.sigmoid()
79.
80.              return gate_inputs
81.
82.      def __clear_masks__(self):
83.          """ clear the edge weights to None """
84.          for module in self.model.modules():
85.              if isinstance(module, MessagePassing):
86.                   module.__explain__ = False
87.                   module.__edge_mask__ = None
88.          self.node_feat_masks = None
89.          self.edge_mask = None
90.
91.      def __flow__(self):
92.          for module in self.model.modules():
93.              if isinstance(module, MessagePassing):
94.                   return module.flow
95.          return 'source_to_target'
96.
97.      def __loss__(self, prob, ori_pred):
98.          """
99.          the pred loss encourages the masked graph with higher
     probability,
100.          the size loss encourage small size edge mask,
101.          the entropy loss encourage the mask to be continuous.
102.          """
103.          logit = prob[ori_pred]
104.          logit = logit + EPS
105.          pred_loss = -torch.log(logit)
106.          # size
107.          edge_mask = torch.sigmoid(self.mask_sigmoid)
108.          size_loss = self.coff_size * torch.sum(edge_mask)
109.
110.          # entropy
111.          edge_mask = edge_mask * 0.99 + 0.005
112.          mask_ent = - edge_mask * torch.log(edge_mask) - (1 -
     edge_mask) * torch.log(1 - edge_mask)
113.          mask_ent_loss = self.coff_ent * torch.mean(mask_ent)
114.
115.          loss = pred_loss + size_loss + mask_ent_loss
116.          return loss
117.
118.      def __set_masks__(self, x, edge_index, edge_mask=None,
     init="normal"):
119.          """ Set the weights for message passing """
120.          (N, F), E = x.size(), edge_index.size(1)
121.          std = 0.1
122.          init_bias = self.init_bias
```

```
123.         self.node_feat_mask = torch.nn.Parameter(torch.randn(F)
      * std)
124.         std = torch.nn.init.calculate_gain('relu') * sqrt(2.0 /
      (2 * N))
125.
126.         if edge_mask is None:
127.             self.edge_mask = torch.randn(E) * std + init_bias
128.         else:
129.             self.edge_mask = edge_mask
130.
131.         self.edge_mask.to(self.device)
132.         for module in self.model.modules():
133.             if isinstance(module, MessagePassing):
134.                 module.__explain__ = True
135.                 module.__edge_mask__ = self.edge_mask
136.
137.
138.     def forward(self, inputs, training=None):
139.         x, embed, edge_index, tmp = inputs
140.         nodesize = embed.shape[0]
141.         feature_dim = embed.shape[1]
142.         f1 = embed.unsqueeze(1).repeat(1, nodesize, 1).reshape(-1,
      feature_dim)
143.         f2 = embed.unsqueeze(0).repeat(nodesize, 1, 1).reshape(-1,
      feature_dim)
144.
145.         # using the node embedding to calculate the edge weight
146.         f12self = torch.cat([f1, f2], dim=-1)
147.         h = f12self.to(self.device)
148.         for elayer in self.elayers:
149.             h = elayer(h)
150.         values = h.reshape(-1)
151.         values = self.concrete_sample(values, beta=tmp,
      training=training)
152.         self.mask_sigmoid = values.reshape(nodesize, nodesize)
153.
154.         # set the symmetric edge weights
155.         sym_mask = (self.mask_sigmoid +
      self.mask_sigmoid.transpose(0, 1)) / 2
156.         edge_mask = sym_mask[edge_index[0], edge_index[1]]
157.
158.         self.__clear_masks__()
159.         self.__set_masks__(x, edge_index, edge_mask)
160.
161.         # the model prediction with edge mask
162.         data = Batch.from_data_list([Data(x=x,
      edge_index=edge_index)])
163.         data.to(self.device)
164.         outputs = self.model(data)
165.         return outputs[1].squeeze(), edge_mask
166.
167.     def get_model_output(self, x, edge_index, edge_mask=None,
      **kwargs):
168.         """ return the model outputs with or without (w/wo) edge
      mask """
169.         self.model.eval()
```

```
170.            self.__clear_masks__()
171.            if edge_mask is not None:
172.                self.__set_masks__(x, edge_index,
        edge_mask.to(self.device))
173.
174.            with torch.no_grad():
175.                data = Batch.from_data_list([Data(x=x,
        edge_index=edge_index)])
176.                data.to(self.device)
177.                outputs = self.model(data)
178.
179.            self.__clear_masks__()
180.            return outputs
181.
182.        def train_GC_explanation_network(self, dataset):
183.            """ train the explantion network for graph classification
        task """
184.            optimizer = Adam(self.elayers.parameters(), lr=self.lr)
185.            if data_args.dataset_name.lower() ==
        'grt_sst2_BERT_Identity'.lower():
186.                split_indices = dataset.supplement['split_indices']
187.                dataset_indices = torch.where(split_indices == 0)
        [0].numpy().tolist()
188.            else:
189.                dataset_indices = list(range(len(dataset)))
190.
191.            # collect the embedding of nodes
192.            emb_dict = {}
193.            ori_pred_dict = {}
194.            with torch.no_grad():
195.                self.model.eval()
196.                for gid in tqdm(dataset_indices):
197.                    data = dataset[gid]
198.                    _, prob, emb = self.get_model_output(data.x,
        data.edge_index)
199.                    emb_dict[gid] = emb.data.cpu()
200.                    ori_pred_dict[gid] = prob.argmax(-1).data.cpu()
201.
202.            # train the mask generator
203.            duration = 0.0
204.            for epoch in range(self.epochs):
205.                loss = 0.0
206.                tmp = float(self.t0 * np.power(self.t1 / self.t0,
        epoch / self.epochs))
207.                self.elayers.train()
208.                optimizer.zero_grad()
209.                tic = time.perf_counter()
210.                for gid in tqdm(dataset_indices):
211.                    data = dataset[gid]
212.                    prob, _ = self.forward((data.x, emb_dict[gid],
        data.edge_index, tmp), training=True)
213.                    loss_tmp = self.__loss__(prob, ori_pred_
        dict[gid])
214.                    loss_tmp.backward()
215.                    loss += loss_tmp.item()
216.
```

```
217.              optimizer.step()
218.              duration += time.perf_counter() - tic
219.              print(f'Epoch: {epoch} | Loss: {loss}')
220.              torch.save(self.elayers.cpu().state_dict(),
       self.ckpt_path)
221.              self.elayers.to(self.device)
222.          print(f"training time is {duration:.5}s")
223.
224.      def get_explanation_network(self, dataset,
       is_graph_classification=True):
225.          if os.path.isfile(self.ckpt_path):
226.              print("fetch network parameters from the saved files")
227.              state_dict = torch.load(self.ckpt_path)
228.              self.elayers.load_state_dict(state_dict)
229.              self.to(self.device)
230.          elif is_graph_classification:
231.              self.train_GC_explanation_network(dataset)
232.          else:
233.              self.train_NC_explanation_network(dataset)
234.
235.
236.      def explain_edge_mask(self, x, edge_index, **kwargs):
237.          data = Batch.from_data_list([Data(x=x,
       edge_index=edge_index)])
238.          data = data.to(self.device)
239.          with torch.no_grad():
240.              _, prob, emb = self.get_model_output(data.x,
       data.edge_index)
241.              _, edge_mask = self.forward((data.x, emb,
       data.edge_index, 1.0), training=False)
242.          return edge_mask
243.
244.      def k_hop_subgraph_with_default_whole_graph(node_idx,
       num_hops, edge_index, relabel_nodes=False, num_nodes=None,
       flow='source_to_target'):
245.          r"""Computes the :math:`k`-hop subgraph of
       :obj:`edge_index` around node
246.
247.          Args:
248.              * node_idx: The central node(s).
249.              * num_hops: The number of hops.
250.              * edge_index: The edge indices.
251.              * relabel_nodes True means that edge_index will be
       relabeled to hold consecutive indices
252.                  starting from zero.
253.              * num_nodes: The number of nodes
254.              * flow: The flow direction of aggregation
255.          Return: :class:`LongTensor`, :class:`LongTensor`,
       :class:`LongTensor`,
256.              :class:`BoolTensor`)
257.          """
258.
259.          num_nodes = maybe_num_nodes(edge_index, num_nodes)
260.
261.          assert flow in ['source_to_target', 'target_to_source']
262.          if flow == 'target_to_source':
```

```
263.            row, col = edge_index
264.        else:
265.            col, row = edge_index  # edge_index 0 to 1, col:
     source, row: target
266.
267.        node_mask = row.new_empty(num_nodes, dtype=torch.bool)
268.        edge_mask = row.new_empty(row.size(0), dtype=torch.bool)
269.
270.        inv = None
271.
272.        if int(node_idx) == -1:
273.            subsets = torch.tensor([0])
274.            cur_subsets = subsets
275.            while 1:
276.                node_mask.fill_(False)
277.                node_mask[subsets] = True
278.                torch.index_select(node_mask, 0, row,
     out=edge_mask)
279.                subsets = torch.cat([subsets,
     col[edge_mask]]).unique()
280.                if not cur_subsets.equal(subsets):
281.                    cur_subsets = subsets
282.                else:
283.                    subset = subsets
284.                    break
285.        else:
286.            if isinstance(node_idx, (int, list, tuple)):
287.                node_idx = torch.tensor([node_idx], device=row.
     device, dtype=torch.int64).flatten()
288.            elif isinstance(node_idx, torch.Tensor) and
     len(node_idx.shape) == 0:
289.                node_idx = torch.tensor([node_idx])
290.            else:
291.                node_idx = node_idx.to(row.device)
292.
293.            subsets = [node_idx]
294.            for _ in range(num_hops):
295.                node_mask.fill_(False)
296.                node_mask[subsets[-1]] = True
297.                torch.index_select(node_mask, 0, row, out=edge_mask)
298.                subsets.append(col[edge_mask])
299.            subset, inv =
     torch.cat(subsets).unique(return_inverse=True)
300.            inv = inv[:node_idx.numel()]
301.
302.        node_mask.fill_(False)
303.        node_mask[subset] = True
304.        edge_mask = node_mask[row] & node_mask[col]
305.
306.        edge_index = edge_index[:, edge_mask]
307.
308.        if relabel_nodes:
309.            node_idx = row.new_full((num_nodes,), -1)
310.            node_idx[subset] = torch.arange(subset.size(0),
     device=row.device)
311.            edge_index = node_idx[edge_index]
```

```
312.
313.        return subset, edge_index, inv, edge_mask
314.
315.    def get_subgraph(self, node_idx, x, edge_index, y,
       **kwargs):
316.        num_nodes, num_edges = x.size(0), edge_index.size(1)
317.        graph = to_networkx(data=Data(x=x, edge_index=edge_
       index), to_undirected=True)
318.        subset, edge_index, _, edge_mask =
       k_hop_subgraph_with_default_whole_graph(
319.            node_idx, self.num_hops, edge_index, relabel_nodes=True,
320.            num_nodes=num_nodes, flow=self.__flow__())
321.        mapping = {int(v): k for k, v in enumerate(subset)}
322.        subgraph = graph.subgraph(subset.tolist())
323.        nx.relabel_nodes(subgraph, mapping)
324.
325.        x = x[subset]
326.        for key, item in kwargs.items():
327.            if torch.is_tensor(item) and item.size(0) == num_nodes:
328.                item = item[subset]
329.            elif torch.is_tensor(item) and item.size(0) == num_edges:
330.                item = item[edge_mask]
331.            kwargs[key] = item
332.        y = y[subset]
333.        return x, edge_index, y, subset, kwargs
334.
335.    def train_NC_explanation_network(self, dataset):
336.        data = dataset[0]
337.        dataset_indices = torch.where(data.train_mask !=
       0)[0].tolist()
338.        optimizer = Adam(self.elayers.parameters(), lr=self.lr)
339.
340.        # collect the embedding of nodes
341.        x_dict = {}
342.        edge_index_dict = {}
343.        node_idx_dict = {}
344.        emb_dict = {}
345.        pred_dict = {}
346.        with torch.no_grad():
347.            self.model.eval()
348.            for gid in dataset_indices:
349.                x, edge_index, y, subset, _ = \
350.                    self.get_subgraph(node_idx=gid, x=data.x,
       edge_index=data.edge_index, y=data.y)
351.                _, prob, emb = self.get_model_output(x, edge_index)
352.                x_dict[gid] = x
353.                edge_index_dict[gid] = edge_index
354.                node_idx_dict[gid] = int(torch.where(subset ==
       gid)[0])
355.                pred_dict[gid] = prob[node_idx_dict[gid]].
       argmax(-1).cpu()
356.                emb_dict[gid] = emb.data.cpu()
357.        # train the explanation network
358.        for epoch in range(self.epochs):
359.            loss = 0.0
360.            optimizer.zero_grad()
```

```
361.                tmp = float(self.t0 * np.power(self.t1 / self.t0,
       epoch / self.epochs))
362.                self.elayers.train()
363.                for gid in tqdm(dataset_indices):
364.                    pred, edge_mask = self.forward((x_dict[gid],
       emb_dict[gid], edge_index_dict[gid], tmp), training=True)
365.                    loss_tmp = self.__loss__(pred[node_idx_
       dict[gid]], pred_dict[gid])
366.                    loss_tmp.backward()
367.                    loss += loss_tmp.item()
368.                optimizer.step()
369.                print(f'Epoch: {epoch} | Loss: {loss}')
370.                torch.save(self.elayers.cpu().state_dict(),
       self.ckpt_path)
371.                self.elayers.to(self.device)
```

GraphMask is a post hoc method that can be used to explain the significance of edges in each graph intelligence layer. In a manner analogous to that of the PGExplainer, it educates a classification model to determine whether or not an edge could be gone down without having an impact on the forecasting made previously. GraphMask, on the other hand, is able to obtain an edge mask for each graph intelligence layer, whereas PGExplainer only concentrates on the feature space. The thrown edges are then overtaken by trainable threshold interconnection, which seem to be vectors sharing the same dimensionality of node embeddings. This helps to make sure that the organization of the graph does not need to be altered. It is worth noting that binary Concrete distribution and the reparameterization trick are used in order to approximate discrete masks. In addition, the classifier is trained utilizing the entire dataset by minimizing a divergence term, which measures the difference between network predictions. This is done in order to ensure that the best results are achieved. In a manner comparable to that of PGExplainer, it is able to significantly improve the "introduced evidence" problem and offer a comprehensive comprehension of the trained graph intelligence models.

ZORRO makes use of discrete masks in order to recognize significant input vertices and attributes of nodes. A greedy method is leveraged to choose vertices or node attributes slowly and carefully to get discrete masks for vertices and features after the algorithm has been given an input graph. ZORRO will choose the node or feature of a node that has the maximum fidelity rating for each step in the process. It is the non-differentiable drawback of precisely defined masks is circumvented because there is no training process implicated in this method. Moreover, because they wear pretty tough masks, ZORRO does not have the "introduced evidence" dilemma that other organizations do. On the other hand, the greedy mask optimization technique might result in local interpretations that are optimal. Furthermore, because masks are created on a case-by-case basis for each graph, the interpretations could not provide a comprehensive understanding of the topic.

The purpose of the causal screening method is to investigate the causal attribution of various edges in the input graph as potential interpretations.

The edge mask for the interpretive subgraph is determined by this. Studying the change in predictions that occurs as a result of including a new edge, also recognized as the causation impact, in the existing explanatory subgraph is the fundamental concept underlying causal attribution. In order to acquire edge masks for each step, it examines the causation impacts of multiple edges and then chooses the edge that has the highest causal effect to add to the explanatory subgraph. This is done so that the edge masks can be generated. To be more specific, it uses something called the individual causal effect, or ICE, to choose edges. This is a method that measures the distinction in mutual information (between the forecasts of initial graphs and the informative subgraphs) after incorporating various edges to the subgraph. Causal Screening is a greedy algorithm that generates discrete masks in the same way that ZORRO does, but there is no training methodology involved. As a result, it overcomes the disadvantage of "introduced evidence" but may be caught in locally ideal interpretations and missing a global perspective.

Using SubgraphX, the authors investigate subgraph-level justifications for graph intelligence. The Monte Carlo Tree Search (MCTS) algorithm is used to quickly narrow down the reason for a forecast to the most relevant subgraph by cutting away unnecessary branches. Furthermore, a Shapley value is used as the incentive of MCTS to quantify the significance of subgraphs, and a practical estimation of the Shapley value is proposed by focusing on relationships within the message-passing domain. SubgraphX does not focus on mask research per se, but its node pruning operations can be seen as various masks to create subgraphs, and the MCTS algorithm could be seen as the mask generating technique. To further improve the mask generation technique, the Shapley values can be used as the goal function. The resulting subgraphs are better suited to graph data and easier for humans to understand than those obtained by other perturbation-based approaches. As the MCTS algorithm searches multiple subgraphs, the computing load is higher.

The python implementation of the SubgraphX is given in the following code snippets:

Step 1: define shapely values

```
1.   #. . . . . . . . . Class imports. . . . . . . . . . . . . . . .
2.   import math
3.   import torch
4.   import networkx as nx
5.   from Configures import mcts_args
6.   from torch_geometric.data import Data, Batch
7.   from torch_geometric.utils import to_networkx
8.   from functools import partial
9.   from collections import Counter
10.  import copy
11.  import numpy as np
12.  from scipy.special import comb
13.  from itertools import combinations
14.  from torch_geometric.data import Data, Batch, Dataset
15.  import os
```

```
16.  from tqdm import tqdm
17.
18.  ####################################################
     ############################
19.  def Model_value_function(gnnNets, target_class):
20.      def value_func(batch):
21.          with torch.no_grad():
22.              logits, prob, _ = gnnNets(batch)
23.              score = prob[:, target_class]
24.          return score
25.      return value_func
26.
27.  def get_graph_build_func(build_method):
28.      if build_method.lower() == 'zero_filling':
29.          return graph_build_zero_filling
30.      elif build_method.lower() == 'split':
31.          return graph_build_split
32.      else:
33.          raise NotImplementedError
34.
35.
36.  class MargSubgraphData(Dataset):
37.
38.      def __init__(self, data, exclude_mask, include_mask,
     subgraph_build_func):
39.          self.num_nodes = data.num_nodes
40.          self.X = data.x
41.          self.edge_index = data.edge_index
42.          self.device = self.X.device
43.
44.          self.label = data.y
45.          self.exclude_mask =
     torch.tensor(exclude_mask).type(torch.float32).to(self.device)
46.          self.include_mask =
     torch.tensor(include_mask).type(torch.float32).to(self.device)
47.          self.subgraph_build_func = subgraph_build_func
48.
49.      def __len__(self):
50.          return self.exclude_mask.shape[0]
51.
52.      def __getitem__(self, idx):
53.          exclude_graph_X, exclude_graph_edge_index =
     self.subgraph_build_func(self.X, self.edge_index, self.
     exclude_mask[idx])
54.          include_graph_X, include_graph_edge_index =
     self.subgraph_build_func(self.X, self.edge_index, self.
     include_mask[idx])
55.          exclude_data = Data(x=exclude_graph_X,
     edge_index=exclude_graph_edge_index)
56.          include_data = Data(x=include_graph_X,
     edge_index=include_graph_edge_index)
57.          return exclude_data, include_data
58.
59.
60.  def marg_participate(data: Data, exclude_mask: np.array,
     include_mask: np.array,
```

```
61.                                  value_func, subgraph_build_func):
62.           """ Calculate the marginal value for each pair """
63.           marginal_subgraph_dataset = MargSubgraphData(data,
          exclude_mask, include_mask, subgraph_build_func)
64.           dataloader = DataLoader(marginal_subgraph_dataset,
          batch_size=256, shuffle=False, pin_memory=True, num_workers=0)
65.
66.          marg_participate_list = []
67.
68.          for exclude_data, include_data in dataloader:
69.              exclude_values = value_func(exclude_data)
70.              include_values = value_func(include_data)
71.              margin_values = include_values - exclude_values
72.              marg_participate_list.append(margin_values)
73.
74.          marg_participates = torch.cat(marg_participate_list, dim=0)
75.          return marg_participates
76.
77.
78.    def graph_build_zero_filling(X, edge_index, node_mask: np.array):
79.          """ subgraph building through masking the unselected nodes
          with zero features """
80.          ret_X = X * node_mask.unsqueeze(1)
81.          return ret_X, edge_index
82.
83.
84.    def graph_build_split(X, edge_index, node_mask: np.array):
85.          """ node spliting-based subgraph building"""
86.          row, col = edge_index
87.          edge_mask = (node_mask[row] == 1) & (node_mask[col] == 1)
88.          ret_edge_index = edge_index[:, edge_mask]
89.          return X, ret_edge_index
90.
91.
92.    def local_shapley(coalition: list, data: Data, local_raduis: int,
93.                      value_func: str,
          subgraph_building_method='zero_filling'):
94.          """ shapley value in case of local neighbor as players """
95.          graph = to_networkx(data)
96.          num_nodes = graph.number_of_nodes()
97.          subgraph_build_func =
          get_graph_build_func(subgraph_building_method)
98.
99.          local_region = copy.copy(coalition)
100.         for k in range(local_raduis - 1):
101.             k_neiborhoood = []
102.             for node in local_region:
103.                 k_neiborhoood += list(graph.neighbors(node))
104.             local_region += k_neiborhoood
105.             local_region = list(set(local_region))
106.
107.         set_exclude_masks = []
108.         set_include_masks = []
109.         nodes_around = [node for node in local_region if node not in
          coalition]
110.         num_nodes_around = len(nodes_around)
```

```
111.
112.        for subset_len in range(0, num_nodes_around + 1):
113.            node_exclude_subsets = combinations(nodes_around,
        subset_len)
114.            for node_exclude_subset in node_exclude_subsets:
115.                set_exclude_mask = np.ones(num_nodes)
116.                set_exclude_mask[local_region] = 0.0
117.                if node_exclude_subset:
118.                    set_exclude_mask[list(node_exclude_subset)] = 1.0
119.                set_include_mask = set_exclude_mask.copy()
120.                set_include_mask[coalition] = 1.0
121.
122.                set_exclude_masks.append(set_exclude_mask)
123.                set_include_masks.append(set_include_mask)
124.
125.        exclude_mask = np.stack(set_exclude_masks, axis=0)
126.        include_mask = np.stack(set_include_masks, axis=0)
127.        num_players = len(nodes_around) + 1
128.        num_player_in_set = num_players - 1 + len(coalition) - (1 -
        exclude_mask).sum(axis=1)
129.        p = num_players
130.        S = num_player_in_set
131.        coeffs = torch.tensor(1.0 / comb(p, S) / (p - S + 1e-6))
132.
133.        marg_participates = \
134.            marg_participate(data, exclude_mask, include_mask,
        value_func, subgraph_build_func)
135.
136.        local_shapley_value = (marg_participates.squeeze().cpu() *
        coeffs).sum().item()
137.        return local_shapley_value
138.
139.
140.    def monte_carlo_shapley(coalition: list, data: Data,
141.                    value_func: str,
        subgraph_building_method='zero_filling',
142.                    sample_num=1000) -> float:
143.        """ estimation of the shapley value according to monte carlo
        sampling"""
144.        subset_build_func =
        get_graph_build_func(subgraph_building_method)
145.
146.        num_nodes = data.num_nodes
147.        node_indices = np.arange(num_nodes)
148.        coalition_placeholder = num_nodes
149.        set_exclude_masks = []
150.        set_include_masks = []
151.
152.        for example_idx in range(sample_num):
153.            subset_nodes_from = [node for node in node_indices if
        node not in coalition]
154.            random_nodes_permutation = np.array(subset_nodes_from +
        [coalition_placeholder])
155.            random_nodes_permutation =
        np.random.permutation(random_nodes_permutation)
```

```
156.          split_idx = np.where(random_nodes_permutation ==
      coalition_placeholder)[0][0]
157.          selected_nodes = random_nodes_permutation[:split_idx]
158.          set_exclude_mask = np.zeros(num_nodes)
159.          set_exclude_mask[selected_nodes] = 1.0
160.          set_include_mask = set_exclude_mask.copy()
161.          set_include_mask[coalition] = 1.0
162.
163.          set_exclude_masks.append(set_exclude_mask)
164.          set_include_masks.append(set_include_mask)
165.
166.      exclude_mask = np.stack(set_exclude_masks, axis=0)
167.      include_mask = np.stack(set_include_masks, axis=0)
168.      marg_participates = marg_participate(data, exclude_mask,
      include_mask, value_func, subset_build_func)
169.      monte_carlo_shapley_value = marg_participates.mean().item()
170.
171.      return monte_carlo_shapley_value
172.
173.
174.  def monte_carlo_local_shapley(coalition: list, data: Data,
      local_raduis: int,
175.                    value_func: str,
      subgraph_building_method='zero_filling',
176.                    sample_num=1000) -> float:
177.      """ estimation of the local_shapley value based monte carlo
      sampling """
178.      graph = to_networkx(data)
179.      num_nodes = graph.number_of_nodes()
180.      subgraph_build_func =
      get_graph_build_func(subgraph_building_method)
181.
182.      local_region = copy.copy(coalition)
183.      for k in range(local_raduis - 1):
184.          k_neiborhoood = []
185.          for node in local_region:
186.              k_neiborhoood += list(graph.neighbors(node))
187.          local_region += k_neiborhoood
188.          local_region = list(set(local_region))
189.
190.      coalition_placeholder = num_nodes
191.      set_exclude_masks = []
192.      set_include_masks = []
193.      for example_idx in range(sample_num):
194.          subset_nodes_from = [node for node in local_region if
      node not in coalition]
195.          random_nodes_permutation = np.array(subset_nodes_from +
      [coalition_placeholder])
196.          random_nodes_permutation = np.random.
      permutation(random_nodes_permutation)
197.          split_idx = np.where(random_nodes_permutation ==
      coalition_placeholder)[0][0]
198.          selected_nodes = random_nodes_permutation[:split_idx]
199.          set_exclude_mask = np.ones(num_nodes)
200.          set_exclude_mask[local_region] = 0.0
201.          set_exclude_mask[selected_nodes] = 1.0
```

```
202.             set_include_mask = set_exclude_mask.copy()
203.             set_include_mask[coalition] = 1.0
204.
205.         set_exclude_masks.append(set_exclude_mask)
206.         set_include_masks.append(set_include_mask)
207.
208.     exclude_mask = np.stack(set_exclude_masks, axis=0)
209.     include_mask = np.stack(set_include_masks, axis=0)
210.     marg_participates = \
211.         marg_participate(data, exclude_mask, include_mask,
    value_func, subgraph_build_func)
212.
213.     monte_carlo_local_shapley_value =
    (marg_participates).mean().item()
214.     return monte_carlo_local_shapley_value
215.
216.
217. def gnn_score(coalition: list, data: Data, value_func: str,
218.               subgraph_building_method='zero_filling') ->
    torch.Tensor:
219.     """ the value of subgraph with selected nodes """
220.     num_nodes = data.num_nodes
221.     subgraph_build_func =
    get_graph_build_func(subgraph_building_method)
222.     mask = torch.zeros(num_nodes).type(torch.float32)
223.     mask[coalition] = 1.0
224.     ret_x, ret_edge_index = subgraph_build_func(data.x,
    data.edge_index, mask)
225.     mask_data = Data(x=ret_x, edge_index=ret_edge_index)
226.     mask_data = Batch.from_data_list([mask_data])
227.     score = value_func(mask_data)
228.     # get the score of predicted class for graph or specific
    node idx
229.     return score.item()
230.
```

Step 2: Build Monta Carlo Tree Search

```
1. #. . . . . . . . Build  Search Tree. . . . . . . . . . . . . .
2. class MCTSNode():
3.
4.     def __init__(self, coalition: list, data: Data,
5.                  ori_graph: nx.Graph, c_puct: float = 10.0,
6.                  W: float = 0, N: int = 0, P: float = 0):
7.         self.data = data
8.         self.coalition = coalition
9.         self.ori_graph = ori_graph
10.        self.c_puct = c_puct
11.        self.children = []
12.        self.W = W  # sum of node value
13.        self.N = N  # times of arrival
14.        self.P = P  # property score (reward)
15.
16.    def Q(self):
17.        return self.W / self.N if self.N > 0 else 0
18.
```

```
19.     def U(self, n):
20.         return self.c_puct * self.P * math.sqrt(n) / (1 + self.N)
21.
22. class MCTS():
23.     def __init__(self, X: torch.Tensor, edge_index:
    torch.Tensor, n_rollout: int,
24.                 min_atoms: int, c_puct: float, expand_atoms:
    int, score_func):
25.         """ graph is a networkX graph """
26.         self.X = X
27.         self.edge_index = edge_index
28.         self.data = Data(x=self.X, edge_index=self.edge_index)
29.         self.graph = to_networkx(self.data, to_undirected=True)
30.         self.data = Batch.from_data_list([self.data])
31.         self.num_nodes = self.graph.number_of_nodes()
32.         self.score_func = score_func
33.         self.n_rollout = n_rollout
34.         self.min_atoms = min_atoms
35.         self.c_puct = c_puct
36.         self.expand_atoms = expand_atoms
37.
38.         self.root_coalition = sorted([i for i in range(self.
    num_nodes)])
39.         self.MCTSNodeClass = partial(MCTSNode, data=self.data,
    ori_graph=self.graph, c_puct=self.c_puct)
40.         self.root = self.MCTSNodeClass(self.root_coalition)
41.         self.state_map = {str(self.root.coalition): self.root}
42.
43.     def calculate_scores(score_func, children):
44.         results = []
45.         for child in children:
46.             if child.P == 0:
47.                 score = score_func(child.coalition, child.data)
48.             else:
49.                 score = child.P
50.                 results.append(score)
51.         return results
52.
53.     def mcts_rollout(self, tree_node):
54.         cur_graph_coalition = tree_node.coalition
55.         if len(cur_graph_coalition) <= self.min_atoms:
56.             return tree_node.P
57.
58.         # Expand if this node has never been visited
59.         if len(tree_node.children) == 0:
60.             node_degree_list =
    list(self.graph.subgraph(cur_graph_coalition).degree)
61.             node_degree_list = sorted(node_degree_list,
    key=lambda x: x[1], reverse=mcts_args.high2low)
62.             all_nodes = [x[0] for x in node_degree_list]
63.
64.             if len(all_nodes) < self.expand_atoms:
65.                 expand_nodes = all_nodes
66.             else:
67.                 expand_nodes = all_nodes[:self.expand_atoms]
68.
```

```
69.                     for each_node in expand_nodes:
70.                         # for each node, pruning it and get the
     remaining sub-graph
71.                         # here we check the resulting sub-graphs and
     only keep the largest one
72.                         subgraph_coalition = [node for node in all_nodes
     if node != each_node]
73.
74.                         subgraphs = [self.graph.subgraph(c)
75.                             for c in nx.connected_
     components(self.graph.subgraph(subgraph_coalition))]
76.                         main_sub = subgraphs[0]
77.                         for sub in subgraphs:
78.                             if sub.number_of_nodes() >
     main_sub.number_of_nodes():
79.                                 main_sub = sub
80.
81.                         new_graph_coalition =
     sorted(list(main_sub.nodes()))
82.
83.                         # check the state map and merge the same sub-graph
84.                         Find_same = False
85.                         for old_graph_node in self.state_map.values():
86.                             if Counter(old_graph_node.coalition) ==
     Counter(new_graph_coalition):
87.                                 new_node = old_graph_node
88.                                 Find_same = True
89.
90.                         if Find_same == False:
91.                             new_node =
     self.MCTSNodeClass(new_graph_coalition)
92.                             self.state_map[str(new_graph_coalition)] =
     new_node
93.
94.                         Find_same_child = False
95.                         for cur_child in tree_node.children:
96.                             if Counter(cur_child.coalition) ==
     Counter(new_graph_coalition):
97.                                 Find_same_child = True
98.
99.                         if Find_same_child == False:
100.                            tree_node.children.append(new_node)
101.
102.                scores = calculate_scores(self.score_func, tree_
     node.children)
103.                for child, score in zip(tree_node.children, scores):
104.                    child.P = score
105.
106.            sum_count = sum([c.N for c in tree_node.children])
107.            selected_node = max(tree_node.children, key=lambda x:
     x.Q() + x.U(sum_count))
108.            v = self.mcts_rollout(selected_node)
109.            selected_node.W += v
110.            selected_node.N += 1
111.            return v
112.
113.        def mcts(self, verbose=True):
```

```
114.            if verbose:
115.                print(f"The nodes in graph is {self.graph.
       number_of_nodes()}")
116.            for rollout_idx in range(self.n_rollout):
117.                self.mcts_rollout(self.root)
118.                if verbose:
119.                    print(f"At the {rollout_idx} rollout, {len(self.
       state_map)} states that have been explored.")
120.
121.            explanations = [node for _, node in self.state_map.items()]
122.            explanations = sorted(explanations, key=lambda x: x.P,
       reverse=True)
123.            return explanations
124.
125.    def reward_func(reward_args, value_func):
126.
127.        if reward_args.reward_method.lower() == 'gnn_score':
128.            return partial(gnn_score,
129.                           value_func=value_func,
130.    subgraph_building_method=reward_args.subgraph_building_method)
131.
132.        elif reward_args.reward_method.lower() ==
       'monte_carlo_shapley':
133.            return partial(monte_carlo_shapley,
134.                           value_func=value_func,
135.    subgraph_building_method=reward_args.subgraph_building_method,
136.                           sample_num=reward_args.sample_num)
137.
138.        elif reward_args.reward_method.lower() == 'local_shapley':
139.            return partial(local_shapley,
140.                           local_raduis=reward_args.local_raduis,
141.                           value_func=value_func,
142.    subgraph_building_method=reward_args.subgraph_building_method)
143.
144.        elif reward_args.reward_method.lower() ==
       'monte_carlo_local_shapley':
145.            return partial(monte_carlo_local_shapley,
146.                           local_raduis=reward_args.local_raduis,
147.                           value_func=value_func,
148.    subgraph_building_method=reward_args.subgraph_building_method,
149.                           sample_num=reward_args.sample_num)
150.        else:
151.            raise NotImplementedError
```

Step 3: Build the SubgraphX explainer:

```
1.    #. . . . . . . . . . Build explainer. . . . . . . . . .
2.    def get_closest_node(results, max_nodes):
3.        """. . . . . . . . . . . . . . . . . . . . . . . . .
4.        . . . . . . . . .   get the top reward graph node . . . . . .
5.        """
6.        results = sorted(results, key=lambda x: x.P, reverse=True)
7.        results = sorted(results, key=lambda x: len(x.coalition))
8.
9.        result_node = results[0]
10.       for result_idx in range(len(results)):
```

```
11.             x = results[result_idx]
12.             if len(x.coalition) <= max_nodes and x.P > result_node.P:
13.                 result_node = x
14.        return result_node
15.
16.  def SubGraphX(max_nodes):
17.        dataset = """read the dataset"""
18.        plotutils = """load data plotting utility"""
19.        input_dim = dataset.num_node_features
20.        output_dim = dataset.num_classes
21.
22.        data_indices = """ fetch data indices"""
23.
24.        gnnNets = """Load Graph Intelligence Models"""
25.        checkpoint = torch.load(mcts_args.explain_model_path)
26.        gnnNets.update_state_dict(checkpoint['net'])
27.        gnnNets.to_device()
28.        gnnNets.eval()
29.
30.        save_dir = os.path.join('./outputs',
31.                                f"{mcts_args.dataset_name}_"
32.                                f"{model_args.model_name}_"
33.                                f"{reward_args.reward_method}")
34.        if not os.path.isdir(save_dir):
35.            os.mkdir(save_dir)
36.
37.        fidelity_metric_list = []
38.        sparsity_metric_list = []
39.        for i in tqdm(data_indices):
40.            #. . . . . . . . . . get data and prediction. . . . . . .
41.            data = dataset[i]
42.            _, probs, _ =
       gnnNets(Batch.from_data_list([data.clone()]))
43.            prediction = probs.squeeze().argmax(-1).item()
44.            original_score = probs.squeeze()[prediction]
45.     # . . . . . . . . . . . . . . . . . . . . . . . . . . . . .
46.            #. . . . . . . . call reward function. . . . . . . . . .
47.            value_func = Model_value_function(gnnNets,
       target_class=prediction)
48.            payoff_func = reward_func(reward_args, value_func)
49.
50.            #. . . . . . . . Get routes and create graph. . . . . . . .
51.            result_path = os.path.join(save_dir, f"example_{i}.pt")
52.
53.            # mcts for l_shapely
54.            mcts_state_map = MCTS(data.x, data.edge_index,
55.                                  score_func=payoff_func,
56.                                  n_rollout=mcts_args.rollout,
57.                                  min_atoms=mcts_args.min_atoms,
58.                                  c_puct=mcts_args.c_puct,
59.
       expand_atoms=mcts_args.expand_atoms)
60.
61.            if os.path.isfile(result_path):
62.                results = torch.load(result_path)
63.            else:
```

```
64.              results = mcts_state_map.mcts(verbose=True)
65.              torch.save(results, result_path)
66.
67.         #. . . . . . . . . local sharply value. . . . . . . .
68.              graph_node_x = get_closest_node(results,
     max_nodes=max_nodes)
69.              masked_node_list = [node for node in list(range(graph_
     node_x.data.x.shape[0]))
70.                             if node not in
     graph_node_x.coalition]
71.              fidelity_metric = original_score - gnn_score(masked_node_
     list, data, value_func,
72.
     subgraph_building_method='zero_filling')
73.              sparsity_metric = 1 - len(graph_node_x.coalition) /
     graph_node_x.ori_graph.number_of_nodes()
74.              fidelity_metric_list.append(fidelity_metric)
75.              sparsity_metric_list.append(sparsity_metric)
76.
77.         # visualization
78.         if hasattr(dataset, 'supplement'):
79.              words =
     dataset.supplement['sentence_tokens'][str(i)]
80.              plotutils.plot(graph_node_x.ori_graph,
     graph_node_x.coalition, words=words,
81.                             figname=os.path.join(save_dir,
     f"example_{i}.png"))
82.         else:
83.              plotutils.plot(graph_node_x.ori_graph,
     graph_node_x.coalition, x=graph_node_x.data.x,
84.                             figname=os.path.join(save_dir,
     f"example_{i}.png"))
85.
86.     fidelity_metrics = torch.tensor(fidelity_metric_list)
87.     sparsity_metrics = torch.tensor(sparsity_metric_list)
88.     return fidelity_metrics, sparsity_metrics
```

Till the time of witting this book, the research efforts were still evolving to improve the performance of quality of perturbation-based explanation using more improved methods such as CF-GNNExplainer, RCExplainer, ReFine, and CF2; you can read more about these methods in Section 9.6.

9.3.3 Surrogate Models

In this section, we introduce the surrogate methods for explaining deep graph models.

9.3.3.1 A Conceptual View

Gradient-/feature-dependent techniques and permutation-dependent methods might be challenging to implement when access to the graph intelligence model system is restricted (e.g., only queries are allowed). One rational approach is to use simpler models (i.e., surrogates) to mimic the targeted graph intelligence models' input-output transformation. The operationally comparable surrogate model may understand the local behavior of the targeted graph intelligence models by taking into account the resemblance between the training examples and the corresponding neighbor. Model independence is a hallmark of surrogate approaches, with variations emerging primarily in neighborhood sampling techniques and human-interpretable surrogate models.

Given the intricate and often nonlinear nature of the interactions that exist between the input vector and the output projections, graph intelligence models are notoriously difficult to comprehend. The surrogate method is a common approach utilized for the purpose of providing example-based interpretations for picture models. The fundamental concept is to make use of a surrogate model that is straightforward and easy to read in order to come up with an approximation of the sophisticated deep model's forecasts for the surrounding regions of the input sample. It is worth noting that these techniques make the assumption that the relationships in the nearby sections of the input instance are simpler and could be effectively caught by a simplified surrogate model. This is an important point to keep in mind. After that, the interpretations derived from the explainable surrogate model are utilized in order to explain the initial predictions. The application of surrogate methods to the graph domain presents a number of challenges due to the discontinuous nature of graph data and the presence of topological information. If this is the case, it is unclear how to characterize the adjacent areas of the input graph and what kinds of intelligible surrogate models would be appropriate.

Not long ago, a number of surrogate techniques have been proposed to generate explanation to the graph intelligence models, such as GraphLime (Huang *et al.*, 2020), PGM-Explainer (Vu and Thai, 2020), and RelEx (Zhang, Defazio and Ramesh, 2021). The workflow of these technologies in its broadest sense is depicted in Figure 9.3. To begin the process of explaining the prediction of a particular input graph, they first gather a local dataset that contains a number of data objects that are neighboring one another and their predictions. After that, they applied an easy-to-interpret model to the data in order to get knowledge of the local data. In the end, the explanations that come from the interpretable model are considered to be the explanations that came from the initial model for the input graph. Although these approaches are conceptually comparable at a high level, the primary distinctions lay in the means through which the local data is acquired and the easily understandable surrogate model is applied to the data.

9.3.3.2 Surrogate Interpretability Methods

Local surrogate models are explainable frameworks that are utilized in the process of providing an explanation for final prediction generated by black box learning solutions. As a concrete implementation of local surrogate models,

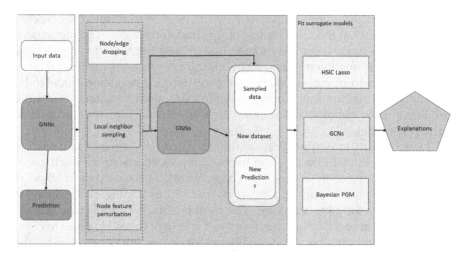

FIGURE 9.3
Generic workflow of surrogate interpretability methods.

the locally interpretable model-agnostic explanations (LIME) (Ribeiro, Singh and Guestrin, 2016) was offered as a possible solution. In order to come as close as possible to the projections of the basic black box model, surrogate explainability methods are trained. LIME places more of an emphasis on learning local surrogate models that can explicate outcome of model as opposed to creating a general surrogate strategy.

The LIME approach is extended to graph intelligence models by GraphLime GraphLime (Huang *et al.*, 2020), which also investigates the relative relevance of various node attributes for the purpose of node classification tasks. If you give GraphLime a target node in the input graph, it will consider the N-hop nearby nodes of that node and their predictions to be its local dataset. A good choice for N is the number of layers in the training graph intelligence models. After that, a nonlinear surrogate model known as the Hilbert-Schmidt independence criterion (HSIC) Lasso is used to the local dataset in order to fit it. Take note that HSIC Lasso is an approach for selecting features that is dependent on a kernel. In conclusion, it is possible to select key features to interpret the HSIC Lasso predictions by using the weights of the various features that are included in the HSIC Lasso. These particular traits have been chosen because they are thought to best explain the initial graph intelligence model forecast. Nevertheless, GraphLime is only capable of providing interpretations for node attributes. It does not take into account the graph structures, like nodes and edges, which are significantly more significant for graph data. Furthermore, GraphLime has been suggested as a means of explaining node classification tasks; however, it can't be immediately used to graph classification tasks.

The python implementation of the LIME (adapted for graph intelligence) is given in the following code snippets:

```
1.    #. . . . . . . . . Class imports. . . . . . . . . . . . . . . . .
2.    import numpy as np
3.    from sklearn.linear_model import Ridge
4.
5.    import torch
6.    from torch_geometric.nn import MessagePassing
7.    from torch_geometric.utils import k_hop_subgraph
8.    #. . . . . . . . . Build explainer. . . . . . . . . . . . . . .
9.    class LIME:
10.       """ LIME explainer - adapted to GNNs
11.       Explains only node features
12.       """
13.
14.       def __init__(self, data, model, gpu=False, cached=True):
15.           self.data = data
16.           self.model = model
17.           self.gpu = gpu
18.           self.M = self.data.num_features
19.           self.F = self.data.num_features
20.
21.           self.model.eval()
22.
23.       def __initial_prediction__(self, x, edge_index, *unused,
      **kwargs):
24.
25.           #. . . . . . . . . . Fetch initial prediction. . . . . . .
26.           with torch.no_grad():
27.               if self.gpu:
28.                   device = torch.device(
29.                       'cuda' if torch.cuda.is_available() else 'cpu')
30.                   self.model = self.model.to(device)
31.                   log_logits = self.model(
32.                       x=x.cuda(), edge_index=edge_index.cuda(),
      **kwargs)
33.               else:
34.                   log_logits = self.model(x=x, edge_index=edge_
      index, **kwargs)
35.               probas = log_logits.exp()

37.           return probas

39.       def explain(self, node_index, hops, num_samples, info=False,
      multiclass=False, **kwargs):
40.           num_samples = num_samples//2
41.           x = self.data.x
42.           edge_index = self.data.edge_index
43.
44.           probas = self.__initial_prediction__(x, edge_index,
      **kwargs)
45.           proba, label = probas[node_index, :].max(dim=0)
46.
47.           x_ = deepcopy(x)
```

```
48.           original_feats = x[node_index, :]
49.
50.       if multiclass:
51.           sample_x = [original_feats.detach().numpy()]
52.
53.           sample_y = [probas[node_index, :].detach().numpy()]
54.
55.           for _ in range(num_samples):
56.               x_[node_index, :] = original_feats + \
57.                   torch.randn_like(original_feats)
58.
59.               with torch.no_grad():
60.                   if self.gpu:
61.                       log_logits = self.model(
62.                           x=x_.cuda(),
      edge_index=edge_index.cuda(), **kwargs)
63.                   else:
64.                       log_logits = self.model(
65.                           x=x_, edge_index=edge_index,
      **kwargs)
66.                   probas_ = log_logits.exp()
67.
68.                   proba_ = probas_[node_index]
69.
70.                   sample_x.append(x_[node_index, :].detach().
      numpy())
71.                   # sample_y.append(proba_.item())
72.                   sample_y.append(proba_.detach().numpy())
73.
74.       else:
75.           sample_x = [original_feats.detach().numpy()]
76.           sample_y = [proba.item()]
77.
78.           for _ in range(num_samples):
79.               x_[node_index, :] = original_feats + \
80.                   torch.randn_like(original_feats)
81.
82.               with torch.no_grad():
83.                   if self.gpu:
84.                       log_logits = self.model(
85.                           x=x_.cuda(),
      edge_index=edge_index.cuda(), **kwargs)
86.                   else:
87.                       log_logits = self.model(
88.                           x=x_, edge_index=edge_index, **kwargs)
89.                   probas_ = log_logits.exp()
90.
91.                   proba_ = probas_[node_index, label]
92.
93.                   sample_x.append(x_[node_index, :].detach().numpy())
94.                   sample_y.append(proba_.item())
95.
96.       sample_x = np.array(sample_x)
97.       sample_y = np.array(sample_y)
98.
99.       solver = Ridge(alpha=0.1)
```

```
100.            solver.fit(sample_x, sample_y)

102.            return solver.coef_.T
```

The python implementation of the GraphLIME is given in the following code snippets:

```
1.   #. . . . . . . . . . . . . Class imports.. . . . . . . . .
     . . . . . . . import numpy as np
2.   from sklearn.linear_model import LassoLars
3.
4.   import torch
5.   from torch_geometric.nn import MessagePassing
6.   from torch_geometric.utils import k_hop_subgraph
7.   #. . . . . . . . . . Build explainer.. . . . . . . . . . . .
8.   class GraphLIME:
9.
10.      def __init__(self, data, model, gpu=False, hop=2, rho=0.1,
     cached=True):
11.          self.data = data
12.          self.model = model
13.          self.hop = hop
14.          self.rho = rho
15.          self.cached = cached
16.          self.cached_result = None
17.          self.M = self.data.num_features
18.          self.F = self.data.num_features
19.          self.gpu = gpu
20.
21.          self.model.eval()
22.
23.      def __flow__(self):
24.          for module in self.model.modules():
25.              if isinstance(module, MessagePassing):
26.                  return module.flow
27.          return 'source_to_target'
28.
29.      def __subgraph__(self, node_idx, x, y, edge_index, **kwargs):
30.          num_nodes, num_edges = x.size(0), edge_index.size(1)
31.
32.          subset, edge_index, mapping, edge_mask = k_hop_subgraph(
33.              node_idx, self.hop, edge_index, relabel_nodes=True,
34.              num_nodes=num_nodes, flow=self.__flow__())
35.
36.          x = x[subset]
37.          y = y[subset]
38.
39.          for key, item in kwargs:
40.              if torch.is_tensor(item) and item.size(0) == num_nodes:
41.                  item = item[subset]
42.              elif torch.is_tensor(item) and item.size(0) == num_edges:
43.                  item = item[edge_mask]
44.              kwargs[key] = item
45.
46.          return x, y, edge_index, mapping, edge_mask, kwargs
47.
```

```
48.     def __initial_prediction__(self, x, edge_index, **kwargs):
49.         if self.cached and self.cached_result is not None:
50.             if x.size(0) != self.cached_result.size(0):
51.                 raise RuntimeError(
52.                     'Cached {} number of nodes, but found
    {}.'.format(
53.                         x.size(0), self.cached_result.size(0)))
54.
55.         if not self.cached or self.cached_result is None:
56.             # Get the initial prediction.
57.             with torch.no_grad():
58.                 if self.gpu:
59.                     device = torch.device(
60.                         'cuda' if torch.cuda.is_available() else
    'cpu')
61.                     self.model = self.model.to(device)
62.                     log_logits = self.model(
63.                         x=x.cuda(), edge_index=edge_index.cuda(),
    **kwargs)
64.                 else:
65.                     log_logits = self.model(
66.                         x=x, edge_index=edge_index, **kwargs)
67.                 probas = log_logits.exp()
68.
69.             self.cached_result = probas
70.
71.         return self.cached_result
72.
73.     def __calculate_kernel__(self, x, reduce):
74.         assert x.ndim == 2, x.shape
75.
76.         n, d = x.shape
77.
78.         dist = x.reshape(1, n, d) - x.reshape(n, 1, d)
79.         dist = dist ** 2
80.
81.         if reduce:
82.             dist = np.sum(dist, axis=-1, keepdims=True)
83.
84.         std = np.sqrt(d)
85.
86.         # (n, n, 1) or (n, n, d)
87.         K = np.exp(-dist / (2 * std ** 2 * 0.1 + 1e-10))
88.
89.         return K
90.
91.     def __compute_gram_matrix__(self, x):
92.
93.         G = x - np.mean(x, axis=0, keepdims=True)
94.         G = G - np.mean(G, axis=1, keepdims=True)
95.
96.         G = G / (np.linalg.norm(G, ord='fro', axis=(0, 1),
    keepdims=True) + 1e-10)
97.
98.         return G
99.
```

```
100.    def generate_explanation(self, node_index, hops,
        num_samples, info=False, multiclass=False, *unused, **kwargs):
101.        # hops, num_samples, info are useless: just to copy
        graphshap pipeline
102.        x = self.data.x
103.        edge_index = self.data.edge_index
104.
105.        probas = self.__initial_prediction__(x, edge_index, **kwargs)
106.
107.        x, probas, _, _, _, _ = self.__subgraph__(
108.            node_index, x, probas, edge_index, **kwargs)
109.
110.        x = x.cpu().detach().numpy()    # (n, d)
111.        y = probas.cpu().detach().numpy()    # (n, classes)
112.
113.        n, d = x.shape
114.
115.        if multiclass:
116.            K = self.__calculate_kernel__(x, reduce=False)
117.            L = self.__calculate_kernel__(y, reduce=False)
118.
119.            K_bar = self.__compute_gram_matrix__(K)
120.            L_bar = self.__compute_gram_matrix__(L)
121.
122.            K_bar = K_bar.reshape(n ** 2, d)
123.            L_bar = L_bar.reshape(n ** 2, self.data.num_classes)
124.
125.            solver = LassoLars(self.rho, fit_intercept=False,
126.                               normalize=False, positive=True)
127.            solver.fit(K_bar * n, L_bar * n)
128.
129.            return solver.coef_.T
130.
131.        else:
132.            K = self.__calculate_kernel__(x, reduce=False)
133.            L = self.__calculate_kernel__(y, reduce=True)
134.
135.            K_bar = self.__compute_gram_matrix__(K)
136.            L_bar = self.__compute_gram_matrix__(L)
137.
138.            K_bar = K_bar.reshape(n ** 2, d)    # (n ** 2, d)
139.            L_bar = L_bar.reshape(n ** 2,)    # (n ** 2,)
140.
141.            solver = LassoLars(self.rho, fit_intercept=False,
142.                               normalize=False, positive=True)
143.            solver.fit(K_bar * n, L_bar * n)
144.
145.            return solver.coef_
```

Integrating the concepts of surrogate techniques and perturbation-based approaches is one of the ways that RelEx investigates the explainability of node categorization models. Provided a targeted vertex and its computing network (*N*-hop neighbors), it first obtains a local data by simply selecting interconnected subgraphs from the computational graph. It then feeds those subgraphs to trained graph intelligence models to acquire their forecasts.

Finally, it outputs the local data. To be more explicit, it begins at the node that serves as the target and then arbitrarly chooses other nodes in a breadth-first search way. Following this, it makes use of a graph convolution model as the surrogate model in order to suit the local data. Take note that in contrast to the surrogate model in LIME and GraphLime, the one found in RelEx cannot be interpreted. Following training, it then implements the perturbation-based techniques that were discussed earlier in order to explain the predictions. Some examples of these methods include producing soft masks or Gumbel-Softmax masks. In contrast to GraphLime, it is capable of providing explanations pertaining to significant nodes. Nevertheless, it comprises various stages of estimation, such as employing the surrogate model to estimate local relationships utilizing masks to estimate the edge significance; as a result, the interpretations are less persuasive and trustworthy. Specifically, the surrogate model is used to estimate local relationships. Moreover, because perturbation-based approaches may be explicitly used to explain original deep graph models, it is not essential to develop another non-interpretable deep model as the surrogate model in order to explicate it. This is because the explanation can be provided by the original model itself. It is also unclear how it can be utilized to complete jobs involving graph categorization.

Moreover, in order to give instance-level interpretations for graph intelligence models, PGM-Explainer constructs a stochastic graph intelligence model. The local dataset is obtained through the randomized disturbance of the node features. To be more specific, whenever PGM-Explainer receives a graph as input, it will arbitrarily tamper with the characteristics of the nodes of some random nodes located within the computing network. The PGM-Explainer will then register a stochastic process for each node in the computational graph. This variable will indicate if the properties of the node are being changed and how that change will affect the graph intelligence model forecasts. A local data can be obtained by carrying out similar methods numerous times in succession. Take note that the local dataset used by PGM-Explainer consists of node variables rather than distinct samples drawn from the nearby graphs. The Grow-Shrink (GS) technique is then utilized to choose the most important dependent variables in order to minimize the amount of the local data. In conclusion, an explainable Bayesian network is utilized to fit the regional dataset and to provide an explanation for the predictions made by the initial graph intelligence model model. PGM-Explainer is able to provide interpretations on graph vertices, but it ignores graph edges, which carry crucial data about the graph's structure. Furthermore, unlike RelEx and GraphLime, the PGM-Explainer may be used to explain not only node classification but also graph classification jobs. This is a significant advantage.

The python implementation of the **PGM_NodeExplainer** is given in the following code snippets:

```
1.  #. . . . . . . . . Class imports.. . . . . . . . . . . . . . .
2.  import networkx as nx
```

```
3.   import math
4.   import time
5.   import torch
6.   import numpy as np
7.   import pandas as pd
8.   from scipy.special import softmax
9.   from pgmpy.estimators.CITests import chi_square
10.  from pgmpy.estimators import HillClimbSearch, BicScore
11.  from pgmpy.models import BayesianModel
12.  from pgmpy.inference import VariableElimination
13.  from scipy import stats
14.
15.  #. . . . . . . . Build explainer. . . . . . . . . . .
16.  class PGM_NodeExplainer:
17.      def __init__(self, model, A, X, ori_pred, num_layers, mode = 0,
     print_result = 1):
18.          self.model = model
19.          self.model.eval()
20.          self.A = A
21.          self.X = X
22.          self.ori_pred = ori_pred
23.          self.num_layers = num_layers
24.          self.mode = mode
25.          self.print_result = print_result
26.
27.      def n_hops_A(self, n_hops):
28.          # Compute the n-hops adjacency matrix
29.          adj = torch.tensor(self.A, dtype=torch.float)
30.          hop_adj = power_adj = adj
31.          for i in range(n_hops - 1):
32.              power_adj = power_adj @ adj
33.              prev_hop_adj = hop_adj
34.              hop_adj = hop_adj + power_adj
35.              hop_adj = (hop_adj > 0).float()
36.          return hop_adj.numpy().astype(int)
37.
38.      def extract_n_hops_neighbors(self, nA, node_idx):
39.          # Return the n-hops neighbors of a node
40.          node_nA_row = nA[node_idx]
41.          neighbors = np.nonzero(node_nA_row)[0]
42.          node_idx_new = sum(node_nA_row[:node_idx])
43.          sub_A = self.A[neighbors][:, neighbors]
44.          sub_X = self.X[neighbors]
45.          return node_idx_new, sub_A, sub_X, neighbors
46.
47.      def perturb_features_on_node(self,feature_matrix, node_idx,
     random = 0, mode = 0):
48.
49.          X_perturb = feature_matrix
50.          if mode == 0:
51.              if random == 0:
52.                  perturb_array = X_perturb[node_idx]
53.              elif random == 1:
54.                  perturb_array = np.random.randint(2, size =
     X_perturb[node_idx].shape[0])
55.              X_perturb[node_idx] = perturb_array
```

```
56.              elif mode == 1:
57.                  if random == 0:
58.                      perturb_array = X_perturb[node_idx]
59.                  elif random == 1:
60.                      perturb_array = np.multiply(X_perturb[node_
     idx],np.random.uniform(low=0.0, high=2.0, size = X_perturb[node_
     idx].shape[0]))
61.                  X_perturb[node_idx] = perturb_array
62.              return X_perturb
63.
64.      def explain(self, node_idx, num_samples = 100,
     top_node = None, p_threshold = 0.05, pred_threshold = 0.1):
65.          print("Explaining node: " + str(node_idx))
66.          nA = self.n_hops_A(self.num_layers)
67.          node_idx_new, sub_A, sub_X, neighbors =
     self.extract_n_hops_neighbors(nA,node_idx)
68.
69.          if (node_idx not in neighbors):
70.              neighbors = np.append(neighbors, node_idx)
71.
72.          X_torch = torch.tensor([self.X], dtype=torch.float)
73.          A_torch = torch.tensor([self.A], dtype=torch.float)
74.          pred_torch, _ = self.model.forward(X_torch, A_torch)
75.          soft_pred =
     np.asarray([softmax(np.asarray(pred_torch[0][node_].data)) for
     node_ in range(self.X.shape[0])])
76.
77.          pred_node = np.asarray(pred_torch[0][node_idx].data)
78.          label_node = np.argmax(pred_node)
79.          soft_pred_node = softmax(pred_node)
80.
81.          Samples = []
82.          Pred_Samples = []
83.
84.          for iteration in range(num_samples):
85.
86.              X_perturb = self.X.copy()
87.              sample = []
88.              for node in neighbors:
89.                  seed = np.random.randint(2)
90.                  if seed == 1:
91.                      latent = 1
92.                      X_perturb = self.perturb_features_on_node(X_
     perturb, node, random = seed)
93.                  else:
94.                      latent = 0
95.                  sample.append(latent)
96.
97.              X_perturb_torch =  torch.tensor([X_perturb],
     dtype=torch.float)
98.              pred_perturb_torch, _ =
     self.model.forward(X_perturb_torch, A_torch)
99.              soft_pred_perturb =
     np.asarray([softmax(np.asarray(pred_perturb_torch[0][node_].
     data)) for node_ in range(self.X.shape[0])])
100.
101.             sample_bool = []
```

```
102.                    for node in neighbors:
103.                        if (soft_pred_perturb[node,np.argmax(soft_
      pred[node])] + pred_threshold) < np.max(soft_pred[node]):
104.                            sample_bool.append(1)
105.                        else:
106.                            sample_bool.append(0)
107.
108.                    Samples.append(sample)
109.                    Pred_Samples.append(sample_bool)
110.
111.                Samples = np.asarray(Samples)
112.                Pred_Samples = np.asarray(Pred_Samples)
113.                Combine_Samples = Samples-Samples
114.                for s in range(Samples.shape[0]):
115.                    Combine_Samples[s] = np.asarray([Samples[s,i]*10 +
      Pred_Samples[s,i]+1 for i in range(Samples.shape[1])])
116.
117.                data = pd.DataFrame(Combine_Samples)
118.                ind_sub_to_ori = dict(zip(list(data.columns),
      neighbors))
119.                data = data.rename(columns={0: "A", 1: "B"}) # Trick to
      use chi_square test on first two data columns
120.                ind_ori_to_sub = dict(zip(neighbors,list(data.columns)))
121.
122.                p_values = []
123.                dependent_neighbors = []
124.                dependent_neighbors_p_values = []
125.                for node in neighbors:
126.
127.                    chi2, p = chi_square(ind_ori_to_sub[node], ind_ori_
      to_sub[node_idx], [], data)
128.                    p_values.append(p)
129.                    if p < p_threshold:
130.                        dependent_neighbors.append(node)
131.                        dependent_neighbors_p_values.append(p)
132.
133.                pgm_stats = dict(zip(neighbors,p_values))
134.
135.                pgm_nodes = []
136.                if top_node == None:
137.                    pgm_nodes = dependent_neighbors
138.                else:
139.                    top_p = np.min((top_node,len(neighbors)-1))
140.                    ind_top_p = np.argpartition(p_values, top_p)[0:top_p]
141.                    pgm_nodes = [ind_sub_to_ori[node] for node in
      ind_top_p]
142.
143.                data = data.rename(columns={"A": 0, "B": 1})
144.                data = data.rename(columns=ind_sub_to_ori)
145.
146.                return pgm_nodes, data, pgm_stats
147.
148.        def generalize_target(self, x):
149.            if x > 10:
150.                return x - 10
151.            else:
```

```
152.                 return x
153.
154.     def generalize_others(self, x):
155.         if x == 2:
156.             return 1
157.         elif x == 12:
158.             return 11
159.         else:
160.             return x
161.
162.     def chi_square(self, X, Y, Z, data):
163.
164.         X = str(int(X))
165.         Y = str(int(Y))
166.         if isinstance(Z, (frozenset, list, set, tuple)):
167.             Z = list(Z)
168.         Z = [str(int(z)) for z in Z]
169.
170.         state_names = {
171.             var_name: data.loc[:, var_name].unique() for
     var_name in data.columns
172.         }
173.
174.         row_index = state_names[X]
175.         column_index = pd.MultiIndex.from_product(
176.             [state_names[Y]] + [state_names[z] for z in Z],
     names=[Y] + Z
177.         )
178.
179.         XYZ_state_counts = pd.crosstab(
180.                 index=data[X], columns= [data[Y]] + [data[z]
     for z in Z],
181.                 rownames=[X], colnames=[Y] + Z
182.             )
183.
184.         if not isinstance(XYZ_state_counts.columns, pd.MultiIndex):
185.             XYZ_state_counts.columns =
     pd.MultiIndex.from_arrays([XYZ_state_counts.columns])
186.         XYZ_state_counts = XYZ_state_counts.reindex(
187.             index=row_index, columns=column_index
188.         ).fillna(0)
189.
190.         if Z:
191.             XZ_state_counts = XYZ_state_counts.sum(axis=1,level
     = list( range(1,len(Z)+1)) )  # marginalize out Y
192.             YZ_state_counts = XYZ_state_counts.sum().unstack(Z)
     # marginalize out X
193.         else:
194.             XZ_state_counts = XYZ_state_counts.sum(axis=1)
195.             YZ_state_counts = XYZ_state_counts.sum()
196.         Z_state_counts = YZ_state_counts.sum()  # marginalize
     out both
197.
198.         XYZ_expected = np.zeros(XYZ_state_counts.shape)
199.
200.         r_index = 0
```

```
201.            for X_val in XYZ_state_counts.index:
202.                X_val_array = []
203.                if Z:
204.                    for Y_val in XYZ_state_counts.columns.levels[0]:
205.                        temp = XZ_state_counts.loc[X_val] *
        YZ_state_counts.loc[Y_val] / Z_state_counts
206.                        X_val_array = X_val_array +
        list(temp.to_numpy())
207.                        XYZ_expected[r_index] = np.asarray(X_val_array)
208.                        r_index=+1
209.                else:
210.                    for Y_val in XYZ_state_counts.columns:
211.                        temp = XZ_state_counts.loc[X_val] *
        YZ_state_counts.loc[Y_val] / Z_state_counts
212.                        X_val_array = X_val_array + [temp]
213.                        XYZ_expected[r_index] = np.asarray(X_val_array)
214.                        r_index=+1
215.
216.            observed = XYZ_state_counts.to_numpy().reshape(1,-1)
217.            expected = XYZ_expected.reshape(1,-1)
218.            observed, expected = zip(*((o, e) for o, e in
        zip(observed[0], expected[0]) if not (e == 0 or math.isnan(e) )))
219.            chi2, significance_level = stats.chisquare(observed,
        expected)
220.
221.            return chi2, significance_level
222.
223.        def search_MK(self, data, target, nodes):
224.            target = str(int(target))
225.            data.columns = data.columns.astype(str)
226.            nodes = [str(int(node)) for node in nodes]
227.
228.            MB = nodes
229.            while True:
230.                count = 0
231.                for node in nodes:
232.                    evidences = MB.copy()
233.                    evidences.remove(node)
234.                    _, p = self.chi_square(target, node, evidences,
        data[nodes+ [target]])
235.                    if p > 0.05:
236.                        MB.remove(node)
237.                        count = 0
238.                    else:
239.                        count = count + 1
240.                        if count == len(MB):
241.                            return MB
242.
243.        def pgm_generate(self, target, data, pgm_stats, subnodes,
        child = None):
244.
245.            subnodes = [str(int(node)) for node in subnodes]
246.            target = str(int(target))
247.            subnodes_no_target = [node for node in subnodes if node
        != target]
248.            data.columns = data.columns.astype(str)
```

```
249.
250.           MK_blanket = self.search_MK(data, target,
        subnodes_no_target.copy())
251.
252.
253.           if child == None:
254.                est = HillClimbSearch(data[subnodes_no_target],
        scoring_method=BicScore(data))
255.                pgm_no_target = est.estimate()
256.                for node in MK_blanket:
257.                    if node != target:
258.                        pgm_no_target.add_edge(node,target)
259.
260.            #   Create the pgm
261.                pgm_explanation = BayesianModel()
262.                for node in pgm_no_target.nodes():
263.                    pgm_explanation.add_node(node)
264.                for edge in pgm_no_target.edges():
265.                    pgm_explanation.add_edge(edge[0],edge[1])
266.
267.            #   Fit the pgm
268.                data_ex = data[subnodes].copy()
269.                data_ex[target] =
        data[target].apply(self.generalize_target)
270.                for node in subnodes_no_target:
271.                    data_ex[node] =
        data[node].apply(self.generalize_others)
272.                pgm_explanation.fit(data_ex)
273.           else:
274.                data_ex = data[subnodes].copy()
275.                data_ex[target] =
        data[target].apply(self.generalize_target)
276.                for node in subnodes_no_target:
277.                    data_ex[node] =
        data[node].apply(self.generalize_others)
278.
279.                est = HillClimbSearch(data_ex,
        scoring_method=BicScore(data_ex))
280.                pgm_w_target_explanation = est.estimate()
281.
282.            #   Create the pgm
283.                pgm_explanation = BayesianModel()
284.                for node in pgm_w_target_explanation.nodes():
285.                    pgm_explanation.add_node(node)
286.                for edge in pgm_w_target_explanation.edges():
287.                    pgm_explanation.add_edge(edge[0],edge[1])
288.
289.            #   Fit the pgm
290.                data_ex = data[subnodes].copy()
291.                data_ex[target] =
        data[target].apply(self.generalize_target)
292.                for node in subnodes_no_target:
293.                    data_ex[node] =
        data[node].apply(self.generalize_others)
294.                pgm_explanation.fit(data_ex)
295.
```

```
296.
297.          return pgm_explanation
298.
299.    def pgm_conditional_prob(self, target, pgm_explanation,
       evidence_list):
300.          pgm_infer = VariableElimination(pgm_explanation)
301.          for node in evidence_list:
302.              if node not in list(pgm_infer.variables):
303.                  print("Not valid evidence list.")
304.                  return None
305.          evidences = dict(zip(evidence_list,[1 for node in
       evidence_list]))
306.          elimination_order = [node for node in
       list(pgm_infer.variables) if node not in evidence_list]
307.          elimination_order = [node for node in elimination_order
       if node != target]
308.          q = pgm_infer.query([target], evidence = evidences,
309.                              elimination_order = elimination_order,
       show_progress=False)
310.          return q.values[0]
```

The python implementation of the **PGM_GraphExplainer** is given in the following code snippets:

```
1.   #. . . . . . . . . Class imports. . . . . . . . . . . . . . .
     . . . . . import time
2.   import torch
3.   import numpy as np
4.   import pandas as pd
5.   from scipy.special import softmax
6.   from pgmpy.estimators import ConstraintBasedEstimator
7.   from pgmpy.estimators.CITests import chi_square
8.
9.   #. . . . . . . . . Build explainer. . . . . . . . . . . . . .
10.  class PGM_GraphExplainer:
11.      def __init__(self, model, graph, num_layers = None,
     perturb_feature_list = None, perturb_mode = "mean", # mean, zero,
     max or uniform
12.          perturb_indicator = "diff", print_result = 1, snorm_n =
     None, snorm_e = None):
13.
14.          self.model = model
15.          self.model.eval()
16.          self.graph = graph
17.          self.snorm_n = snorm_n
18.          self.snorm_e = snorm_e
19.          self.num_layers = num_layers
20.          self.perturb_feature_list = perturb_feature_list
21.          self.perturb_mode = perturb_mode
22.          self.perturb_indicator = perturb_indicator
23.          self.print_result = print_result
24.          self.X_feat = graph.ndata['feat'].numpy()
25.          self.E_feat = graph.edata['feat'].numpy()
26.
27.      def n_hops_A(self, n_hops):
```

```
28.              # Calculate n-hops adjacency matrix
29.              # Use the same implementation given in PGM_NodeExplainer
30.
31.      def perturb_node_features(self, feature_matrix, node_idx,
     random = 0):
32.
33.          X_perturb = feature_matrix.copy()
34.          perturb_array = X_perturb[node_idx].copy()
35.          epsilon = 0.05*np.max(self.X_feat, axis = 0)
36.          seed = np.random.randint(2)
37.
38.          if random == 1:
39.              if seed == 1:
40.                  for i in range(perturb_array.shape[0]):
41.                      if i in self.perturb_feature_list:
42.                          if self.perturb_mode == "mean":
43.                              perturb_array[i] =
     np.mean(feature_matrix[:,i])
44.                          elif self.perturb_mode == "zero":
45.                              perturb_array[i] = 0
46.                          elif self.perturb_mode == "max":
47.                              perturb_array[i] =
     np.max(feature_matrix[:,i])
48.                          elif self.perturb_mode == "uniform":
49.                              perturb_array[i] = perturb_array[i] +
     np.random.uniform(low=-epsilon[i], high=epsilon[i])
50.                              if perturb_array[i] < 0:
51.                                  perturb_array[i] = 0
52.                              elif perturb_array[i] >
     np.max(self.X_feat, axis = 0)[i]:
53.                                  perturb_array[i] =
     np.max(self.X_feat, axis = 0)[i]
54.
55.
56.          X_perturb[node_idx] = perturb_array
57.
58.          return X_perturb
59.
60.      def batch_perturb_node_features(self, num_samples,
     index_to_perturb,
61.                                      percentage,
     p_threshold, pred_threshold):
62.          X_torch = torch.tensor(self.X_feat, dtype=torch.float)
63.          E_torch = torch.tensor(self.E_feat, dtype=torch.float)
64.          pred_torch = self.model.forward(self.graph, X_torch,
     E_torch, self.snorm_n, self.snorm_e)
65.          soft_pred = np.asarray(softmax(np.asarray(pred_torch[0].
     data)))
66.          pred_label = np.argmax(soft_pred)
67.          num_nodes = self.X_feat.shape[0]
68.          Samples = []
69.          for iteration in range(num_samples):
70.              X_perturb = self.X_feat.copy()
71.              sample = []
72.              for node in range(num_nodes):
73.                  if node in index_to_perturb:
```

```
74.                          seed = np.random.randint(100)
75.                          if seed < percentage:
76.                              latent = 1
77.                              X_perturb =
     self.perturb_node_features(X_perturb, node, random = latent)
78.                          else:
79.                              latent = 0
80.                      else:
81.                          latent = 0
82.                      sample.append(latent)
83.
84.              X_perturb_torch =  torch.tensor(X_perturb,
     dtype=torch.float)
85.              pred_perturb_torch = self.model.forward(self.graph,
     X_perturb_torch, E_torch, self.snorm_n, self.snorm_e)
86.              soft_pred_perturb =
     np.asarray(softmax(np.asarray(pred_perturb_torch[0].data)))
87.
88.              pred_change = np.max(soft_pred) -
     soft_pred_perturb[pred_label]
89.
90.              sample.append(pred_change)
91.              Samples.append(sample)
92.
93.          Samples = np.asarray(Samples)
94.          if self.perturb_indicator == "abs":
95.              Samples = np.abs(Samples)
96.
97.          top = int(num_samples/8)
98.          top_idx = np.argsort(Samples[:,num_nodes])[-top:]
99.          for i in range(num_samples):
100.             if i in top_idx:
101.                 Samples[i,num_nodes] = 1
102.             else:
103.                 Samples[i,num_nodes] = 0
104.
105.         return Samples
106.
107.     def explain(self, num_samples = 10, percentage = 50,
     top_node = None, p_threshold = 0.05, pred_threshold = 0.1):
108.
109.         num_nodes = self.X_feat.shape[0]
110.         if top_node == None:
111.             top_node = int(num_nodes/20)
112.
113. #        Round 1
114. Samples = self.batch_perturb_node_features(int(num_samples/2),
     range(num_nodes),percentage,
115.
     p_threshold, pred_threshold)
116.
117.         data = pd.DataFrame(Samples)
118.         est = ConstraintBasedEstimator(data)
119.
120.         p_values = []
121.         cand_nodes = []
```

```
122.
123.            target = num_nodes # The entry for the graph
        classification data is at "num_nodes"
124.        for node in range(num_nodes):
125.            chi2, p = chi_square(node, target, [], data)
126.            p_values.append(p)
127.
128.            number_cands = int(top_node*4)
129.            cand_nodes = np.argpartition(p_values, number_cands)
        [0:number_cands]
130.
131.    #        Round 2
132.            Samples = self.batch_perturb_node_features(num_samples,
        cand_nodes, percentage,
133.
        p_threshold, pred_threshold)
134.            data = pd.DataFrame(Samples)
135.            est = ConstraintBasedEstimator(data)
136.
137.            p_values = []
138.            dependent_nodes = []
139.
140.            target = num_nodes
141.            for node in range(num_nodes):
142.                chi2, p = chi_square(node, target, [], data)
143.                p_values.append(p)
144.                if p < p_threshold:
145.                    dependent_nodes.append(node)
146.
147.            top_p = np.min((top_node,num_nodes-1))
148.            ind_top_p = np.argpartition(p_values, top_p)[0:top_p]
149.            pgm_nodes = list(ind_top_p)
150.
151.            return pgm_nodes, p_values, cand_nodes
```

9.3.4 Decomposition Explanation

9.3.4.1 Conceptual View

Decomposition methods, which evaluate the value of input characteristics by decomposing the initial model's forecasts into many terms, are another common way to describe deep image classifiers. These models estimate the significance of attribute values. After that, the terms are considered to be the significance ratings of the attributes that relate to them being input. These methods conduct an in-depth analysis of the model parameters to discover the connections that can be made between the characteristics of the input space and the forecasts of the outcome. It is important to keep in mind that the conservative aspect of these approaches stipulates that the total number of decomposed elements must have the same value as the score that was initially predicted. Nevertheless, because graphs comprise nodes, edges, and node characteristics, it is hard to actually apply such approaches to the graph domain. The process of assigning scores to the various edges of a graph is not a simple one, despite the fact that these edges carry essential topological information that could not be disregarded.

In recent times, a number of different decomposition approaches have been developed in order to understand deep graph intelligence models. These methods include layer-wise relevance propagation (LRP) (Schwarzenberg *et al.*, 2019), GNN-LRP (Schnake *et al.*, 2021), and excitation BP (Pope *et al.*, 2019b). These decomposition methods are designed with the intention of constructing scored decomposition rules in order to distribute forecast scores across the input space. Figure 9.4 illustrates the workflow that is typically associated with these technologies. These techniques back propagate the prediction score from the output layer all the way down to the input layer, distributing it layer by layer. The forecast made by the model is utilized as the first target score, and this procedure begins at the output layer. After that, the rating is broken down into its component parts and sent to the neurons in the layer below it in accordance with the decomposition criteria. They are able to get important scores for node characteristics by repeatedly carrying out these operations until they reach the input space. These significance ratings can then be merged with one another to indicate edge significance, node significance, and walk significance. It is important to note that none of these techniques take into account the activation functions that are used in graph intelligence models. The scoring decomposition criteria, the perspective of decomposition, and the objectives of explanation are the primary areas in which these various approaches diverge from one another.

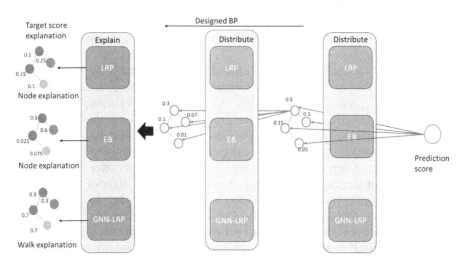

FIGURE 9.4
Generic workflow of the decomposition-based interpretability methods.

9.3.4.2 Decomposition Methods

The LRP method extends the capabilities of the original LRP technique to deep network models. It does this by breaking the output prediction score down into a variety of distinct node significance ratings. The rule for the decomposition of the rating is constructed based on the concealed features and weights. The score of a target neuron is approximated using a linear formula, and it is based on the ratings of the neurons in the layer below it. Inherently, the neuron that contributes the most to the activation of the target neuron will be awarded a larger percentage of the total score for the target neuron. If the adjacency matrix is not regarded as a component of the graph intelligence model during the post hoc explication phase, the neighboring matrices will acquire deconstructed scores, which will render the conservative property invalid. This is done to ensure that the conservative condition is satisfied. The explanatory findings acquired using LRP are more reliable than those obtained using other methods since LRP is directly produced based on the model parameters. On the other hand, it is only able to investigate the significance of individual nodes and could be used to graph structures like subgraphs and graph walks, both of which are significantly more vital to the comprehension of graph intelligence models. Besides, the usage of such an algorithm necessitates an in-depth comprehension of the modeling techniques; as a result, its applicability to non-expert users, including academics working in multiple fields, is restricted. In addition, excitation BP shares a similar idea as the LRP algorithm but is developed from the view of the law of total probability. It defines that the probability of a neuron in the current layer is equal to the total probabilities it outputs to all connected neurons in the next layer. Then the score decomposition rule can be regarded as decomposing the target probability into several conditional probability terms. Note that the computation of excitation BP is highly similar to the z+-rule in LRP. Hence, it shares the same advantages and limitations as the LRP algorithm.

GNN-LRP is a study that looks at the significance of various graph walks. When conducting neighborhood information aggregation, it is more cohesive to the deep graph intelligence models since graph walks correspond to message flows. It does this by treating the graph intelligence model as a function and providing a perspective of high-order Taylor decomposition so that the score decomposition rule can be developed. The Taylor decomposition, when evaluated at root zero, is shown to include only terms of order T, where T is the number of layers present in the trained graph intelligence models and each term equates to a graph walk with T steps, according to a theoretical demonstration. After that, concepts of this nature might be considered to be the importance scores of graph walks. Because it isn't conceivable to directly calculate the high-order derivatives provided by the Taylor expansion, GNN-LRP also uses a back propagation approach to estimate the T-order terms. This is because it is not possible to immediately calculate the high-order derivatives. Take note that the GNN-LRP algorithm's back-propagation calculations work in a way that is analogous to the LRP technique. GNN-LRP, on the other hand, allocates scores to various graph walks rather than assigning them to individual nodes or edges in the graph. It keeps a record of the routes taken by the distribution processes as they move from one layer to the next. These walks are believed to be separate from one another, and the scores are derived from the nodes that correspond to each of the walks. Despite the fact that GNN-LRP has a strong theoretical foundation, the approximations that it uses in its operations could not be entirely correct. In additional to this, the computation cost is quite significant due to the fact that each walk is analyzed on its own. In addition, it is difficult for non-specialists to use, particularly in multidisciplinary fields, due to the fact that the back propagation rules must be developed for various models and graph intelligence model versions. This presents a challenge for multidisciplinary fields.

9.4 Model-Level Explanations

The explanation of graph intelligence models is provided by model-level methods that are independent of any particular input sample. These explanations are high-level and describe generic behavior. They are not dependent on any particular input. When contrasted with techniques at the instance level, this path has seen significantly less exploration. The XGNN (Yuan *et al.*, 2020) approach, which is centered on graph generation, is the only model-level technique that currently exists. Model-level techniques, as opposed to instance-level methods, strive to provide broad perspectives and high-level comprehension in order to explain deep graph models. To be more specific, they investigate what kinds of input graph topologies can cause a given graph intelligence model behavior, such as increasing the accuracy of a target prediction. A common path to take when attempting to gain model-level interpretations for image classifiers is known as input optimization. Due to the fact that it is not possible to immediately apply it to graph models because of the discontinuous graph topology information, it becomes more difficult to describe graph intelligence models at the model level. As a result, it is still an essential topic, although receiving less attention from researchers. XGNN appears to be the only model-level method that is currently available for describing graph intelligence models to the greatest of our knowledge (Yuan *et al.*, 2022).

XGNN is an explanation that looks to use graph creation to provide light on graph intelligence models. It trains a graph generator so that the generated graphs can maximize a targeted graph forecast rather than directly optimizing the graph that is inputted into the system. After that, the created graphs are considered to be the explanations for the target prediction, and it is anticipated that these graphs will include graph structures that are discriminatory. In XGNN, the generation of the graph is approached as a reinforcement learning issue instead. The generator makes a prediction at each stage regarding how an edge should be added to the existing graph. After that, the created graphs are fed into the trained graph intelligence models in order to collect feedback that may be used to train the generator using policy gradient. Besides, a number of graph rules have been included to make it more likely that the explanations will be valid as well as understandable to humans. For instance, the rule for chemical data can be stated as the node degree of an atom not being allowed to surpass its maximal chemical valency. This is an instance of how the rule could be applied. In addition, XGNN allows the user to place a maximum limit on the size of the created graphs, which helps to ensure that the final interpretations are clear and concise. Take note that XGNN is a generic framework for the development of model-level interpretations, which allows any appropriate graph generation technique to be used. Additionally, the explanations are of a broad nature and offer a comprehensive comprehension of the trained graph intelligence models. However, the suggested XGNN only illustrates its success in explaining graph classification models, and it is uncertain whether XGNN can be applied to node classification tasks. This is an essential approach for future studies to investigate, as it proves the importance of the direction.

9.5 Interpretability Evaluation Metrics

The lack of ground realities makes it difficult to entirely trust evaluations of visualization outcomes regarding the reasonableness of explanations to humans. It's also a time-consuming manual process for humans to examine the outcomes of each input sample when comparing the performance of various explanation approaches. The subjective nature of human cognition also plays a large role in evaluations, which is not acceptable. As a result, criteria for evaluation are fundamental for the investigation of explanatory strategies. An effective metric would be the one that evaluates findings from the model's perspective, such as checking to see if the provided explanations are consistent with the model. Many newly proposed evaluation measures for generated explanations are discussed in this section.

9.5.1 Fidelity Measure

The generated explanations must be devoted to the underlying AI solution by recognizing the key features necessary to the AI algorithm, not the targeted audience. For instance, the Fidelity+ (Pope *et al.*, 2019a) performance measure was recently designed to compare this. Subjectively, if significant input features recognized by explanation methods are discriminatory to the AI model, removing these features should cause the forecasts to substantially differ. Fidelity+ is thus described as the variation in accuracy between the last and fresh forecasts after filtering significant input features (Hooker *et al.*, 2019; Pope *et al.*, 2019a). Let G_i denote the ith input and $f(\cdot)$ representing the AI algorithm that need to be interpreted in formal terms, and the outcome can be represented as $\bar{y}_i = argmax \ f(G_i)$. The explanations can then be thought of as a hard importance map m_i, with each element indicating whether the corresponding feature is important or not. It is worth noting that the generated explanations for methods (Gonzalgo, Stephenson and Thompson, 2011; Anonymous Authors, 2021) are discrete masks that can be used directly as the importance map. Furthermore, if the importance scores for methods (Ying *et al.*, 2019; Huang *et al.*, 2020) are constant ideals, the significance of the metric m_i could be acquired using thresholding and normalization. Therefore, the *Fidelity* + prediction accuracy score can be calculated as

$$Fidelity +^{acc} = \frac{1}{N} \sum_{i=1}^{N} \left(1\left(\bar{y}_i = y_i\right) - 1\left(\bar{y}_i^{1-m_i} = y_i\right)\right), \tag{9.4}$$

where y_i denotes the initial forecasting of input i and N denotes the number of inputs. $1 - m_i$ denotes the opposite mask that means eliminating the significant input features, and $\bar{y}_i^{1-m_i}$ denotes the outcome obtained by passing new input to trained AI algorithm $f(\cdot)$. If $\bar{y}_i$ and y_i are equal, the indicator function $1\left(\bar{y}_i = y_i\right)$ returns 1; otherwise, it returns 0. It should be noted that the *Fidelity* $+^{acc}$ metric investigates the change in prediction accuracy. The *Fidelity* + of probability can be defined by focusing on the predicted probability:

$$Fidelity +^{prob} = \frac{1}{N} \sum_{i=1}^{N} \left(f(G_i)_{y_i} - f\left(G_i^{1-m_i}\right)_{y_i} \right), \tag{9.5}$$

where $G_i^{1-m_i}$ denotes the new input formed by retaining features of G_i relying on the complimentary mask $1 - m_i$.

It is significant to mention that *Fidelity* $+^{prob}$ tracks the transformation in forecasted probability, which is more delicate than *Fidelity* $+^{acc}$. Increasing scores for both performance measures allows improved explanation outcomes and the identification of more key features (Pope *et al.*, 2019a; Guidotti *et al.*, 2020). The *Fidelity* + measurement investigates forecasting transformation by removing important features. Conversely, the measurement *Fidelity* – experiments forecast to change by retaining significant input features while discarding insignificant ones. Intuitively, notable features should encompass contextual power, resulting in forecasts that are equivalent to the previous forecasts even when insignificant features are eliminated. Formally, the measurement *Fidelity –* can be calculated as follows:

$$Fidelity +^{acc} = \frac{1}{N} \sum_{i=1}^{N} \left(1\left(\bar{y}_i = y_i\right) - 1\left(\bar{y}_i^{m_i} = y_i\right) \right), \tag{9.6}$$

$$Fidelity +^{prob} = \frac{1}{N} \sum_{i=1}^{N} \left(f\left(G_i\right)_{y_i} - f\left(G_i^{m_i}\right)_{y_i} \right), \tag{9.7}$$

where G_i^m is the new graph created by retaining significant features of G_i relying on explanation m_i, and $\bar{y}_i^{m_i}$ is the fresh forecasting. It is worth noting that for both *Fidelity +^{acc}* and *Fidelity +^{prob}*, smaller values indicate that less important information is deleted in order to improve the explanations outcomes.

9.5.2 Sparsity Measure

Better explanations should be sparse, capturing only the major significant input features while ignoring the irrelevant features. Sparsity is an indicator that shows such an estate. It particularly represents the ratio of features chosen as significant by explanation techniques (Pope *et al.*, 2019a). Formally, given the input G_i and its tough significance map m_i, the Sparsity measurement can be estimated as

$$Sparsity = \frac{1}{N} \sum_{i=1}^{N} \left(1 - \frac{|m_i|}{|M_i|} \right), \tag{9.8}$$

where $|m_i|$ symbolizes the total of significant input features recognized in m_i, and $|M_i|$ embodies the total number of features in G_i. A higher score indicates that the explanations are sparser and seem to encapsulate only the major significant input details.

```
1.   #. . . . . . . . Class imports. . . . . . . . . . . .
2.   import torch
3.   import torch.nn as nn
4.   from typing import List, Union
5.   from torch import Tensor
6.   import numpy as np
7.   import cilog
8.   from torch_geometric.nn import MessagePassing
9.
10.  def control_sparsity(mask, sparsity=None):
11.      r"""
12.      . . . . . . . . Inputs: . . . . . . . . . . . . . .
13.      1) The mask to be transformed
14.      2) The sparsity to be controlled i.e., 0.7, 0.5
15.      . . . . . . . .Output: . . . . . . . . . . . . . . .
```

```
16.      The converted mask in which top (1 - sparsity) values are
    assigned infinity.
17.      """
18.      if sparsity is None:
19.          sparsity = 0.7
20.
21.      _, indices = torch.sort(mask, descending=True)
22.      mask_len = mask.shape[0]
23.      split_point = int((1 - sparsity) * mask_len)
24.      important_indices = indices[: split_point]
25.      unimportant_indices = indices[split_point:]
26.      transformed_mask = mask.clone()
27.      transformed_mask[important_indices] = float('inf')
28.      transformed_mask[unimportant_indices] = - float('inf')
29.
30.      return transformed_mask
31.
32.
33. def fidelity(ori_probs: torch.Tensor, unimportant_probs: torch.
    Tensor) -> float:
34.
35.      drop_probability = ori_probs - unimportant_probs
36.
37.      return drop_probability.mean().item()
38.
39.
40. def fidelity_inv(ori_probs: torch.Tensor, important_probs: torch.
    Tensor) -> float:
41.
42.      drop_probability = ori_probs - important_probs
43.
44.      return drop_probability.mean().item()
45.
46.
47. class XCollector(object):
48.
49.      def __init__(self, sparsity):
50.          self.__related_preds, self.__targets = {'zero': [],
    'masked': [], 'maskout': [], 'origin': []}, []
51.          self.masks: Union[List, List[List [Tensor]]] = []
52.
53.          self.__sparsity = sparsity
54.          self.__fidelity, self.__fidelity_inv = None, None
55.          self.__score = None
56.
57.
58.      @property
59.      def targets(self) -> list:
60.          return self.__targets
61.
62.      def new(self):
63.          self.__related_preds, self.__targets = {'zero': [],
    'masked': [], 'maskout': [], 'origin': []}, []
64.          self.masks: Union[List, List[List[Tensor]]] = []
65.
66.          self.__fidelity, self.__fidelity_inv = None, None
```

```
67.
68.     def collect_data(self,
69.                        masks: List [Tensor],
70.                        related_preds: dir,
71.                        label: int) -> None:
72.
73.         if self.__fidelity or self.__fidelity_inv:
74.             self.__fidelity, self.__fidelity_inv = None, None
75.             print(f'#W#Called collect_data() after calculate
    explainable metrics.')
76.
77.         if not np.isnan(label):
78.             for key, value in related_preds [label].items():
79.                 self.__related_preds[key].append(value)
80.
81.             self.__targets.append(label)
82.             self.masks.append(masks)
83.
84.
85.     @property
86.     def fidelity(self):
87.         if self.__fidelity:
88.             return self.__fidelity
89.         else:
90.
91.             zero_mask_preds, mask_out_preds, masked_preds,
    one_mask_preds = \
92.                 torch.tensor(self.__related_preds['zero']),
    torch.tensor( self.__related_preds ['maskout']), \
93.                 torch.tensor(self.__related_preds ['masked']),
    torch.tensor ( self.__related_preds ['origin'])
94.
95.             self.__fidelity = fidelity(one_mask_preds,
    mask_out_preds)
96.             return self.__fidelity
97.
98.     @property
99.     def fidelity_inv (self):
100.        if self.__fidelity_inv:
101.            return self.__fidelity_inv
102.        else:
103.
104.            zero_mask_preds, mask_out_preds, masked_preds,
    one_mask_preds = \
105.                torch.tensor(self.__related_preds ['zero']),
    torch.tensor(self.__related_preds ['maskout']), \
106.                torch.tensor(self.__related_preds ['masked']),
    torch.tensor(self.__related_preds ['origin'])
107.
108.            self.__fidelity_inv = fidelity_inv (one_mask_preds,
    masked_preds)
109.            return self.__fidelity_inv
110.
111.    @property
112.    def sparsity(self):
113.        if self.__sparsity:
```

```
114.            return self.__sparsity
115.        else:
116.            raise ValueError(f' You can control and initialize your '
117.                             f'Sparsity once you initialize that
     class rather than computing it.')
```

9.5.3 Stability Measure

Furthermore, better explanations need to be more consistent. Intuitively, when tiny differences to the input are made without influencing the forecasts, the explanations should stay constant. The previously approved Stability measurement assesses the stability of an explanation technique (Sanchez-Lengeling et al., 2020). Based on a given input G_i, the explanations m_i are considered the ground truth. The input G_i is then perturbed by slight differences, to yield a new input $\ddot{G}_i$. It is significant to mention that G_i and $\ddot{G}_i$ must have the same forecasts. The explanations of $\ddot{G}_i$ are then acquired, signified as m_i. We can calculate the Stability score by looking at the difference between m_i and $\acute{m}_i$. The lower value shows that the explanation method is more durable and resistant to noisy information. Furthermore, because some input formats are sensitive, hence, determining the appropriate number of perturbations may be difficult.

9.6 Case Study

The interpretability is essential pillar of responsible graph intelligence since it has been becoming a major concern for business and data owners. In response to this concern, both academia and industry are interesting to practically investigate the techniques necessary to explain the decision made by the graph intelligence models. Motivated by that, the supplementary materials of this chapter are designated to provide a holistic implementation of different interpretability methods discussed in the previous sections on real-world case studies for different graph tasks. The supplementary materials of this chapter also provide the readers with recommendations for further reading about the content of this chapter. The repository of supplementary materials is given in this link: https://github.com/DEEPOLOGY-AI/Book-Graph-Neural-Network/tree/main/Chapter%209

References

Anonymous Authors. (2021) 'Hard Masking for Explaining Graph Neural Networks', in *International Conference on Learning Representations 2021*, pp. 1–12.

Baldassarre, F. and Azizpour, H. (May 2019) 'Explainability Techniques for Graph Convolutional Networks.' Retrieved from http://arxiv.org/abs/1905.13686.

Dabkowski, P. and Gal, Y. (2017) 'Real Time Image Saliency for Black Box Classifiers', in *Advances in Neural Information Processing Systems*. doi: 10.48550/arXiv.1705.07857.

Gonzalgo, M. L., Stephenson, A. J. and Thompson, I. M. (2011) 'Causal Screening To Interpret Graph Neural Networks', *Education* 2, pp. 1–13.

Guidotti, R. *et al.* (2020) 'Explaining Image Classifiers Generating Exemplars and Counter-Exemplars from Latent Representations', in *AAAI 2020 – 34th AAAI Conference on Artificial Intelligence*, 13665–13668. doi: 10.1609/aaai.v34i09.7116.

Hooker, S. *et al.* (2019) 'A benchmark for interpretability methods in deep neural networks', in *Proceedings of the 33rd International Conference on Neural Information Processing Systems*, pp. 9737–9748.

Huang, Q. *et al.* (2020) 'GraphLIME: Local Interpretable Model Explanations for Graph Neural Networks.' *arXiv Prepr. arXiv2001.06216*. Retrieved from http://arxiv.org/abs/2001.06216.

Luo, D., Cheng, W., Xu, D., Yu, W., Zong, B., Chen, H., & Zhang, X. (2020). Parameterized explainer for graph neural network. Advances in neural information processing systems, 33, 19620-19631. https://proceedings.neurips.cc/paper/2020/hash/e37b08dd3015330dcbb5d6663667b8b8-Abstract.html

Pope, P. E. *et al.* (2019a) 'Explainability Methods for Graph Convolutional Neural Networks', in *Proceedings of the IEEE Computer Society Conference on Computer Vision and Pattern Recognition*, 10764–10773. doi: 10.1109/CVPR.2019.01103.

Pope, P. E. *et al.* (2019b) 'Explainability Methods for Graph Convolutional Neural Networks', in *2019 IEEE/CVF Conference on Computer Vision and Pattern Recognition (CVPR)*, IEEE, 10764–10773. doi: 10.1109/CVPR.2019.01103.

Ribeiro, M. T., Singh, S., and Guestrin, C. (2016) '"Why Should I Trust You?" Explaining the Predictions of Any Classifier', in *NAACL-HLT 2016 – 2016 Conference of the North American Chapter of the Association for Computational Linguistics: Human Language Technologies, Proceedings of the Demonstrations Session*. doi: 10.18653/v1/n16-3020.

Sanchez-Lengeling, B., Wei, J., Lee, B., Reif, E., Wang, P., Qian, W., ... & Wiltschko, A. (2020). Evaluating attribution for graph neural networks. Advances in neural information processing systems, 33, 5898–5910.

Schlichtkrull, M. S., De Cao, N. and Titov, I. (October 2020) 'Interpreting Graph Neural Networks for NLP With Differentiable Edge Masking'. Retrieved from http://arxiv.org/abs/2010.00577.

Schnake, T. *et al.* (2021) 'Higher-Order Explanations of Graph Neural Networks via Relevant Walks', *IEEE Transactions on Pattern Analysis and Machine Intelligence*. doi: 10.1109/TPAMI.2021.3115452.

Schwarzenberg, R. *et al.* (2019) 'Layerwise Relevance Visualization in Convolutional Text Graph Classifiers', in *EMNLP-IJCNLP 2019 – Graph-Based Methods for Natural Language Processing – Proceedings of the 13th Workshop*. doi: 10.18653/v1/d19-5308.

Vu, M. N. and Thai, M. T. (2020) 'PGM-Explainer: Probabilistic Graphical Model Explanations for Graph Neural Networks', in *Advances in Neural Information Processing Systems*.

Ying, R. *et al.* (2019) 'GNNExplainer: Generating Explanations for Graph Neural Networks', in *Advances in Neural Information Processing Systems*. doi: 10.48550/arXiv.1903.03894.

Yuan, H. *et al.* (2020) XGNN: 'Towards Model-Level Explanations of Graph Neural Networks', in *Proceedings of the ACM SIGKDD International Conference on Knowledge Discovery and Data Mining.* doi: 10.1145/3394486.3403085.

Yuan, H. *et al.* (February 2021) 'On Explainability of Graph Neural Networks via Subgraph Explorations.' Retrieved from http://arxiv.org/abs/2102.05152.

Yuan, H. *et al.* (2022) 'Explainability in Graph Neural Networks: A Taxonomic Survey', *IEEE Transactions on Pattern Analysis and Machine Intelligence*, pp. 1–19. doi: 10.1109/TPAMI.2022.3204236.

Zhang, Y., Defazio, D., and Ramesh, A. (2021) 'RelEx: A Model-Agnostic Relational Model Explainer', in *AIES 2021 – Proceedings of the 2021 AAAI/ACM Conference on AI, Ethics, and Society.* doi: 10.1145/3461702.3462562.

10

Toward Privacy Preserved Graph Intelligence: Concepts, Methods, and Applications

10.1 Introduction

With the superior performance of graph neural networks (GNNs) in modeling graph-structured data, they have found widespread use in many fields, including security-related ones like wireless communication, traffic forecasting, malware detection, and fraud detection. In spite of their prodigious potential in promoting humans in different real-world applications, a recent literature demonstrated that graph intelligence methods are vulnerable to the leakage of confidential information, are exposed to adversarial attacks, are black-boxes, and could succeed to amplify social bias from training observations, leading to the accidental damage to the individuals and society. For instance, prior research shows that attackers can manipulate graph intelligence methods to produce the desired result by making small adjustments to the training graph. Graph intelligence models, trained on social network, may reinforce harmful bias in society because they internalize prejudice. As a result, graph intelligence models in which users may have faith are emerging as a means of protecting themselves from the potential harm posed by the models itself. This chapter follows the previous chapter by providing in-depth exploration of different aspects of responsibility of graph intelligence models such as privacy, robustness, and fairness. To enrich the knowledge of the readers about each of these aspects, a fine-grained taxonomy is designed to categorize the corresponding methods and devise the generic outlines for the various types of trustworthy (Dai *et al.*, 2022).

In spite of the success the graph intelligence had in modeling graphs, there are growing worries regarding the ability of graph intelligence methods to be trusted. To begin, graph intelligence models are susceptible to attacks that can either steal confidential data or alter the behaviors of the model. These attacks can have an impact on both. Hackers, for instance, are able to use the embeddings of nodes in social networks to infer information about the nodes' attributes as well as information about their friendships. By inserting malicious nodes into the network, they can also easily deceive the graph intelligence into giving target forecasting to a node. Second, there are issues with the fairness and interpretability of the graph intelligence models themselves. To be more explicit, graph intelligence models have the potential to amplify the bias present in the training data, which can lead to discrimination against people of particular genders, skin colors, and other sensitive protected characteristics. In conclusion, it can be challenging to make sense of the predictions generated by the graph intelligence because the underlying model has a significant degree of nonlinearity. Graph intelligence methods are also unreliable due to the fact that they cannot be interpreted, which significantly restricts the applications for which they can be used. These shortcomings provide a significant barrier to the use of graph intelligence in real-world applications, particularly in high-stake contexts like those found in the healthcare and financial industries. As a result, the question of how to construct reliable graph intelligence models has emerged as a central one.

Recent discussions within the European Union have resulted in the development of a set of recommendations for trustworthy artificial intelligence (AI) systems. According to the guidelines, a trustworthy AI should comply with four moral values: having respect for human autonomy, preventing harm, being fair, and being interpretable. AI systems are mandated to adhere to human-centric design guidelines and consider leaving valuable opportunity for human decision respect the principle of human autonomy. As a result, this chapter does not place a primary emphasis on that particular path of responsible graph intelligence. According to the principle of prevention of harm, AI systems ought to be technically robust and guaranteed that they are not open to the use of malicious intent, which corresponds to the robustness and privacy aspects of our survey. In order to adhere to the principle of fairness, it is necessary for AI systems to guarantee that individuals and groups will not be subjected to unfair bias, discrimination, or stigmatization. In order to meet the requirements for interpretability, the decision-making process of the AI must be both transparent and explainable. It is important to emphasize that the four facets are not independent of one another in any way. For example, the adversary could introduce bias into the training data in order to undermine the integrity of the model or confuse the graph intelligence explainer model. The explanations that are offered by methods of explainable graph intelligence can also be beneficial in other domains. In addition, by conducting an analysis of the explanations, we are able to determine whether or not the model, currently being used, produces biased predictions. As a result, it is essential to investigate the relationships that exist between these aspects in order to finally develop graph intelligence that are reliable and satisfactorily address the concerns of robustness, privacy, fairness, and explainability simultaneously.

Within the scope of this chapter, we also include some discussion regarding the interactions between the various facets of trustworthiness in regard to the upcoming instructions. In recent years, there has been a proliferation of papers focusing on various aspects of responsible graph intelligence in response to the rising demand for reliable graph intelligence. For instance, a graph intelligence that is resilient against the perturbations introduced by attackers has been developed. In addition, privacy-preserving graph intelligence models have been proposed for use in a variety of real-world applications, such as financial analysis, with the goal of preventing the disclosure of confidential information. Fair graph intelligence and understandable graph intelligence have also become popular topics as a means of addressing worries regarding the reliability of graph intelligence. There have been multiple investigations conducted into the robustness and comprehensibility of graph intelligence. However, none of them go into sufficient detail about the dependability of graph intelligence, which should also cover the aspects of privacy and fairness. They do not include the emerging directions and techniques such as scalable attacks, backdoor attacks, and self-explainable graph intelligence, which are discussed in this survey, for the aspects of robustness and explainability either. On the other hand, it focuses primarily on the methods of building trustworthy AI systems using i.i.d. data. Trustworthy AI that was developed for i.i.d. data cannot be used to process graph-structured data in general because of the complexity of the graph's topology and the implementation of message-passing mechanisms in graph intelligence.

10.2 Privacy Threats for Graph Intelligence

The impressive results of graph intelligence rely on the big data in the same way that deep learning (DL) algorithms for images and texts do. Users' private information is gathered in order to train robust graph intelligence models for use in healthcare, banking systems, and bioinformatics services. The functional magnetic resonance imaging of the brain is one of the applications of graph intelligence. Furthermore, the model owner may make available the query application programming interface (API) service for disseminating the learned information by graph intelligence methods. Commonly, the pretrained graph intelligence models are shared with outside parties for the purposes of knowledge distillation or other downstream tasks. Nevertheless, the security of private and sensitive information is being jeopardized by the collection and use of private data for training graph intelligence, the application service, and model release.

To begin, most graph intelligence models are developed in a centralized fashion, wherein all user data and models are stored in a single location. Sensitive attributes collected may be compromised in the event of a data breach or unauthorized use if a central server is used. For example, in 2021, a hacker forum published, for free online, the personal information of half a billion Facebook users. Second, privacy attacks can result in sensitive user data being exposed through either model release or the services themselves. The privacy of users of, say, an online service for diagnosing brain diseases is seriously at risk because of membership inference attacks, which can identify the individuals included in the dataset used for training. In addition, several privacy attacks, including link extrapolation and feature inference, have been shown to successfully rob the pretrained model of its users' personal details. In order to build trust, it is essential to create graph intelligence that respects users' privacy.

Multiple studies have explored the preservation of the privacy of DL solution. Nevertheless, they are devastatingly devoted to the confidentiality problems associated with standard i.i.d. data like vision data and textual data. Unfortunately, these studies seldomly examine the privacy attacks and defense techniques on the graph data, even though these techniques are confronted with the topological information of graph data and the message-passing method of graph intelligence methods. Thus, this section provides in-depth exploration of the privacy attacks in graph intelligence and the design of privacy-preserved graph intelligence to guard against different privacy threats.

This subsection presents a fine-grained taxonomy for categorizing the privacy attacks on graph intelligence based on the intended confidential information. The discussion also argues different scenarios of the attacker's available intelligence for directing and triggering privacy attacks. In the same context, this section introduces a detailed description of the prevailing techniques for privacy attacks (see Figure 10.1).

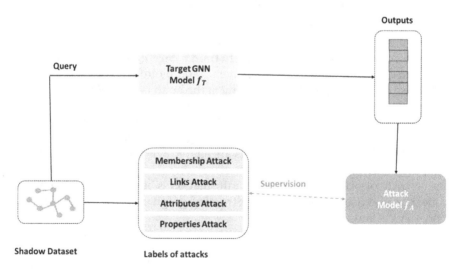

FIGURE 10.1
Illustration of generic framework for privacy attacks on graph intelligence methods.

(Adapted from Dai *et al.*, 2022.)

When hackers target graph intelligence methods, they're trying to get at data that shouldn't be publicized. The membership, sensitive properties of nodes, and connections between nodes are all examples of training graph-related target information. Additionally, some adversaries seek to steal the parameters of graph intelligence models. There are generally four types of privacy assaults depending on what the attacker knows about the target.

- **Membership inference attack:** The attackers' goal in a membership inference assault is to establish whether or not the target sample is a component of the training dataset. To illustrate this point, let's say that in order to investigate how COVID-19 spreads, researchers decide to train a graph intelligence model on the social networks of COVID-19 patients. The membership inference attack has the capability of determining whether or not a targeted subject is part of a training patient network, which can lead to information about the subject being leaked. In contrast to the nature of the i.i.d. data, the format of the target samples might either be graphs or nodes. For the purpose of node classification, for example, the target samples can be subgraphs of the local graph that is associated with the target node, or they can simply contain the node properties. The graph that needs to be classified serves as the target sample for the graph classification tasks.

- **Reconstruction attack:** The objective of the reconstruction assault, which is often referred to as a model inversion attack, is to determine the confidential information contained inside the input graph. Reconstruction attacks on GNNs can be broken down into two categories: building restoration, in which the attacker attempts to deduce the constructions of target instances, and attribute reconstruction, already recognized as a feature inference attack, in which the attacker attempts to extrapolate the characteristics of target instances. This is possible due to the fact that graph-structure information is constituted of graph configuration and node features. In most cases, it is necessary to have the embeddings of the target samples in order to carry out the reconstructive attack.

- **Property inference attack:** The goal of a property inference attack is distinct from that of a feature reconstruction attack in that it is to deduce data characteristics that are not represented as attributes. For instance, one might wish to deduce the ratio of women to males in an online community, even though this information is not present in the properties of the nodes themselves. The attacker might also be concerned with architecture attributes like the degree of nodes, which refer to the number of users that the intended users have in common with others on a social media platform.

- **Model extraction attack:** This attack intends to retrieve information from the intended model by first learning another version that acts in a manner that is analogous to that of the targeted one. It is possible for it to concentrate on several facets of the model information, which leads to the model distillation process having two objectives:
  i. The objective of the adversary is to acquire a model with a performance that is close to that of the targeted model.
  ii. The adversary makes an effort to imitate the decision space of the intended model.
  A model extraction attack could, in turn, endanger the security of a model for an API service and could be a foothold for a broad range of adversarial and privacy attacks.

10.3 Threat Models of Privacy Attacks

In order to undertake privacy threats, the attackers typically need to acquire an ancillary understanding of the GNN and/or dataset that they are targeting. In this part, we will present the classification of attack scenarios of privacy attacks in terms of the experience of the attackers. Generally, an attacker's information of the threat model could be divided into two configurations, and this division is determined by whether or not the parameters of the target GNN are known. These two configurations are black-box and white-box attacks.

- **White-box attack:** Adversaries in a white-box scenario can acquire training parameters. To be successful, assaults might require information beyond just the trained graph intelligence models themselves, like the nodes or graphs to be exploited in inference attacks or a shadowing database, namely a database that shares particular distribution as the training database of the targeted graph intelligence. Pretrained models graph intelligence, whose models have been made available to the public, is susceptible to a white-box assault. Additionally, it is useful throughout the federated training procedure, whenever intermediary calculations exist.

- **Black-box attack:** In a black-box attack, as opposed to a white-box attack, the parameters of the targeted graph intelligence are undisclosed; however, the structure of the targeted graph intelligence and hyperparameters throughout learning might well be disclosed. In this configuration, it is generally permissible for adversaries to inquire about the targeted graph intelligence model in order to obtain the forecasting scores or embeddings of the examples that were inquired. To carry out black-box attacks, you will need shadowed databases in addition to the targeted nodes and graphs, just as you will need these things to carry out white-box assaults. An example of real-world use of the black-box privacy attack is the targeting of the API service that transmits the results of the graph intelligence models in response to user inquiries.

10.3.1 Methods of Privacy Attack on GNNs

There are many different design strategies for privacy assaults, but one of the most prevalent is called a supervised privacy attack. The use of the shadow database and the outcome of the intended models in order to obtain the supervision necessary for learning a privacy attack mode, which could be explained as a coherent model and is illustrated in Figure 10.2 are the fundamental principle underlying supervised privacy attack methods.

Membership inference attack: The objective of this attack is to determine whether or not a targeted instance was used in the learning of the targeted model. The overfitting of the network to the training data results in the prognosis matrices (expected labeling distributions) of the training samples and the test samples covering various sample spaces. This overfitting of the model is what causes the eavesdropping of membership information. Therefore, the prediction vector can be used by an adversary to determine whether or not a data sample was part of the training samples. The majority of typical method for acquiring knowledge of a membership inference attack model is to make

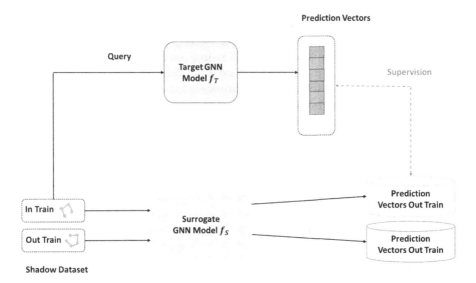

FIGURE 10.2
Illustration of generic shadow training scheme for membership inference attacks.

(Adapted from Dai *et al.*, 2022.)

use of shadow training, which entails obtaining supervision for membership inference and training an attack model. Figure 10.2 depicts the process of shadow learning in its entirety. During the shadow training process, a portion of the shadow dataset is used to train a surrogate model to behave in a manner that is analogous to that of the targeted model.

On i.i.d. data, the membership inference attack has previously been subjected to a substantial amount of research. In recent times, membership inference attacks on graphs have garnered an increasing amount of interest. These attacks generally adhere to the same scheme of shadow training, which has been successful for GNNs in recent times. Another approach that was examined for use in node classification tasks was membership inference depending on subgraphs of the local network associated with the target node. To make it more explicit, the shadow database is presented in the shape of a graph that is derived from the same underlying distribution as the graph that was employed for learning purposes. As the shadow model, a graph convolution network (GCN) has been implemented. The attack on targeted instances was thus investigated by other research efforts, in which the attackers are solely supplied with node attributes. The most significant distinction is that they are able to complete the graph classification problem using that kind of attack.

Reconstruction attack: As was said before, the objective of a reconstruction attack is to deduce the sensitive properties or linkages contained within the targeted databases. Because GNNs communicate with one another via message passing, the learnt node/graph embeddings are able to take into account both the properties of nodes and the architecture of graphs. The knowledge can therefore be reconstructed using the node embeddings that have been learnt by the targeted GNN using the current restoration attack approach. The embeddings might not be accessible for certain implementations, but it is possible to acquire the forecast array of an example through inquiring the targeted model. This is in contrast to the situation in which the embeddings are accessible.

All of the strategies that have been discussed thus far concentrate on blackbox parameters. Nevertheless, with the emergence of pretraining GNN and federated training, both of which exchange the learning gradients, whitebox reconstructive attack approaches also begin to gain much interest. For instance, the GraphMI (Zhang *et al.*, 2021) paper suggests reconstructing the mapping function in a white-box environment, which refers to a situation in which the parameters of the trained model are already determined. If there is as little difference as possible between the genuine node labeling and the estimates made using recreated matrix, then the original adjacency matrix and the recreated adjacency matrix A will have a high degree of similarity. Moreover, the graph topology is modified so that reliable forecasts can be obtained from the GNN model while still adhering to the feature smoothing criterion.

Property inference attack: The initial stages of this assault have not yet been completed. An initial attempt is made to deduce the characteristics of a target graph based on the embedding of that graph.

Model extraction attack: The goal of the model extraction attack is to figure out how to operate a surrogate model that acts in a manner that is comparable to the target model. The membership inference attack, which is illustrated in Figure 10.2, also takes into account the training procedure for a surrogate model. In most cases, the adversary will begin by conducting a query on the targeted model in order to gather estimates based on the shadowed database. After that, it trains the surrogate model for model extraction assaults by using the shadowed database and the predictions that correlate to it. Using this approach as a guide, current research has looked into GNN model harvesting attacks using various degrees of understanding about the targeted model's shadowed database and trained network. For instance, the generic framework of model extraction is used throughout the training process on the shadowed database, which contains graph topologies. In the event that the shadowed database does not provide any organization, the absent graph topologies could initially be learned.

10.4 Differential Privacy for Graph Intelligence

The privacy of graph intelligence solutions can be protected using a broad range of methods that enable performing a trustworthy big data analysis (statistical analysis, representational learning, data mining, etc.) while ensuring the privacy of model and training data. Among these methods, differential privacy (DP) has been achieving wide acceptance in the different application domains (Jiang *et al.*, 2021; Li *et al.*, 2022; Sajadmanesh and Gatica-Perez, 2020, 2021).

DP is a more up-to-date approach to cybersecurity, and its advocates argue that it protects personal data far more effectively than more conventional ways. Let's figure out the best way to protect people's privacy in a consistent manner.

Through the use of DP, researchers and database analysts are afforded an easier means of accessing and analyzing data stored in dataset that may include personally identifiable information without compromising the privacy of those whose data is being accessed. This can be accomplished by ensuring that the information provided by the data contains only the barest minimum of distracting elements. The newly added distraction is sufficiently large to be able to preserve the subject's privacy, while, at the same time, being constrained enough to ensure that the information obtained by analysts may still be put to good use. Think of a person who is debating whether or not to agree to have their information stored in a dataset. It could be a patient determining whether or not to allow their medical records to be used in a study, or it could be a survey respondent weighing whether or not to share their opinions. An effective privacy concept will reassure individuals that sharing their data won't negatively affect them in the long run. Although perfect privacy cannot be assured, the odds of having your privacy compromised are significantly reduced. DP delivers exactly this feature.

A straightforward explanation of DP would state that it makes data anonymous by deliberately introducing noise into the dataset. It gives data specialists the ability to do any and every feasible (valuable) statistical analysis without revealing any personally identifiable information. These databases contain the information of thousands of individuals, which helps solve public concerns and also contain data regarding the persons themselves.

Given two datasets $\mathcal{D}$ and $\mathcal{D}'$, a randomization mechanism $M[\cdot]$ is considered to work on the dataset to generate a particular output. The mechanism $M[\cdot]$ can be said to be differentially private if the output is almost indiscernible for every sample from $M[\mathcal{D}]$ and $M[\mathcal{D}']$. More officially, a mechanism $M[\cdot]$ is stated *differentially private* if for all subgroups of output $\mathcal{S} \subset \text{Range}[M]$ and datasets $\mathcal{D}$ and $\mathcal{D}'$.

$$Pr(M[\mathcal{D}] \in \mathcal{S}) \leq \exp[\epsilon] Pr(M[\mathcal{D}'] \in \mathcal{S}). \tag{10.1}$$

When the method is applied to a database, the factor ϵ regulates how much variation there can be in the results between the two neighboring datasets and quantifies the amount of privacy that is compromised as a result. When values of ϵ are close to zero, it implies providing less loss of privacy, whereas greater values correlate to only limited guarantees of privacy. If the meaning of this definition isn't immediately clear, that's okay. Several simple examples will be provided later in this course to help illustrate these concepts. In this chapter, we first recast the concept of DP in terms of differences.

There is a strong relationship between ϵ-DP and the divergences that can occur between different probability distributions. A divergence is a measurement of the difference in probability distributions that are obtained from two different samples. If the distributions are equivalent, it equals zero, but it increases in size if there is any significant difference between them. As the output of mechanism $M[\cdot]$ is determined in a randomized fashion, there is a probability distribution across it. Differentially private status is only conferred upon the mechanism when, and only when, the following conditions are met:

$$\text{div}[M[\mathcal{D}] \| M[\mathcal{D}']] \leq \epsilon \tag{10.2}$$

datasets $\mathcal{D}$ and $\mathcal{D}'$ differ by at most a single record. In the above formula, div $[\cdot \| \cdot]$ denotes the Renyi divergence of order $\alpha = \infty$.

One can expect to pay a mean premium of a factor $\exp[\epsilon]$ of more than if they did not want to join in a dataset wherein accessibility was ϵ-differentially private. However, these relationships and assurances may be used to calibrate based on the sensitiveness of the information and the requirements of the analysis, making what is otherwise a difficult problem much more manageable.

The Laplace mechanism: Here, we'll take a look at one of the more traditional DP methods. The Laplace mechanism introduces randomness into the outcome of a consistent dataset operation. If you want to hide the true outcome of a calculation and protect the privacy of its inputs, you can do what we call "plausible deniability" and randomly select a reply to a binary question (Gong *et al.*, 2020).

Let $f[\cdot]$ represent a deterministic procedure of data that yields a single number. One possible use is to a keep track of how many records meet a certain criterion. The methodology of Laplace mechanism works by injecting noise to $f[\mathcal{D}]$ as follows:

$$M[\mathcal{D}] = f[\mathcal{D}] + \xi, \tag{10.3}$$

where $\xi \sim Lap_\xi[b]$ denotes a sample drawn from a Laplace distribution with magnitude b. The Laplace mechanism is ϵ-differentially private with $\epsilon = \Delta f / b$. The symbol Δf represents a factor known as the sensitivity that relies on the functionality $f[\cdot]$.

This relationship could be analyzed by breaking it down into its component parts. Larger volumes of noise may better protect one's privacy but doing so comes at the cost of a reaction that is less precise. The scale factor of the Laplace distribution determines this and thus causes the answer supplied by to be less accurate for greater values. This is governed by the weighting factor. In this instance, the compromise between precision and discretion is made quite clear. Nevertheless, the degree of privacy provided for a stable value of b relies on the task $f[\cdot]$. To justify that, one may think about injecting Laplacian noise with $b = 1$ to (1) a function calculating the mean of income set of workers in pounds and (2) a function calculating the mean of heights of workers in meters. Given that the anticipated scale of the income function is much greater than that of the height function, the fixed added noise will have relatively less effect for the income function.

Therefore, the level of noise needs to be adjusted such that it is proportional to the characteristics of the function. Those characteristics are caught by Δf which is a constant that defines the degree to which the output of $f[\cdot]$ could differ with the adding or elimination of a single element. Formally, Δf is the ℓ_1 sensitivity of and is defined as

$$\Delta f = \max_{D, D'} \| f[\mathcal{D}] - f[\mathcal{D}'] \|_1 \tag{10.4}$$

where $\| \cdot \|_1$ denotes the ℓ_1 norm $\mathcal{D}$ and $\mathcal{D}'$ and varies in just single component.

There is more than one mechanism that can lead to DP, not just the Laplace mechanism. It is possible to employ the exponential method in order to deliver differentially private responses to questions that don't have numerical solutions. For example, "what color of eyes do most people have?" and "which municipality has the highest prevalence of cancer?" are examples of such questions. It is also helpful for building better processes for performing numerical computations such as determining the median, mode, and mean of a set of data.

Gaussian mechanism: The Gaussian mechanism produces results by supplementing the signal with Gaussian noise rather than Laplacian noise, and the amount of noise produced is determined by the ℓ_2 sensitivity rather than ℓ_1. Because additive Gaussian noise was far less prone to taking on extreme values than Laplacian noise and is often tolerated by downstream analysis, the Gaussian mechanism is convenient (Liu, 2019). Unfortunately, the Gaussian process only meets a lesser type of DP known as (ϵ, δ)-DP. This is an unfortunate limitation. An $M[\cdot]$ mechanism is said to be "differentially private" in a formal sense if and only if

$$Pr\big[M[\mathcal{D}] \in \mathcal{S}\big] \leq \exp[\epsilon] Pr\big[M[\mathcal{D}'] \in \mathcal{S}\big] + \delta, \tag{10.5}$$

for all subgroups of output $\mathcal{S} \subset \text{Range}[M]$ and datasets $\mathcal{D}$ and $\mathcal{D}'$ that differ by at most single component. DP is stronger in the sense that it limits privacy loss even in worst case situations that could result in big amounts of noise being required. On the other hand, (ϵ, δ)-DP permits for possibly large privacy violations but only with probability δ. Unofficially, you can think of an ϵ-DP mechanism as being (ϵ, δ)-DP with probability.

In a nutshell, DP guarantees that an adversary is not able to consistently infer whether or not a certain individual is contributing to the database query, even with unbounded computational capacity and access to every record in the database except for that specific individual's data. DP runs by injecting some kind of statistical noise to the data either to their inputs or to the output. According to where the noise is injected, DP is categorized into two categories—local and global.

Local DP: When using local DP, individual (input) data points are contaminated with random noise. Let's say we're interested in seeing how much cash the typical person has on hand in order to purchase an online course. Now opportunities are as follows: some may not have to disclose out the actual amount. This is where local DP comes in; rather than asking for the precise amount, we simply ask participants to add a random number (noise) between −100 and +100 to the cash they are now holding and report the sum. Thus, if "X" possessed $30, we could calculate exactly how much money he or she has by adding a random number, say −10, to it: $30 + (−10) = $20. Therefore, their confidentiality will be protected. In this case, the noise can be applied either directly to the database or to the individual datasets before being uploaded to the database, as seen earlier (Wang *et al.*, 2020; Zheng, Hu and Han, 2020).

It's also possible to calculate the odds of a coin toss using a method called "randomized response," which is commonly employed in the social sciences to gain insight into broad patterns of forbidden behavior when it's unclear whether or not the collected data are reliable. For instance, a survey that asks, "Have you ever committed theft?"

Following the assumption of a binary "Yes" or "No" response to the following query: to begin, I would suggest flipping a coin twice. Second, if the initial coin toss yields a "Yes" or "No" result, it can be considered that answer to be accurate. Third, if the first toss of the coin comes up heads, the solution is determined by the second toss. The person must now respond "Yes" if the coin lands on its head and "No" if it comes up tails. When it comes down to it, we' do not actually give the person a say in the matter. Here's where we sprinkle in some "randomness."

Consider the odds of a "yes" answer from someone who has never stolen anything before in their life. That can only occur if the second coin flip also results in a heads result. That's because if the initial coin flip had resulted in heads, the respondent would have claimed to have never stolen anything in their life. If the first coin is flipped and comes up heads, the person will answer "yes," even though the correct answer is "no." Therefore, each individual is now shielded by "plausible deniability" thanks to the introduction of noise or unpredictability. Each individual is shielded from harm in a significant way. In addition, the "actual statistics" are merely averaged with a 50% chance; thus, we may retrieve the underlying statistics with reasonable precision. Given this, if we take a large sample and find that 60% of respondents gave a positive answer, we can infer that the true distribution is centered around 70%, as 70% averaged with 50% (coin flip) = 60%, which is the result we received.

Unfortunately, by resorting to averaged numbers, we sacrifice some precision in exchange for increased anonymity. The higher the level of privacy (plausible deniability), the less reliable the findings will be. How about the benefits? By hiding the true value from the dataset's primary collector (the "data curator"), sensitive information can be safeguarded. An individual's reliance on the integrity of the data curator or the database owner (in this case, Bob) is not required. Since each user must contribute noise to their own data, the total noise is substantially larger. Moreover, a larger number of users are usually required to obtain meaningful findings. To counteract this, epsilon is typically set to a large value in real-world applications.

Global DP: When using global DP, noise is appended to the database's query results as a final step before they are made available to a third party. The results of a database query are distorted, the data organizer aggregator. By taking these precautions, the data curator ensures that the personal information of database users remains secure. The database owner and data curator can be relied upon. All sensitive information is stored in the database, and only the data curator has access to the actual raw data. To the point, add little to no noise and yet-received useful information can be achieved by using a small epsilon. But users need to feel comfortable enough with the data collector to feel comfortable sharing their data with it. Since the aggregator could be a shady business or government agency, achieving that goal might be tricky. As an added bonus, the global model stores all of the information in a single location. The possibility of a catastrophic failure rises, as in the case where the aggregator is compromised, and all the data is exposed (Jiang *et al.*, 2021).

Keep in mind that if you can trust the database owner, the only difference between local and global DP is that the latter produces more precise outcomes while retaining the same level of anonymity. But this can only work if the database's owner can be relied upon. That is, the owner/curator of the database must appropriately inject noise and safeguard data confidentiality.

10.5 Federated Graph Intelligence

The year 2016 marked the beginning of widespread dissemination of the notion of federated learning (FL). The core idea behind it is to train DL models on various datasets that are distributed over multiple devices or entities, which might assist to safeguard local data privacy to some level. Since that time, FL has undergone tremendous progress and has emerged as a prominent area of study interest within the AI discipline (Wahab *et al.*, 2021). The development mostly reaps the benefits of the following three aspects:

1. The fast success of DL: The widespread and fruitful implementation of machine learning technologies is one of the most important factors contributing to the development of FL. In the most recent few decades, technologies based on machine learning have been used with great success in a variety of fields, including language processing, image processing, and biometrics, to name just a few of these fields.

2. The exploding growth of big data: The exploding growth of big data has been a driving force behind the development of FL. Huge quantities of data are produced each day in a variety of contexts, including but not limited to social networks, the Internet of Things (IoT), microgrids, e-commerce, health-care facilities, and banking systems. This tendency has, on the one hand, not only helped to advance the field of DL, but, on the contrary, it has also presented traditional DL with serious challenges. Learning a global model while simultaneously addressing the privacy issues related with big data has become an increasingly difficult task due to the fact that big data is typically stored in multiple systems by various entities. Because of this, traditional methods of DL are getting less efficacious, and FL is being regarded as an evolving option.

3. Global privacy regulations: The legal regulations for the protection of data privacy have been a driving force behind FL's lightning-fast growth. In recent years, there has been an increase in the number of data breaches, which poses a significant risk to the privacy of users' data. As an illustration, in 2019, more than 540 million records of Facebook users that were stored on Amazon's cloud service were made public, which resulted in significant ethical and legal complications. As a result, numerous legal regulations have been established to protect the private user data of internet users. Some examples of these regulations include the California Privacy Rights Act (Determann and Tam, 2020) in the United States of America, the Singapore Personal Data Protection Act in Singapore (Yongquan, 2017), and General Data Protection Regulation (GDPR) in the European Union (Hoofnagle, van der Sloot and Borgesius, 2019). These kinds of regulations have been a considerable driving force behind the advancement of FL, particularly the FL that protects users' privacy.

For the construction of smart and privacy-enhanced IoT systems, the idea of FL has been introduced relatively recent times. Practically speaking, FL is a decentralized cooperative AI solution that enables data training through the coordination of several machines with a centralized server. This is accomplished without the need to share realistic training data. For instance, in autonomous IoT networks, several connected devices could collaborate with an aggregator (such a server) to train DL model (e.g., graph intelligence model). These IoT devices could take on the role of workers (see Figure 10.3).

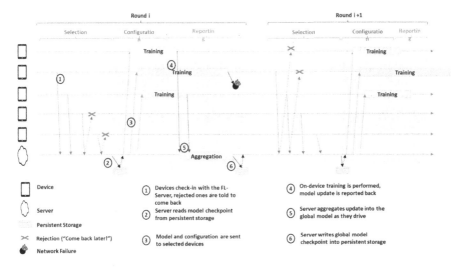

FIGURE 10.3
Generic federated learning protocol.

(Adapted from Lim *et al.*, 2020.)

The core concept of FL is that it should be possible for a huge number of end devices or hosts that are holding local data samples, which also are referred to as clients, to individually and cooperatively train a single DL model with need for disclosing any of original data. A coordinating device, also known as a parameter server, will then compile the participation made by each of the clients, from which it will deduce an upgraded model. This model will then be distributed to the clients who are taking part in the activity, so that they may take the advantage of the clients' prior training experiences and be capable of pursuing their own personal training knowledge in subsequent rounds.

To be more explicit, the aggregator will initially begin the process of creating a global model with learning parameters. Each client obtains the most recent version of the model from the parameter server, updates its own version of the model—for example, by stochastic gradient descent (SGD)—making use of its personal local training data, and then offloads its own version of the update to the parameter server.

After that, the parameter server brings together all of the local model updates and builds a brand new, more accurate global model. The parameter server is able to improve the quality of the learning while simultaneously reducing the amount of user privacy that is compromised as a result of the use of the computational power of distributed clients. After that, the local clients will calculate their next local update while simultaneously downloading the most recent global update from the parameter server. This process will continue until the global learning is finished.

FL is able, thanks to its cutting-edge operational philosophy, to provide a number of significant benefits for IoT applications, including the following:

- **Protection of data privacy:** FL does not necessitate the raw data for training at the coordinator. Thus, some measure of data privacy is guaranteed, and the likelihood of disclosure of confidential personal information to an outside entity is reduced. The privacy preservation capability of FL is a great option for developing smart and secure IoT technologies in the wake of extremely strict data privacy reservation regulations like the GDPR (Tamburri, 2020). In continuation of the previous point, it is not necessary for users' raw data to be uploaded to the cloud. This improves user privacy and minimizes the likelihood of eavesdropping to some degree, presuming that FL participants and servers do not engage in malevolent behavior. In point of fact, if users' privacy is improved, they will be more inclined to participate in collaborative model training, which will allow for the development of superior inference models.

- **Low-latency network communication**: With FL, communication delays that are caused by offloading are less of an issue because IoT data is not sent to the server. As a result, it reduces demands on the network in terms of spectrum and transmits power during the data-training phase. Machine learning (ML) models are able to undergo dedicated training and updates when FL is used. While this is going on, serious decisions, such as action recognition, could be carefully made at the edge devices or end devices if the edge-computing architecture is being used. When choices are taken in the cloud before being transmitted to the machines at the end of the chain, the result is a latency that is far less than that. This is absolutely necessary for time-sensitive applications such as self-driving vehicles, where even the tiniest delays might pose a serious risk to the driver and passengers.

- **Efficient network bandwidth**: There is a reduction in the quantity of data that must be uploaded to the cloud. Participating devices, for instance, do not transmit the raw data in order to have them processed; rather, they just transmit the updated model parameters in order to have them aggregated. As a consequence of this, the costs of data communication are greatly reduced, and the strain placed on backbone networks is alleviated (Imteaj *et al.*, 2022).

- **Enhanced learning quality**: FL has the capability to improve the rate of convergence of the ultimate training procedure and deliver greater learning prediction performance. This is something that could not be accomplished by using centralized AI strategies with insufficient information and restrained computing resources. FL does this by attracting a large amount of computational resources and diversified sets of data from a network of IoT devices. In exchange, FL also boosts the sustainability of mobile communication systems owing to the dispersed learning characteristic of the algorithm (Nguyen *et al.*, 2023).

The paradigm of FL is significantly distinct from that of centralized (centralized) DL, and it presents extra one-of-a-kind issues in the following areas:

- Connectivity: When participating in FL, client devices are usually disconnected or on a connection that is either slow or expensive. This indicates that the connectedness in FL is restricted, and that the method for choosing clients to engage in the federated training can be skewed toward specific scenarios (e.g., local time zone, device being charged or not) (Nguyen *et al.*, 2021).

- Communication: In FL, there is no original data that is required to be shared with any centralized server, which decreases the quantity of data that has to be carried through the network. This is due to the fact that no original data is required to be exchanged with any central server. The fact that the machine learning model is trained in a distributed manner; however, it necessitates that numerous model updates be sent between the servers and the clients across a considerable number of iterations. This results in increased transportation cost.

- Data privacy is maintained with FL since the training is carried out locally on each user's device; therefore, the raw data is never transferred off of it. In spite of this, the threat of initiating inference attacks that try to extrapolate confidential material from the training data of users who are participating in a cooperative model increases when there are more individuals engaging in the model (Wu *et al.*, 2022).

- Decreased latency and waiting times: One benefit of FL is that it allows decision-making algorithms to be trained locally on edges or end devices rather than in the cloud. This results in a decrease in both of these factors.

- Massive distribution: It is anticipated that the number of clients that take part in the federated training will be much more than the typical number of training samples taken by each client.

- Statistical heterogeneity: Given that the training data on each client device is dependent on its own consumption habits, the local data of one client in FL is not presumed to be indicative of the entire data distribution. This is due to the fact that the training set on each client device is dependent on its own consumption habits. Similarly, because customers use their products or applications to varied degrees, the quantity of the local datasets that are associated with each customer tends to be unique.

In a typical FL platform, there are two primary roles: clients, who are responsible for their own local training data, and a server, which is in charge of coordinating the entirety of the training procedure and keeping the global model updated without having access to the clients' sets of data. In spite of the fact that there is typically just one server, the number of clients can sometimes be rather enormous. In most cases, the procedure of developing an FL includes three essential phases as follows:

- Phase 1: *initialization of federated settings.* The weights of the global mode and the hyperparameters are both initialized by the server after the first step. This includes a number of clients, a number of communication rounds, optimizer, and batch size, epochs. After that, it begins the process of activating the clients, broadcasting the global model after it has been initialized, and distributing computation duties to particular selected clients (see Figure 10.4).

- Phase 2: On the customer service side, local model training and updates are provided. First, the selected clients receive the most recent global information (such as weights or gradients) that has been transmitted by the server, and then they use their local datasets to update the individual parameters of their local models, where *t*

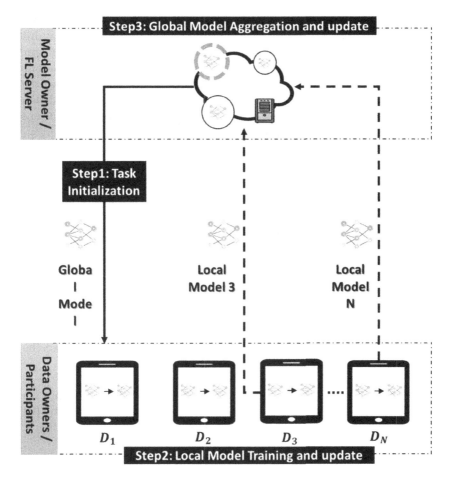

FIGURE 10.4
Generic procedure for federated training under server-client paradigm.

represents the index of the most recent communication round. After they have finished the local training, the next step is for them to submit their local information (such as weights or gradients) to the server so that it may be used in the parameter's aggregation process. During the phase of local training, the objective of the client that is picked in each round is to minimize the value of some loss function in order to get the optimal local model parameters.

- Phase 3: *Global aggregation at the server side.* Following the aggregation of the incoming local information that was transmitted by the chosen clients, the server then delivers the upgraded information back to the clients so that they can participate in the subsequent training session. The objective is to minimize the global objective functions in order to find optimal values for all of the global model parameters.

This section summarizes the current FL methods according to a categorization based on data partitioning and communication architectures. Given matrix D_i as the training data saved at the client i and sample $d = \left(d_{ID}, d_{feature}, d_{label} \right)$ **from** this dataset such that $d \in D_i$ denotes a data sample of D_i, whereby $d_{ID} \in X_i^{ID}$, $d_{feature} \in X_i^{feature}$, and $d_{label} \in X_i^{label}$ represent the *sample identifier*, set of features, and label, correspondingly. There are three different data partitioning scenarios that can occur depending on the distributions of the data instances in both identifier and feature space.

- Scenario-1: Horizontal segmentation of training data. The training data hosted by the participants shares the same feature space; however, they vary in ID spaces, such that, $X_i^{feature} = X_j^{feature}$, but $X_i^{ID} \neq X_j^{ID}$. In most cases, this circumstance takes place in the same field. For instance, student records from several educational institutions typically share the same feature area but have distinctively distinct ID spaces.

- Scenario-2: Vertical segmentation of training data: The training data hosted by the participants shares the same ID space; however, they vary in the feature spaces, such that $X_i^{ID} = X_j^{ID}$, but $X_i^{feature} \neq X_j^{feature}$.

- Scenario-3: Hybrid segmentation of training data: The training data hosted by the participants neither shares the feature space nor the ID spaces.

On the basis of the previous data segmentation, the FL approaches could be broken down into three different types. Federated transfer learning (FTL), horizontal FL, and vertical FL are the main types of FL.

10.5.1 Horizontal FL

Horizontal FL offers an appropriate solution to train deep networks using data distributed according to Scenario-1, in which the training sets of the clients share the same feature space but vary in ID spaces. The way can be expressed as follows:

$$Horizontal\ FL\text{:} = \left(X_i^{feature} = X_j^{feature} \right); \left(X_i^{ID} \neq X_j^{ID} \right)\ for\ all\ D_i\ \&\ D_j;\ i \neq j\ (10.6)$$

In horizontal FL systems, all learning clients work together to collaboratively train a global FL model by using their local datasets (see Figure 10.5). These datasets have the same feature space but vary from one another in sample space. Because each client has access to the exact same data, it is possible for them to train locally using the same AI model (e.g., linear regression or support vector machine. Every client in a horizontal FL system locally trains its own AI model so that it may compute a local update. The calculated local update can be concealed by employing encryption or DP methods,

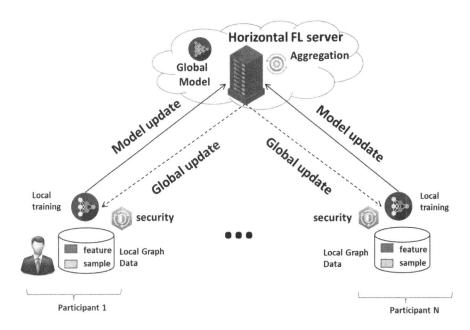

FIGURE 10.5
Systematic visualization of horizontal FL paradigm.

which will result in an increase in the system's overall level of safety. After that, the server compiles the latest global update without needing immediate access to the clients' local data by compiling all of the local updates that have been sent in by the clients. In the final step, the server relays the global update to each and every client in preparation for the subsequent iteration of local-ized learning. The procedure described above will continue to iterate until either the loss function converges or an accuracy level that is satisfactory is reached. Wake-word detection is one example of horizontal FL that can be found in applications for the IoT, such as voice assistants in smart homes. In this scenario, clients speak the same sentence (located in the feature space) on their mobile phones using a variety of distinct voices (located in the sample space). Following this, a parameter server takes the local speaking updates and averages them to produce a global model for voice recognition.

Communication designs in horizontal FL primarily fall into one of two categories: client-server designs and peer-to-peer systems. Computing is cen-tralized in a client-server design, which makes sense given that there is one server that is responsible for directing the entirety of the training procedure. Since there is no centralized server in the peer-to-peer topology, decentral-ized computation is used. For each training cycle, a different client would be arbitrarily chosen to take on the role of server.

Client-server paradigm. The setup in question is also referred to as central-ized FL. In a conventional client-server paradigm for a horizontal FL system, the asset of n clients (participants) works together with the assistance of the server (coordinator) to train a machine learning model. The implicit premise of this paradigm is that the clients are truthful, whereas the server is truthful, yet inquisitive. As a result, the protection of information leaks in this FL paradigm centers on the interchange of model parameters between clients and the server, and the training process comprises the following five fundamental phases:

- Phase 1: The coordinator performs initialization for the hyperparameters and parameters of model (this may be graph intelligence model) then broadcasts the initial calculations to the carefully chosen participants.

- Phase 2: The carefully chosen participants collaboratively train the local models in a privacy-preserving manner, by using their local private data to update the learning parameters (i.e., local updates). Then, the local updates of each participant are uploaded to the coordinator in either synchronous or asynchronous fashion.

- Phase 3: The coordinator performs safe aggregation of received parameters from participants according to predefined aggregation scheme such as weighted averaging.

- Phase 4: The coordinator transmits the recently aggregated parameters back to the participants.

- Phase 5: The participants decrypt the received parameters and update their local parameters and continue training.

During the course of this training process, the model parameter that is being traded can either be a model weight or a gradient. When it comes to the model weight, the participants communicate their locally computed weights to the coordinator, which then compiles all of the weights it has received and communicates the results back to the participants. The advantages of using this kind of technology include the fact that it is not necessary for them to synchronize frequently and that they can tolerate losing updates. One drawback is that there is no assurance of convergence. Concerning the model gradient, the participants communicate their locally computed gradients to the coordinator, and the coordinator then combines all of the gradients it has received before communicating them back to the participants. The benefits of using these kinds of approaches include providing precise information regarding gradients and ensuring convergence. The cost of communication and the requirement for a connection both require a reliable form of communication, which is a disadvantage.

Peer-to-peer paradigm. A decentralized FL is another name for this peer-to-peer paradigm. In contrast to the client-server design, this paradigm does not include a central coordinator. Each participant privately trains a DL model using its own local dataset in this paradigm. The participant then upgrades its model using the model information obtained from other participants and communicates the updated model information to the other participants. Therefore, the prevention of information leakage in this FL architecture centers on ensuring safe communication between participants. This objective can be accomplished by implementing several security solutions, such as a cryptography system that is founded on public keys. In addition, since there is no centralized coordinator, an established protocol ought to be made available in advance in order to coordinate the procedure of training. A cyclic transfer and a random transfer are the two types of protocols that are available in this paradigm (Lim *et al.*, 2020).

- Cyclic transfer. In this protocol, the participants are arranged in a form of rounded chain $\{p_1, p_2, ..., p_n\}$. Participant p_1 transmits its present local parameters to the participant p_2. Participant p_2 acknowledges the incoming parameters information from p_1 and makes use of its local dataset to upgrade the accepted model information and later transmits the updated parameters of its local model to the following participant p_3. Once the model converges or execution constraint is satisfied, the training operations terminate.

- Random transfer. Under this protocol, a participant p_k arbitrarily chooses a participant p_i with equivalent likelihood and transmits the parameters information to p_i, which accepts local updates from p_k and makes use of the local training data to update the accepted local updates, and then arbitrarily chooses a participant p_j with the same probability and transmits the upgraded model parameters to participant p_j. The above procedure is conducted instantaneously among n participants till the model converges or execution constraint is satisfied.

10.5.2 Vertical FL

Vertical FL is an appropriate choice to train deep models (such as GNNs) making use of training data belonging to the distribution scheme stated Scenario-2, which means that the data is sharing the same ID space but not the same feature spaces. This way, the vertical FL can be formulated as follows:

$$\text{Vertical FL:} = \left(X_i^{feature} \neq X_j^{feature} \right); \left(X_i^{ID} = X_j^{ID} \right) \text{ for all } D_i \ \& \ D_j ; i \neq j \quad (10.7)$$

In contrast to horizontal FL, vertical FL solves the problem of shared AI model learning in a network of clients that share the same sample space but have distinct data feature spaces. This is illustrated in Figure 10.6. In vertical FL, an approach based on entity alignment is used to aggregate overlapping instances from client accounts. Using various forms of encryption, these samples are merged to educate a general AI model. One instance of vertical FL

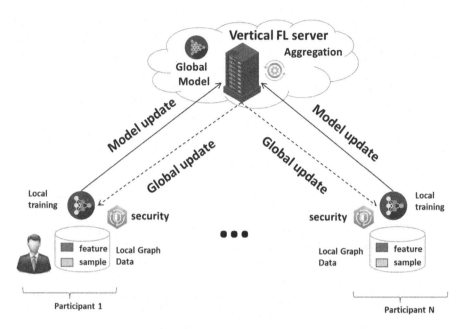

FIGURE 10.6
Systematic visualization of vertical FL paradigm.

that may be used in IoT applications is the common learning model that can be used by different organizations in a smart city. For instance, e-commerce enterprises and financial institutions can use this model. In a smart city, an e-commerce corporation and a bank that serve city customers (the same sample space) can join a vertical FL procedure to collaborate training a deep model using their data sources, such as historic user payments at e-commerce companies and user account balances at banks. For example, an e-commerce corporation could use the consumer payment history of its clients, while a bank can use the consumer account balance of its clients. Vertical FL is capable of determining the best possible customized loans for each individual client using this model, which is based on the consumer's history of internet purchases.

For vertical FL, there are mainly two communication *Paradigms*: an architecture with a third-party coordinator and an architecture without a third-party coordinator.

Paradigm with third-party coordinator. Suppose that participant p_1 and participant p_2 cooperatively train a deep network making use of their local training sets, and participant p_1 posses label data applied to train the public model. Participants p_1 and p_2 are truthful but curious with respect to each other. For ensuring the data privacy is maintained throughout the training procedure, a truthful third-party coordinator p_3 is integrated to manage the training. This is a fair hypothesis, for the reason that p_3 could be official agencies, for instance, governments. Thus, the working methodology of vertical FL system composed of five primary working phases as follows:

- Phase 1: Aligning ID. For the reason that there are various identifiers in the two training sets of the participants p_1 and p_2, the vertical FL paradigm initially necessitates making use of encryption-dependent ID alignment methods to validate the generic IDs without uncovering the confidential data of participants p_1 and p_2. Those share data examples are later exploited for training the vertical FL framework.

- Phase 2: Participant p_3 engenders an encryption key couple and transmits the open key to participants p_1 and p_2.

- Phase 3: Participants p_1 and p_2 perform encryption to their intermediary outcomes and interchange that information.

- Phase 4: Participants p_1 and p_2 each compute encoded parameters and combine a mask. Participant p_1 also computes an encoded loss. Then, participants p_1 and p_2 transmit the encoded outcomes to participant p_3.

- Phase 5: Participant p_3 decrypts the accepted calculations and transmits the deciphered parameters and loss back to participants p_1 and p_2. Then, participants p_1 and p_2 unmask the parameters and upgrade the parameters of model.

Paradigm without third-party coordinator. Suppose that participant p_1 and participant p_2 collaboratively train a machine learning model using their local datasets, and participant p_1 has label data used for training the global model. Participants p_1 and p_2 are honest-but-curious ones to each other. To prevent privacy leakage, such a vertical FL system must have the following seven main steps:

- Phase 1: Aligning ID. An ID placement method is initially adopted to validate the shared IDs between participants p_1 and p_2. After that, the shared data examples are used to train a vertical FL system.

- Phase 2: Participant p_1 creates an encoding key couple and transmits the generic key to participant p_2.

- Phase 3: Participants p_1 and p_2 initialize their model weights.

- Phase 4: Participants p_1 and p_2 each compute their incomplete linear forecasters, and participant p_2 transmits its forecaster outcome to participant p_1.

- Phase 5: Participant p_1 computes the model residue, encodes the residue, and transmits it to participant p_2.

- Phase 6: Participant p_2 computes the encoded parameters and transmits the masked parameters to participant p_1.

- Phase 7: Participant p_1 decrypts the masked gradient and sends it back to participant p_2. Then, participants p_1 and p_2 update their model locally.

10.5.3 Federated Transfer Learning (FTL)

FTL is an appropriate option to train learning model making use of data distributed according to Scenario-3, where the data has a variety of ID spaces and feature spaces or only carries out a small number of co-incidence examples (see Figure 10.7). This could be designated as follows:

$$FTL: = \left(X_i^{feature} \neq X_j^{feature} \right); \left(X_i^{ID} \neq X_j^{ID} \right) \text{ for all } D_i \& D_j; i \neq j \quad (10.8)$$

FTL approaches can be broken down into three distinct types according to the classification of transfer learning: instance-dependent FTL, feature-dependent FTL, and parameter-dependent FTL (Lo *et al.*, 2021).

- The instance-dependent FTL makes the assumption that some of the labeled examples in the data pertaining to the source domain could be reweighted and used once more for the purpose of training in the target domain. For the horizontal FL, the data of various clients might well have distinct distributions. As a consequence, the efficiency of learning methods that are trained on these data may suffer considerably. One option would be to dynamically adjust some of the chosen training examples and then use those reweighted instances again to train the model. This would help alleviate the distribution discrepancy.

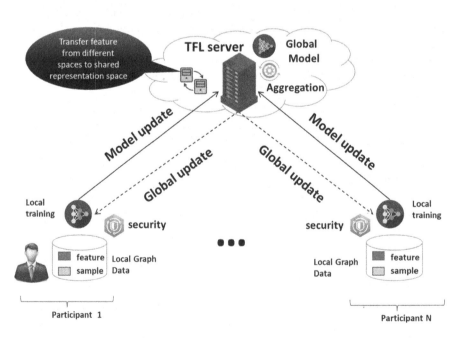

FIGURE 10.7
Systematic visualization of federated transfer learning paradigm.

When it comes to the vertical FL, the aims of various customers may be distinct from one another. Additionally, the ID realignment in the vertical FL may have an adverse effect on the FTL, which is referred to as negative transfer.

- *Feature*-dependent *FTL*: In order to properly encode the transformation information required to go from the source domain to the target domain, feature-dependent FTL strives to reduce domain divergence and develop a "strong" feature representation for the target domain. The feature map could be generated for the horizontal FL by optimizing the greatest mean difference among the various datasets of customers. This will allow for the best possible results. The feature map could be constructed for the vertical FL by reducing the difference between the features of alignment examples found in distinct data.

- *Parameter*-dependent *FTL*: In order to efficiently encode the transformation information, parameter-dependent FTL seeks to make use of shared parameters or previous distribution of hyperparameters between the models of the source domain and the models of the target domain. Before beginning work on the horizontal FL, a global model that is shared by multiple clients would be first trained using their respective dataset. After then, any client is able to finetune their own local model by applying the pretrained global model to their own local data. When it comes to the vertical FL, predictions that have been built on alignment data samples can be used to infer minor flaws or labels for non-aligned data samples of clients. After that, by training the model on the larger datasets, one can get a model that is more precise (Yin, Zhu and Hu, 2021).

10.6 Open-Source Frameworks

There are many different frameworks and pieces of software available to choose from when it comes to putting FL into practice in the real world. On the other hand, when it comes to proofs-of-concept and experiments, opensource frameworks are frequently sufficient. The goal and characteristics of the underlying use case have a significant impact on the option that should be selected. When developing a FL solution, it is vital to take into account a number of key aspects, including the number of times you want to apply it, the requirements for standardization, the requirements for security, as well as the needs for support and maintenance. In this part, a high-level overview of the most cutting-edge open-source frameworks for FL is presented for your perusal.

10.6.1 TensorFlow Federated

TensorFlow Federated is a free and open-source library that was presented by Google to design and train learning algorithms (i.e., graph intelligence models) in a collaborative setting on distributed data (Li *et al.* 2021). TensorFlow Federated was intended to make doing public research and experiments easier, and it federates training resources across multiple organizations. TensorFlow Federated is made up of two major application programming functionalities, namely Federated Core, which is a development tool for successfully implementing distributed computation, and FL layer, which enables integrating prevailing DL algorithm into TensorFlow Federated without attempting to address the methodology of federated machine learning algorithms (i.e., graph intelligence models). Federated Core is a development tool for implementing distributed computation, and an FL layer enables incorporating existing deep learning algorithm into TensorFlow Federated.

10.6.2 FedML

FedML (He *et al.*, 2020) benchmark framework and open research library is designed to speed up the process of developing FL solutions. It does this by establishing three various computational frameworks, including mobile on-device training, distributed training, and standalone simulation, which all work together to make it possible for many parties to conduct experiments in any scenario. For each paradigm, a unique set of federated algorithms is built. Some examples of these algorithms include FedAvg, FedOpt, FedNova, FedRobust, and FedNAS. SDK for GPUs, cellphones, and IoT devices that are not only lightweight but also compatible with multiple platforms. It affords a regulated and comprehensive benchmark dataset for the non- i.i.d. context, which can be used for fair comparison, and it facilitates different algorithmic research with flexible and generic API architecture and standard implementations. A platform for intelligent MLOps operations is designed to make collaboration and deployment easier in the real world. It provides support for a variety of DL tasks, including Federated Natural Language Processing (FedNLP), Federated Computer Vision (FedCV), and Federated IoT (FedIoT). This compatibility is powered by the architecture of FedML Core. FedML provides help for the implementation of Pytorch. Another one of FedML's distinguishing characteristics is that it comes equipped with a topology manager that is capable of supporting a diverse selection of network topologies. This feature makes it simple to adapt FedML to a variety of federated configurations. FedGraphNN (He *et al.*, 2021) is an open FL benchmark system that is built on FEDML. It was provided by the work x, which was driven by current achievements in the field of graph intelligence. FedGraphNN can aid research on federated GNNs. FedGraphNN is constructed on a unified formulation of graph FL, and it includes a broad variety of datasets originating from a variety of fields, popular GNN models, and FL algorithms, in addition to providing secure and effective system support. In particular for the datasets, the FedGraphNN collected, preprocessed, and split a total of beyond 30 datasets originating from seven different domains. These datasets include those that were publicly available as well as those that were expressly obtained, such as those from hERG and Tencent.

10.6.3 Federated AI Technology Enabler (FATE)

FATE (Liu *et al.*, 2021) is being touted as the first open-source industrial-grade FL framework. It is being hosted by the Linux Foundation, and its purpose is to enable organizations to learn from one another's data in a cooperative manner while still maintaining the data's confidentiality and safety. Implementing a variety of encryption and multi-party computing (MPC) approaches, such as SecretShare MPC Protocol (SPDZ), Fake encryption, Affine Homomorphic encryption (HE), RSA encryption, Paillier encryption, and others, helps support secure computation protocols. Learning can take place under both horizontal and vertical data partitioning using FATE. FATE provides two different deployment modes: solo, which is used for installations on a single host, and Cluster, which is used for installations on several nodes. It suggests putting the machine learning and DL solution in place using Docker Compose and Kubernetes. Because it only supports certain backends, such as TensorFlow and Pytorch, the FATE cannot be declared to be framework agnostic in its current state because it has already been defined.

10.6.4 IBM Federated Learning

IBM FL is a Python framework that is open-source and can be used to build FL solutions using any ML/DL frameworks (such as Keras, PyTorch, and Tensorflow). Additionally, it supports a variety of learning topologies, including supervised learning, unsupervised learning, and reinforcement learning (e.g., DQN, DDPG, and PPO). It does this by putting in place a number of sophisticated aggregation algorithms, such as Iterative Averaging, FedAvg, Gradient Averaging, Coordinate-wise median, Fed+, FedProx, and Shuffle Iterative Averaging, in order to accumulate the local updates that come from a variety of IoT parties. Modifications to these methods could speed up the convergence, reduce the amount of time needed for training, improve model security, and many other benefits. It provides support for a few fairness strategies (such as Local Reweighing, Global Reweighing, and Federated Prejudice Removal), all of which improve the FL process by helping to reduce bias.

10.6.5 Flower

Flower (Beutel *et al.*, 2020) is an open-source framework for constructing FL solutions. It is intended to meet the requirements outlined in this chapter, and it may be downloaded for free. First, it must be modifiable in such a way that it can support a wide variety of federated configurations that are tailored to the specific requirements of each use case. Second, it must be expandable in such a way that the AI research was taken into consideration when it was constructed. Therefore, the variety of modules that can be used to develop more advanced systems can be expanded and replaced. Third, it is framework-agnostic, which means that it can be used with any ML framework. For example, it can be used with TensorFlow, TFLite, PyTorch, MXNet, Hugging Face Transformers, JAX, scikit-learn, PyTorch Lightning, or even raw NumPy for users who enjoy computing gradients by hand. Fourth, it is credible, in the sense that it was written while keeping the possibility of future maintenance in mind. Fifth, it must be interoperable, meaning that it should function well on a variety of operating systems and diverse edge devices.

10.6.6 Leaf

Leaf (Caldas *et al.*, 2018) is a benchmarking platform that can learn in federated settings and supports a range of intelligent applications. These applications include multi-task learning, FL, on-device learning, and meta-learning. Leaf is an open-source project. Open-source datasets, benchmark algorithms (such as minibatch SGD and FedAvg), and statistical metrics make up the constituent parts that make up the whole. The modular design is used as the basis for LEAF's architecture, which makes it easier to operate and more adaptable to a variety of experimental conditions.

10.6.7 NVIDIA Federated Learning Application Runtime Environment (NVIDIA FLARE)

NVIDIA FLARE is a software development kit that is open-source, domain-agnostic, and extensible. It enables researchers and practitioners to extend the prevalent machine learning and DL solutions (such as TensorFlow, Nemo, RAPIDS, and PyTorch) to develop a federated system and supports platform developers in developing a secure, privacy-preserved, and distributed multi-party cooperation. NVIDIA FLARE was created by NVI. Because it is built on a componentized architecture, NVIDIA FLARE gives researchers the ability to customize workflows to meet their requirements and swiftly experiment with different design configurations. When it comes to protecting the privacy of federated systems, NVIDIA FLARE is equipped to handle the deployment of both DP and HE. The aggregation algorithms FedAvg, FedProx, and FedOpt are all supported in NVIDIA FLARE. It features two different training procedures, which are known as the scatter and gather workflow and the cyclic workflow.

10.6.8 OpenFL

OpenFL (Reina *et al.*, 2021) is a framework written in Python that is free to use and open-source. It was developed by Intel Labs and the Intel IoT Group. It provides support for the training of statistical DL models without regard to the underlying framework, such as TensorFlow or PyTorch. It is compatible with a variety of aggregation algorithms, including FedAvg, FedProx, FedOpt, and FedCurv. At the moment, it supports and offers two techniques to construct federated experimentation, which are known as the workflow reliant on the Director and the workflow based on the Aggregator. There are two different kinds of nodes included in the architecture of the OpenFL network topology: aggregators and collaborators. Every member of the federation is classified as either a collaborator or an aggregator node according to their specific role. A dataset that is owned by a participant is stored inside a collaborator node by that participant. The machine learning model is locally trained on the hardware of the collaborator node in question. The dataset is not transferred away from the collaborator node at any point. A compute node that is trusted by all of the collaborator nodes is referred to as an aggregator node. In a star architecture, the collaborator nodes connect directly to the aggregator node rather than going through any intermediate nodes. The aggregator establishes a connection to the collaborator nodes using mutually authorized transport layer security network connections and remote procedure calls (gRPC).

10.6.9 PaddleFL

PaddleFL is an FL framework that is open-source and is built on PaddlePaddle. It enables distributed training and flexible structuring of training jobs on Kubernetes. It provides support for the vertical FL and horizontal FL, which are the two principal FL schemes. In general, PaddleFL comprises two different components, which are referred to as federated learning with MPC and Data Parallel. Distributed data owners are able to engage in federated training using federated algorithms, such as FedAvg, differentially private SGD, and SecAgg, when using Data Parallel. This enables distributed data owners to work together. PFMPC was chosen to provide secure training and prediction based on several protocols, including PrivC and mixed protocol (named ABY3), both of which are advancement opportunities MPC methods. This decision was made in order to implement PFMPC.

10.6.10 PySyft and PyGrid

PySyft (Ziller *et al.*, 2021) is a python open-source framework for constructing FL systems that may be secured with encrypted computation (such as MPC and HE) as well as DP techniques. PySyft was developed by the PySyft foundation. It was developed by the OpenMined community, and its primary functionality relies on DL models that have either PyTorch or TensorFlow as their implementation. PySyft supports installation on OS X, Linux, and Windows, each of which is a different sort of operating system. PySyft is capable of performing computations in a couple of different modes. The first mode, known as dynamic mode, operates on data that has not yet been seen. The second mode, known as static computations, creates a graph of calculations that can be run at a later time in a number of different computing environments. PySyft configures end-devices to function as virtual workers so that federated training can be simulated. Next, the data is dispersed throughout the virtual workers, and a PointerTensor is constructed to preserve the configuration of the data, which includes ownership information and the place where it is stored. PySyft declares objects and models to be in simulation mode in this way; consequently, it is likely to conclude that PySyft is not willing to be applied in industrial products that involve communication across networks. This conclusion is likely to be reached due to the fact that PySyft declares simulation mode for objects and models. Because of this, you might require still another library known as PyGrid. PyGrid is a peer-to-peer network of data sources that can collaborate to train AI models on the web, mobile devices, edge devices, and many kinds of terminals by using PySyft. It is also possible to define it as the central server for carrying out both data-centric and model-centric FL. PyGrid comprises these three separate components. To begin, there is the domain, which is where a Flask application was used to safely store both the models and the training data. Second, there is the worker, which is a transitory compute instance that is handled and processed by data under the management of domain modules. Third, there is the network, which is an application written in Flask that can monitor and control a variety of domain modules.

10.6.11 Sherpa.ai

The Sherpa.ai (Rodríguez-Barroso *et al.*, 2020) was released and proposed as an open-source framework for secure federated computing and DP. It executes secure computing protocols to offer regulation-acquiescent data partnership, simplifies experimentation and research, and delivers a modular method to improve scalability by means of federated methods, tools, and models (Ziller *et al.*, 2021). Sherpa.ai was conceived as an open-source framework for secure federated computing and DP. It enables collaborative training of models based on distributed training data, transmitting the local changes of the models in order to safely aggregate the final model, as did earlier frameworks. Sherpa.ai is not only limited to a single category of models or tools, but rather incorporates a wide variety of machine and DL models that can be used with any data. These models may discover complex relationships between data points. It also gives the capability to connect FL with various types of DP, which ensures that the confidentiality of locally stored data is maintained during the training process. The application of these strategies can assist the developers in preventing hostile agents from interfering in the communication of local parameters. As a result, the malicious agent will be unable to trace the information back to the source data. Sherpa.ai offers additional services such as subsampling methods, adaptive DP, sensitivity sampler, and federated attack simulations.

10.7 Case Study

The privacy-preservation is essential pillar of responsible graph autoencoders graph intelligence since it has been becoming a major concern for business and data owners. In response to this concern, both academia and industry are interesting to practically investigate the steps and techniques necessary to make the graph intelligence learn and operate in privacy-preserved manner. Motivated by that, the supplementary materials of this chapter are designated to provide a holistic implementation of different privacy-preservation mechanisms discussed in the previous sections. The implementations of these mechanisms are trained and evaluated on real-world case studies for different graph tasks. The supplementary materials of this chapter also provide the readers with recommendations for further reading about the content of this chapter. The repository of supplementary materials is given in this link: https://github.com/DEEPOLOGY-AI/Book-Graph-Neural-Network/tree/main/Chapter%2010.

References

Beutel, D. J. *et al.* (2020) 'Flower: A Friendly Federated Learning Research Framework'. doi: 10.48550/arXiv.2007.14390.

Caldas, S. *et al.* (2018) 'LEAF: A Benchmark for Federated Settings', [Online]. Available: http://arxiv.org/abs/1812.01097.

Dai, E. *et al.* (2022) 'A Comprehensive Survey on Trustworthy Graph Neural Networks: Privacy, Robustness, Fairness, and Explainability', [Online]. Available: http://arxiv.org/abs/2204.08570.

Determann, L. and Tam, J. (2020) 'The California Privacy Rights Act of 2020: A Broad and Complex Data Processing Regulation that Applies to Businesses Worldwide', *Journal of Data Protection & Privacy*, 4(1), pp. 7–21.

Gong, M. *et al.* (2020) 'A Survey on Differentially Private Machine Learning [Review Article]', *IEEE Computational Intelligence Magazine*. doi: 10.1109/MCI.2020.2976185.

He, C. *et al.* (2020) 'FedML: A Research Library and Benchmark for Federated Machine Learning', [Online]. Available: http://arxiv.org/abs/2007.13518.

He, C. *et al.* (2021) 'FedGraphNN: A Federated Learning System and Benchmark for Graph Neural Networks', [Online]. Available: http://arxiv.org/abs/2104.07145.

Hoofnagle, C. J., van der Sloot, B. and Borgesius, F. Z. (2019) 'The European Union General Data Protection Regulation: What it is and what it Means', *Information and Communications Technology Law.* doi: 10.1080/13600834.2019.1573501.

Imteaj, A. *et al.* (2022) 'A Survey on Federated Learning for Resource-Constrained IoT Devices', *IEEE Internet of Things Journal.* doi: 10.1109/JIOT.2021.3095077.

Jiang, H. *et al.* (2021) 'Applications of Differential Privacy in Social Network Analysis: A Survey', *IEEE Transactions on Knowledge and Data Engineering.* doi: 10.1109/TKDE.2021.3073062.

Li, Q. *et al.* (2021) 'A Survey on Federated Learning Systems: Vision, Hype and Reality for Data Privacy and Protection', *IEEE Transactions on Knowledge and Data Engineering.* doi: 10.1109/TKDE.2021.3124599.

Li, Y. *et al.* (2022) 'Break the Data Barriers While Keeping Privacy: A Graph Differential Privacy Method', *IEEE Internet of Things Journal.* doi: 10.1109/JIOT.2022.3151348.

Lim, W. Y. B. *et al.* (2020) 'Federated Learning in Mobile Edge Networks: A Comprehensive Survey', *IEEE Communications Surveys & Tutorials,* vol. 22, no. 3, pp. 2031–2063. doi: 10.1109/COMST.2020.2986024.

Liu, F. (2019) 'Generalized Gaussian Mechanism for Differential Privacy', *IEEE Transactions on Knowledge and Data Engineering.* doi: 10.1109/TKDE.2018.2845388.

Liu, Y. *et al.* (2021) 'Fate: An Industrial Grade Platform for Collaborative Learning with Data Protection', *The Journal of Machine Learning Research,* 22(1), pp. 10320–10325.

Lo, S. K. *et al.* (2021) 'A Systematic Literature Review on Federated Machine Learning: From a Software Engineering Perspective', *ACM Computing Surveys.* doi: 10.1145/3450288.

Nguyen, D. C. *et al.* (2021) 'Federated Learning for Internet of Things: A Comprehensive Survey', *IEEE Communications Surveys and Tutorials.* doi: 10.1109/COMST.2021.3075439.

Nguyen, D. C. *et al.* (2023) 'Federated Learning for Smart Healthcare: A Survey', *ACM Computing Surveys.* doi: 10.1145/3501296.

Reina, G. A. *et al.* (2021) 'OpenFL: An Open-Source Framework for Federated Learning', [Online]. Available: http://arxiv.org/abs/2105.06413.

Rodríguez-Barroso, N. *et al.* (2020) 'Federated Learning and Differential Privacy: Software Tools Analysis, the Sherpa.ai FL Framework and Methodological Guidelines for Preserving Data Privacy', *Information Fusion,* vol. 64, pp. 270–292. doi: 10.1016/j.inffus.2020.07.009.

Sajadmanesh, S., & Gatica-Perez, D. (2020). When differential privacy meets graph neural networks. arXiv preprint arXiv:2006.05535.

Sajadmanesh, S. and Gatica-Perez, D. (2021) 'Locally Private Graph Neural Networks', in *Proceedings of the 2021 ACM SIGSAC Conference on Computer and Communications Security.* doi: 10.1145/3460120.3484565.

Tamburri, D. A. (2020) 'Design Principles for the General Data Protection Regulation (GDPR): A Formal Concept Analysis and its Evaluation', *Information Systems.* doi: 10.1016/j.is.2019.101469.

Wahab, O. A. *et al.* (2021) 'Federated Machine Learning: Survey, Multi-Level Classification, Desirable Criteria and Future Directions in Communication and Networking Systems', *IEEE Communications Surveys & Tutorials.* doi: 10.1109/COMST.2021.3058573.

Wang, T. *et al.* (2020) 'A Comprehensive Survey on Local Differential Privacy Toward Data Statistics and Analysis', *Sensors (Switzerland)*. doi: 10.3390/s20247030.

Wu, C. *et al.* (2022) 'A Federated Graph Neural Network Framework for Privacy-Preserving Personalization', *Nature Communications*, vol. 13, no. 1, p. 3091. doi: 10.1038/s41467-022-30714-9.

Yin, X., Zhu, Y. and Hu, J. (2021) 'A Comprehensive Survey of Privacy-Preserving Federated Learning: A Taxonomy, Review, and Future Directions', *ACM Computing Surveys*. doi: 10.1145/3460427.

Yongquan, B. W. (2017) 'Data Privacy Law in Singapore: The Personal Data Protection Act 2012', *International Data Privacy Law*. doi: 10.1093/idpl/ipx016.

Zhang, Z. *et al.* (2021) 'GraphMI: Extracting Private Graph Data from Graph Neural Networks', in *Proceedings of the Thirtieth International Joint Conference on Artificial Intelligence*. doi: 10.24963/ijcai.2021/516.

Zheng, H., Hu, H. and Han, Z. (2020) 'Preserving User Privacy for Machine Learning: Local Differential Privacy or Federated Machine Learning?', *IEEE Intelligent Systems*. doi: 10.1109/MIS.2020.3010335.

Ziller, A., Trask, A., Lopardo, A., Szymkow, B., Wagner, B., Bluemke, E., ... & Kaissis, G. (2021). Pysyft: A library for easy federated learning. Federated Learning Systems: Towards Next-Generation AI, 111–139.https://link.springer.com/chapter/10.1007/978-3-030-70604-3_5

Index

Note: Page numbers in italics refer to figures.

Printed in the United States
by Baker & Taylor Publisher Services